Tomorrow's History

Selected Writings of Simon Zadek, 1993–2003

Dr Simon Zadek

Simon is Chief Executive of the international non-profit organisation, AccountAbility. He serves or has served on numerous Boards and Advisory Councils, including that of the Global Alliance for Workers and Communities, the State of the World's Commission for Globalisation, the ILO's World Commission on the Social Dimensions of Globalisation, the UN Commission for Social Development Expert Group on CSR, and the founding Steering Committee of the Global Reporting Initiative. He is currently a Senior Fellow at Harvard University, and was previously Visiting Professor at the Copenhagen Business School, the Development Director of the New Economics Foundation, and founding Chair of the Ethical Trading Initiative. In 2003 he was named one the World Economic Forum's 'Global Leaders for Tomorrow'.

He works directly with numerous global corporations, focusing mainly on the integration of corporate responsibility into core business strategy, most recently including Anglo American, Barlow World, Gap, Nike and Novo Nordisk. He is also currently convening and co-chairing several initiatives, including a multi-sector alliance working on the transition of the textiles and garment industry following the end of the Multi-Fibre Arrangement; and co-chairing the British Standards Institute's Sustainability Standard Technical Committee.

simon@accountability.org.uk

Peter Raynard

Peter is an independent author and editor and long-time associate of AccountAbility. He has written and co-written on a range of subjects concerning the accountability and social responsibility of private, public and non-governmental organisations. These include: *The Future of Sustainability Assurance* (2004), *Towards a Croatian Business Agenda for Corporate Social Responsibility* (2004), *CSR: Implications for Small and Medium Enterprises in Developing Countries* (2002) and *Business and Poverty: Bridging the Gap* (2002).

He is currently editor of AccountAbility's journal *AccountAbility Forum*, published by Greenleaf Publishing. Previously he was Head of Third Sector Organisations at the New Economics Foundation, where he worked for six years.

peter@raynard.fsnet.co.uk

About AccountAbility

AccountAbility's mission is to promote accountability for sustainable development. As a leading international professional institute, AccountAbility provides effective assurance and accountability management tools and standards through its AA1000 Series, offers professional development and certification, and undertakes leading-edge research and related public policy advocacy. AccountAbility has embraced an innovative, multi-stakeholder governance model, enabling the direct participation of its organisational and individual members who span business, civil-society organisations and the public sector from different countries across the world.

www.accountability.org.uk

tomorrow's
history

Selected Writings of Simon Zadek,
1993–2003

Simon Zadek
co-edited by Peter Raynard

Greenleaf
PUBLISHING

AccountAbility
institute of social and ethical accountability

2 0 0 4

Published by Greenleaf Publishing Limited
Aizlewood's Mill
Nursery Street
Sheffield S3 8GG
UK
www.greenleaf-publishing.com

Printed on paper made from at least 75% post-consumer waste
using TCF and ECF bleaching.
Printed in Great Britain by William Clowes Ltd, Beccles, Suffolk.
Cover by LaliAbril.com.

British Library Cataloguing in Publication Data:
    A catalogue record for this book is available from the British Library.

Hardback: ISBN 1874719 86 1
Paperback: ISBN 1874719 85 3

contents

acknowledgements

Acknowledging people with whom I have collaborated over a ten-year period is, if nothing else, a test of memory. Firstly, I would like to thank all the co-authors of the writings that make up this anthology. They are: Franck Amalric, Jutta Blauert, Elena Bonfiglioni, Helle Dossing, Mike Edwards, Maya Forstater, Christian Haas, Sanjiv Lingayah, Alex MacGillivray, Malcolm McIntosh, Mira Merme, Philip Monaghan, Peter Raynard, Catherine Rubbens, John Sabapathy, Tracey Swift, Pauline Tiffen, Stephen Thake, Chris Tuppen and John Weiser.

Then there are the many other people who have contributed indirectly to the work, which includes Gavin Andersson, Dr Ariyaratne, Maggie Burns, Paul Burke, Geoff Bush, Barry Coates, Peter Cornelius, Lisa Curtis, Tom Delfgaauw, Maria Eitel, Paul Ekins, John Elkington, Richard Evans, Murdoch Gatward, Sue Gillie, Barbara Goodwin, Niels Hojensgard, Vernon Jennings, Hannah Jones, Georg Kell, Caroline Knowles, Mark Lee, Jens Erik Lund, Ed Mayo, Paul Monaghan, Jane Nelson, Alan Parker, Peter Pruzan, Vicky Pryce, Maria Sillanpää, Mangalam Srinivasan, David Sogge, Ros Tennyson, Jim Tomlinson, Nigel Twose, Maneto Valdemar, David Wheeler and, perhaps most of all, my father, Peter Zadek.

I would also like to thank Peter Raynard for being such an amazing editor and, more importantly, friend and guide. Thank you to Martin Cooper for his tireless efforts in obtaining the permissions from the original publishers. And also thanks to Mira Merme for her views on the chapters to include and comments on drafts of the first chapter, and for just being there. A particular mention must go to colleagues at AccountAbility, with whom I have enjoyed working with over the past few years, and who have inspired and perspired in almost equal measure. Finally, thanks to John Stuart and staff at Greenleaf Publishing for agreeing to publish this anthology, and then doing just that.

Simon Zadek
August 2004
London

introduction
writing by candlelight

Publishing a collection of my writings was meant to be easy, a matter of connecting the bits into some semblance of a coherent whole. In practice, the task proved more complex. It soon became clear that my work needed to be understood in the context of the evolution of a wider area of thinking, debate and practice. Looking back from today, we might call this area 'corporate responsibility'. Viewed from the early work looking forward, the area is better described as Schumacher's 'economics as if people mattered'. Either way, the excitement and challenge in assembling this anthology has been less to do with a review of my writing and more about using it as a lens through which to better understand how ideas have impacted on a decade of people's work in promoting more responsible business and economy.

This broader perspective led me to the more basic question about the terms on which ideas made a real difference. This question teases and haunts all those who try to make change by shaping tomorrow's ideas. Why do some become mainstream policy and practice, while others languish in the margins of debate, condemned to be history's junk DNA? After all, cars and telephones seemed peculiar accessories in their early development stages, as did most of today's commonplace and most profoundly influential technologies. Frederick Hayek, pre-eminent intellectual architect of the neoliberal revolution, seemed decidedly cranky when he published his seminal book *The Road to Serfdom* (Hayek 1944) on the heels of the recession-ridden European 1930s. The ideas of intellectual giants such as Einstein, Freud and Marx were considered eccentric at best in their formative years.

Why do some ideas fail to make a difference? Is it a sign that social Darwinism is alive and well? After all, innovations like the long-forgotten 'pet rock' (today we have e-pets), the fashionable toy of the late 1980s, or Clive Sinclair's doomed three-wheeled car, hardly count as lost opportunities for making a better world? Or was there something more sinister afoot—vested interests favouring one solution over another, irrespective of the public good? After all, Arthur Koestler argued in his provocative book *The Case of the Midwife Toad* (Koestler 1971) that Darwin's triumph over his arch-foe, the French scientist Lamarck, had more to do with intrigue and deceit than a reward to good science, or the rule of fact over fiction. Political analysts such as Noam Chomsky, John Pilger or even their young pretender George Monbiot, are supremely skilled at asserting the presence of conspiracies behind the façade of democratic accountability.

The pieces in this anthology have been largely written by candlelight. They have been written on planes, trains, and at weekends, with little expectation that they would be read, or that they described things that would become common currency and make a difference. Yet many of these pieces describe social innovations that have mainstreamed, often with such unlikely name tags as sustainability indicators, stakeholder dialogue, social auditing, corporate social responsibility, ethical and fair trade, and responsible competitiveness. They crystallise much of my work over the past ten years, in working with others to mainstream ideas that at the time, it seemed, would never interest a journalist, for example, on anything but the quietest of news days. The writings reflect my involvement with organisations such as the New Economics Foundation, a pioneer in the development of modern social auditing, sustainability indicators, community finance and much more. They illustrate my involvement in setting up the UK-based Ethical Trading Initiative, and Account-Ability (where I am presently the CEO), and in working with companies such as The Body Shop and Ben & Jerry's through to Nike, BT, and many others. Most importantly, they illuminate the efforts of an eclectic group of people across the globe with whom I have had the great pleasure to work with, many of whom are co-authors of the pieces in this anthology.

Writing about tomorrow's ideas is partly about sensing the pulse of change before it happens. Placing bets on which ideas will be tomorrow's facts is certainly a simpler enterprise than trying to slipstream ones that might otherwise fail. But the real reward comes when one goes beyond this in contributing to bridging the margin into the mainstream. John Elkington coined the term 'triple bottom line' in 1994.[1] Although he had not originated the underlying idea of sustainable development, his innovation simplified a complex idea for the business community. In doing this, he created a vehicle that helped to move the abstract utopia of sustainable development into the concrete realities of day-to-day business. The adoption of the term 'social audit' by Traidcraft and The Body Shop in the early 1990s, both working with our team at the New Economics Foundation, aimed to give a professional feel to their decision to report on their social as well as their financial performance. They did not invent the term, which has a history going back to the early years of the 20th century. But their decision marked the early days of an extraordinary transformation in how business is accounting for itself.

We are convinced that ideas count. But we are less clear about when, why, and how much. This first chapter reflects briefly on these questions by reference to some of the stories behind the material contained in this book. It will almost certainly frustrate the curious and engaged reader, since it does little more than sketch a topic that is worthy of far more. This limitation reflects the fact that I remain unclear as to what role the ideas that have evolved in my area of work really do or will play in making a real difference. As Mao Tse Tung allegedly said when asked about the significance of the French Revolution, 'it is too early to tell'. In this sense, this chapter maps 'work in progress'—a more serious intellectual enterprise waiting to be done that explores the impact of ideas in transforming the role of business and economy in the 21st century.

One thing leads to another

First looks can be deceptive. When in 1982 I proposed a PhD topic to my professor at the London School of Economics that explored economics through an analysis of feminist science fiction, he smiled benignly and suggested instead that I turn my attention to the history of the steam engine. I offered this again as my topic for postgraduate scholarship to the University of Oxford, and was politely asked to 'think again'. Years later, I got my way, and in 1992 published my PhD thesis as *An Economics of Utopia* (Zadek 1993a). My thesis set out a way of thinking about an economics that shifted us from a focus on resource allocation based on market scarcity to one rooted in ethical discourse between those impacted by arising decisions. Tellingly, the secondary title was *Democratising Scarcity*, which in many ways sums up my view and interests in reshaping the discipline and practice of economics. How can we, in short, shape the economy—the use of scarce resources— to the will and needs of people? Looking back, it is easy to see this as the precursor to work on accounting methodologies based on stakeholder dialogue. This subsequently became the basis on which AccountAbility's AA1000 Series was built,[2] impacting in turn on the way in which I approached, for example, my work with the Global Reporting Initiative.[3]

But looking back can deceive, creating 'facts' out of fiction, rather than turning ideas into realities. My thesis is a case in point. On the face of it, the work that I (and others) have done since that time appears to have followed a well-ordered plan. But the reality is of course quite different. My thesis was completed by candlelight. In its writing, it was largely unconnected from many of the exciting developments that were emerging over the same period in the fields of alternative economics and corporate responsibility. The thesis may well have influenced my thinking and practice. But, truth be told, it was in no way part of the main thrust of intellectual thinking that was at that time reshaping the ways in which we understand our world.

My introduction to the New Economics Foundation (NEF) in 1993 was through James Robertson's work on religion and economics. I am a great fan of E.F. Schumacher's seminal book, *Small is Beautiful: Economics as if People Mattered* (Schumacher 1973), a crucial part of NEF's intellectual lineage. Most well known in his book is the chapter 'Buddhist Economics', where he describes an approach to economics influenced by Buddhist teaching and practice. I had been interacting for some years with a Sri Lankan NGO called Sarvodaya Shramadana. Led by its charismatic leader, Dr Ariyaratne, it sought to integrate a self-grown blend of Buddhism and Gandhi's philosophy into its community programmes. Like many NGOs at the time, the organisation was struggling with the challenges of growth and scale, trying to reconnect the ever-more thinly spread link between its originating values and its work on the ground. I was fascinated by these challenges, and concerned at the absence of any serious work on how large-scale organisations could fit into an alternative economics paradigm. NEF's newly appointed Executive Director, Ed Mayo, became convinced of the value of building a programme of research in the light of my argument that an alternative economics without a progressive approach to large-scale organisation would simply not fly. And so it was that I joined this band of merry men (and it was all men at that time), cramped into a small room, above a sweatshop off Brick Lane in London's East End.

The resulting programme, *Value-Based Organisation*, was a study of the links between organisational performance, values and accountability. The basic hypothesis was that organisational performance was grounded in its values, and that values were expressed not by what it said on the door but by the organisation's underlying rule structures. The focus was on the NGO community, an orientation that has remained important today, as reflected in a piece included in this anthology, first published in the magazine, *Alliance*, 'Civil Governance and Accountability: From Fear and Loathing to Social Innovation'. In addition to Sarvodaya Shramadana, we worked with some amazing organisations, including UNITAS, the network of non-profit organisations working on sustainable agriculture in Bolivia; the Mexican eco-anarchist group GEA; and the Christian fair-trade organisation Traidcraft. We developed a number of tools to help us assess whether and how organisations' values were consistent with the way they worked, and vice versa.

Few of these tools saw the light beyond their research application and coverage in an NEF publication, *Value-Based Organisation* (Zadek 1996). The reason for this marginalisation was not, however, to do with their limitations, but rather the success of our work with Traidcraft, and in particular with their head of external relations, Richard Evans. Traidcraft, working with community trading organisations from all over the world, challenged us to work with them in answering just one question: 'are we "fair"?' Drawing on learning from the programme, we co-developed a social audit tool that integrated stakeholder engagement into a process of multi-dimensional planning and evaluation. At the core of this tool was the vision that stakeholders' voices—rather than only the financial value of market-based transactions—should be the basic currency of any robust accounting system, both at the design stage when the questions concerned who to talk to and how, and then in the development of performance metrics and reporting. Our politics and philosophy was in essence that the quality of stakeholder engagement was *the* quality test of an effective social audit, rather than just an informative 'add-on'.

The Latin American components of the *Value-Based Organisation* programme had some unexpected consequences. Working with Jutta Blauert from the UK Institute of Latin American Studies, we connected her skills and networks focused on sustainable agriculture and rural development with our work on alternative economics, organisational values, accounting and accountability. We ended up collaborating in a two-year study group entitled 'Mediating Sustainability', exploring how grass-roots organisations amplified their voice to the policy level in government and business. The results of this work, one of the first to explore how NGOs impacted on public policies, are summarised in 'The Art of Mediation' drawn from the book *Mediating Sustainability: Growing Policy from the Grassroots*.

As part of this, we came into closer contact with key players from the international movement for 'participatory development', including Robert Chambers, author of the seminal book, *Farmers First* (Chambers *et al.* 1989), then at the Institute of Development Studies at the University of Sussex. NEF's growing engagement with the business community made this relationship difficult in the initial stages, given this network's concerns over the impact of multinationals on development. But this resistance declined as it became clear how much there was to learn from each other. Their work on participatory development at a community level was in effect the 'horizontal' equivalent of our approach to social auditing which was intended to work 'vertically' within large, modern organisations. Our work on systems and metrics proved useful to those working at community level who focused on the empowerment aspects of engagement and dialogue. Social auditing in turn benefited from our interaction with the participatory development movement, for example, in learning from techniques for community planning and evaluation.

Bringing together the worlds of community-based empowerment and corporate accountability is, today, a well-trodden path. But this was far from the case when in 1994 NEF convened a meeting of local community organisations, international research activists and a host of people from the OECD, the UN and the World Bank at Toynbee Hall, a venue buried deep within London's impoverished East End. The meeting was billed as being about measuring sustainable development, and resulted in the two-volume publication, *Accounting for Change: Indicators for Sustainable Development*, co-authored with Alex MacGillivray (Zadek and MacGillivray 1994). On the first day, I recall how the participants quietly observed each other, wondering what lay behind an agenda littered with presentations and discussions about measurement. On the second day, a more fruitful war of words broke out, with the focus of attention on the pros and cons of technocratic measures (what we subsequently called 'cold' indicators), as compared to community-led metrics ('hot' indicators).

This spectrum of measures from hot to cold has proved a crucial axis along which social (more than environmental) accountability has become measured and, in many ways, contested. The idea was that the hotter indicators were those embedded within a particular conversation, relationship or set of circumstances. Their value was not their objectivity but rather the bridge they created between different people and interests, such as a mining company and a community. The strength of such metrics was, then, their 'inter-subjectivity', reflecting the language of my PhD, *An Economics of Utopia*. The colder the indicators, on the other hand, the more they could serve across many conversations, and so provide information to people who were not direct participants. Hot indicators tended at that time to be favoured by those who saw change as a political process, while cold indicators were advocated by those with a more managerial perspective.

Mediating between hot and cold indicators, reconceptualised in 'Beyond Fourth-Generation Evaluation', lies at the heart of the approach to social and subsequently sustainability accounting and reporting that emerged over this period. On the one hand, the challenge was to create metrics that legitimised and enabled the professional management of non-financial aspects of performance. On the other hand, the process of building and applying metrics was seen as the Trojan Horse through which to empower employees, communities and other stakeholders that had historically been excluded from decision-making. The key was to navigate between these options, connecting performance management and measurement with stakeholder engagement through the development and promotion of one integrating methodology.

This idea was outlined in its contemporary form in 1993 in the publication *Auditing the Market: A Practical Approach to Social Auditing* (Zadek and Evans 1993).

This pamphlet, co-authored with Richard Evans, outlined in simple terms the 'accounting principles' required to build and apply social metrics through stakeholder dialogue. Like most 'great social innovations', we rapidly discovered that it had already been invented. Social accounting and auditing has a fascinating and important history, elements of which are summarised in Chapter 15, 'Accounting works: a comparative review of contemporary approaches to social and ethical accounting', co-authored with Peter Raynard. But this history is largely theoretical. Numerous publications laid out the art of social auditing as it should or could be, but not how it was, with notable exceptions such as the work of Charles Medawar through Social Audit Limited. Crucially, the importance of the 1993 and subsequent publications—for example, the book co-edited with Peter Pruzan and Richard Evans, *Building Corporate Accountability: Emerging Practices in Social and Ethical Accounting, Auditing, and Reporting* (Zadek *et al.* 1997)—was that they offered not only philosophy and concepts but practical examples of the messy realities of companies trying to do it.

Silence largely greeted the early work emerging from Traidcraft and NEF. The corporate community crassly dismissed social auditing as being 'for the likes of The Body Shop and Ben & Jerry's, not for *real* companies'. The professional auditing companies, today of course all competing for business in this growing market, were unanimous in agreeing that 'there would be no significant market for this kind of service'. Ironically, civil-society organisations in the main also gave these early experiences short shrift, dismissing them as public relations and irrelevant to the cause of corporate accountability. There were a few, quite unexpected, takers. Reuters, oddly, picked up the story. After an (unexpected) visit to NEF's offices, they posed the question in their news release: 'Is it possible', they asked, 'that up some rusty old steps in London's East-end lies a still-hidden innovation [social auditing] that one day might fundamentally change the business landscape?' It felt like Christmas.

But this all changed in late 1995. Years of hard campaigning by NGOs and labour organisations about working conditions in global supply chains of premium brands such as Disney and Nike were paying off. Companies were seeking a public truce by agreeing to the principle that they had some responsibility for the working conditions of those employed by other companies from which they were buying products. Let no one tell you otherwise, this was an immensely important breakthrough in the history of corporate accountability.

The irony of this success was the difficulty it created for many labour-focused NGOs. Companies, true to form, raised the practical question, 'If we are to be accountable, we have to account—how can this be done?' NGOs were basically clueless, and labour organisations were hardly better. It is one thing to campaign but quite another to know how best to manage labour conditions across enormous, sprawling global supply chains. In the UK, a group of development and human rights NGOs formed a small task group to look at this issue, led by Oxfam, Christian Aid and the World Development Movement. Looking around to find any civil-society organisations that had any relevant practical expertise, they came upon NEF. We of course knew very little about labour standards issues, since this area of work had been left to our (now defunct) sister organisation, New Consumer (the UK equivalent to the US-based Council on Economic Priorities, now also defunct). But we did know something about social auditing.

One year later, the Labour Party swept into power in the UK. As Clare Short took up her position as Secretary of State for International Development, her civil servants presented her with options for new investments. High on the agenda was a proposal to support a multi-stakeholder initiative to work out how best to make codes of conduct in global supply chains work to improve labour standards. Behind this proposal lay a gruelling year of tough negotiations between the parties. It was not just who was at the table that was innovative, although the combination of international labour, big business and NGOs was certainly 'news'. What was extraordinary was that the initiative was designed not to set and enforce codes but to create a collaborative platform to learn how to implement codes effectively. The partners had built sufficient trust between each other to be willing to risk a relatively open-ended engagement in an environment where every other initiative around the world was focused on standards and compliance. And so the Ethical Trading Initiative was born.

Looking back, innovation seems so well organised. The pathways that transport ideas from the mainstream to the margin seem elegant and rational, their impact signalling their timeliness as much as their inherent qualities. Leadership in this world is recognisable, usually individualised, and invariably original and brilliant. But this version of the history of ideas should be dismissed as either a malicious or misguided fairy tale. Certainly, the role of particular people should not be underestimated. Ideas are certainly elevated by individuals' insights and energies. But, beyond this, I suspect we need to seek insight from the coincidences of the moment. People find themselves in the right place at the right time, applauded for advancing ideas that would have been (and often were) dismissed as lunatic ravings just moments before. Mainstreaming ideas can perhaps best be understood as an 'associational' process, a sort of institutional poetry rather a linear, scientific transmission.

One thing does indeed lead to another.

Mainstreaming paradoxes

Today, the air is thick with the buzz of corporate responsibility leaders, innovators and practitioners. Conferences and publications on the topic are in abundance, the tip of an iceberg that has become a fast-growing industry. Many of those companies and service providers most vocal in distancing themselves from the early experimentation have proved the strongest advocates of sustainability reporting, often winning applause and coveted awards in the process. Even companies from controversial sectors such as alcohol, tobacco and gambling have joined the party— running up bills of tens of millions of dollars in demonstrating their new-found enthusiasm for dialogue and transparency.

In one sense, little of this is new. The role of business in society has always been the subject of public debate, policy and practice. Our histories are littered with experiments of businesses 'doing good'. After all, the mother of industrialisation, England, gave birth not only to the world's industrial sweatshops, but socialising entrepreneurs such as Robert Owen, and the modern co-operative movement. Indeed, some of our most democratic innovations—notably the labour movement— were built on a vision of making business more responsible.

But the fact that there is a rich lineage to our work does not reduce the particularities of the moment. Today's experience of corporate responsibility exists in a particular context, and has important, distinct characteristics. Emerging from the troubled waters of globalisation, its focus has in truth not been on 'business' per se, but 'big business' of the multi- and transnational variety. The main provocateurs of change have been the new breed of transnational civil-society organisations—the NGOs—filling a perceived void left by both governments and the labour movement. The 'credible threat' that encourages change has also a particular, contemporary variant. This is more closely linked to the vulnerability of businesses' intangible assets than to the traditional threat of disrupting production. Its early stages in the 1990s were associated with perceived shortfalls in the role of the state, particularly in terms of the adequacy and enforcement of statutory regulation.

Core to the specifics of the moment has been the emergence of what I, and others, have dubbed 'civil regulation' as a route to setting business norms and punishing those companies that fail to meet them. This is best framed in terms of non-statutory policies and codes, negotiated through engagement with key stakeholders, as described in the chapter 'Civil Regulation', taken from my book *The Civil Corporation: The New Economy of Corporate Citizenship* (Zadek 2001a). Civil regulation is in many ways the essence of 'amateurism' in its original sense (i.e. activities not undertaken for financial reward). Yet it is this amateurism that is profoundly transforming the very professions that have so desperately sought to remain aloof from such activity. Edward Said's Reith Lectures on the role of the intellectual in many ways reflect the thinking behind this agenda (Said 1994).

A clear example of this is the impact civil regulation has had on the dramatic growth in the disclosure of non-financial performance, which has driven demands for new standards for accounting, auditing and reporting. These demands are increasingly being embraced by professionals, including accountants and auditors, often sensing new markets to build and exploit. Yet their professional bodies have been the fiercest defenders of traditional boundaries to their disciplines, their methods and, by implication, their authority. In this case, this resistance has catalysed the creation of new institutions representing new visions and interests, and associated methods. AccountAbility (originally the Institute of Social and Ethical AccountAbility) was born out of precisely such demands, in this case for a professional institute that could promote social and sustainability thinking and practice in the development of tomorrow's accounting, auditing and reporting standards. Mainstreaming ideas has turned out to have as much to do with legitimising these new institutions as it has been about smart thinking.

Mainstreaming corporate responsibility is clearly not just a matter of business complying with human rights and other societal norms, and neatly packaging it all in an annual sustainability report. Certainly we should celebrate good practice in these areas. And, yes, we should highlight the great success of some companies in addressing, for example, the complexity of labour standards in global supply chains. But if these 'good practices' are the essence of corporate responsibility, we must conclude that it is little more than an interesting experiment, perhaps a short-term palliative to satisfy public expectations of what business should be account-able for.

The alchemy of success certainly needs us to take advantage of opportunism and innovation through leadership practice, as popular thinking about 'tipping points' makes clear. Leadership is part of how change happens. It is crucial to our learning, and to showing others what is possible. But 'extra-ordinary' practice is also a sign of an idea's continued marginal status. After all, we do not (or should not) give prizes to companies for producing accurate financial statements, or for achieving accept-able health and safety records.

The mainstream is characterised by what is unexceptional and unnoticed.

The alchemy of success requires that the mechanics of, say, corporate responsi-bility are no more than symptoms, or at best reflect changes that can underpin the mainstreaming process. There are several macro-changes that support the view that corporate responsibility is part of a deeper transformation in our society: the emergence of a global civil society linked inextricably to the globalisation of markets; the increasingly visible levels of inequity, poverty and environmental insecurity; and the underlying loss of trust in the institutions we have built to govern us, to create private goods and services, and deliver public goods such as health and security. There are also numerous more business-specific shifts taking place: the extension of business into the delivery of public services, and the management and ownership of what were previously public assets; and the transformation in the ways in which businesses are managed and economic value created, with a far greater focus on 'networked' people and institutions requiring cohesive values and higher levels of trust. These underlying changes have been amply documented by many contemporary commentators.

We can see these underlying changes play themselves out in specific spheres of corporate responsibility. It is barely a year or so since a deal was struck under the auspices of the World Trade Organisation (WTO) that allowed generic versions of patented drugs for certain diseases, notably HIV/AIDS, to be produced and traded across borders for sale in poor countries. This outcome had been deemed 'incon-ceivable' just a year earlier as the collective power of the global pharmaceutical industry applied its muscle in the South African courts. The launch of the UN Global Compact in July 2000 was greeted by many with concern and derision in equal measure. For some, particularly labour and human rights organisations, it was 'too soft'. For others, notably the bulk of the US business community, it was in all but name a perversion of the natural order, and a definite 'no-no' in the eyes of their omnipotent legal advisors. Just three years on, the Compact is not only alive but very much kicking. Thousands of companies, the majority from developing coun-tries, have pledged their allegiance to its original nine principles (now ten), which in all but name mirror many of the UN's core Conventions.[4] Some argue it is easy to pledge allegiance, but many more begin to wonder if these are the formative stages of new pieces of the global governance puzzle.

These early signs of deeper change do not, at this stage, however, warrant too much celebration. The instinct and practice on the part of much of the business community is to continue to profit through the irresponsible externalisation of social and environmental costs. This is perhaps best symbolised by the failure to date of the Doha Trade Round to deliver the end of the EC's and US's poverty-inducing agricultural subsidies, and the Bush Administration's almost-mesmerising trashing of the Kyoto Treaty and other profit-limiting environmental controls. Our enthusiastic embrace of progress in some areas of corporate responsibility should certainly not blind us to the warnings of less-optimistic fellow travellers such as Naomi Klein and David Korten.

The truth, of course, is that both progressive and truly ghastly things can and do happen at the same time. Indeed, they can be authored by the same communities, and even at times by the very same actor. The idea that change happens by one thing stopping to allow another to begin is simply misguided. The value of John Elkington's inspiring optimism is not diminished by the accuracy of George Monbiot's revelations about the business community, just as Naomi Klein's hard-edged critique is not blunted by Mark Moody-Stuart's embracing spirit.

As progressive ideas struggle to find water and light, there is simultaneously and without contradiction cause for both hope and despair.

Momentary coincidences

Mainstreaming is rarely about common interests, despite optimistic rhetoric to the contrary. Ideas become mainstream most effectively when the interests of players with very different visions and aims **coincide momentarily in practice**.

The art of 'momentary coincidences' was highlighted in work on partnerships with Ros Tennyson and others from the International Business Leaders Forum, published as *Endearing Myths, Enduring Truths* by the World Bank-facilitated Business Partners for Development initiative (Zadek 2001c). We offered a list of ten myths about partnerships, and what we felt were the corresponding truths. Arguably the most important concerned the role of shared vision and aims of participants in tri-sector partnerships. Influenced by the work of Mancur Olsen, particularly his seminal book, *The Logic of Collective Action* (Olsen 1971), we argued that a key **endearing myth** was that:

> Successful partnerships are primarily shaped around a common or shared long-term vision or aim.

The **enduring truth**, on the other hand, we argued as being that:

> Successful partnerships are those shaped around common or shared activities that first and foremost deliver against the legitimised individual aims of each partner.

The *realpolitik* of momentary coincidences creates opportunities for getting things done. Branded businesses increasingly took responsibility for labour standards in their (purely contracted) global supply chains because of the need to defend reputations. But times change, and we now see the chase for improved labour standards acquiring new energy because companies require more participative factory conditions to profit, for example, from 'lean manufacturing' principles and practices. Stakeholder engagement, initially seen by many businesses (and it still is) as an unacceptable erosion of the rights of management to manage, has increasingly become 'just another aspect of management' in mainstream practice.

But the pragmatism of mainstreaming involves compromise. The environmental movement of the 1980s was the enemy of the business community until it became clearer that the eco-efficiency element of the agenda was both manageable within a traditional business model, and indeed potentially profitable. The cost, however, was the surgical separation of what was mainstreamed from the (to some) problematic, eco-justice element. NGOs such as Friends of the Earth, after a decade of successfully mainstreaming some environmental issues, are now turning their focus back to the eco-justice agenda. An equivalent for corporate responsibility has been its almost complete de-link with the sustainable consumption agenda to which it was wedded in the '90s. We face the implications of this de-linking when we challenge the underlying problems with the 'Wal-Mart' business model that seeks to deliver ever-cheaper products to relatively impoverished urbanised consumers. Ensuring that companies such as Wal-Mart get, for example, 'labour standards right' is important, but really misses the point when it comes to a radical agenda for remodelling our markets towards a sane and sustainable economics.

As partnerships have mainstreamed, similarly the limits of 'momentary coincidences' have become more apparent, raising concerns in many quarters as to their impacts. Criticism of initiatives such as the UN Global Compact by development and human rights organisations and the labour movement exemplify such concerns, as the potential for leveraging resources and momentum can distract us from asserting the need to change the rules of the game. Partnerships should not be automatically understood as an advancement of the cause of progressive change, or indeed the opposite. More usefully, they can be seen as reflecting a moment in time where the balance of power between the parties makes a consensual framework for action suited to the principal partners. Such partnerships can become institutionalised and so endure, such as the UN Global Compact, or national initiatives such as the Ethical Trading Initiative or AccountAbility. But such institutions remain ephemeral, and can just as easily disappear if the balance of power shifts, and the interests of one party are better served in other ways.

We see, for example, that business has grown weary of the pressures to partner 'at all costs', and is increasingly challenging the competencies and legitimacy of their would-be civil collaborators. Work commissioned by Business for Social Responsibility (BSR), and published in 2002 as *Working with Multilaterals* (Zadek 2002), explored through the eyes of business the experience of partnering with UN agencies. Although politely moderate, the report was taken to be a resounding critique of the UN's own accountability. Business found the UN largely unprofessional and unaccountable in its partnership dealings, an experience confirmed by many non-business actors involved in this crucially important institution. The focus on corporate accountability in debate about UN–business partnerships was understandable, but missed the point, the report argued. Holding companies to account in partnerships required strong public and civil partners, and above all impeccable accountability and performance credentials on their part, both of which were in short supply.

Inventing tomorrow's history

John Maynard Keynes famously argued that what stops us creating positive futures is not a shortage of good ideas but our inability to let go of the past. Being the bearer of 'tomorrow's bad tidings' is an unwelcome role. UN officials were furious that *Working with Multilaterals* challenged the UN's basis of accountability. Concerns expressed in 'Looking Back from 2010' over the inadequacy of NGO accountability were met with a stony silence by NGO leaders angry that they had somehow been betrayed from within their own ranks. Advocates of partnerships were not happy at 'Partnership futures', published at the time of the Johannesburg Summit, because of the bleak scenario it presented for the possible future role of partnerships in development.

But it is not only the bad tidings that are resisted. My writings consistently highlight the potential for progressive change, but the challenges underlying this potential are also resented and resisted by those who should know better. It is, ironically, the civil activists who more than others have resisted the idea that the business community should have a social purpose. The argument in 'Ethical trade futures' that companies could be a key pathway through which progressive public policies could be achieved was met with derision and irritation by labour activists. At a meeting in Chicago convened by the McArthur Foundation, one Latin American activist argued, 'keep it simple, let them [business] stick to their knitting in trying to make a profit, and leave governments and us to regulate and challenge them'.

Resistance to change is pervasive, and it is a wonder that anything important changes at all. My reflections, set out in the preceding pages, offer three interconnected reasons.

- The first is that **'one thing leads to another'**, creating an associational process combining coincidence with the role of people in change.

- The second concerns the **mainstreaming paradox**, where ideas mainstream because of their connection to the underlying logic of its context, economic or otherwise.

- And finally, the notion of **'momentary coincidences'** that give energy to ideas despite the very differing broader interests of their advocates.

These reasons are neither new nor complete, and may well be incorrect in many instances. But together they have helped me to understand a little about the bit of history that I am honoured to be part of and, with others, contribute to.

Section I
the economics of utopia

1
a matter of need*

Human Scale Development: Conceptions, Applications, and Further Reflections. By Manfred Max-Neef with contributions from Antonio Elizalde and Martin Hopenhayn. London: Zed Books, 1992, Apex Press, New York). 114 pp. £36.95 hb, £14.95 pb.

A Theory of Human Need. By Len Doyal and Ian Gough. London: Macmillan, 1991. 365 pp. £35.00 hb, £10.99 pb.

Development is about needs: the need to survive, to eat, for shelter, for environmental and social security, and many aspects of community. Development is about the satisfaction of these needs, particularly for those who are not getting enough. But what are these 'basic needs'? Are they defined in absolute terms—protein intake, for example—or in relative terms, such as 'enough to participate in what others are doing'? Does drinking Coca-Cola, driving a car, or taking up arms against one's neighbour satisfy a need, a desire, or are these just mistakes or aberrations?

These questions, while not new, are nonetheless serious, particularly for those who find themselves as directors, arbitrators, or facilitators of 'need'-related changes ranging from the villages of India to the slums of London. The roles of participatory research and indigenous knowledge, for example, hang on a thread of what one believes constitutes legitimate need. So, too, does the case for universal rights and norms of social justice, with its associated plethora of 'alternative' social, economic and environmental indicators. Without some sense of how to establish and reach agreement about the nature of basic or fundamental needs, it is difficult to make decisions about which needs to satisfy and how, whether within the formulation of national social policy, or international or local development initiatives.

This matter has recently been addressed in two books, *A Theory of Human Need* by Len Doyal and Ian Gough, and *Human Scale Development: Conception, Application and Further Reflections* by Manfred Max-Neef with contributions from Antonio Elizalde and Martin Hopenhayn. Both challenge the current relativist vogue in analysing needs. Both assert the intelligibility of universal needs, while supporting the cause of pluralism. Both challenge the prevailing despondency and apathy of post-modern, post-1980s' debate and practice by setting out concrete normative approaches. Both books are, quite simply, necessary reading for anyone interested

* From a book review, in *Environmental Values* 3 (1994), pp. 83-85. © The White Horse Press, Isle of Harris.

in the theory and practice of social change, as confirmed by the considerable acclaim accorded to them within their respective circles.

Doyal and Gough set out with the ambitious aim of demonstrating that 'a coherent, rigorous theory of human need must be developed to resurrect an acceptable vision of social progress and to provide a credible alternative to the neo-liberalism and political conservatism which has caused serious harm to so many within the capitalist world' (p. 3). This aim is pursued with deadly intent over the following 300 pages, which offer wide-ranging insights into some philosophical and practical underpinnings of the analysis of needs. Central to their argument is that 'basic needs are linked to the avoidance of serious harm . . . [which] . . . is . . . understood as the significantly impaired pursuit of goals which are deemed of value by individuals' (p. 50). The avoidance of 'serious harm' in turn requires a combination of procedural and substantive conditions, which Doyal and Gough derive theoretically from a brief but pointed critical application of the works of key contemporary philosophers, notably Rawls, Habermas and Sen. These conditions focus on physical health and autonomy, the latter concerning in particular mental 'health', cognitive development, and economic opportunity. These conditions allow one, they argue, to transcend the double-binds established by both cultural relativism and one of its philosophical bedfellows, utilitarianism. In this way it is possible to achieve a clear statement of human rights rooted in a coherent and theoretically consistent statement of basic needs.

Doyal and Gough are quite rightly not satisfied to offer merely intellectual neatness or completeness, since their interests transparently concern the practice of political economy. They take it upon themselves to show that their theoretical discourse translates into the empirical jungle of applied social analysis. Thus, the penultimate section of the book discusses the relationship between their theoretical propositions, and the range of intermediate goods, or 'satisfiers', through which people in practice might experience adequate satisfaction of basic needs. This section includes a review of a fascinating assortment of social, economic and environmental indicators that the authors feel could be used in the application of their underlying argument.

The core text of Max-Neef and his colleagues on the matter of need spans precisely 41 pages of well-spaced text, a minor fraction of that provided by Doyal and Gough. Not surprisingly, therefore, Max-Neef's approach does not delve seriously into the philosophical spheres in which he is implicitly rooted, or which he chooses to challenge. At the same time, *Human Scale Development* is as ambitious as Doyal and Gough's work, and approaches development with a comparable political stance. Max-Neef's aim is '[to provide] . . . a conceptual framework that shows a way out of the sterile confrontation between traditional developmentalism and neo-liberal monetarism' (p. viii). The two texts also coincide in their view of universal needs, 'fundamental human needs are finite, few and classifiable . . . [and] . . . are the same in all cultures and in all historical periods'. 'What changes, both over time and through cultures,' Max-Neef continues in implicit agreement with Doyal and Gough, 'is the way or the means by which the needs are satisfied' (p. 18).

Max-Neef's and Doyal and Gough's arguments are not, however, the same. Max-

Neef defines 'fundamental needs' along two axes: *existential* (Being, Having, Doing and Interacting), and *axiological* (Subsistence, Protection, Affection, Understanding, Participation, Idleness, Creation, Identity and Freedom). Economic goods, or also, for example, activities and states of mind, can be placed in cells of a 'Matrix of Satisfiers' linking existential and axiological aspects of fundamental needs. Food and shelter, for example, might be placed in the cell that links Subsistence and Having. Passion, imagination and curiosity, similarly, might be expressions of the relationship between Being and Creation.

Max-Neef's approach, while less rigorous in theoretical terms, is more comprehensive than Doyal and Gough's framework in allowing for qualitative factors to be taken into account. It also offers the possibility of analysing not only 'positive' satisfiers, but also goods and activities that prevent the satisfaction of fundamental needs. Thus, matrix cells can be filled (all too easily) with 'destroyers' (which annihilate the possibility of satisfaction over time), 'pseudo-satisfiers' and 'inhibiting satisfiers'. Max-Neef is therefore directly addressing the Coca-Cola question, and so offers a means of classifying significant negative aspects of the equation of 'development', such as censorship, and the over-exploitation of natural resources.

A third and most important distinguishing feature of Max-Neef's approach is its focus on the community, rather than the individual. Doyal and Gough draw inspiration from Kant's conception of 'autonomy', which concerns most directly the condition of the individual (or an aggregate of individuals). Max-Neef, on the other hand, focuses on the need to 'encourage increasing autonomy in (and through) the emerging social movements' (p. 10). Thus, whereas both arguments support the proposition of universal needs, Doyal and Gough choose ultimately to offer a menu of universal measures of the satisfaction of the individual's basic needs, while Max-Neef emphasises the role of the 'community' in defining its own 'matrix of needs'.

This difference in approach (individual versus community autonomy, and universal versus local indicators) is partially complementary. Doyal and Gough have not attempted to describe the process of social change, whereas Max-Neef's approach is essentially a tool for community-specific, political–therapeutic processes, i.e. the whole participatory paradigm (Chambers *et al.* 1989). Similarly, Max-Neef's emphasis on the role of the community in the self-definition of needs does not necessarily conflict with Doyle and Gough's cross-community analysis of outcome, or indeed the need to constrain community agendas if they prove to be—in Max-Neef's own terminology—reflections of, rather than liberation from, dominating 'collective pathologies'.

There is a sense, however, in which the two approaches do potentially conflict. Doyal and Gough broadly build on, and contribute a theoretical basis to, the growing body of work on alternative social and economic indicators (Anderson 1991; Ekins 1992). Much of this work is certainly an improvement on traditional measures of 'success' that have dominated the mainstream economic development debate. However, such measures are also problematic in purporting to offer not only universal measures of social change, but 'objective' measures of whether and when such change is 'good' or 'bad'. The concern is that even the best-intentioned attempts to provide universal measures of well-being or social improvement have proved vulnerable to the degrading effects of their adoption and misuse by bureaucracies and professionals (Chambers 1993). Such interests respond defensively towards any serious attempt to legitimise conceptions of 'success' that directly conflict with their own concerns. The resistance of governments and businesses alike to allowing meaningful participative processes in the selection and production of environmental indicators is an obvious case in point.

This concern is not directed at the intent of Doyal and Gough, whose political interests are clear. They would surely support the relevance of local perspectives articulated through locally generated indicators, whether along the lines suggested by Max-Neef or in other ways (Zadek 1993b). However, while the assertion of universal indicators clearly attempts to win the high ground on an ambitious scale, the support of the rights of communities to evolve their own perspectives may ultimately be a more effective strategy of empowerment—and will certainly always be a necessary component of it. Thus, the danger of universalised indicators undermining local initiative is not a reason for abandoning any such approach, but rather underlines the need to consider strategy with some care.

The two books reviewed here are relevant in a period marked by increasing dismay and despondency at the failure of a development model that has been readily applied to the 'third world' on the basis of the twofold misconception that it was right for 'them', and that it has already proved right for 'us'. Doyal and Gough's fascinating philosophical and empirical discourse offers insight into this critical area, and a mass of material that can underpin the evolution of more-coherent social and economic policy and praxis and, by implication, political processes. Max-Neef's approach is an equally powerful challenge to the core 'development paradigm' which continues to dominate the mainstream approaches to the formulation and implementation of social and economic change. His refutation of the notion that we have to be passive (complaining) recipients and implementers of conventional wisdoms is no less than an open invitation to anyone involved in social change—which of course includes us all—to reappraise the place of economic goods and processes in the context of our real needs, and to act on the basis of such a reappraisal.

Max-Neef and his colleagues, and Doyal and Gough, take us forward in addressing this critical area at the level of praxis and theory. Both books reviewed offer their own insights as well as together highlighting tensions between different perspectives and approaches. Both must be basic reading for anyone interested and concerned about what we are to do, and how we are to think, in the 'post-development' era.

2
the *practice* of buddhist economics?[*]

The question

Over recent years there has been an increased interest in the relationship between religion and that most down-to-earth subject: economics. The reason for this developing debate is in itself of considerable interest, and is certainly relevant here. It concerns the central question of whether we can believe any longer that the secular trajectory of economic development typical of industrialised countries is sustainable over the long—or possibly over the not so long—term. One mirror image of this question is whether the role of 'religion' or faith, in some shape or form, offers a basis for evolving more effective mechanisms for survival, let alone reasonable levels of well-being, for the majority.

This chapter is part of this evolving debate. Its starting point is the able contributions made by Frederic Pryor in this journal[1] about the relationship between economics and Buddhism (1990, 1991). The possibility is explored of taking the debate beyond his focus on the canonical texts into the heartland of Buddhism, 'practice' itself. Indeed, the broad proposition here is that Buddhism offers considerable insight into our economic conditions and practices, but that an appreciation of these insights requires that one takes one's starting point as the 'practice' rather than the purely theoretical or ethical aspects of Buddhism.[2]

The 'practice' of Buddhist economics

Pryor states at the beginning of his first paper ('A Buddhist Economic System—In Principle') that his 'discussion of ideas in the formal Buddhist canonical sources

[*] First published in the *American Journal of Economics and Sociology* 52.4 (October 1993). © Blackwell Publishing, Oxford.

does not tell us anything very specific about how Buddhism is actually practised today' (1990: 340). Pryor maintains this focus in his second paper ('A Buddhist Economic System: In Practice'), despite its declared interest in 'practice' rather than 'principle' (1991: 17). Pryor's work is an important contribution to the field, since it is necessary to explore the literal meaning of original texts with respect to matters of ethics and their possible implications for economic practice.[3] However, this approach also has its limitations. Texts (even 'original' ones) are produced in a particular social, political and economic context. Their interpretation therefore needs to take account of both our understanding of that context, and the context in which we find ourselves today. The comments in this chapter are therefore an attempt to edge sideways towards such an approach as a contribution to building bridges between the relationship of the texts to economics (as done by Pryor), and some of the day-to-day 'realities' of economic and spiritual life. That is, since Buddhism is fundamentally concerned with a set of values realisable only through 'practice', let us turn towards the puzzling question of what might be **the practice of Buddhist economics**.

On organisation

Most traditions of social analysis argue that the well-being of individuals and groups is intimately related to the ethics and rationale of social organisation. The Buddha, on the other hand, is often viewed as seeing increased well-being as arising from only individual practice, rather than through the development of particular forms of social organisation. Indeed, the Buddha, argues Pryor, 'had little concern for society as such and little conviction of its possible improvability' (1991: 20). The implication of this apparent divergence of approach has been that the meaning of the 'small-scale' philosophy implicit in Buddhist economics (Schumacher 1973) has remained largely divorced from serious analysis of larger-scale, modern society.

This divorce is not, however, either necessary or desirable. One route to establishing some relationship between the two is to consider the link between Buddhism and the organisation of 'community'.[4] Chakravarti, for example, argues that the Buddha modelled the Sangha (the orders of the monks) on the *ganasangha* (Chakravarti 1992). The *ganasangha* were one sort of political, territorial 'clan' that existed in what is now northern India around the time of the Buddha, about sixth century BC. Two key features of these clans were that its members exercised a collective power,[5] and held all assets as common property. The organisation of decision-making in the Sangha broadly follow the same lines: 'no social divisions are recognised—there is the metaphor of people who come, and like the four streams, merge together. Decision is through consensus. You try to accommodate all points of view, but if that fails, then the majority opinion counts' (Chakravarti 1992: 16). This world of the monks is to be contrasted, argued Chakravarti, to the *janapadas*, the world of the laity. Decision-making in this lay world was dominated by the kings and the *ganapathis* (the owners of property who never work for anyone else). Here, decision-making structures were strictly hierarchical, and included little or no process of consultation with the wider populace.

It is wrong to conclude, therefore, that the practice of Buddhism does not offer insights into the matter of social organisation, even if Pryor is right in arguing that the canonical texts do not suggest that the Buddha *advocated* one or other form. In particular, the form of social organisation of the Sangha described by Chakravarti suggests that communal, non-hierarchical forms of decision-making were seen as offering an aid in discarding the pressures of desires rooted in the self (ego), and thus an aid to achieving *nibbana* (nirvana). Thus, whilst the Buddha saw the process of production (and reproduction) as key elements in the generation of greed and the loss of compassion (Chakravarti 1992: 16), he also saw that **the actual structure of decision-making could support or impede a transcendence of these existential shackles**. Pryor certainly recognises this. So, although he insists that the Buddha understood that social conditions could never be *fundamentally* bettered, he agrees that they 'might help or hinder humans in their search for *nibbana*' (1991: 20).[6] However, Pryor's decision to focus on the texts rather than practice draws him away from exploring this in more detail.

Buddhist action

That Buddhism concerns first and foremost the 'practice of being' rather than any 'philosophy of becoming' is reflected in the historical roots of the notion of Sangha. It is therefore critically necessary to consider the implications of the Buddha's signposts in today's society. It is in the real achievements of people attempting to act in the imperfect world according to the tenets of Buddhism that offers the only meaningful understanding into what Buddhism does or does not contribute to our manner of living. The difficulty of this approach, of course, is that the records are so diverse. The experiences of communities influenced by Buddhism range from the inspirational direction taken by the community of exiled Tibetans through to the role of Buddhist nationalism in the current civil war raging in Sri Lanka (Chapela 1992). The limits of this chapter, and of the author, do not allow for any comprehensive assault on this daunting subject. However, it is possible to offer a simple illustration of how Buddhist principles are applied in pursuit of social transformation.

The illustration draws from the experience of the Sarvodaya Shramadana Movement ('Sarvodaya') in Sri Lanka. Sarvodaya is a community organisation working to improve the situation of people in rural areas throughout Sri Lanka (Zadek and Szabo 1993). Important here is that the philosophy and imagery through which Sarvodaya's aims and approach are articulated are drawn from a combination of Gandhian and Buddhist principles (Ariyaratne 1985; Macy 1984). Underpinning Sarvodaya's work is the view that social action and change must seek to achieve spiritual transformation, and so bring forward both compassion and wisdom in people's social relationships, and also in their relationships to themselves and nature (Batchelor and Brown 1992).

The critical feature of Sarvodaya's method is embodied in its approach to village-level consultation and mobilisation. Sarvodaya has evolved a process of decision-making at village level which would in secular 'development vocabulary' be called **participative decision-making** (Chambers 1992; Max-Neef *et al.* 1991). This includes, for example, meetings of the entire village in **family gatherings**, and the formation of groups within the village (women, youth, elders, etc.), who are then encouraged to articulate their own needs and the path by which those needs might be achieved (usually with some technical, organisational or material help from Sarvodaya). That is, the way to break the vicious circle of poverty, loss of dignity, passivity, and ultimately selfish attitudes towards others, **has everything to do with the process of decision-making** within the community. Where it was possible to create more open and equal dialogue between the members of the community, and sometimes outsiders, this supports a process of growing self-awareness of needs and capacities, a recovering of self-dignity, and ultimately spiritual development.

The important place of 'economic development' in Sarvodaya's work arose from the very real needs of its constituencies in the rural areas of Sri Lanka (Ariyaratne 1988; van Loon 1990). The explosion of violence in Sri Lanka from the early 1980s, in particular, further accentuated an already declining economic situation through-out the country, which struck most deeply at the weakest members of the community (Athukorala and Jayasuriya 1991). At the same time as recognising this need, Sarvodaya continued to view improvements in material standards of living as instrumental to achieving a broader sense of well-being. However, this perspective, while consistent with the Movement's Buddhist beliefs, proved difficult to act out in practice. As the material lacking of village communities became more extreme, Sarvodaya came increasingly under pressure to act in practice more like a service-delivery agency, offering credit, business development advice, etc., rather than attempting to maintain the links between economic and broader spiritual develop-ment [Perera *et al.* 1992; Zadek and Szabo 1993].

Whether Sarvodaya has been successful in its economic and broader activities is a matter of considerable debate. Some point to the lack of definitive material advancement of its village partners as a sign of failure; others argue that the disruptions caused by the civil war makes such observations of little worth, and that material advancement is in any case not the key indicator of success. This chapter does not attempt to adjudicate in this debate, since it is not intended as an evalu-ation of the organisation's work. However, the chapter does illustrate the types of actions and forms of organisation that might arise from people rooted in Buddhist perspectives, and the kind of tensions that can built up around such approaches.

The practice of Sarvodaya

It is fundamental to Buddhism that 'practice' does not only concern external 'actions', however laudable, such as those described above. Practice in Buddhism concerns the matter of one's own level of development, which is then reflected in one's actions, rather than vice versa. It is therefore useful to briefly consider the matter of Sarvodaya's practice as reflected by its own processes of organisation and decision-making.

It is useful to return in this context to Chakravarti's description of the traditional organisational forms of the Sangha and the laity. Sarvodaya embodies a curious mixture of both forms. The Sarvodaya model clearly attempts to replicate in some ways the design intended for the Sangha, particularly those aspects that stress the communal basis of decision-making. However, this model was, as we have said, designed with the community of monks in mind, not the laity. Thus, the model was considered in the context of the separation of monks from the processes of production and reproduction, which is of course precisely *not* the situation of the village communities with which Sarvodaya is engaged. That is, the Sarvodaya model of village-level decision-making draws its inspiration from the Buddhist texts, but applies it 'out of context' in terms of a literal reading of those texts. This should not be taken as a criticism. Rather, it highlights the need to consider the 'practice' rather than only the texts of Buddhism when attempting to understand what is its relationship with the very practical world of economics.

What becomes apparent in looking at the decision-making processes in the core of Sarvodaya itself (rather than what happens in the villages with Sarvodaya facilitation) is a lack of what would conventionally be understood as participation or formal consultation. So, for example, although there is a form of *family gathering* that occurs at the headquarters of Sarvodaya, the deference of the mass of Sarvodaya workers towards its President—Dr Ariyaratne—and senior managers limits the possibility of serious grievances or policy issues being fully aired. More generally, the organisation has a hierarchical decision-making structure that enforces the rights of managers at the centre to make decisions, without ensuring formalised feedback processes, let alone any constituted rights of Sarvodaya workers to participate in the process of formulating these decisions.

Great care must be taken in analysing these broad observations to avoid a denigrating caricature, or equally a rose-tinted ideal, to supplant a meaningful analysis of the relationship between the practice of Buddhism and social organisation. Two particular approaches have constituted the historical pattern of analysis of Sarvodaya. The first, which is broadly the argument of those within the organisation, is that it is the pressures from the international donor community to professionalise and become a 'delivery mechanism' for aid that has resulted in this top-down form of decision-making. In this sense, the organisation form is seen as a Western transplant that has little or nothing to do with Sri Lanka or Buddhism. There is, indeed, considerable evidence to support this analysis as a partial—but not a complete—explanation (Zadek and Szabo 1993). International donors have been particularly influential since the early '80s, dominating key processes of organisational change up to the current time.

The second viewpoint, held by many of Sarvodaya's opponents, is that its autocratic form of organisation has evolved from the very social structures that it aspires to oppose, and the (ego-based) interests that its Buddhist tenets renounce. There is also some support for this argument. It is clear that traditional patterns of paternalism are at work within the organisation. This reflects, rather than opposes, some of the least attractive features of traditional society in Sri Lanka. Certainly this is the case regarding the acceptance of the principal of hierarchy and the place of women within that hierarchy.

A third view, and that held by the author, is that while the two preceding views are both valid as partial explanations, a further factor is at play which, while more difficult to describe, needs to be appreciated for any thorough analysis of the relationship between Buddhism, economics and social organisation. This other factor might be referred to as a 'state of receptivity', but would be seen within Buddhism as concerning the matter of compassion. It is certainly the case, for example, that Dr Ariyaratne takes many important decisions himself, often without any formal or explicitly structured process of consensus seeking. At the same time, there is little doubt as to his concerns for the rights and well-being of villagers, or people at lower levels within Sarvodaya. The question needs to be asked whether it is necessary to consider the importance of a non-structural variable which concerns the extent to which a person or organisation has developed a *receptivity* towards others, a condition that might be seen to be an aspect of compassion.

This third view would be largely unacceptable to most Western social analysts. A compassion not reflected structurally in institutionalised rights and practices would be seen as paternalistic in the extreme, from these perspectives, and so worthy only of rejection and replacement. At the same time, it is precisely whether such formal structures of democracy really mean that there is real social participation that is increasingly being questioned, particularly in the 'newly democratised countries' of Eastern Europe and elsewhere. Furthermore—and almost certainly as a part of this questioning process—there is a steady growth in research geared towards inter-pretations of communication patterns that do not rely solely on formalised, 'tangible' structural relationships (Levin 1989; Varela *et al.* 1992). However, while such works are both scholarly and radical attempts to describe these non-structural relationships, they continue to be viewed with some scepticism by those that approach the subject without any engagement in the practice being discussed.

The relationship between Buddhism and social organisation cannot be under-taken effectively without some movement of the analysis towards an approach that looks at the practice of those concerned, both in action and—more importantly—within themselves as individuals and as groups. There are problems in interpreting Buddhist-inspired attempts at social organisation, such as Sarvodaya, because any real initiative reflects many aspects of society, both good and bad. More important, perhaps, is that the practice of Buddhist economics requires that one move beyond an analysis that focuses only on formal aspects of social relationships, one that looks at the immediate terms of the relationships being considered, which may include aspects that one might call empathy, or receptivity.

Macroeconomic Buddhism

This analysis of practice can be taken forward into an analysis of macroeconomic change. Pryor (1991) begins this task through the use of a straightforward macroeconomic model. The more that the laity give to monks, he argues, the less will the economy grow. Furthermore, if reaching *nibbana* depends on being freed from the conditions of production and reproduction (i.e. requires one to be a monk), then the best strategic approach to pursue in maximising the number of people in a society that can reach *nibbana* is to ensure that the economy grows fast. In this way, he concludes, it will be able to support increasing numbers of *nibbana*-seeking (but otherwise unproductive) monks. There is—in short—a trade-off between some enlightenment now, and more enlightenment in the future.

There is an inclination when faced with a model of this kind to dismiss it for its simplified nature and mechanically determined conclusions. However, Pryor has clearly (if somewhat brutally) articulated an argument that, partly because it has a distinguished lineage, should be taken seriously (Weber 1958). There are several ways in which Pryor's proposition can be viewed. Firstly, the argument is empirically non-trivial in that significant proportions of total income are known to be transferred to the temples in Buddhist societies. Suksamran (1977), for example, reports that this proportion can and has been as high as 55% of the total income of some communities in Thailand. Indeed, the widest-held view of the impact of Buddhist-influenced behaviour is, as Ling states, that 'surplus material resources are devoted to economically unprofitable ends' (1980: 580). It is, however, incorrect to assume that resources transferred to the 'monk sector' should be treated entirely as 'consumption'. Ebihara (1966), for example, reports that some resources passing through the 'monk sector' in Cambodian peasant society are used to provide social services, such as healthcare and education, which would likely be made available through another route in a non-Buddhist society. Indeed, traditional development theory supports the view that such 'social' expenditures are critical components of long-term investment strategies, a view that could quite easily be incorporated into a somewhat more complex version of Pryor's macroeconomic model (World Bank 1990). Ebihara continues that a further proportion of such resources flows directly into construction and other economic activities. Such expenditures should also be interpreted differently from straightforward consumption, even if it is temples rather than factories that are being built. Public policy theory acknowledges, for example, the potential significance of public works expenditure on private-sector investment decisions and training, apart from the direct multiplier effects.

A somewhat different perspective concerns what Pryor refers to as **radiation**. Radiation concerns the effect on society of giving resources to the monks, irrespective of its use. Thus, he states that, 'buddhists hold that any appropriate dhammic action inevitably leads to an increase of the material welfare of the community' (1991: 18). Pryor offers an interesting although ambiguous mixture of interpretations of the meaning or root of radiation. Firstly, he quotes Reynolds and Clifford's argument that, 'as a result of the monk's pure and selfless actions, the laity flourish' (Reynolds and Clifford 1980: 62), but does not attempt to explain exactly what is meant by this. Secondly, although he notes that the king legitimises his position through giving (selflessly) to the monks, he makes no attempt to examine what might be the relationship between this legitimising process and economic success. Most interesting of all is his reference to Liebenstein's notion of **x-efficiency**. Liebenstein, it will be recalled by students of economics, developed the notion of x-efficiency to describe a reason for changes in productivity that could not be explained by resort to traditional production functions that treated labour as a determinate input into production. In particular, Liebenstein argued that there was a positive effect on productivity if the 'atmosphere' was right, which concerned people's idea of fairness, of being 'attended to', and other factors. Most important of all, however, was that his argument with the marginalists was not that this required an additional variable to be added to their production function, but rather that the whole idea of a marginal analysis based on the premise of labour as being a determinate production input was flawed.

It would be fair to say that Liebenstein was from the same tradition as other liberal institutional economists in paving the way towards an opening of *micro*economics to management studies. However, of relevance here is that these lessons did not translate into methodological innovations in *macro*economics. Thus, while Pryor offers an interesting perspective in raising the analogy of Buddhist radiation and Liebenstein's x-efficiency, his rapid switch to a macroeconomic analysis does not allow him to explore the implications of his insight. To be precise, Liebenstein's point suggests that the economist who is interested in understanding the dynamics of wealth production must consider the determinants of labour productivity not only with respect to changes in the labour–capital ratio (which is essentially the realm in which Pryor has confined his analysis), but also *in respect to labour itself*. That is, the relevant variable becomes a numerator with output per unit of, say, labour time, with a denominator again being some measurement of labour, only this time one that allows for qualitative variation. This was the critical point that Liebenstein was trying to get across, a point consistently misunderstood at the time, and which appears to have been missed—or at least ignored—by many to the current day.

In considering the possible effects of Buddhism on the economic performance of a society, the discussion has concentrated on influences of 'Buddhist behaviour' on the process of wealth creation. More specifically, it has been assumed that wealth or income is the endogenous variable to be maximised subject to a variety of possible 'constraints', particularly the behavioural outcomes of Buddhism. The discussion above has demonstrated that there is far greater ambiguity in the influence of Buddhism on the process of wealth creation even if we assume that this is the sole interest of economics. It is simple to demonstrate—at least within the context of Pryor's model—how Buddhism might have a positive long-run effect on wealth creation through its impact on investment in education, health and other public infrastructure. So, it is as well to lay one particular ghost to rest: **there is no *necessary* reason why the Buddhist practice of Sangha that channels material resources to the monks should slow the process of wealth creation.** Whether it does or does not requires careful research, often in areas and with interests not subject, like Liebenstein's x-efficiency, to direct observation, let alone quantification. In any case, such work should consider not only the economic fortunes of the Buddhist communities that are economically less industrialised—such as Sri Lanka and Cambodia—but also those that are leaders in the production of material wealth, notably Japan.

Buddhism and material welfare

The foregoing discussion may tell us something about the historical process of economic change and its relationship to institutional forms of Buddhism. However, it tells us little, arguably, about *Buddhist economics*. The key to understanding the foundation of Buddhist economics is to understand the place of well-being derived from material possessions in the 'practice' of Buddhism. Buddhism acknowledges the need for production and consumption, and accepts that this involves processes of negotiation, trading, acquisition of capital, and so on. At the same time, Buddhism challenges the individual (and society as a whole) to contextualise these processes in Buddhist values, including for example the idea of Right Thought, Action and Livelihood. Most importantly, economic welfare is seen within Buddhism as being instrumental in achieving spiritual advancement, as Louis van Loon points out in his essay entitled 'Why the Buddha did not Preach to the Hungry Man' (1990). Whereas the essence of modernist thinking is to view all pre-capitalist values as instrumental to either enabling or impeding economic growth, Buddhist economics turns this equation on its head and insists rather that economic development must cohere with Buddhist values.

This Buddhist challenge to modernist thinking has its support from development theory that argues that economic development, in order to be sustainable and meaningful, needs to take account of the value system within which such developments are taking place. Thus, 'a non-instrumental treatment of values draws its development goals from within the value system to which living communities still adhere' (Goulet 1980: 484-85). In developing the philosophy and practice of Sarvodaya, Dr Ariyaratne stated that their aim was to catalyse a process of social and economic change at the village and national levels that would be in 'harmony with *moral and spiritual ends*' (1982: 48). To achieve this, he continues, it is necessary to recognise that 'the economic component of development is but one aspect of development, it is a means to an end, therefore the means adopted should be relevant to the desired ends' (1982: 48).

Concluding meditations

Pryor concludes that Buddhism is most likely to be a constraint to economic performance, unless of course the monks agree with Pryor that rapid economic growth is the most effective route to liberating everyone from production and so setting them on the path to *nibbana*. Furthermore, although Pryor highlights some of the ethical implications of his reading of Buddhism, he concludes that Buddhism has little insight to offer with regard to matters of social organisation.

This chapter offers a somewhat different perspective. Firstly, we have suggested that Buddhism does offer direction on the critical issue of social organisation, as we have illustrated from both the actions and the 'practice' of Sarvodaya. At the core of this direction is the importance of self-awareness (mindfulness) as individuals working within a group, and self-awareness of the group itself in terms of its attitude and behaviour towards others. This translates most generally into the characteristics of compassion and wisdom, but will have particular forms in different contexts. Secondly, the review of Pryor's macroeconomic analysis suggests that there is no *necessary* reason for assuming that giving gifts to the monks should reduce economic performance, particularly in the long run. More importantly, however, is the view that it is a confusion to judge the 'effectiveness' of Buddhism in encouraging economic *growth*, when the underlying tenets of Buddhism placed all (non-subsistence) forms of economic activity as instrumental to other ends.

The relationship between Buddhism and economics is part of a wider debate concerning the role of spiritual beliefs in the economic sphere. This debate in turn is understood as being part of an ongoing process of questioning how best to understand and act in this sphere. It can be hoped that the participants of these linked debates will continue to contribute within the spirit of the subject under consideration: namely, in a manner that is sensitised to the guidance offered by Buddhism, or other spiritual or secular models. This sense, more than anything else, concerns the need to know the practice rather than the theory of the maps being considered, and the critical need to contextualise economic activities and ideas *within*, rather than outside of, such practice.

3
an economics of utopia
democratising scarcity*

there are the politicians and the priests, the ayatollahs and the economists, who will try to explain that reality is what they say it is. Never trust them; trust only the novelists, those deeper bankers who spend their time trying to turn printed paper into value, but never pretend that the result is anything more than a useful fiction.

Malcolm Bradbury, *Rates of Exchange*, p. 8

the severance of reality from fantasy . . . is a political and epistemological strategy whereby a prevailing state of affairs . . . is immunised from . . . events that threaten to transform prevailing power relationships.

Robert Spiegelmann, *Abundance and Scarcity: A Methodology of Reading Social Theory*, p. 136

Economics and utopia

Economics is the study of what we make and what we consume; how we value things, and how and why we deal with each other in the way that we do, at least in the material realms. Economics has always existed in that humans have always been concerned with how to organise the means of production and distribution for the purpose, at least in part, of consumption. However, the subject of mainstream economics as it is perceived today—what we might call **modern economics**—has a more specific lineage. Modern economics is understood to be the study of what we *actually* do and the way we *actually* behave. In laying claim to this distinction, modern economics sees itself as the quintessential *science* of social investigation. This concern with what *is*, rather than what *might* or *ought* be, arises from the

* Avebury Press, Aldershot, 1993 (no longer in print). © Simon Zadek.

methodological distinction between the neutral observation of the positivist—to which it lays claim—and the prescriptive perspective of the normative proposition. That is, the self-image of modern economics is of a neutral, detached, universal language through which the truth regarding Reality can be discerned.

Utopia, to the contrary, is conventionally thought of as being about the implausible, idealistic fantasy. From this viewpoint, it is everything that is unobservable, unquantifiable, unprovable; it is overtly prescriptive, it is a 'fancy' of the thinking subject. In that utopia is seen as concerning an ideal, it is also within the tradition that distinguishes between the positive and the normative method. Utopia is understood as concerning what *should* be, and how we *ought* to behave, rather than what *is*. Utopia at best is seen as giving us inspiration by offering some unambiguous direction; utopia is the unquestionable goal that will not be, and for some should never be, reached.

Economics and utopia offer certain insights into nature, our nature, and the nature of our interaction. Both claim nature as their support, whether it be an atomistic existence, or an interwoven reality. Modern economics emphasises a perspective of struggle, of competition, and of the need for exclusive self-interest. This is the world of antagonistic classes of people, economising individuals, economic trees, competitive particles, and self-interested genes. Utopia, on the other hand, emphasises the interconnected dimensions, the world of the liberated spirit and the enlightened being; loving, kind, generous; not only out of obligation imposed through externalised morals or ethical codes, but out of a different sense of relationship, an insight of reciprocity and co-operation, an actual rather than a proscribed interdependence being the 'natural' order.

The conventional meaning and distinction between the concepts of **modern economics** and **utopia** can therefore be introduced as being that:

- **Economics aspires to be about the Now**, explaining what has happened in the past and what might happen in the future on the basis of historical data—the **Past Now** and the **Future Now**.

- **Utopia is about what is Nowhere**, describing what is desirable on the basis of speculative insight concerning the past and the future—the **Past Nowhere** and the **Future Nowhere**.

Such distinctions between the subject of modern economics and utopia are a part of the foundations of modernism, foundations that bound the spheres of the positive and the normative, of what is and what ought to be, of the *Now* and *Nowhere*. This chapter argues that this traditional distinction between economics and utopia is both a misconception and a deception. The scientific method is not value-free; it is unambiguously ambiguous; fact is indeed often stranger than fiction, and fiction often more closely approximates fact than do naturalistic perceptions of some reality. Modern economic theory is arguably a fantastical abstraction from our real material circumstances, whereas fantasy can offer startling insights into all-too tangible aspects of our economy. Furthermore, the distinction between fact and fiction also serves to delineate mainstream views from challenging information and associated perspectives, marginalising the latter in the process. Modern economics, for example, is highly resistant to new forms of

economic theory and praxis that confront the heart of its own method and associated assumptions, particularly those concerning human behaviour and viable
forms of social organisation (Daly and Cobb 1990; Ekins and Max-Neef 1992). These
forms of action and beliefs are more often than not dismissed as the 'utopian
ramblings of confused ideologues', whereas modern economics is understood as the
best possible (or at least the only possible) reality.

The erroneous distinction between economics and utopia is explored through
three aspects of modern economics, and their relationship to conceptions of utopia,
its conception of markets and of human nature, and its method of analysis. However, the classic conflictive approach to challenging the hegemony of economics is
rejected here, since it merely reinforces the underlying false dualism of fact and
fiction ('which is more real than the other?'). Rather, the approach adopted here is
to challenge the very dualism itself by offering a reading of modern economics as a
utopian perspective *simultaneous* to its literal, or literally intended, sense. The
relevance of such a reading is that it challenges not merely modern economics'
literal depiction of reality on positivist or normative grounds, but at the root of its
method and its basis of legitimisation. Where economics is understood to be as
fantastical, idealistic and introspective as other forms of 'speculative insights' that
may be dubbed 'utopian', it is possible to begin to level the playing field of discourse
and praxis, and work more openly towards achieving preferred forms of socialisation.

Harmonious perfection of economics' markets

Perfect competition—like all of modern economics—describes a world of markets
where goods and services are exchanged for the purpose of consumption or use in
the production process. Perfect competition has the particular characteristic that no
one actor has significant influence on the movements of the market, and in
particular on the prevailing price (Koutsoyiannis 1975; Layard and Walters 1978).[1]
The implication is that resources are allocated through this market in the 'most
effective' manner subject to costs and preferences. Goods and services are provided
at the least possible cost; and 'welfare' of the participants in the market is maximised,[2] subject to initial conditions such as the distribution of income, capabilities
and circumstances.

A crucial aspect of perfect competition is the point of equilibrium. The market
equilibrium, say, for the producer, occurs at the point of intersection of its marginal
and average costs with the market demand curve, the latter being an aggregate of
the infinite number of downward-sloping demand curves that reflect the preferences of individual consumers. The point at which trading takes place—that is, the
price and quantity at which goods are exchanged—is then the point of intersection
of these 'curves', which is the equilibrium. Disturbances to this equilibrium are of a
short-term nature, given the assumptions of perfect competition. The entry of more
producers or consumers into the market, for example, makes no difference to the
state of balance because there are already an effectively infinite number of both

consumers and producers in the market. A technology shift, a change in tastes, habits or other circumstance will 'move the market' to a new equilibrium. Indeed, since all non-equilibrium positions are inaccessible within the terms of the model itself, the model of perfect competition describes a market—and indeed a 'world'— that comprises only the point of 'perpetual' equilibrium.

Notions of equilibrium

A market described in the terms outlined above is seen to be, as the name suggests, the essentially (or perfectly) *competitive* environment. Equilibrium arises through a balance of the competitive 'forces' or pressures that market participants use against each other. From this perspective, perfect competition reflects a Hobbesian view of nature and our natural state as being inherently competitive, a philosophical viewpoint summed up as 'dog eats dog'.

Such a market might be seen by some as reflecting (our) nature, and might be deemed 'perfect' in some particular sense. However, it would to many have little if anything to do with utopia, which is more usually understood to be concerned with social 'harmony' and 'peace', rather than the balancing of conflict or competition. However, the description of perfect competition need not only be read in the literal form preferred by both its advocates and enemies; it can also be read in terms of the metaphoric images that it evokes, particularly in its expressions of balance. Support for the view of 'equilibrium' in modern economics as a utopian 'artifact' comes, for example, from Ralf Dahrendorf. Dahrendorf argues that utopias are characterised by their belief in the possibility of social equilibrium. In such models:

> social change is an abnormal, or at least an unusual, state, one that has to be accounted for in terms of deviations from a 'normal', equilibrated system (1968: 126).

The flaw in such a viewpoint, he argues, cannot be resolved through resort to shifts in the point of equilibrium, since the shortfall of such models concerns the very notion of equilibrium itself. For Dahrendorf, then, the preferred alternative to 'utopian' models of social equilibrium is the model of social conflict. Of interest here is the way Dahrendorf sets the harmonious and conflictive approaches against one another, rather than the 'accuracy' of his arguments. For another way of looking at the two approaches is as qualitatively different and intimately related perspectives on the same story. So, in the case highlighted here, Dahrendorf's conflictive model is the literal expression of competition in the market, whereas the model of equilibrium is reflected simultaneously as a 'utopian' expression of peace, stability and harmony.

This point can also be understood through reference to Dahrendorf's co-option of quantum theory to illustrate his own argument. He calls the 'indeterminacy principle' as a witness to (rather than a proof of) his rejection of models of equilibrium as being utopian.

> The indeterminacy principle in modern physics, which is again nothing but a useful assumption without claim to any reality other than operational, has been taken as a final refutation of all determinist philosophies

> of nature. Analogous statements could be made about the equilibrium
> model of society (1968: 124).

This argument is intended to support his view that the very notion of equilibrium evokes a sense of stability that is 'utopian' rather than rooted in the actual terms of our social and biophysical lives. For Dahrendorf, the distinction he is so anxious to enforce is one of actual 'fact' and actual 'fiction'. However, the flaw in his own argument is revealed through use of the very same correspondence to quantum physics from which he draws. His use of the analogy suggests the opposition of 'equilibrium' and 'indeterminacy' (i.e. because the world is indeterminate, we cannot talk about equilibrium). It would be equally correct, however, to use the analogy in a somewhat different manner in associating the categories of 'equilibrium' and 'conflict' as being equivalent to the quantum world of waves and particles. This is arguably a more appropriate reading of the sense in which indeterminacy is understood as an *observation*, rather than an instability in the object itself (Bohm 1980). In this case, equilibrium is not opposed in any sense to the proposition of indeterminacy, but is one of the possible ways of perceiving the 'data' or world. This approach accords more closely to the argument presented here in that we are not proposing that the 'competitive' expression within perfect competition is 'fact' and the sense of harmony is 'fiction', or indeed vice versa. Rather, we are suggesting that the model is capable of and does articulate both aspects, while—importantly— acknowledging only one.

Normative equilibria

Perfect competition is clearly a simplification of the world as we understand it. This in itself does not represent a problem, since all theoretical constructs seek insight through simplification of one sort or another. However, perfect competition is more than a mere simplification because it has normative as well as descriptive or predictive dimensions. So, for example, a market dominated by one or a few suppliers or consumers will be judged according to the degree of efficiency of resource allocation in that market as compared to what would have occurred under perfect competition. This deviation between what would have occurred under perfect competition and what empirically seems to have actually occurred or would theoretically have occurred in a different form of market (monopoly, monopsony, oligopoly, etc.) is, however, not seen simply as a *difference*, but is seen as a *loss*. Thus, perfect competition is the market structure that maximises social welfare subject to the utility preference maps and the initial resource distribution of the market participants. Deviations from conditions of perfect competition reduce social welfare 'below its maximum potential'. Thus, the description of perfect competition is an exposition (for its proponents) of the way the world *should* rather than *could* work.

> competitive equilibrium thus appears as a lost reality to which we ought
> to return so that everything may go better for us . . . or an ideal yet to be
> realised (Godelier 1966: 53).

Perfect competition is a perfect world that will never be attained in its literal form, but one that carries with it those critical characteristics of harmony both between participants and with nature. Perfect competition is not merely a theoretical simplification for the purpose of prediction; it is a proposition of an ideal. Here then is a clear case of one of the core aspects of what constitutes a classical idea of utopia.

The suggestion that perfect competition (or its contemporary forms in general equilibrium analysis) constitutes a normative proposition receives support not only from opponents of modern economics such as Godelier, but from within the core of the paradigm itself. Thus, as Arrow remarked in his Nobel Lecture:

> In my own thinking, the model of general equilibrium under uncertainty is as much a normative ideal as an empirical description (Arrow 1972: 30).

Similarly, Hahn argues that the model of general equilibrium:

> Serves a function similar to that which an ideal and perfectly healthy body might serve a clinical diagnostician when he looks at an actual body (Hahn 1984: 308).

Thus, argues Roy, there is little choice but to conclude that Hahn and Arrow, and more probably a large portion of mainstream economists, are neo-Platonists. That is, although they do not see themselves as being concerned directly with a particular perception of some ideal person, language or culture, they do have an idea of 'ideal economic agents trading at ideal prices' (Roy 1989: 85), which implies an associated conception of what is 'ideal'.[3]

Best of all possible worlds

Perfect competition is only one part of modern economics. The subject of economics has, in the last century or so, generated more sophisticated derivatives of the basic model, which focus on the various states of 'imperfection' in the market that can exist across the range from oligopoly, to monopoly and monopsony situations. In these 'second-best' scenarios, the implications are examined of such factors as incomplete knowledge and the costs of acquiring information, of discontinuities in production scales, financial, legislative and other barriers to entry, and so on. On this basis, the modern economist claims that reality is approached more and more as the extremities of the base model of perfect competition are carved away.

The utopian aspects of modern economics do not ultimately depend, however, on the level of complexity of the subject's models. The basic model of supply and demand remains the same throughout all of the variations in particular market structures, and so remains underpinned by the essential feature of equilibrium, or what we have otherwise called harmony. Thus, for example, it is true that the introduction of some technology development or change in taste may in models of 'imperfect' competition move the point of intersection of supply and demand to levels of price and quantity different from those reached in perfect competition. However, the fundamental basis of that intersection remains identical, a position of perpetual equilibrium or balance.[4] That is, the utopia of modern economics is reflected in the notion of equilibrium itself, and is unaffected by the choice of, and is equally apparent in *every*, market model.

The idealisation of the notion of equilibrium is also maintained across all of the models in modern economics. In our discussion of perfect competition, we noted that it was a state or arrangement of economic affairs that was being advocated; it was essentially a normative proposition. This is also the case for all other models in modern economics, in that equilibrium is the best possible situation that can be achieved *given* the market structure. The point of equilibrium, for example, under conditions of monopoly, may be suboptimal to the efficiency and welfare conditions that might be achieved under alternative market conditions, such as perfect competition. However, the point of equilibrium within the model of monopoly is the best outcome given that market structure. Thus, since the models always 'exist' in practice at the point of equilibrium, modern economics describes outcomes as the 'best of all possible worlds'. That is, modern economics views points of market equilibrium as the best possible situations that could arise in the circumstances, irrespective of the market structure.

Idolising resource efficiency

The final issue concerning the utopian nature of the market equilibrium in modern economics is the actual ideal 'state' that it implies. The critical feature of the point of equilibrium is that it is where maximum **resource efficiency** is achieved.[5] The question of to *what extent* this is 'true' is not at issue here, although in general terms modern economics depicts a hierarchy of optimisations in respect to this criterion with perfect competition at the pinnacle. Furthermore, the issue of *whether* or not this is a suitable criterion on which to base a conception of 'the best' is not considered here.

What is at issue is that this criterion for optimisation is **not subjected to doubt** within modern economics. That is, the assumption of the appropriateness of 'resource efficiency' as the ultimate interest of economic activity, and its privilege within the economic sphere over other possible criteria, is just that, an *assumption*. One person, or indeed all people, may consider it to be an eminently sensible assumption; but that is not the point. The point is that it cannot be subjected to question within the sphere of modern economics (Zadek 1992). To present this in another way, the criterion that forms the basis for an idealisation of equilibrium (and for a hierarchy of preferred states of equilibrium across different market forms) *transcends* modern economics in not being open to question.[6] To ignore the source of criteria adopted (and similarly the method in which they are applied) is to treat such a source (and method) as 'transcendent', in the sense of some unquestioned basis on which decisions are taken or activities played out (Bateson 1987).[7] This unquestioned nature (and implied unquestionability) of the assumption of resource efficiency as the essential criterion within modern economics represents a further critical constituent of its utopia form; a statement of the sacred.

The economic utopian

The vision in modern economics outlined in the last section of harmony and balance, perfection, overtly normative perspectives, and finally the unquestioned nature of the social goal of resource efficiency, all support the proposition that the subject embodies some idealisation that most would deem utopian. Our reading of this utopian 'shadow' embedded within modern economics should not be understood as being in opposition to a more conventional reading of its competitive features. Rather, it complements such a reading in adding an unacknowledged but powerful level of 'positive' symbolism to what might otherwise be a drab or even disturbing vision of the market economy.

Missing from the analysis so far, however, is any appraisal of the treatment by modern economics of the individual. Such an appraisal is absolutely necessary since it is its particular perception of human nature that ultimately underpins its theoretical constructs of the market, and people's actions within it. Furthermore, it is often around alternative projections of human nature and behavioural practice and potential that the traditional opposition to modern economics forms. It is here again that the dualism of fact and fiction that serves to legitimate modern economics and marginalise alternative formulations becomes apparent and needs to be explored.

The economic person

The individual in modern economics has a number of particular characteristics. Most obvious are the characteristics of 'rationality' in two particular senses: internal consistency of choice, and maximisation of self-interest. It is perhaps not surprising that the battle with modern economics concerning perceptions of human behaviour has mainly focused on the latter aspect of assumed rationality. It is this aspect that consolidates the polarisation of reasonably well-defined intellectual and political camps (Zadek 1992). However, we turn in this chapter to the former aspect of rationality, internal consistency, since it serves as a clear illustration of the proposition being explored here.

The interest here, then, is in what is being portrayed through the articulation of the very idea of internal consistency, rather than whether the notion is a reasonable interpretation of rationality or reality. In its simplest terms, the notion that the economic individual is rational in this sense can be interpreted as implying that he or she knows fully their needs at each point in time; knowing in particular what trade-off between options is most appropriate to satisfy those needs (Sen 1982).[8] So, although a person's needs may change over time, they possess from their first to their last breath the same ability and inclination to make decisions on a 'rational' basis in the sense described above. In these senses, the individuals that make up the population of modern economics are all identical.

Individuals in modern economics are also identical in that they are all free from all characteristics that cannot be articulated in a manner intelligible to the market. The market can only receive certain signals, prices and quantities for a given product. Other signals must either be converted into these terms, or must be ignored altogether; the market is by definition devoid of any non-commodity relationships. By this is not only meant that people only relate through their products but also that the characteristics of those products can only be articulated in modern economics in terms of price and quantity. Modern economics, however, is uninterested in these relationships unless they are referred through price and quantity. This is precisely why Godelier argues that aspects of the passing of gifts generally do lie outside of the sphere of modern economics, even though quantity and *value* may be quite apparent (Godelier 1966).

There are three main differences between individuals in modern economics, as well as the necessary similarities discussed above. Firstly, **inherited circumstances** are the different economic and social circumstances into which each person is born. Inequalities are acknowledged in terms of wealth and wealth-generating circumstances, such as class, gender and ethnicity. However, these inequalities form the entry point into the economic sphere, and are therefore only analysed in terms of their material effect rather than their source and substance. Secondly, **inherited characteristics** are the 'inherent' qualities that each person has: their looks, their 'intelligence', their 'creativity'. Again, these factors are acknowledged within modern economics, but act only as entry-point differentiations rather than being analysed within the subject itself. Finally, **revealed preferences** are formed in part by inherited circumstances and characteristics, and so, like these factors, are determined largely outside of the scope of modern economics. Social persuasion in the construction of preferences is sometimes acknowledged—such as advertising—but, because of the assumed economic rationality of the individual, this acknowledgement does not undermine the use of the individual and revealed preferences as the core of the theoretical framework.

Individuals in modern economics are, however, not simply different, but *have* to be different for their interaction within the bounds of the market to function. Thus, as Lionel Robbins states about the nature of economic generalisations:

> the main underlying assumption is the assumption of the schemes of valuation of the different economic subjects. But this . . . is really an assumption of one of the conditions which must be present if there is to be economic activity at all. It is an essential ingredient of our conception of conduct with an economic aspect (Robbins 1935: 37-38).

The individual in modern economics therefore has some quite distinct, generic characteristics. On the one hand, they are all identical in being rational in the two senses described above, and can furthermore articulate that rationality in terms intelligible to the market. On the other hand, they are all different in that they are able to determine a basis for trade through differentiated preferences, production possibilities and costs.

Finally, before passing on to the matter of any 'utopian' characteristics of these interesting people, it is worthwhile reminding ourselves what they do with their time. The role of the individual in the economic society is to enter the market where preferences are revealed to enable the task of exchange to take place. Thus, modern economics describes the ebb and flow of necessarily differentiated but strangely similar human beings. These people, with their personalities defined through their revealed preferences and the interaction of these preferences with one another, comprise a gigantic collage of supply-side and demand-side opportunity costs. These human beings spend their lives in a process of entering and leaving different markets, a life of perpetual negotiation in the context of absolute rationality.

The utopia of economic being

How is one to interpret this description of people's behaviour? Is it 'merely' a simplification, an ideologically rooted caricature, or a proposition of a preferred state of 'being'? The opponents of modern economics would point to this vision of the individual as a basis for an indictment of the subject.

> We need an economics that benefits not just Economic Man, but real men and women who have the capacity to live a life of values, integrity and wholeness (Lutz and Lux 1988: 84).

For Lutz and Lux, the individual painted by modern economics is a reflection of the discipline's miserable, reductionist perspective on the human condition. On the other hand, there are a mixture of views that support this image of the individual. There are those that take the vision in quite literal terms. Stigler, for example, takes this position in viewing people as self-interested, utility maximisers. This view, he argues

> is the prevalent one found by economists not only within a wide variety of economic phenomena, but in their investigation of marital, child-bearing, criminal, religious, and other social behaviour as well (Stigler 1981: 176).

Friedman, on the other hand, would argue that the issue does not concern whether or not these are 'realistic' descriptions of how people are, but whether the models based on these descriptions yield 'good' predictions (Friedman 1953).

It is not the concern here to debate the pros and cons of different ways of describing people. Rather, we wish to argue that, while the traditional opposition to the vision of modern economics is not wrong, it is limited in its understanding of the discipline's multi-dimensional language. Modern economics, like all languages, must be viewed as having a profusion or hierarchy of different levels at which it communicates information. It is only by acknowledging these different levels that it becomes possible to uncover the complex patterns of imagery that any particular language uses to instil meaning within its form and content.

We would suggest that there is one undervalued or ignored aspect of the vision of the individual embedded within modern economics: namely, a utopian vision. This vision is not accurate in the literal sense implied by Stigler; is not purely reductionist in the manner described by Lutz and Lux; and is not only instrumental to the purpose of prediction in the sense meant by Friedman. Rather, it is that the individual in modern economics is free from the trauma of confusion in matters of choice. The first level of that freedom is described by the condition of 'internal consistency'. This condition, it will be recalled, implies that people are able to unambiguously rank all of their options, at least in cardinal terms. Therefore, this condition rejects, for example, Maslow's view of a hierarchy of *incomparable* needs

(Maslow 1954), which can only be 'resolved' through resort to some mechanism of choice that cannot be described in linear, logical terms. Humanist economists such as Lutz and Lux have used Maslow's model in an attempt to reconstruct the economic individual as 'reasonable' rather than rational (Lutz and Lux 1988). However, whereas Lutz and Lux would see their initiative as aiming to make a contribution to a more 'humane' vision of people in economics, the argument here points out that the viewpoint of modern economics is what in other languages would be seen as the ultimately liberated person. Krishnamurti, for example, follows the tradition of Eastern philosophy in arguing that the error of the Western model is to see 'choice' as having a close resemblance to 'freedom'; 'where there is confusion there is choice. Where there is no confusion, there is no choice' (Krishnamurti 1972). The individual in economics makes no choice whatsoever in the sense meant by Lutz and Lux, since there is a transparent hierarchy of needs and priorities that does not have to be 'determined' since it, quite simply, exists. This hierarchy, or ranking, is— it will be recalled—established by the three exogenous factors of inherited circumstances and characteristics, and revealed preferences. Each of these factors is determined outside of the model of modern economics: i.e. the individual in modern economics has an uncanny (if unintended) resemblance to Krishnamurti's state of liberation, a liberation rooted in a transcendence of the confusion of choice.

The full irony of this resemblance becomes even more apparent when we turn to the question of relationships between these liberated individuals. The process of interaction in the market is, as we have described, underpinned by the preconditions of similarity and difference. In that Robbins confirms that the differences establish a basis for economic activity, the similarities establish a mechanism through which differences are resolved. Crucial here to our story is that the process of resolution of the differences between people is entirely predetermined. The 'terms of trade' that determine their economic relationship are established outside of the model. It is hard not to draw a negative view of this vision. This view is summarised in the 'biological' equivalence of the process of interaction described in modern economics, as depicted so graphically by Bernard Mandeville.

> Vast numbers thronged the fruitful hive;
> Yet those vast numbers made 'em thrive;
> Millions endeavouring to supply
> Each other's lust and vanity (Mandeville 1714: 18).

The image of the individual in modern economics is therefore utopian in that he or she goes through life with no sense of doubt in the choices that face him or her. The role of this individual is to make 'decisions' in this unconfused state. Choices are not, however, of the form that we normally face—namely, between incommensurable options—but rather are choices between clearly ranked priorities. Deciding between choices, therefore, is more a matter of calculation on the basis of transparent parameters. As a result, relationships between individuals in modern economics are equally clear. These individuals enter into arrangements for the exchange of goods and services on the basis of a general method, and a set of characteristics specific to each individual that are predefined to the system. On this basis, it is unnecessary to view these exchange relationships as requiring any decision of substance, since the outcome is predetermined prior to the outset of the relationship. That is, people in modern economics have unneurotic, unambiguous relationships, the nature of which are 'transcendently' established. On this basis, therefore, the individual in modern economics is truly utopian.

Utopian method in economics

The previous two sections have focused on the manner in which modern economics idealises both individuals and their context (the market). There is a further sense in which modern economics is utopian, which concerns not so much its descriptive aspects as its *method* and associated *source* of understanding.

On utopian and economic method

The first stage of an exploration of the relationship between utopia and the method of modern economics is to agree on what one is looking for. Is there, after all, a method that can be deemed 'utopian'? In one sense the answer is clearly no. The notion of utopian is multifaceted. Some would define the term within the limits of literature, while others would consider it in relation to sociology or political philosophy. Some would see it in terms of content, while others would consider it in terms of form or function (Levitas 1991). Each one of these perspectives implies a different method, which seems to deny the possibility of establishing any fixed relationship between utopia and method.

In another sense, however, the answer may be yes; that is, it may be possible to define more clearly what is *not* utopian method. We would suggest here that the key characteristic of what utopian method *is not* is positivistic, or what Ernst Bloch calls *practicism*, which can be simply defined as one that focuses entirely on the logical interpretation of 'data' collected through 'direct observation of events' that is taken to *be* the Reality or Truth (Bloch 1938–47). Utopias resort to every form of method apart from Bloch's practicism. So, for example, the tradition of utopian literature makes use of many forms of 'correspondence' (metaphor, analogy, etc.). The philosophical traditions of utopia tend to be rooted in the language of rationalism. Particularly important is that many forms of the utopian traditions make use of the 'subjective' as a legitimate channel for the communication of understanding of both actual and potential circumstances. So, for example, much of the feminist 'science fiction' utopias view the nature of women's oppression through the subjective experiences of women.

Modern economics, on the other hand, presents itself as an impersonal, objective reflection of the world. It adopts the tools of 'simple observation', and so claims a 'scientific' status. Modern economics does not intend to prove its core propositions through anecdotal evidence, as it might see the work of anthropologists, or through the screen of a particular political perspective, as some would view, say, sociological analysis. Modern economics may get its viewpoints and predictions right or wrong, but in both cases its self-perception is one of a dignity realised through methodological rigour. That, at least, is the public face of the discipline.

The rhetoric of modern economics

This public view of the methodological differences between economic and utopian 'method' is erroneous. The implicit basis or method of modern economics is in practice qualitatively closer to our understanding of utopian method than seems possible from the public face of modern economics. This basis is a discourse that translates perspectives often acquired in terms that are not compatible with the 'black and white' dictates of positivism, although they are subsequently 'translated' into the modernist language of scientific objectivity without due reference to (or admission of) their original source.

An analysis of the manner in which the subject of economics articulates its viewpoint requires an examination of the rhetoric of economics. McCloskey's work was the first explicit attempt to use a rhetorical approach to examine the validity of economic argument. McCloskey's underlying hypothesis was that much of economics is in practice underpinned not by its apparent rigour, but rather by a more value-laden, introspective method.

McCloskey's starting point is to identify the 'modernist' paradigm (what here has been called at various stages the scientific method) as that methodology that seeks to distinguish itself from the experiential realm.

Scientific reality	Humanistic reality
Fact	Value
Truth	Opinion
The demarcation line*	
Objective	Subjective
Rigorous	Intuitive
Precise	Vague

* McCloskey 1986: 52

FIGURE 1   THE SCIENTIFIC REALITY—HUMANISTIC REALITY RELATIONSHIP

> Modernism views science as axiomatic and mathematical and takes the realm of science to be separate from the realm of form, value, beauty, goodness, and all unmeasurable quantity (1986: 6).

This viewpoint, argues McCloskey, creates a demarcation line between the Us that are part of the Modernist world, and the Them, who reside in the world of metaphysics, morals, personal conviction, and most of all doubt.

Modern economics places itself firmly within the left hand of the rectangle—the Scientific Reality. This classification, however, does not reflect the practice of economic methodology. McCloskey illustrates this in his discussion of the Law of Demand (which states quite simply that, when prices for a good go up, demand falls, and vice versa). The law is a fundamental part of modern economics.

> Belief in the Law of Demand is the distinguishing mark of the economists . . . Economists believe it ardently (1986: 59).

To be 'ardent', however, is really not a scientific position, at least not according to the mythology of the scientific method to which modern economics purports to adhere. McCloskey argues that economists have used a range of methods to demonstrate the existence of such a law. At one end of the spectrum are the public tools of economics, in particular econometrics, more straightforward statistics, and some experimental tests. All of these three forms of 'proof' are scientific in their nature, and are the tools that therefore underpin the discipline's claim to the status of science. However, these tools have been used to only limited effect in a long-standing and intensive effort to 'prove' the basic thesis of modern economics, the Law of Demand. Statistical tests on economies and markets, and some experimental work, have all failed to provide anything but weak confirmation of the hypothesis, or indeed outright rejection. At best, argues McCloskey:

> The modernist (scientific) arguments yield mixed results (1986: 58).

However, McCloskey continues, this weakness in results of economics' publicly legitimated methods has done nothing to make economists uncertain about the 'truth' of the Law of Demand. Rather, they have rooted their 'ardent belief' in alternative method, including: introspection ('what would I do if the price of petrol doubled?'); thought experiments ('what would someone else do if the price of petrol doubled?'); narrative case studies (much like anthropologists, only in a much less structured manner since economics has little formal method that it can apply in a case study approach); the lore of the business community ('if business people say it is like that, who can disagree?'); the lore of the academy ('who would disagree with professors who argue it to be the case?'); and, most of all, through analogy ('if you accept that it is true for ice cream, then it must be true for petrol'). The modernist argument, continues McCloskey, would be that these latter methods are merely supportive to the primary, scientific research. However, this is far from the case, for value judgements and metaphysical assumptions are an integral part of the scientific methods themselves.

> they [scientific methods] too depend on analogies (the market is just like this demand curve), metaphysical propositions (the time series is a sample from all possible universes), and traditional authority (we have always assumed finite variance of the error term) (1986: 61).

McCloskey drives home his central argument with a welter of illustrations. Modern economics, he argues, far from being Modernism's model pupil, is a paradise of metaphors. Its language of 'auctioneers', 'invisible hands' and 'velocities' cannot with any conviction be a language of literal description. The market has but a few rather irrelevant auctioneers, the invisible hands remain above all else invisible, and it cannot be said that money really moves at any literal velocity whatsoever.

This failure to appeal to the 'objective circumstances' indicated by the data should not be seen as a sign of failure of method. Such signs of apparent 'failure' rather reveal what we all actually do. We all combine qualitatively different ways of seeing in our expression of what we might arrogantly argue to be the truth. Numbers and statistics subversively combine with beliefs and childhood memories to form 'results'. Such beliefs include a world, or indeed a universal, view—a view that is largely unproven and indeed unprovable in any modernist sense. Modern economics does not lie outside of this complex formation of qualitatively diverse data that make up a seemingly coherent and homogeneous viewpoint. As such, modern economics cannot be *a priori* readily distinguished from any other form of speculation, and certainly cannot be deemed characteristically pragmatic in its approach. Modern economics, whether the elegant version of perfect competition or its more complex derivatives, carries within it most 'unscientific' methods in that it incorporates personal and group ideals.

It is tempting to conclude from this that to describe modern economics as a science is a misnomer. Far from it: the mistake is rather to imagine science as we do. In distinguishing scientific from, say, humanistic realities, we paint a picture that is both inaccurate and unhelpful. Not only is economics not a science but nor is a science a science, in the sense of it being objective, or value-free and free from introspection.

> Economics is a collection of literary forms, not a science. Indeed, science
> is a collection of literary forms, not a science. And literary forms are
> scientific (McCloskey 1986: 55).

Thus, it is not that economics is not about what actually happens but rather that it is offering a view of what happens in the same way that we all do, by constructing a subjective perspective based on a range of different levels of sensibility, which may of course include 'data' collection and 'statistical analysis'. However, these as well as other aspects of its method are essentially forms of introspection, and in particular extrapolations based on personal experiences.

McCloskey's innovative work extends beyond the simple framework that has been presented here, as does the methodological resources from which he draws. However, what we have offered is sufficient for the intended purpose; McCloskey's work illustrates the double-edged misnomer in understanding modern economics as 'scientific'. Firstly, it rarely has succeeded in proving even its most basic hypothesis at a level of rigour that would be commensurate with the strict dictates of positivism. Secondly, 'science' itself is caricatured in this way, and should rather be seen as a synthetic method of which positivism is only one part. In this sense, the method of modern economics should not be set in opposition to the utopian method.

The utopia in modern economics

We are informed and often persuaded that the essential feature of modern economics is that it is about what actually happens; it faces reality fair and square, and does not allow wishes and dreams to influence its pragmatic perspective.

This proposition has been effectively challenged in this chapter through an exploration of the utopian dimensions of three interrelated aspects of modern economics. The first considers the context of the marketplace, which tends inexorably towards equilibrium. This equilibrium is not merely described but is advocated as the preferred point of existence. This aspect of the subject's utopian leaning features across the entirety of its method, not only the pinnacle of its idealisation, that being perfect competition. The justification for such advocacy is a 'transcendent' one in that it refers to the unquestioned normative proposition: the preferability of 'resource efficiency'. The second aspect of the subject's utopian leaning is its image of people and their relationship. The individual in economics is unambiguous as to its interests and its approach to decision-making, even though it may be both selfish and monotonously mechanical in its calculations. The economic individual in this specific sense depicts the holy grail of liberation in our personal and social spheres. Finally, the language used by economists reflects an interjection of 'non-scientific' perspectives into economic analysis. Thus, modern economics is ultimately utopian in that it draws from the rich language of metaphor and its associated variants.

To propose a utopian nature of modern economics is to assert, on the face of it, a very different perspective to most utopians and utopian theorists. Furthermore, such a proposition might sit uneasily with many of modern economics' strongest critics. It is certainly true that the approach taken here is very different from the traditional perspectives offered by these groupings. However, the founding concerns underlying their and my arguments are, I would suggest, very similar.

Asserting the utopian nature of modern economics firstly acts to reveal, and so ultimately to reduce, its hegemony over other forms of social discourse: an hegemony that is enforced by a false distinction between fact and fiction, normative and positivist, etc.

> the severance of reality from fantasy . . . is a political and epistemological strategy whereby a prevailing state of affairs . . . is immunised from . . . events that threaten to transform prevailing power relationships (Spiegelmann 1982: 136).

Such privileging of certain forms of language has, of course, its reasons. These reasons are substantive in the sense that they emerge from the actual social relationships within which power and interests are vested and sustained. Clearly it would be absurd to imagine that a mere 'revealing' of this hegemony through the approach adopted in this chapter would itself act of an effective counter-action. However, in addressing the matter of the privilege of modern economics as a language through which we understand our economic context, this chapter at least contributes to clearing the way for a more open dialogue between different methods or languages of understanding in the theory and practice of economics.

The power of modern economics does not, however, merely lie in its supposedly pragmatic approach. It not only asserts its positivist form but *simultaneously* makes use of language (equilibrium, harmony, clarity, etc.) that implicitly projects itself as a utopian project. This projection, which has been explored in this chapter, directly contradicts its literal expressions of competition and self-interest, and yet should not be understood as coincidental or contradictory to the subject's central ideological propositions and concerns. That is, modern economics achieves a supreme juggling feat of asserting positivist supremacy while at the same time achieving hegemonic influence within the utopian realm of our fantasies and aspirations.

This chapter has suggested that an exploration of the utopia that is modern economics offers insights into the means by which the subject achieves legitimacy by reinforcing a false dualism concerning itself and conceptions of utopia, while at the same co-opting the very language of utopia to its own ends. The three windows through which we have explored this phenomenon are each enormous and complex in their own right, and we have done little more than glimpse through them to illustrate the underlying proposition. Together, however, these glimpses demonstrate the relevance of the issue, and the potential of the approach adopted in its investigation.

Section II
civil society, power and accountability

4
looking back
from 2010[*]

Once upon a golden age . . .

It all came to a head in the second half of the 1990s, although the underlying roots have a far earlier origin. The 1980s had been a golden era for what was then known as the 'non-governmentals'. From relative obscurity, NGOs became a centre of attention. They offered a vision of an active and responsible civil society under-pinned by flexible, effective and accountable institutions. They offered, in short, themselves.

And they were accepted. They symbolised what the by-now emasculated state sectors could no longer provide—moral representation of the excluded. They were guardians of faith of a people's democracy, latter-day Davids exposing the grubby, ineffectual and at times destructive deeds of marauding Goliaths. By the end of the 1980s, the NGOs—private aid agencies foremost among them—were a force that could not be ignored. Well financed and publicly acclaimed, they took on roles from providers of state-funded services to legal challenges of corporate and state activities. Then the 1990s dawned...

Globalisation and its malcontents

As you will recall, this was intended to be the period when the globalisation of trade and community would be realised via the General Agreement on Tariffs and Trade (GATT) agreement, CNN and the global shopping arcade on the Internet. It's quite strange to think about that dream in retrospect, given what actually happened.

---

[*] First published in *Compassion and Calculation: The Business of Private Foreign Aid*, edited by David Sogge. © Pluto Press (1996), London.

The severe recession created by the globalisation adventure had the same effect on NGOs as it did on their main sparring partner, the corporate sector. They were, after all, both products of the same underlying process. It was therefore logical that they should share the same patterns of development. During the early 1980s, many private aid agencies had over-expanded. In the leaner times of the 1990s, most agencies saw financial shortfalls as the heart of the problem. Agency staff's livelihoods began to compete for importance with the livelihood strategies being promoted for the world's poor, many of whom had meanwhile become clients, customers, users and, of course, 'partners'.

Agency leaders began to echo the corporate solution: retrenchment for survival. The extremities of the movement's early proponents were replaced by the managerial style of the period, 'corporate neoliberalism'. Downsizing and de-layering was the order of the day, albeit smothered in the NGO language of decentralisation and empowerment. The same management consultants who had helped to construct the Babylonian aid edifices of the 1980s returned to advise solemnly on how to take them down again. This time, however, they had added redundancy counselling services to their colourful brochures, and talked intently about inter-agency competition, the returns from cold-call invasive marketing, and the need for a couple more serious crises in the South to make up for the funding shortfall.

Charity money, however, proved addictive. When they had it—money, that is—there seemed to be more and more strings attached. When they didn't have it, their enormous bureaucracies (and their many dependent subcontractors) grew hungry, angry and frightened. Substance abuse and real dependencies had set in during the 1980s. More and more of the stuff was needed even though it was clear that the more they had the more were the values and other strengths of the NGOs compromised in its use.

Transnationals face south

Particularly dire was the situation of the Northern transnational agencies—or what were known as 'development non-governmentals' or 'private foreign aid agencies'. They had built up enormous organisations and associated financial commitments during the early neoliberal period. They had extended their scope through development programmes, lobbying and campaigning, and, in particular, disaster relief work. The official aid system of governments and international agencies, and the public, had willingly funded these moral crusades through promises of increased efficiency, effectiveness and an approach to participation that evaded the problematic role of the state, especially those democratically elected.

This helped propel the meteoric growth in the number of Southern NGOs who implemented the projects and kept pushing the cause of decentralisation and delegation so as to get more of the power over the funds. These Southern bodies had by the early 1990s outgrown their subordinate status. They were demanding a more-than-equal share of the cake. The agencies found themselves limited to an ever-diminishing set of activities. Funding from governments and international agencies flowed directly to the growing cadre of Southern NGOs, who in turn took the international stage by storm. They insisted on direct representation rather than the earlier indirect routes to power through their Northern colleagues. Some Southerners launched their own fundraising organisations in Europe and North America, particularly following the success of the newly elected African National Congress in attracting money directly. No part of the agencies' operations were safe at that time from the deadly pincer movement of invasive funding pressures and the rising of the South.

Matters of measurement

Meanwhile the agencies fell prey to a serious case of measurement neurosis. New and expensive forms of accounting were introduced just at the time the agencies were cutting and downsizing. Measuring impact became a sort of institutional pass-the-parcel exercise. Funding agencies weaved an increasingly crazed, bureaucratic nightmare around their 'clients' in response to their own internal pressures. Agencies spent more and more time and money to fulfil these reporting requirements, and thus had to reduce the time and energy available for getting the job done. Agencies passed the buck to their Southern partners, instilling the same fear around reporting requirements that had been imposed on them. The facts of poverty became buried under a wealth of conceptual transformations. Impact assessment became an industry unto itself. Talk of indicators, targets and evaluation processes became the newspeak of the age, often substituting for the facts of power relations, exploitation and poverty.

The changes resulting from the crisis in the 1990s unfortunately came about largely despite the strands taken by many agencies. A few medium-sized agencies moved towards new forms of accountability. But these relatively minor cases had no real ripple effect because of the obstinacy of the largest agencies, most marked in the so-called 'Seven Brothers'.

Drawing their nickname from the term 'Seven Sisters' applied by Anthony Sampson to the seven largest oil companies, the Seven Brothers were a group of private transnational aid agencies that directly or indirectly controlled about 60% of the funds passing from North and South via non-governmental hands. They dominated much of the lobbying space created during the 1980s, so they set the agenda in the media campaigns for hearts, minds and money. The fortunes of the NGO community lay in the image that these few organisations created for the public, state and, to a lesser degree, the corporate sector.

The resistance to change shown by the Seven Brothers and other agencies meant that the first real changes came about involuntarily, not via internal reflection and change of heart. The underlying structural issues became a crisis for the agency community when some of the more embarrassing aspects became public. It almost seemed a corollary of the increasing legitimacy of agencies in the eyes of the official aid establishment. From there, it was mostly downhill. A number of spirited journalistic investigations were undertaken—particularly from the TransOceanic

Institute, a renowned, European tabloid-style research institute based in the Netherlands. The book produced by this institute included a series of disclosures about malpractice, shoddy performance and outright cynical behaviour in high-profile agencies (TransOceanic Institute 1996). These disclosures were, as many of those in the know have since argued, unrepresentative. However, the damage was done, and the floodgates opened.

The immediate effect was the outbreak of a fierce public debate in Europe and North America, with numerous allegations and counter-allegations flying through the media. Kinder critics portrayed the agencies as bloated bureaucracies in which well-meaning ethical and political initiatives had been buried in a paperchase and a sweaty morass of circular consultation. Enemies derided them as a self-serving elite unwilling to submit themselves to the very forms of accountability that they insisted on for others. Amidst this invective and confusing debate, officials working for government and international bodies quietly secured themselves. Programme approvals were mysteriously delayed and existing programmes were placed on hold pending the completion of some obscure technicality. This bureaucratic retreat did not remain secret for long, and, when publicised, it precipitated a steep decline in publicly raised funds.

A major joint review of agency funding was ordered by the World Environment Organisation; its sister company, the World Bank; the anti-corruption agency based in Berlin, Transparency Incorporated, and a consortium of corporate sponsors. The European Commission and the United Nations eagerly scrambled to join this consortium, albeit as junior partners, because they saw it as a way of distracting scrutiny by the international community. The contents of this joint review report, 'Development Challenges for the 21st Century: The Role of the Non-Governmentals', were pretty ghastly, with accusations of ineptitude combined with crass naïveté verging on corruptness-by-error (World Economic Organisation/World Bank 1998). The outcome of this review was all too predictable. Funding declined dramatically, and in a number of cases the accreditation rights—the lifeblood of these organisations by then—to major national and international policy was withdrawn.

There was, it must be said, some malicious exaggeration in the response of governmental and international bodies. For over a decade, bureaucrats and technicians for these organisations who had been repeatedly held to moral account by small, badly organised agencies finally had their chance to take revenge for earlier humiliations such as the Wapenhans critique of the World Bank, and the legal ruling against the British government over the tying of funds for the Pergau Dam in Malaysia to their purchase of arms. Here finally was the opportunity to beat the agencies with their own moralising stick.

It is ironic that moralism was the one weapon that the private aid agencies had not reckoned could be used against them. They should have been warned by the media campaigns waged against a number of so-called 'ethical businesses' over this period. Even more ironic, perhaps, was that the bureaucrats who took their revenge in this way were drawn from among the same people, who, only a decade or so earlier, had built their own careers by supporting the emerging non-governmental giants. These international bureaucrats had become a roving expert on how to work with any type of agency. They ran newly emerged, assertive departments within organisations that were otherwise more or less moribund. Many of these bureau-cracies in fact came originally from the agencies themselves, the very organisations that had become their clients and contractors. This made it all the more sad to see how quickly they turned away from the agencies, playing a central part in naming the very deficiencies that they had been so central in creating.

The agencies were in a shambles, as a domino effect tore through their ranks. Already demoralised by retrenchments that had alienated many of their Southern partners, the Seven Brothers met together in closed sessions to find a common approach to this problem. The central issues, they agreed, were legitimacy and accountability. The essential challenge was, broadly, 'What gives an organisation the right to take funds with the stated aim of doing good for others?' What could guarantee in the 'eyes of the beholder' that the organisation really intended to do what it said? How could one ensure that this was what the intended recipients of this wealth of goodness really wanted? Success was, of course, important. However, public opinion polls taken at the time showed that most people in the North did not really believe that the facts of poverty in the South would significantly change, certainly not at any large-scale level. Similarly, an in-depth survey commissioned by Shell and carried out by the World Environmental Organisation highlighted the fact that 'success' was understood as a demonstration of trying the best one could in difficult circumstances, not demonstrating significant positive outcomes.

Southernising

A radical 'Southernisation' process began as a way of rebuilding legitimacy. Southern NGOs had not suffered the same sort of undressing in the media as had the agencies (another interesting story which seems to be coming to the surface at the moment). It was therefore possible for the agencies to regain at least some of their lost legitimacy in the eyes of the North—and so their funding—by demonstrating the increased control over decision-making by NGOs.

A series of mergers between key Northern agencies and Southern NGOs started taking place. Those agencies who failed to merge, or who failed to merge quickly enough, found themselves subjected to predatory 'asset stripping' of people, programmes and funding sources by other NGOs from the North and South. Most of those with the 'ride it out' philosophy eventually had to change tack. A number of them left it too late and had to close their doors for good.

Biting the hand that once fed

The old adage 'It never rains, it pours' proved to be devastatingly applicable in this period. The controlled 'mergers' were, in most cases, sufficient to move the new organisations onto a new plateau of stability, but the South was still restless. The experiences in the mid-1990s of mass demonstrations against GATT in India, and the uprising in Chiapas following the signing of North American Free Trade Agreement (NAFTA), offered a taste of one form of resistance to what was seen as the high-handed approaches taken by agencies in the South. The embarrassment caused by these demonstrations, and the small but well-publicised loss of lives of agency officials and demonstrators (particularly in one awful case where agency officials turned out to be armed, and fired on a peaceful demonstration in a fit of fear), pushed agencies that had been slow on their feet to appreciate the need for change.

But then, a number of community organisations in the South suddenly began bringing cases against agencies to the international courts. Most accused the agencies of expropriating personal and community-based information for fundraising, and then using the money for unrelated purposes. Others charged them with making 'false promises'. (An interesting study of this period suggests that this strategy was the brainchild of a consortium of Southern companies interested in acquiring aid-funded contracts then in the hands of Northern agencies. These companies, it appears, were being fed with information and legal advice by a large Northern advertising agency, Media Development Inc., which was building a reputation in public fundraising for Southern development-oriented organisations.) Legal history was made where peasant and urban communities shrewdly used intellectual property rights legislation and privacy laws. Some high-profile agencies found that their opponents were the very organisations with whom they had campaigned against GATT regulations on intellectual property rights. The merger strategy took on a more urgent note, so as to co-opt community organisations that posed the greatest legal danger. This led to the establishment of offshore legal registration in several NGO havens, notably Norway and Switzerland.

The end of non-profits

The idea of non-governmentalism, it will be recalled, was to enable a balance of autonomy from the state; an orientation towards non-financial gains; and a governance structure that sought to secure accountability in relation to stated aims. Exactly how this was achieved varied from place to place, but broadly built on the idea of 'trusteeship' associated with do-good organisations. That is, the trustees who effectively had the only legal right to direct the organisation were chosen by a group that usually acquired this right through historical precedent, and were representative only in the sense of having legitimised concern for the same issues as the organisation.

The trustee model, in its various forms, was legitimate only until it was really tested. It could not withstand the pressures of a complex matrix of activities involving large volumes of resources, and major conflicts of interest regarding the use of these resources. Most of all, it became subject to challenge the moment the overall legitimacy of the agencies became open to doubt.

It became widely accepted that the traditional model of agency ownership—which was basically no formal ownership at all, leaving effective ownership in the hands of elected officials—was inadequate. In 1999, drawing partly from a government-sponsored in-depth analysis of the non-governmental sector in the UK, produced in 1994 (HMSO 1999; Knight 1994), a law was passed through the English Parliament marking the end of non-ownership status for all but a few (rather archaic) cases. The agencies, of course, resisted. They took the English government to the European Courts in an effort to overturn this shift in legal status. The European Court not only confirmed the original judgement but made strong recommendations that the approach be pursued at a European level. The counter-move had backfired. By the turn of the century, the whole notion of 'non-governmental' as a form of (non)-ownership was effectively over.

New forms of accountability

It would be gratifying to be able to say that a new form of ownership arose phoenix-like from the ashes to support appropriate forms of accountability for non-governmental organisations. This did not happen, although there was a period of intense and often very creative innovation in new forms of accountability and ownership. Rather, a range of existing models of accountability were taken up by different NGO-like organisations.

Institutional–federalism

This was probably the most common form adopted. It was quite similar to the 'Europe of the Regions' model that had been rejected by the European Union in the mid-1990s. Each part of newly merged organisations acquired a vote according to various possible measures of size: the more conservative organisations tended to weight votes according to monies provided, whereas the more radical organisations gave weight to how many people each part represented. The heads of the parts, many of which were in the South, made up the Board of Directors. This approach seemed to work particularly well for those organisations that were in practice controlled by their staff, since it tended to consolidate decision-making within the organisation's (extended) boundaries, rather than extending decision-making to outside institutions, groups and individuals. This model was therefore often preferred by agencies oriented towards service delivery rather than advocacy and campaigning.

Block-vote model

Some NGOs went for a variation of the block-voting formulae adopted by numerous political parties and trade union movements in the 'socio-corporate' era of the 1960s and 1970s. World Services International (WSI), for example, created a voting structure that gave funder stakeholders an aggregate block vote of 25%, community organisations (the intended beneficiaries) about 55%, and staff the remaining 20%. At the time, this approach seemed particularly attractive to agencies wishing to secure long-term funding relationships with a small number of institutional sources, and to focus activities on a small and stable number of communities. It was also an approach of relevance to agencies faced with legal action from the South, as was the case for WSI.

The WSI experience was particularly interesting in how subsequent power battles shifted the effective locus of control back towards staff. The model they adopted should have given the community organisations effective control. However, the staff and funders managed from the outset to operate a divide-and-rule approach which gave them effective power. When this no longer functioned, the staff themselves organised a workers' 'buy-out' (with support from the funders), leaving WSI in its current well-known form as the only agency workers' co-operative, in many ways resembling the institutional–federal model. WSI now provides a range of services, in practice doing a lot of cheap subcontract work for other agencies.

One-person one-vote model

Of the large agencies, TransFam adopted the most radical approach of all, a one-person one-vote system across their one million members. This was not, it must sadly be said, because they were the most radical organisation prior to the period of change. It was TransFam, some may recall, that became the focal point of mass demonstrations in the late 1990s, and had to cope with the largest number of litigations. Eventually, faced with imminent bankruptcy, TransFam signed the famous Delhi Accord in 2001. The over-3,000 closely typed pages of the Accord spelled out a deal whereby TransFam would become owned by all those people who had received grants directly through them over a specific period. In return, the various litigations were dropped, and the relatively widespread intimidation of TransFam's officials ceased. It was quite a depressing affair at the time; today it is seen as a low point in the collapse of the dinosaurs. It is somewhat ironic therefore that the TransFam model is now seen as the most radical to emerge from that period.

Enter the NICs

In that period there were, however, a set of organisations that voluntarily embraced radical transformations in accountability and ownership. These are the so-called 'New Internationalist Conglomerates' (NICs). These did not form a coherent community of organisations, but were a motley category that had acquired the name 'NICs' along the way, largely because of the ways in which they coped with the crisis of the 1990s.

The NICs did, however, have a few fairly common characteristics. Firstly, although most of them were originally Northern NGOs, they were different from aid agencies of the traditional resource-transfer school. They grew out of operational, educational and lobbying work within and usually about their own communities and countries. Thus, although they did have an international profile, they brought with them a distinctly and unashamedly Northern internationalist perspective. This Northern root also meant that the NICs had a different sense of accountability. The intended beneficiaries of the private aid agencies had only limited access to the Northern media. But the beneficiaries and collaborators of the NICs could make their views heard in exactly those institutional spaces where the NICs could most easily be confronted and, if necessary, held to account. Thirdly, the NICs were generally smaller and younger than the mainly middle-aged agencies. They thus suffered much less from institutional inertia, bureaucratisation and internal vested interests.

But the really critical difference was that the NICs were of the information rather than the development age. Hence their other nickname, the 'New Information Consolidators'. They generated and shared knowledge, not funds. They moved information, not freight. They fostered development education, research, lobbying and campaigning, rather than funding physical projects.

These features gave the NICs an altogether different organisational form. In them, authority was far less hierarchically organised, since generating and sharing knowledge was much more about reciprocal relationships and respect. Their relationships with each other and with beneficiaries tended to be far more open-ended, involving less dependencies, fewer reporting structures and, in general, a far higher level of voluntarism. The NICs did not therefore face the same sorts of difficulties encountered by other types of agency, particularly those that emerged before early neoliberalism, during the development period.

Conclusions and lessons

The last 20 years have been quite remarkable. Looking back, it seems quite obvious that the changes should have been expected. However, at the same time it was all pretty unexpected. Even those most committed to change had got stuck in a visionless vision, one that was able to see what was wrong, but just couldn't discern what to do. Everyone seemed to be looking for the 'Big Story' and missed the massive events that were unravelling on their own doorstep. That is, until these events stood up and slapped them in the face.

This should not really be a surprise. It is difficult to see problems clearly when you are right in the middle of it all. This is not merely due to ignorance or malice. We often prefer to hang on to redundant utopias. Our certainties of what is wrong are not matched by a clarity of what would be an achievable 'right'. This state of 'perplexity', as Manfred Max-Neef describes it, is the 'outcome of a situation for which we cannot recognise a precedent, which has kept us in a dead-end alley and barred the road to imaginative, novel and bold solutions' (Max-Neef et al. 1991). The only route forward, Andre Gorz confirms, is to 'find a new utopia, for as long as we are the prisoners of the utopia collapsing around us, we will remain incapable of perceiving the potential for liberation' (Gorz 1989).

This story is a lesson for us all. We may be pleased at the changes that have taken place: the new forms of private aid agencies, and the NICs. But history challenges us all not to repeat the incredibly myopic behaviour of the late twentieth century. After all, it might have turned out very differently, and may still do so in the future.

5
which globalisation?[*]

Globalisation, the market and civil regulation

Advocating globalisation as the way to address social and environmental challenges is like recommending antibiotics to deal with a virus. Antibiotics clear everything in their path, but simply cannot solve viral problems. But they sure do a lot of damage in the process.

The downside of globalisation are not 'just temporary effects' as claimed by its supporters. Neither the social democratic nor the communitarian models can withstand the pressures of globalisation, which systematically undermines traditional family, state and community-based mutual support contracts and practices. Similarly, in terms of the environment, the positive technological advances are diminished by the impact of inadequate regulation. In addition, there is the irreversible environmental damage caused by the sheer scale of the increases in production, trade and consumption, as set out in the recent World Wide Fund for Nature Report, *Dangerous Curves: Does the Environment Improve with Economic Growth?* (1996).

There is a need to acknowledge the positive effects of increased trade between nations. The newly industrialised countries would certainly not be enjoying their current economic prosperity without export-led growth—sustained economic growth does alleviate poverty. Gross wastage and inefficiencies such as exists in state-run industries from Moscow to Dar-es-Salaam can be challenged and reduced through increased competition. The creative energies of people previously trapped within these stagnant institutions can be released through trade liberalisation and privatisation.

But the most undervalued positive effect of globalisation has been on ordinary members of society. Vast and fluid international networks of individuals and civil organisations are creating an organic ethics that is creating a framework of 'civil regulation'. This is not vested in statutory form, since the state increasingly refuses to act in any way that will constrain the negative effects of the international flow of capital. Rather, civil regulations are rooted within a language that the most power-

* This article was first published in *Development* Volume 40(3), September 1997. *Development* (ISSN 1011-6370) is the journal of the Society for International Development (www.sidint.org). © 1997 Society for International Development, Rome.

ful global actors, multinationals, understand only too well—that of the market.

It turns out that ordinary people are not merely consumers, but people willing to selectively withhold consumption. The public are not just pension or insurance holders, but people wanting savings to be invested for social and environmental as well as (and for) personal good. The public are not merely staff to be employed (or not), but holders of a creativity and energy that is demanding to be harnessed through deeper relationships and commitments.

It turns out that globalisation needs people, and that in their turn people have a broad set of needs that is now being voiced—through the market—where such voices count. It turns out that people are the virus that globalisation cannot control.

And civil regulations work. Witness the growing list of global giants that have moved towards compliance, as recently documented in a New Economics Foundation report, *Open Trading: Options for Effective Monitoring of Corporate Performance* (1997a). Secrecy is no longer an option, as Texaco and the Swiss banks have found to their cost in recent months. Shell has finally turned its back on its treasured stance of measured political neutrality; Nike and Reebok accept the principle of their performance being verified by NGOs. British Telecom, Grand Metropolitan and others have announced their intentions to undertake and report social audits of their activities.

Civil regulations have a further source of legitimacy: the lavish demonstration of alternative approaches to building businesses and economies. Communities are regaining their ability to create economic institutions and processes over which they have control, not only at local but also at national and international levels. The list of community economics options set out in a recent New Economics Foundation 'guidebook' for the UK, *Community Works* (1997b) illustrates just this. Community banks and enterprises, local currencies, community-based planning systems and fairly traded products are no longer marginal. More people in the UK do voluntary work than have a 'job'. Over half a billion people in the world belong to membership-based economic enterprises. This is increasingly the stuff of the financial pages of Western newspapers, rather than the 'weekend news'.

Corporations and community-based civil institutions understand better than governments and their multilateral equivalents that there is a new social contract in the making. It is not vested with the legal legitimacy of a social clause within the World Trade Organisation (WTO) framework, or the pomp and ceremony of a G7 resolution. It is a social contract formulated on the streets, and agreed in anxious company boardrooms, within risk-averse investment houses, and ultimately at the 'point of sale'.

Organisations such as the World Bank and the OECD could well have a role to play in these processes, as could governments. But these actors must appreciate that their withdrawal from any serious developmental role in the 1980s has undermined their credibility, and in most instances demonstrated their lack of insight and competency.

Because of this, these ageing institutions cannot be judge or jury, or even arbiter or mediator. Their role must be to observe, encourage and, where appropriate, facilitate dialogue and negotiation between the actors that count, corporations that make and deliver goods and services, and other civil institutions that are increasingly setting the terms for these activities.

6
consumer works*

co-written with Franck Amalric

Why consumption?

What is the distinction between sustainable consumption and sustainable development? At first glance, the answer seems obvious: sustainable development is a broader concept than sustainable consumption. The latter only focuses on one element of the overall system: consumption itself. A closer examination of the debate defies this apparently straightforward distinction. Discussions about sustainable consumption turn out to include everything that we might expect to see embodied within the broader concept of sustainable development, including the entire social and ecological process of production, distribution, trade, actual consumption, and its after-effects. It seems on second glance that, when someone calls for 'a sustainable approach to consumption', they are calling for 'sustainable development' itself.

But there is a difference between sustainable consumption and sustainable development, and it is not merely a semantic one. The difference comes on what are the critical points of change to edge development along a sustainable path. The interest in consumption reflects a recognition that, although the *structural* driver of our current system is capital accumulation and profit, the *transforming* driver may well lie elsewhere: namely, in the sphere of consumption.

* This article was first published in *Development* 41(1) (March 1998). *Development* (ISSN 1011-6370) is the journal of the Society for International Development (www.sidint.org). © 1998 Society for International Development, Rome.

Some propositions

Consumption is a fundamental ingredient of sustainable development

Our basic human needs—nutrition, clothing, shelter and energy—depend on consumption of material resources. Beyond the meeting of these basic needs, consumption is a central, although not the only, ingredient that can enhance people's quality of life. Making more effective use of health and education products and services, for example, can enhance people's control over their lives, and their long-term health and security. So consumption is not a 'bad' per se. Instead, we need to distinguish among the different forms of consumption, and their role in advancing or constraining our way down the sustainable development path.

Consumption need not be positive in terms of sustainable development

In a world characterised for some by ever-expanding choices in available products and services, people may choose to consume products and services that ultimately constrain their development, either directly or indirectly. Some drugs, for example, undermine health, thereby reduce the chances of a long and healthy life for those who consume them. We know that smoking kills, but cigarette production reached a record high of 5,535 billion in 1995, a 100% increase since 1966 (*Guardian*/WWF 1997). Indeed, cigarettes may not only directly damage the health of the smoker but sometimes they are purchased at the expense of other badly needed goods and services. Manfred Max-Neef, in what has become a classic text, *Human Scale Development* (Max-Neef *et al.* 1991), describes various possible effects of consumption on 'real needs', including the 'negative satificers' that constrain the ability to meet the deeper needs of not only food and shelter but also, for example, a sense of belonging.

Consumption can mould sustainable development through its relationship to patterns of trade, production and the state of the environment

The relationship between consumption and sustainable development clearly goes beyond the direct effects of consumption on those who consume. It concerns in particular the social and environmental dimensions embedded within the chains of production and trade, which underpin patterns of consumption. Within these expansive realms lie gross inequalities in income and opportunities. Just as the corporations seek to influence the consumption patterns of those who can afford to pay the financial price, they have an enormous influence on the structures of production and trade that subsume people and the environment on terms that are unacceptable from the perspectives of social justice and environmental sustainability.

We now see the result of increased consumption worldwide. Internationally traded products sold in industrial countries such as toys, sportswear and food products are often produced using workers earning remarkably low wages, including often the exploitative use of child labour which reduces the opportunity for formal education, and can reduce their quality of health. Demand for hardwood forest products undermines the ecological resources that have historically provided sustainable livelihoods for communities located in these regions of the world. The 'disposable consumer economy' can lead to patterns of pollution that damage some people's health in the short term, and constrain longer opportunities for many more.

Consumption can be an active process involving conscious, collective choices and actions, and so extends well beyond what are often seen as passive processes of acquiring goods and services

Consumption has collective as well as individual dimensions. Some of these are 'involuntary' dimensions, in that people are encouraged to consume in order to further their relative status and with little regard for the consequences for others and the environment. Other aspects of collectivity around consumption are, however, of a more active variant. Conscious civil action can and does influence consumption patterns and, through consumption, influence the lives of those involved in production and trading chains. Such actions form one of the many bases on which democratic processes can be strengthened. More generally, they can realise the potential of the human development of economically weaker individuals and groups.

Understanding Factor X

The need for new political approaches in addressing the vision and imperatives of sustainable development is also underlined by 'factor'-based arguments in the arena of consumption analysis, particularly work focused on the environmental dimensions of consumption. Notable among these has been the work of the Wuppertal Institute, Friends of the Earth and others, which concluded that the industrial nations need to reduce their energy use by up to 90% in order to get back towards a sustainable development path—the so-called **Factor 10** proposition. More recent has been the work of Amory Lovins and others, who have concluded that we could achieve a fourfold increase in energy efficiency ('double the wealth, halve the energy use') using existing technology—the so-called **Factor 4** proposition (von Weizsäcker et al. 1997). Yet, despite our knowledge that there is both a problem and possible solutions, most of us continue—as individuals, communities and nations—to pursue courses of action detrimental even to our own interests as well as those of others.

People and communities resist change. Often, they resist the language and ideas of change until there is simply no choice but to embrace what is staring them in the face. This is what Manfred Max-Neef refers to as a state of perplexity. Showing people that Factor 4 is a real possibility, or that Factor 10 is a real need, rarely turns out to do the trick, at least not on its own. This lack of responsiveness is not—as we often perhaps arrogantly think—because we have not made ourselves clear what 'we know to be true'. There is a step between understanding the basic story about sustainable development (and even one's own destructive role) and becoming an agent in the process of change. This is the space within which we need to work. Following the recent vogue for 'factors' of one kind or another, we might call this gap **Factor X**.

To talk about Factor X is a way of distinguishing the end-state that many of us map out as a desired future from the complex process of change that we need to understand and engage in. When we say 'externalities count, and must be counted', we are not providing a solution, but merely an eloquent way of understanding and articulating the problem. When we say 'increase prices to take account of and so reduce these externalities', we are again not offering a solution, but at best a technique that will be useful when the real solution is to hand. We can understand the nature of solutions as being those actual or potential processes and events that empower those who are willing to act, and thereby strengthen the sense of the arising need to act by those who currently do not.

It is in this context that we can best understand the subject of consumption, and its relevance to the political and environmental project of sustainable development. The sphere of consumption is a place where passivity, cynicism and many other disabling features of our time can be effectively challenged, thereby enabling people to believe that action is possible, and positive effects achievable.

For this to be possible will increasingly mean working with the very dynamic processes that are more often seen to represent the core of the problem, or at least its reflection—such as status-oriented consumption, South-to-North mimicry, and the reorientation of production towards wealthier, non-local markets. The 'political consumer'—and her cousins the ethical investor, the reluctant employee and the questioning daughter or son—are rarely liberated from an interest in status, but are able to see how it can be achieved through other means. Seeking to 'do away' with these things may seem desirable to some. However, such a strategy is often likely to be counter-productive, if only because the very constituencies we seek to represent will, faced with the choice, too often reject our views and roles.

The sphere of consumption is fraught with problems, dilemmas and often ghastly paradoxes. However, it is one possible place where the inertia and double-binds embodied within Factor X can be overcome, allowing real progress to be made.

Civil action turns the sphere of consumption into a political terrain, one that is still not fully exploited at a time when the more traditional political spheres have proved barren in the push for sustainability. Hence, if the national political debates or international forums are no longer fertile territory for voicing our practical concerns over sustainability, we may view the realm of consumption as somewhat more encouraging.

Households, communities and webs

Households and individuals are clearly the base 'unit' out of which all other forms of organisation are constructed. While civil action is a collective process, the collective actions in most cases consist of a large number of decisions made at the individual or household level. Individual and household action (through consumer boycotts, for example) in redefining personal consumption patterns is emerging as a current trend for wealthier consumers, particularly in Europe and North America. The phenomenon sometimes known as 'down-shifting' has generated a range of supporting initiatives.

Local communities. Many of the most extraordinary cases of collective action emerge from the community. Visioning processes engage people in thinking through what services and amenities can be of critical importance to the community, or how best to measure and communicate what progress is made over time. Agenda 21 has provided a particular catalyst for these processes in recent years, encouraging the development of a host of tools. As the FAO concluded in relation to these and other, similar initiatives: 'It is becoming increasingly clear that large sections of Third World cities are only surviving because of the input of their underprivileged citizens and that good governance can only be achieved if the traditional decision makers give the poor majorities who are building the city a seat at the negotiating table' (FAO 1997).

Webs. There has been a dramatic increase over the last five years in international collective action through consumption involving both poorer producers and workers, and those wealthier communities with influence over production and trade by virtue of their vast purchasing power. At the micro scale, the 'fair-trade movement' has enabled small-scale, community-based producers to offer goods more directly to high-income consumers in industrial countries. At a more macro scale, international action has tended to focus on the behaviour of transnational corporations operating in a relatively unregulated environment in terms of their social and environmental externalities. Also important has been resistance to the rash of new international regulatory frameworks and institutions (e.g. NAFTA, WTO).

BOX 1 SITES OF CIVIL ACTION ON CONSUMPTION

Does consumer action *really* work?

The argument that consumption is or can be a key sphere to achieve progress through civil action can and should be challenged. Perhaps the most important challenge is that consumer action is the prerogative of the rich. Poorer individuals and communities cannot use this mechanism to fight for change because they have insufficient purchasing power to influence dominant institutions, which deliver goods and services. There are too few alternative sources of much-needed goods and services that allow, for example, isolated rural communities to withdraw their often meagre purchasing power from particular suppliers.

From this perspective, as Raff Carmen (1998) and others eloquently argue, production remains the heartland of where workers and poorer producers can gain some leverage over their circumstances, either through resistance or the development of more autonomous, localised, production processes.

It is certainly true that poorer communities are far less able than wealthier people to use the threat of the withdrawal of their consumption as a leverage for progressive change. There are, however, many examples of effective mobilisation by poorer communities against the state and corporations based on action around key areas of consumption. Direct, collective, political action in the urban shanty towns of Latin America is commonplace as a means of gaining control over the supply of clean water and electricity. When a million farmers in India marched against the GATT, the focus of their discontent was on the growing signs that they would have to purchase their seed in a future world where the variants they had nurtured for generations were either patented or unavailable. We can understand consumption, therefore, in its broader form as 'expenditure', which embraces what economists might traditionally deem to be 'investment'. Similarly, we can see that consumer action can be understood to include far more, say, than the threat of boycott, in that it also encompasses a broader range of civil actions 'outside' of the narrow commodity market that nevertheless are focused on securing the right and ability to acquire and consume appropriate products and services on reasonable terms.

There has, furthermore, been a dramatic increase over the last five years in what we might think of as 'lent consumer power'. This is (usually international) collective action involving, through consumption, both poorer producers and workers, and those wealthier communities that have influence over production and trade by virtue of their vast purchasing power. The peasant communities of Casanares in Colombia have gained some leverage over the company British Petroleum because their international networks have challenged the company's 'ethics' in markets where such a challenge counts. Similarly for Shell in Nigeria, and companies such as GAP and Nike for the treatment of workers in the factories worldwide.

At the micro scale, the 'fair-trade movement' has enabled small-scale, community-based producers—often of basic products such as textiles and crafts, coffee and tea—to offer goods directly to high-income consumers in industrial countries through the mediation of non-profit 'alternative trade organisations'. Consumers have been encouraged to acknowledge and be more informed about the world of the producer, and to select only those products where the producers have some say over labour conditions and pay (Zadek and Tiffen 1996). Even areas of action that appear at first glance to be principally about production often turn out to depend on change in the realm of consumption. The success of local community enterprise or local currencies, for example, usually depend on a combined shift in production and consumption patterns (NEF 1997b). So the argument that consumer action is the prerogative of the rich is not really the case, although the role of collective purchasing power is clearly a critical element. So how far can we actually go?

The more common examples of consumer-based civil action show that consumers or consumer-based organisations can play the role of watchdog with some effectiveness. They can ensure that transnational companies, for instance, respect some basic rules of behaviour (NEF 1997a). It is unclear, however, whether consumer civil action can go beyond a watchdog role, and actually bring about far-reaching structural transformations.

Are the small number of exciting cases of 'fair trade' still in existence because they have not been sufficiently effective for the business community to find them worthwhile undermining? Similarly, the examples of civil actions influencing the behaviour of large companies could be seen simply as a series of one-off cases allowed only because their ad hoc and limited nature meant that they could be accommodated by business and the state.

It is also unclear what type of political alliances can be made, even informally, in the consumer sphere, and how they differ from political alliances made elsewhere. The consumer sphere opens a political terrain that cuts across national state boundaries, and potentially undermines the role of the state, rather than securing and rebuilding it. Conversely, politics is often pointed out as one thing that has not been globalised. In fact, political parties tend to remain nationally based, as it has occurred even in the context of the European Union. This feature of politics may be circumvented, at least to some extent, by rendering more political some social spheres which have already a global reach—the consumption sphere, for example. Finally, of course, is the matter of the natural environment. Civil actions can result in poorer and marginalised communities gaining more, and in some cases those who over-consume in environmental terms using less. But, as Nick Robins and Sarah Roberts (1998) ask, do these actions and their effects even scratch the surface of the challenge of living within our environmental limits?

Concluding remarks

Nothing guarantees *a priori* that civil action around consumption will serve the project of sustainable development. What is also clear is that there are no *a priori* limits to the potential scope of civil actions. Civil action within the sphere of consumption (or, more accurately, within the broader sphere of civil expenditure, including, for example, the sphere of investment) can remould markets to the needs of social justice and environmental sustainability. This is not necessarily a matter of ridding us of the desire to consume for status, as, for example, David Loy and Jon Watts (1998) argue from a Buddhist perspective. Rather, it is to see that the basis for acquiring status and also self-esteem can be reoriented towards consumption (and investment) patterns that are more consistent with the tenets of sustainable development.

It is therefore possible that the flotilla of civil actions against companies are a part of the early foundations of a broader, organic framework of 'civil regulations' that will over time become an integral part of the governance of each and every aspect of business. For this to be possible requires that we deepen our tools for mobilising citizens as consumers, and that we strengthen their solidarity with those who do not have leverage through their purchasing power. Also critical is that we build an increasingly sophisticated approach to dealing with the business community, strengthening our ability to challenge reckless and destructive behaviour, and similarly learning how to reward those companies that seek to do business more responsibly. In this way, it may indeed be possible that what is achievable through civil action will continue to grow, and that over time new standards of behaviour within the market will thereby be set.

civil regulation*

GAP sales are down and executives are quitting, or moving on to 'spend time with family'. Of course, there was no mention of our campaign (the protests, the letters, the teach-ins) to expose GAP Inc.'s sweatshop abuses and how we may have had something to do with GAP's losses. We should [nevertheless] see this as a victory and take credit for the disorientation that we have caused this company.[1]

[While] not investigated in a scientific way . . . the negative press referring to specific incidents is not proved to have a long-term negative effect on the price of the company's shares.[2]

Friedman comes of age

Today, the corporate citizenship test is being applied to more and more parts of the business. As corporate citizenship becomes increasingly significant in terms of policy commitments and practices, there are growing calls for proof by all stakeholders—customers, employees, suppliers, governments, communities and, indeed, shareholders. Shareholders, of course, want to know what are its financial bottom-line effects. But other stakeholders are also increasingly concerned about the business case, rightly seeing this as a measure of the viability of corporate citizenship. Even the most anti-business lobby realises that virtuous but uncompetitive companies will not stay the course. The business case, in short, counts.[3]

At its crudest level, the proposition states that 'being good is good for financial performance'. It suggests that social and environmental gains can deliver financial benefits by producing, for example, business-relevant reputational, productivity and efficiency effects (Utting 2000: 7). The win–win proposition is certainly evocative. It suggests that the corporate community will produce social and environmental dividends through its successful long-term pursuit of profit. It evokes a sense of ethics into what increasingly appears at best an amoral evolution in global market

* First published in *The Civil Corporation: The New Economy of Corporate Citizenship.* © 2001 Earthscan Publications, London.

❝The company's commitment is in part a matter of reinforcing their positive reputation to the general public and the various layers of government with which they regularly interact given the nature of their business❞ (Nelson and Zadek 2000).

Suez Lyonnaise des Eaux

❝If we are the leading corporate citizen, it will do several things for us. It will create an image for Ford that is different from others, and in a cluttered and crowded marketplace in which differentiation is hard to obtain. If we achieve this, we will attract better employees and the highest caliber of people out of universities. They're going to want to come work for a company like Ford❞ (Ford Motor Company 2000).

William Clay Ford Jr, Ford Motor Company

❝It is our belief that this commitment to environmental protection, social progress, and shared economic benefit will give us preferred access to gold projects around the world, thus ensuring our continued success and growth❞ (Placer Dome 2000).

Placer Dome

❝To deny that our neighbours have a genuine stake in the company is to deny not only the reality of their lives, but also their ability to obstruct, delay and even stop the growth of our airports❞ (British Airports Authority 1999: 2).

Sir John Egan, BAA plc

❝We believe that our commitment to contribute to sustainable development holds the key to our long-term business success...Society is still exploring exactly how to put sustainable development into practice but it is clear that we are on a journey and not aiming at a known end-point. For Shell this journey is part of our transformation to become 'top performer' of first choice❞ (Shell 1999: inside front cover).

Shell International

❝We recognize that we will have to be sensitive in our development of retail units in the cities, taking greater account of the diversity of our client base and employees. These are the factors that will define our success in achieving future growth❞ (quoted in Nelson and Zadek 2000).

Ahold

❝Concern is sometimes expressed that 'corporate social responsibility' has no clear business benefits and could destroy shareholder value by diverting resources from core commercial activities...However, the WBCSD supports the view that a coherent CSR strategy based on sound ethics and core values offers clear business benefits❞ (WBCSD 1999: 2).

World Business Council for Sustainable Development

BOX 2 WHY COMPANIES DO THE RIGHT THING

capitalism. Indeed, it suggests a *necessary* convergence of financial success with societal good—a domesticated Darwinism at its very best.

Milton Friedman famously stated that the sole responsibility of business was to maximise financial returns to shareholders (Friedman 1970). Corporate citizenship has been taken as a challenge to this assertion and associated practices. Alice Tepper-Marlin, the President of the Council on Economic Priorities, in reflecting on a decade over which corporate citizenship emerged as a major field of activity, concluded:

> Milton Friedman, the prime advocate of the position that the responsi-
> bility of business is exclusively to maximize profit for shareholders, has
> lost the debate (CBI 1999: 2).

Actually, the reverse may be true. The 'profits with principles' argument underlying the traditional corporate citizenship proposition is more a sophisticated restatement than a refutation of Friedman's position. Friedman always said that businesses should comply not only with the law but also with the norms and expectations of the societies within which they operate. From this perspective, the win–win proposition more or less restates this in saying that business should address new social norms embodied in the idea of corporate citizenship and through this can maximise its long-term financial performance.

The win–win proposition is as provocative as it is evocative. David Korten argues that 'real ethics' costs real money, i.e. that there is a trade-off between profits and principles. For this reason, he continues, truly ethical companies are necessarily pushed out of a competitive market (Korten 1995). For Korten and other critics of corporate behaviour, the win–win proposition is at best a muddle by well-meaning individuals, and at worst a well-orchestrated deception that covers up the underlying growth of corporate power.

The win–win proposition lies at the heart of the confusion over the role and impact of business in society. The view that there need be no trade-off between financial profitability and being responsible to society and the planet is, plainly, a nonsense if it is argued to be always and everywhere correct. It is remarkably simple to identify cases of business behaviour that are immensely profitable and cannot even with a stretch be argued as 'ethical'. Destructive drugs (legal or otherwise), child prostitution, laundering funds stolen by politicians, and weapons of war designed to maim or kill civilians all come to mind as relatively uncontentious cases in point. More disputed examples of questionable business practice adorn our newspapers on a daily basis, ranging from animal testing and the use of genetically modified organisms through to products and services that offer protection against pregnancy. In practice, 'sharp' and immensely profitable dealings exist in all spheres of business.

Advocates of corporate citizenship circumvent these stark examples by arguing that such irresponsible companies will not survive in the long run. Mark Goyder, Director of the UK-based Centre for Tomorrow's Company is a case in point. He asserts that tomorrow's successful companies will *necessarily* be those that are 'inclusive' in the way they deal with their stakeholders (Goyder 1998). But even someone so committed to the win–win proposition acknowledges that 'being responsive to key stakeholders' does not mean *all* stakeholders, and almost certainly does not mean those most in need who have little or no power to impact on the business. The win–win proposition clearly emphasises the need for business to take into account those stakeholders that can impact on the financial bottom line. This is quite different from the more difficult question of the responsibility of business to solve pervasive social and environmental problems. After all, would companies such as Liz Claiborne, Adidas and even Levi Strauss have addressed the issue of child labour and other dimensions of labour standards in its global supply chains had these worker-stakeholders not been 'lent power' by campaigning organisations that threatened to disrupt the company's reputation in its principal markets?[4]

The cruder representations of the profits-with-principles proposition come dangerously close to being tautological or untestable beliefs. Empirical testing must ultimately allow it to be confirmed or refuted, and more importantly to determine under what conditions the proposition may be true. The empirical dilemmas are many. It is certainly difficult to generalise from company to company, sector to sector, and country to country. Nike and Levi's both experienced significant falls in earnings during the late 1990s. Yet they have almost diametrically opposite corporate citizenship reputations. Over the same period, Nike was subjected to a long-running worldwide campaign by NGOs for its alleged failure to secure the appropriate treatment of labour in its global supply chain. Levi's, on the other hand, was consistently celebrated for its social responsibility programmes, winning for example the coveted Corporate Conscience award from the New York-based Council on Economic Priorities (CEP).

The same disconnect between financial and corporate citizenship performance can be observed in the energy sector. Shell under-performed financially throughout the late 1990s compared to its main sector competitors, BP and Exxon (now ExxonMobil). However, it would be a misread of the evidence to attribute this to its miscalculation over Brent Spa, or to its alleged malpractice in Nigeria. Similarly, Shell's poor financial performance over that period cannot convincingly be attributed to the fact that it at the same time became a leader in 'triple bottom line' reporting. Equally for BP, there is no obvious reason why its short-term, measured financial success should have anything directly to do with the company's progressive and much-noted decision to exit the Global Climate Coalition.[5]

The lack of any simple connection between financial, and social and environmental performance, can be further observed in the fate of the two 'ethical business' icons emerging from the sixties, Ben & Jerry's Homemade and The Body Shop International. Both showed more than healthy financial results for many years, building strong positions in profitable niche markets based in large part on perceptions of their social and environmental performance as part of their customer offering. More recently, however, both have fared poorly in financial terms, despite maintaining a strong social and environmental performance (Body Shop 1998).

Doing good clearly does not guarantee financial success over any reasonable time-frame, just as being less-than-ethical does not guarantee financial disaster. Understanding the relationship, if any, between financial and other measures of performance clearly requires a more in-depth exploration of the business drivers underlying corporate citizenship.

Civil regulation in theory

The most visible driver that translates social and environmental 'goods' into positive market signals and related financial gains is *civil regulation* (Murphy and Bendell

1997). Corporations are increasingly under pressure from NGOs and other organisations to drive enhanced social and environmental performance standards through the business process. This includes elements within their own organisational and legal boundaries—for example, in relation to their own staff—and increasingly down global production chains and up towards and indeed beyond the point of consumption. These pressures come in the form of activist campaigning which aim to damage companies' market performance by undermining their reputation (Zadek and Amalric 1998).

Civil regulations in the main involve collective processes, albeit often through loose forms of social organisation. They are the manifestations of essentially political acts that can affect business performance through their influence on market conditions. In their early stages, civil regulations are quintessentially organic and often volatile systems of rules. Indeed, they can best be understood as non-statutory regulatory frameworks governing corporate affairs. They lie between the formal structures of public (statutory) regulation, and market signals generated by more conventional individual and collective preferences underpinned by the use and exchange value of goods and services. How this early stage of civil regulation transforms into more stable rule frameworks—the essence of the proposition underlying the Mecca pathway—is returned to in later chapters.[6]

There have been several celebrated international cases of civil regulation in the last two decades. Probably the longest-lasting campaign has been against the Swiss food giant Nestlé for its alleged approach to marketing baby milk substitutes in developing countries.[7] In terms of human tragedy caused by a single event, the case of Union Carbide in Bhopal, India, is probably the most significant and longest-running campaign. In recent times, the most celebrated case has been the campaign against Shell, first against its attempts to dispose of the Brent Spa oil platform in the Atlantic, and then for events surrounding its massive operations in Nigeria. Of equal significance has been the campaign against McDonald's. In France and India this has focused centrally on the company's alleged role in undermining cultural traditions embedded within food and eating habits. Elsewhere, and in the case of the celebrated court case, the issues have revolved more around environmental and animal rights issues. The anti-Nike campaign, probably the most vociferous, widespread and extended campaign against any single company in recent decades, has most come to symbolise the essence of the movement against globalisation and multinationals. Finally, although in no way exhaustively, there has been the largely European campaign against Monsanto in the late 1990s, the company most visibly involved in the promotion of agricultural processes and products involving genetically modified organisms.

The thinking behind civil regulation is that the reputation of companies can be damaged by civil action to a degree that will affect their business performance. This relationship is characterised in its most simple form in Figure 2. As the company's ethical behaviour as perceived by key stakeholders improves, so does its financial performance, and vice versa (an increase/reduction in reputation of the amount 'A' based on perceived ethical behaviour leads to an increase/decrease in financial performance of the amount 'B'). There are various reasons why this might be the case. Staff may be more motivated when the company for which they work is not the subject of public criticism. Governments may be more at ease in granting plan-

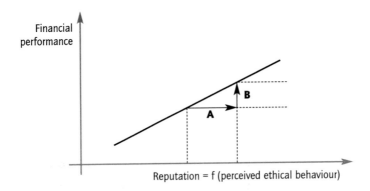

FIGURE 2 CIVIL REGULATION IN THEORY

Source: Zadek and Forstater 1999

ning permission, renewing operating licences, or choosing not to pass constraining public legislation. Customers, particularly for retail companies, will buy their products, and investors are less nervous. In simple terms, the steeper the line in Figure 2, the greater the financial gains from perceived ethical behaviour, and vice versa.

The people speak out

Show-stopping campaigns such as those against Nike, Monsanto and Shell—as well as many others of lesser fame—have all basically had this relationship in mind: 'Hit them till it hurts, and then they will change for the better.' Certainly many of the more radical campaigning and development NGOs think that it works. An email announcement on the anti-GAP listserv declared:

> *Business Week* reported that over the last year GAP sales are down and executives are quitting, or moving on to 'spend time with family'. Of course, there was no mention of our campaign (the protests, the letters, the teach-ins) to expose GAP Inc.'s sweatshop abuses and how we may have had something to do with GAP's losses. We should [nevertheless] see this as a victory and take credit for the disorientation that we have caused this company.

The significance of the cut-and-thrust element of civil regulation appears to be strongly supported by opinion polls of people's views who, as consumers, employees and voters, are the final arbiters in defining what is and is not acceptable business behaviour.[8] Significant were the results of the May 1999 Millennium Poll on consumer expectations of corporate social responsibility which was conducted by Environics International in collaboration with the Prince of Wales Business

Leaders Forum and The Conference Board. It covered 23 countries on six continents—a total of 25,000 interviews. The survey found that, across the globe, roughly two in three consumers want companies to go beyond their historic role of making a profit and obeying laws, and in particular want business to contribute more to achieving broader societal goals. Over one in five consumers reported having actually (and almost as many again have considered) rewarding or punishing companies in the previous year, based on their perceived social and environmental performance (Environics 1999).

These findings are broadly confirmed in many other studies. An opinion poll on public attitudes in Europe towards business was conducted on behalf of CSR Europe in the last quarter of 2000.[9] The findings are consistent across Europe.

a. Over half of Europeans surveyed in 12 countries considered that business does not pay enough attention to their social responsibilities.

b. Over one-quarter of those surveyed said that they had engaged in one or other activity in the previous six months that either introduced ethics into actual consumer purchase decisions or else made such views known by other means.

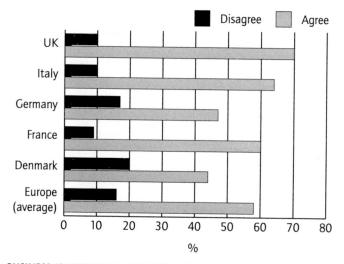

FIGURE 3 BUSINESS IS NOT PAYING ENOUGH ATTENTION TO ITS SOCIAL RESPONSIBILITIES

As part of the Environics Millennium Poll, The Conference Board surveyed 1,000 Americans in 1999. Of these, 42% said that they held companies completely or partially responsible for helping to solve social problems such as crime, poverty and lack of education. Fully one-third said that companies should focus on setting higher ethical standards, going beyond what is required by law, and actively helping build a better society for all. The Conference Board, similarly, found that consumers stated their willingness to back up their expectations with action: 46% of respondents said that they had made a purchase decision, or spoken out, in favour of a company because of a positive perception of its social responsibility; 49% of respondents said that they had decided not to purchase a product or service from a company, or had spoken critically of a company, because it did not meet their standard for being a socially responsible company (Conference Board 1999: 9-13).

Fleishman Hillard, similarly, in a 1999 survey of about 4,000 Europeans aged 15 or older, found that 86% would be more likely to purchase a product from a company 'engaged in activities to help improve society' (Fleishman Hillard 1999). A recent report on ethical consumerism in the UK commissioned by The Co-operative Bank found that increasing numbers of citizens as consumers both expected more from corporations, and felt as consumers and holders of pension funds that they could do more to affect corporate behaviour (Cowe and Williams 2000). Cone Inc. conducted a convincing study in partnership with Roper-Starch Worldwide that explored the impact of cause-related activities on customer loyalty and brand image (Cone Inc. 1999). The study found that:

- Nearly two-thirds of Americans, approximately 130 million consumers, report they would be likely to switch brands (66% in 1993; 65% in 1998) or retailers (62% 1993; 61% 1998) to one associated with a good cause.

- Eight in ten Americans have a more positive image of companies who support a cause they care about (84% 1993; 83% 1998). Education, crime and the quality of the environment were designated as the top social concerns for business to address in local communities.

Finally, for the more technically minded, a study purporting to show a clear link between aspects of good corporate citizenship, consumer behaviour and reputation was undertaken by Walker Information as part of the Council on Foundations report on corporate citizenship (Council on Foundations 1996). This study used survey data to develop correlation coefficients between reputation, brand loyalty, economic value and its definition of 'societal value'. The last included: treatment of employees, caring about the environment, strong ethics, and financial stability.

Walker Information published results for two companies, a manufacturer and a retailer. The results for the manufacturer (Figure 4) showed that a 1-unit increase in societal value led to a 0.27-unit increase in company reputation. A 1-unit increase in economic value led to a 0.34-unit increase in company reputation. A 1-unit

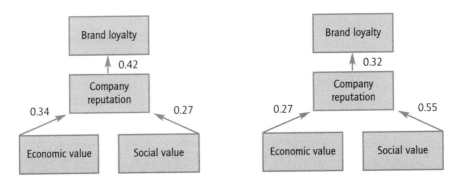

FIGURE 4 MANUFACTURER BRAND   FIGURE 5 RETAILER BRAND

increase in company reputation led to a 0.42-unit increase in brand loyalty. The results for the retailer (Figure 5) showed that a 1-unit increase in societal value led to a 0.55-unit increase in company reputation. A 1-unit increase in economic value led to a 0.27-unit increase in company reputation. A 1-unit increase in company reputation led to a 0.32 unit increase in brand loyalty.

Money talk

Financial performance, and so also share prices, can be vulnerable to public outcry. There is considerable evidence that share prices can be affected when the issue concerns the direct health and welfare of the consumer. The cases of Perrier and Coca-Cola come to mind, both of which suffered financially through consumer reaction to concerns over contaminated products. The high-profile crisis faced by Monsanto is also a case in point. The financial significance of the public actions against genetically modified organisms only took hold where the campaign's focus shifted from the plight of subsistence farmers in developing countries to consumer health (the 'Frankenstein foods' campaign initiated in the UK). There can also be observed financial effects when very specialised issues become entwined in national consciousness—such as animal rights issues in the UK. Public disquiet at stories of animal abuse at Huntingdon Life Sciences Laboratories has in the past demonstrably depressed the company's share value, and more recently has been associated with doubts over the continued existence of the company.[10]

But the more generalised argument that corporate citizenship is good for business because of the impact of civil regulation, although enticing, is simply not true in its crudest form. Even the very high-profile civil campaigns against the likes of Shell, Nestlé and Nike have had little or no demonstrable effect on share prices or dividends. One unpublished study investigating the connection between market value, social/ethical performance and negative press in cases of Nike, Nestlé and Shell concluded:

> [While] . . . not investigated in a scientific way . . . The examples show that the negative press referring to specific incidents is not proved to have a long-term negative effect on the price of the company's shares.[11]

The available evidence is that, with few exceptions, the media-effective attacks on these companies' reputations caused no significant, sustained impact on their share prices. As Michael Hopkins, summing up his own attempt to map corporate social and environmental responsibility against financial performance, concludes:

> the company that did worst in [my social responsibility] rankings—News International—actually had the largest share price rise. Clearly, the public's purchasing of shares is still not greatly affected, as yet, by the companies' level of social responsibility (Hopkins 1998).

For those readers with a predilection for graphs (particularly economists among you), I have supported the remainder of this section with a series of graphical

Electrolux was faced from the late 1980s with concerted action from Greenpeace and other environmental non-profit organisations over the damaging effects of CFCs on the world's climate and in particular on depletion of high-level ozone. Initially the company spent considerable resources seeking to demonstrate their 'innocence'. By the early 1990s, civil pressure had begun to affect sales as customers increasingly sought CFC-free products. Eventually, concluded the company's environmental manager:

> When the stock price depended on our ability to come up with CFC-free refrigerators, of course, managers considered the issue important (quoted in Strannegård and Wolff 1998: 55).

The case of Electrolux is repeated daily across the world in a myriad of different ways. Political action creates a perceived business risk—in this case, through the potential for reduced sales.

BOX 3 CONSUMERS' CARING *CAN* COUNT

representations that builds on the basic visualisation of civil regulation set out in Figure 2. So Figure 6 suggests that, while many companies respond to civil regulation *as if* it is a powerful financial driver (shown by the steep curve, CC), the financial markets respond in a manner that suggests that they are far less concerned that perceived ethical behaviour impacts on the financial bottom line (shown by the flatter curve, DD).

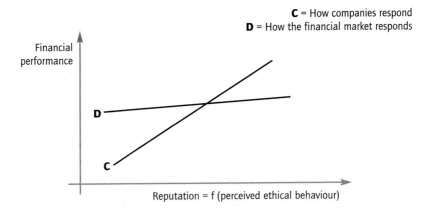

C = How companies respond
D = How the financial market responds

Financial performance

Reputation = f (perceived ethical behaviour)

FIGURE 6 DIVERGENT MARKET RESPONSES

The 'Goyder Effect'

So, the apparent paradox is that companies often respond *as if* civil regulation really counts, whereas the financial markets rarely seem to really care. There are a number of possible explanations for this. The first is that companies respond to the pressures of civil regulation because they (think they) know better than the financial markets in predicting long-term performance. Thus, the more horizontal,

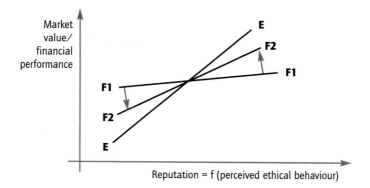

FIGURE 7 THE GOYDER EFFECT

flatter line (F1F1 in Figure 7) indicates the lack of responsiveness by the financial markets given their preoccupation with short-term returns. The steeper curve (EE), on the other hand, reflects companies' longer-term view of the critical relationship.

If the companies are correct, the response curve of the financial markets will eventually swivel towards a steeper slope to reflect new information about financial performance.[12] This would be the view of proponents of the view that 'being good is good for business (in the long term)'. Indeed, we might call this the 'Goyder Effect' in recognition of the key roles played by Mark Goyder and before him his father, George Goyder, in setting out and promoting the argument for 'inclusivity' as a precondition for a long-term successful business strategy (M. Goyder 1998; G. Goyder 1961).

The 'Korten Effect'

The alternative view is that companies are systematically overestimating the financial significance of reputational losses through perceptions of ethical misdemeanours, and vice versa. There are several possible reasons for such overestimation. Important here is that this growth has not been matched by tools and procedures for fully understanding how such intangibles develop and can best be managed. As reported by Susan Fry Bovet in PR Week, only 25% of companies with revenues above US$500 million have formal systems for measuring reputation (Bovet 1999). This has given considerable influence within companies to 'reputation teams' dedicated to the protection of brand values, a key element of intangible assets. These teams will tend to overrate the importance of ethics-based reputational value, both as a means of minimising risk for their companies, and in some cases as a means of enhancing their own importance within the organisation. As a reputation manager from a major UK multinational commented, 'the harder the NGOs come at us, the easier my job gets'.

If the financial implications of reputational gains or losses are indeed not (as) significant as often construed, then the financial markets will eventually trade down companies that over-respond to civil regulation. Eventually, following the

Desert pathway,[13] global corporate citizenship will be squeezed out of companies wishing to survive. We might call this the 'Korten Effect', given David Korten's forceful critique of corporate citizenship (Korten 1997). In graphical terms, this can be represented as companies' response curves swivelling from their highly responsive, steep slope to a flatter, less responsive, state, as set out in Figure 8.

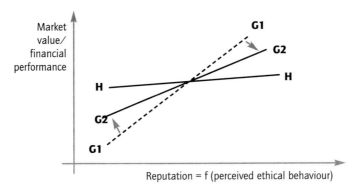

FIGURE 8 COMPANIES ADJUST TO BUSINESS REALITIES

Beyond civil regulation?

Civil regulation is a fickle driver of good corporate citizenship. Clearly, people care, and some act with their feet in their roles as consumers, investors, employees and voters. But the investment community as a whole does not in the main take this either as a serious threat or opportunity, at least to date. The fact that some high-profile companies are responding *as if* civil regulation is important to their financial futures can clearly be read in different ways, the most marked distinctions hopefully captured in the descriptions of the Korten and Goyder Effects. Of course the fact that market leaders do respond in this way can and does in some instances in itself create futures where good corporate citizenship counts. The unknown yet to be explored is how much, how robust and to what effect.

What is clear is that the sheer force of people's stated concerns is not in itself sufficient to drive companies to better practices. Equally clear is the fact that those companies that do act as if good citizenship is an important ingredient of success have increasingly articulated strong business cases which go well beyond the cruder cut-and-thrust of pressure-based civil regulation.

8

civil governance
and accountability
from fear and loathing
to social innovation*

The extraordinary rise to influence of NGOs over the past two decades has been the twentieth century's most important progressive social innovation. And it is this more than anything else that has driven concerns about NGO accountability. As *The Economist* asked, following the failure in Seattle in November 1999 to initiate a new round of trade liberalisation negotiations under the auspices of the World Trade Organisation: 'Are citizens groups . . . the first steps towards an international civil society (whatever that might be)? Or do they represent a dangerous shift of power to unelected and unaccountable special-interest groups?'

In its presentation of this story, *The Economist* was certainly conservative, perhaps somewhat reactionary, and arguably hypocritical in its criticism of NGOs' evocative communication style (note, for example, the provocative cover photo of a poor, black child, with a challenge as to whether NGOs were addressing poverty or causing it). But none of this lessens the fact that the concerns raised about NGO accountability are right and proper.

Put simply, the concern is that NGOs, unlike elected governments and owned businesses, lack an adequate, clearly defined basis on which they can be held to account. Their networked relationships and public profile can certainly provide crucial elements of pressure and oversight. But these mechanisms are rightly seen as inadequate governance for a form of organisation that has become so important in influencing individual attitudes and public and private policy and practice.

*   First published in *Alliance* Volume 8(4) (December 2003). © 2003 Allavida, London. This piece makes reference to articles that also appeared in that issue.

The debate so far

These concerns have a rich history, involving sometimes sophisticated but more often confused and acrimonious debate. This debate covers an eclectic blend of issues and aspects, ranging from straightforward concerns about performance voiced by both intended beneficiaries and funders, through to the murky worlds of corruption and tax relief, skimming across to the select issue of how richer NGOs invest their funds, and back again to the age-old question of whether or in what ways NGOs should be regulated. Much of this debate has been ably documented in many books and articles: for example, Michael Edwards's long list of publications on the topic going back more than a decade, and David Sogge's mid-1990s publication *Compassion and Calculation*, which brought together thoughtful essays relevant to the matter.

The continued success of NGOs in punching above their weight is raising the accountability stakes yet further. Testimony to this has been the recent outpouring about the topic, ranging from national and grass-roots initiatives emanating from civil society itself—for example, in India and the Philippines; through to progressive-leaning publications such as the recent report by SustainAbility, *The 21st Century NGO* (2003); across to clearly politically motivated assaults from the likes of the American Enterprise Institute. Peter Shiras's article in the following pages offers a penetrating summary of this debate in a specific US context.

The challenge, in short, is simply summarised by Michael Edwards, writing in 2000: 'The challenge for NGOs is to show that they can put into practice the [accountability] principles that they campaign for in others' (Edwards 2000b).

How adequate is NGO accountability?

It has to be said that much of what passes for accountability within the NGO community is just not adequate. A recent survey by Environics International highlighted the public's low level of trust in business and governments. NGOs scored very high on the trust index, only bettered by the 'armed forces'. Activists have focused (with glee) on businesses' poor trust ratings in this and other similar surveys. Sadly, few have questioned the basis on which NGOs top the popularity lists, or asked whether such a position is warranted or sustainable.

It is simply true that companies (particularly those that are publicly listed), and to a greater degree many (elected) governments, have more structured accountability mechanisms than the vast majority of NGOs, even if we believe that these mechanisms can deliver inappropriate outcomes. NGOs' retort to this comparison is often that their 'values and commitment' are an adequate basis for accountability. These facets of NGOs are of course important, but their representation in this debate confuses individual and organisational accountability: people come and go, and their views change over time, while organisational accountability needs to be embedded in the fabric of an organisation's rules, norms and adopted standards.

This view, furthermore, wrongly presents the benefits of commonly shared goals as an adequate substitute for having to account for performance and outcomes.

Few NGOs are obliged or voluntarily choose to publish systematic, externally audited accounts of their performance (although this is what NGOs call for from others). Their senior managements and board members are rarely challenged by supporters (or even members, in those rare cases where there are any), and almost never have to stand for election or any other form of external scrutiny except where financial fraud has been uncovered. Accountability to intended beneficiaries tends to be informal—they are empowered to participate, but in few instances are given rights over resources beyond those already allocated to them. Accountability to funders is often far too bureaucratic, and yet personalised and archaic, with resources being allocated too often on the basis of relationships and fashion rather than on the cold facts about past and future likely performance.

An accountability gap

Not to put too fine a point on it, there is an NGO accountability gap. But these facts and concerns do not justify the nonsensical claim that 'NGOs are unaccountable', just as it is absurd to say the same about the business community. The NGO community, a vague name for an extraordinarily heterogeneous group of institutions, has a long history of experimenting with many forms of accountability that others have since copied. The business community did not invent stakeholder engagement, after all. Its roots go to the 'participatory development' paradigm advocated and practised by NGOs around the world since the mid-1970s, marked by Robert Chambers's seminal book, *Farmers First* (Chambers *et al.* 1989). The development of performance indicators with those who are affected is another civil invention, since imitated for better and worse by corporate consultants and many others. Much of the early 'social accounting and auditing' undertaken by the UK-based New Economics Foundation was originally focused on NGO evaluation and accountability before it was transhipped into the field of corporate accountability.

Credit must therefore be given where it is due. But this does not remove the fact that there remains for most NGOs an accountability gap. This gap, worryingly, is largely unattended, and indeed often deliberately ignored or marginalised, by NGOs themselves. At a private meeting I attended with a group of CEOs of major NGOs, one of them expressed the following view: 'People believe us, so why fix something if it is not broken? Anyway, if we try to do something, people will assume that there is a problem, and then we are in real trouble.' Such comments could have come from the CEO of any major corporation a decade ago, but would be rare to hear today from a more seasoned and well-informed business community.

That is not an argument for a semi-literate witch-hunt. After all, many of us have just spent almost a decade convincing people that there are more effective ways to transform the business community than to pursue it as if it were evil. Of course, it is partly fear of such a witch-hunt that puts off the NGO community from doing enough itself about the accountability gap. Yet ironically it is exactly this kind of response (or lack thereof) that puts the matter in the hands of those who are least interested in the continued vibrancy of civil society.

Is NGO accountability unique?

One of the questions core to the debate is whether NGOs have specific accountability issues and needs. Some would argue that all NGO-specific rules and regulations are misplaced since NGOs must simply abide by the more general legal frameworks governing, for example, fraud and disclosure. Many argue that general regulatory frameworks, combined with the often arduous reporting requirements to donors, and accountability driven by the public limelight in which many NGOs operate, is more than enough accountability for one lifetime. Others argue, on the other hand, that NGOs face unique accountability challenges.

The central dilemma is that mission-driven accountabilities are often to people, 'intended beneficiaries', who have little influence and in general no power over the organisation, while contractual accountabilities, where the power lies, in general resides with people at the other end of the pipeline, the funders. Both Ali King's and Sarah Hobson's articles, drawing on the cases of the Zurich Community Trust and the International Development Exchange, highlight the possibilities of vesting more decision-making in grantees. But these experiences do not signal changes in the underlying power relationship between funder and grantee. It is important not to confuse changes in responsiveness and terms of engagement with changes in accountability. From this perspective, trustees/board members and NGO management face, and will continue to face, an accountability dilemma quite different from that faced by their equivalents in business or public institutions. Mission-aligned goals and underlying, institutionalised accountabilities generally run in very different directions. More than anything else, this frames the need for specific debate and solutions on the topic of NGO accountability.

Learning from other sectors

This does not mean that NGOs cannot learn from developments in business and public-sector accountability. Quite the reverse. The growing incidence of corporate social and sustainability reporting[1] has refuelled those advocating a comparable level of NGO transparency. The raging debate about corporate governance, equally, offers important lessons that can be transferred to the NGO community, notably on board director responsibilities and competencies. The emerging practice of public–private partnerships offers another rich terrain for cross-sectoral learning, as highlighted by Ken Caplan's and Pedro Roxas's articles. Both point out the accountability dilemmas in 'cross-sectoral partnerships' involving businesses and NGOs seeking to deliver complex blends of commercial and development gains. The accountability challenges represented by these partnerships, both authors rightly argue, will in the coming years create both insight and pressure to formalise NGO accountability.[2]

Vision not fear

It goes without saying that 'no one size fits all' when it comes to accountability mechanisms. But we can note some broad opportunities for change. The ACCESS initiative (see Box 4) is a case in point, recently launched with the specific intention of developing an international approach to appropriate NGO reporting. This initiative does not actually take accountability as its starting point. Rather, it argues that the terms on which NGOs will be financed in years to come will require increased performance-based reporting. Furthermore, ACCESS recognises the positive performance driver that enhanced, appropriate accountability can bring with it, a fact pointed out by several articles in the following pages. The challenge, ACCESS argues, is to understand and work with the changing relationship between accountability, performance and resourcing—a point reinforced by Jaime Faustino and Barnett Baron's article.

ACCESS aims to increase significantly the quality and quantity of social investment—donations, grants, loans, equity, in-kind support and volunteering—for sustainable development by and for the world's poor. It aims to do this by building *a generally accepted reporting standard for civil-society organisations*. The ACCESS sponsors have come together from diverse geographic and institutional settings. Its members include leading figures from social entrepreneurship, grantmaking foundations, public development agencies, commercial finance, business consulting, and corporate social responsibility.

ACCESS Reporting, which is being created through participatory action research, will be complemented by ACCESS Learning, an independently managed capacity-building programme to strengthen organisations using or seeking to use ACCESS Reporting.

In addition to developing its own reporting standard, ACCESS is also facilitating a Global Dialogue on NGO Transparency, Accountability and Performance. This will bring together small groups of carefully selected participants from CSOs, foundations, public donor agencies and the business community over a two-year period to review the current situation and address future needs for accountability and transparency in CSOs as a means of enhancing their ability to secure adequate resources. The aim is to move from analysis/perspectives to practical and innovative approaches to accountability systems, including but not limited to the ACCESS reporting standard.

BOX 4 ACCESS

Adequate NGO accountability must emerge from vision about the future of civil society, not fear for it. It does not help to scaremonger, accuse or run away. As with the collective endeavours in advancing corporate accountability, what are needed are approaches to accountability for NGOs that make sense of their roles and associated responsibilities. Most of all, NGOs need to continue their tradition of social innovation, applying it to this crucial stage in their own collective development. AccountAbility itself, for example, has tried to innovate in building its own process of governance and accountability (see Box 5). We have paid particular attention to the need to strengthen the roles, professionalism and accountability of our three-part governance structure, a need emphasised in both Marilyn Wyatt's and Balázs Sátor's articles. Although specific to its circumstances, and certainly not perfect, we believe this model offers insights that might be relevant to other NGOs (and indeed businesses and public agencies). Much more is needed from NGOs on this front: experiments in accountability that really push the boundaries of what new forms of organisation can deliver. Failure to do this will carry a heavy price. Success, on the other hand, will act as a stimulant to civil society and its credibility in leading broader changes in the years to come.

AccountAbility's approach to governance and accountability is an attempt to build a framework of accountability that seeks to effectively balance governance structure and process, stakeholder engagement and process, accounting and reporting, and of course performance.

We are a non-profit organisation. We have members who are empowered to vote their representatives onto our Council once every three years. The Council is made up of business, service providers, academics and civil-society members. It has the right and responsibility to set strategy and policies. AccountAbility has an Operating Board, which is the legal board with fiduciary duty. It currently includes five non-executive and one executive director (the CEO). Interestingly, our governance model complies with most of the toughest corporate governance codes.

The Board is responsible to the Council for overseeing the implementation of strategy. Our non-executive directors are paid, which in a stroke ends the 'patronage by the great and good' model that has proved so damaging to good NGO governance. This push for director professionalism and accountability also means we have service contracts against which their performance is periodically assessed, and they have to stand down and seek re-election at our Annual General Meeting. We publish the attendance records at Council and Operating Board, and have time limits on how long a Council member can remain in place.

The third piece of our governance infrastructure is our Technical Committee, which oversees the development of our standards work, the AA1000 Series. This Committee is co-chaired by representatives from the Council and the Operating Board to ensure strategy and fiduciary perspectives are adequately represented in its deliberations and decisions over this core area of our work.

We seek to account to our stakeholders for our activities and decisions. We publish our financial accounts, and the minutes of our Council and Operating Board meetings. We have produced 'Account-Ability Accounts' for two years. These accounts report on the results of structured dialogue with our Council, members, staff and volunteers, partners and funders. Furthermore, it reports targets and performance metrics in relation to each of our four strategic policies and six enablers. The draft accounts are made available to our members and debated at our AGM, before going to the Board and Council for assessment and sign-off.

BOX 5 ACCOUNTABILITY'S ACCOUNTABILITY

9
practical people, noble causes*

co-written with Stephen Thake

People throughout the world are having to respond to change on an unprecedented scale. Inequality has risen to the point where the world's richest 350 people have fortunes greater than the combined wealth of the poorest 45% of the world's population (Bissio 1997). The urbanisation of agricultural societies and the emergence of newly industrialised economies has created in the last 20 years a world of 1.5 billion new urban dwellers, who are legitimately seeking the material benefits that so far have been enjoyed only in industrialised countries.

Technological and organisational developments have had profound effects on many of the older industrialised economies. These have precipitated a dwindling of their manufacturing dominance and an erosion of their status. Coping with the fallout from these changes is dominating and will continue to dominate the agendas of these countries for decades, if not centuries, to come.

The consequences of these changes impact on the individual, the family, the village, town, city and national state alike. They create and expose gaps in the fabric of society. It is now possible to see what happens when the centre of gravity of economic activity moves on. Large parts of our cities and towns are laid waste, production plants and distribution centres are closed. The affluent retreat within increasingly heavily protected enclosures or abandon urban areas altogether. The poor are concentrated in what are fast becoming economic refugee camps. Within a few streets life chances, educational prospects, employment opportunities, income and house prices plummet.

Traditional responses are failing. Democratic capitalism has not had to contend with these problems before. Democratic capitalism, throughout the world, has been dominated by two governing tendencies, broadly defined as Left and Right. Both traditions recognise that modern capitalism is no longer, in its current form, an efficient mechanism for distributing the wealth that it creates. Both, however, believe that those problems can be solved through continued economic growth, in the belief that it 'allows all the ships to rise on the tide'. The debate has been about how much growth was necessary or achievable and who should benefit from the wealth that the growth had generated.

* © 1997 New Economics Foundation, London. This is a summary of the full report.

Innovative solutions are desperately needed. Unless we can find ways to secure a minimum acceptable level of quality of life for the bulk of the world's population within a framework of social justice and environmental sustainability, the future will be bleak. It requires a new way of thinking, of being, of relating to each other both close at home and far afield.

The age of the entrepreneur

This is the age of the entrepreneur. Historically, an entrepreneur was a promoter of musical entertainments.[1] More recently, the concept of the entrepreneur has been incorporated into the lexicon of the commercial sector.

It is now understood that the success of business depends on the innovation of entrepreneurs. In the commercial sector, entrepreneurship is highly regarded. It is the ability to see and exploit new opportunities for financial gain. Companies rise or fall on their ability to stay innovative and entrepreneurial. Entrepreneurs in the commercial sector tend to be highly prized mavericks who have to survive and rise above a world dominated by those whose responsibility it is to manage and stabilise. They are the visionaries who see and exploit opportunities before others.

The concept of the entrepreneur has now been broadened to encompass those who embark on new ventures with boldness and energy, for reasons other than financial gain. Entrepreneurs are thus found within public-sector institutions and charitable organisations as well as in business. Possibly the quintessential example of this is (the late) Michael Young, Lord Young of Dartington. Credited with the initiation of at least 30 socially oriented organisations, notably the Open University, Michael Young was, as Malcolm Dean argues, possibly the most brilliant and well-known social entrepreneur in the UK in the 20th century.[2]

Social entrepreneurship

Social entrepreneurs share similarities with each other and with commercial entrepreneurs. They are both opportunist and eclectic. They are both practical and visionary. They are both analytical and creative. The management guru, Peter Drucker, in *Innovation and Entrepreneurship* (Drucker 1994), identifies a number of practices that are applicable to social and other entrepreneurs alike, including:

- A focus on vision and opportunity

- The creation of a culture of enterprise

- The development of a constituency which continues to suggest innovative and entrepreneurial ideas

Social entrepreneurs are driven by a desire for social justice. Social entrepreneurs do not create personal wealth for themselves, they create common wealth for the wider community. They build social capital in order to promote social cohesion.

Who are social entrepreneurs?

The independent think-tank, Demos, in its recent publication, *The Rise of Social Entrepreneurs*, offers one definition of social entrepreneurs that adds substance beyond the idea of there being 'good people' (Leadbeater 1996: 19-20):

- They excel at spotting unmet needs and mobilising under-utilised resources to meet these needs.

- They are driven and determined, ambitious and charismatic.

- Social entrepreneurs are driven by a mission, rather than the pursuit of profit or shareholder value.

- In the private sector it is quite possible to be a successful entrepreneur without being at all innovative. In the social sector it is far more likely that an entrepreneur will also be an innovator.

Ashoka, an international charity, identifies 'social entrepreneurs and provides them with the equivalent of venture capital to launch them on their careers'.[3] Ashoka has been a pioneer in the field of social entrepreneurs. It has focused on working in the less-industrialised world and in Eastern Europe. Rather than raise funds for aid programmes, it identifies outstanding individuals already working in their country for social change. Once selected, it elects the individual to the Ashoka Fellowship for life and provides a stipend for an average period of three years.

Ashoka sees the 'ethical' purpose of social entrepreneurs as a distinguishing characteristic. However, Ashoka goes further in offering a more detailed description of the types of people who fit this classification:

- **Creative:** finding radical and effective solutions to social problems.

- **Entrepreneurial:** presenting their project, negotiating their needs, commanding support for their idea and winning resources effectively.

- **Agenda-setting:** demanding that their ideas or proposals will make a major difference when successfully implemented.

- **Ethical:** ensuring that public money granted is well used; that ideas are not corrupted by vested interests and that their full commitment is available for the project. Award winners must be good role models for others in their community.

Although interest in social entrepreneurial activity is a recent phenomenon, social entrepreneurs have always been with us. The early Cistercian monks cultivated great swathes of inhospitable countryside. In doing so, they strengthened local economies in ways that have been sustained to this day. The early pioneers of the co-operative movement were some of the social entrepreneurs of the early and middle years of the first Industrial Revolution. So too was Lord Rowton, who, as Disraeli's Private Secretary, established through the mechanism of 5% philanthropic bonds the capital to build the massive hostels for working men that for over half a century dominated the skyline of parts of Bermondsey, Vauxhall, Hammersmith and Camden in London.

Where are social entrepreneurs?

Social entrepreneurs exist across all sectors. There is often a greater affinity between social entrepreneurs working in very different areas than there are between social entrepreneurs and the people around them. Hence social entrepreneurs from different sectors are able to initiate and maintain constructive dialogue, while other cross-sectoral meetings are held back by the barriers of caution and suspicion. This was one of the notable findings in a study by the New Economics Foundation of Ashoka Fellows in South Africa (Zadek 1996). This empathy and understanding based on a sense of common experience does begin to indicate that there are indeed some common traits among social entrepreneurs from diverse backgrounds and involved in very different work.

Social entrepreneurs are becoming prominent in the commercial sector. Companies such as The Body Shop in the UK and Ben & Jerry's Home-Made Ice Cream in the USA are obvious examples of the principles of social entrepreneurs being taken forward within a contemporary commercial environment. People such as Anita Roddick and Ben Cohen have sought to remould the commercial animal into a form that can effectively address social and environmental as well as financial objectives.[4]

This blending of commercial and non-commercial aims and actions can be seen not only with companies that sell cosmetics and ice-cream but within the most conservative of all sectors, the financial community. From the South Shore Bank in Chicago, USA, to the Social Investment Forum in the UK, new organisations have been inspired to challenge conventional financial institutions about the ways in which they lend, the people to whom they lend and the very way in which they understand their roles in society. Each and every one of these more recent financial initiatives has been inspired in particular by the experience of the Grameen Bank in Bangladesh. Central to this inspiration has been the story—or, more properly by now, the legend—of its founder, Professor Muhammad Yunus. Professor Yunus has come to epitomise in many ways those people who have turned their backs on the ethos and practice of their professions (in the case of Professor Yunus, the economics profession), while drawing liberally where relevant on their previous experience to underpin often radically new directions. In this case, as in many others, many if not all of the community development financial institutions established around the world in the last decade have also been driven by these 'new professionals', as Robert Chambers from the Institute of Development Studies has named them. In this sense, people such as Pat Conaty of the Aston Reinvestment

Trust in Birmingham in the UK, Vijay Mahajan from BASIX in Hyderabad in India and Coro Strandberg of VanCity Savings and Credit Union in Vancouver, Canada, are all part of a growing international cadre of social entrepreneurs, who learn from and inspire each other. This is what Bill Drayton, the founder and President of Ashoka, identifies as the emerging 'profession of public innovators'.

Social entrepreneurs working within a commercial environment are not confined, of course, to overtly 'alternative' institutions. In the UK, for example, the initiative launched by the Royal Society for the Encouragement of the Arts, *The Tomorrow's Company Inquiry*, brought forward not merely a wish-list of what life might be, or even a casebook full of good stories, but a host of people working within the heartland of the commercial sector who want, and in many instances are already leading, real changes in the way business is done (RSA 1995). Similarly, the recent report by the Prince of Wales Business Leaders Forum on the role of business in international development, *Business as Partners in Development*, identified social entrepreneurs working within the business community as much as it sought to describe companies, programmes and initiatives (Nelson 1996). Business in the Community co-ordinates campaigns that link together senior business leaders to work around the areas of race, education, economic development, environment and 'Opportunity 2000'.

Social entrepreneurship exists within the public-sector institutions, but has always struggled to thrive. Public-sector institutions are formed around the need to deliver services and are dominated by the need to maintain internal consistency. As long as there are those who receive the services provided and yet others on the waiting list, there is always work to do. The importance of public institutions and departments is frequently measured by the size of their budgets. But their activities are not readily measured against a profit-and-loss account. Their constituencies are diverse and are infrequently asked to register their opinion on the services provided. Local authorities and central governments seek a continued mandate every four or five years for a wide basket of services, none of which are specifically voted on. This is a process that is not conducive to innovation or entrepreneurial activity.

Public-sector institutions over the last 20 years have been subject to a massive culture change which has made them more favourable to innovation. Central government departments have been asked 'Why do they exist?' rather than 'What do they do?' There has been a predisposition to limit government expenditure, to set specific objectives and to quantify the outcomes of investment. It has been a period of rapid innovation during which government has learned from its experience and constantly reformulated its specific objectives.

There have been massive changes in the delivery of services and in the relationships and perceptions that go along with this. Local authorities have gone from being the single 'provider' of services to their 'clients' to being the 'regulator' of a multitude of private firms providing services to 'customers'.

Social entrepreneurial activity has been prompted by these changes at three levels. First, it has given rise to a new breed of senior officers, such as Heather Rabbatts in Lambeth and Sylvie Pierce in Tower Hamlets, who are steering organisations that have lost direction to focus back on course. Second, the increasing importance given to the environmental impact of public spending, including waste disposal, energy consumption and pollution control, requires a rethinking of how public services are delivered. Third, change has been prompted by the recognition that the local authority is a minority stakeholder within the community. There is within the municipal sector an acceptance that its function is to release energies and to empower local communities rather than to control them (Corrigan 1997). The devolution of authority to local groups and neighbourhood associations, the break-up of massive housing departments and the creation of independent housing management and ownership organisations are all examples of social entrepreneurial activity in local authorities. This has led to a marked improvement in the quality of life of people who previously were seen as mere recipients of public services.

The traditional voluntary sector is averse to risk and entrepreneurial activity. Voluntary and charitable sectors have been oriented towards service provision even more than the public sector. Moreover, they are frequently service providers of last resort and hence from this monopolistic position they are not obligated to offer choice and can impose their own value systems. Traditionally, the major charities have often existed within a world of their own. They raised money through public donations and private endowment, to provide services to meet the needs of their particular client groups.

Changes in the world in which charities work have prompted many charitable organisations to face up to change. The advent of the National Lottery has provided an alternative means of funding charitable works. Traditional organisations that have not evolved to meet the changing needs of their client groups are increasingly seen to be remote and potentially damaging. Others that have failed to respond to expanding need are becoming marginal. Social entrepreneurs in the voluntary sector such as Sheila McKechnie (first at Shelter and now at the Consumers' Association) and Stuart Etherington (at the National Council for Voluntary Organisations) are changing old organisations and creating new ones that are more accountable to the communities they serve.

New and renewed forms of community action have begun to emerge. Community action has developed along fault-lines of mainstream economic and social policy, and generally seeks to address both problems that have remained unaddressed for generations as well as those that have been thrown up as a consequence of the current upheavals. Many new initiatives that address the problems that face communities have emerged from those communities themselves and have been championed by social entrepreneurs from within the community, whose vision, energy and skills have been critical in ensuring the success of these innovative solutions.

Community-based social entrepreneurs

It is possible to describe common characteristics of social entrepreneurs, although the formulations offered are unlikely to enable you to spot them in the street. Finding common features does not mean, however, that they all have the same needs. A wealthy and successful social entrepreneur such as Anita Roddick, or one that is as famous as Jonathon Porritt, is unlikely to have quite the same needs as a social entrepreneur who is unknown, unemployed and very possibly quite unemployable in any normal work environment. This needs gap is likely to be all the wider if the latter is someone from a marginalised community, whether so because of religion, race or the simple fact of poverty.

Community-based social entrepreneurs are those who work in the community and suffer the same kinds of discrimination they are trying to overcome for others. They are critical to the success of most community-based initiatives and are a breed of leaders who blend street activism with professional skills, visionary insights with pragmatism, and ethical fibre with hard, tactical thrust.

Community-based social entrepreneurs work in villages, small towns and in the great conurbations. In urban areas, they work in peripheral, suburban and inner-city locations. They operate as individuals and they can also be found in community-based housing associations, community development trusts, settlements, health centres, churches, mosques, temples and synagogues, as well as in primary and secondary schools and single-purpose support groups. They are also found providing legal and financial advice, and in training agencies as well as within the bodies that seek to represent the community and those that work within it.

They focus on self-help and mutual aid and promote co-operation within neighbourhoods and in partnerships with other stakeholders. They work with minorities and represent their interests to the majority. They also work with sections of the majority community which have become marginalised from the mainstream.

Understanding community-based social entrepreneurs

Just as architects and building surveyors look at the physical capital of society and see where it is damaged and in need of repair, so community-based social entrepreneurs look at a community's social capital. They are able to see a tear here, a hole there and places where the fabric of society has become threadbare. Just like their physical counterparts, community-based social entrepreneurs are able to devise remedies, fill voids, refurbish and renew. But social capital is not merely there to be understood, or even to be repaired or rebuilt. Encouraging people to work together—using and building social capital—is to achieve common goals. Whether it be to open a hospice, encourage small businesses, build a home or reawaken people's confidence, community-based social entrepreneurs are expert at making relationships work.

Community-based social entrepreneurs empower others. Individuals working from within the community cannot work in isolation. Their success is predicated on a combination of lasting relationships and fast-moving alliances. Productive leadership in this context is therefore rarely of the 'John Wayne' variety. People at the forefront of new initiatives invest enormous energy in building or tapping into 'social capital', which, according to US sociologist James Coleman, is 'the ability of people to work together for common purposes in groups and organisations' (Coleman 1988). Lack of work and income and the associated loss of status and identity lead to personal and communal senses of hopelessness, isolation and depression. Community-based social entrepreneurs fill the void left where traditional youth programmes and sports activities have been withdrawn or have failed to engage local people.

The new generation of community-based social entrepreneurs is engaged in the development and introduction of programmes focused on self-help, self-worth, leadership, education and positive health. For example, physical recreation is seen not just as an end in itself but also as a stepping stone on the way to other forms of participation and personal development. Community-based social entrepreneurs can also be seen working with the elderly, the terminally ill, those who have learning difficulties or those who have a long-term illness or physical disability, as well as with their carers. Their purpose is to enable people who usually are seen as being economically and socially inactive and a drain on society to live as full and engaged lives as they feel comfortable with.

Social entrepreneurs create 'space' for creativity and celebration. Some community-based social entrepreneurs tap into the great fund of creativity, enquiry and enjoyment that is present in all of us. Capital and revenue funding have been obtained for music and video centres, community arts projects, computer technology centres and singing, drama and dance projects, confirming that culture is a shared experience and not confined to art galleries, museums, theatres and concert halls. It has given scope for artists with communication skills to complement their technical and creative abilities. These artists, chosen by local people, listen to their stories and build their hopes and fantasies into their work. They also work directly with people, enabling them to express and develop their own skills and talents.

These acts of celebration take place in empty buildings and left-over spaces as well as purpose-built community centres and church halls. They explode into the public domain as murals, art works, sculptures, carnivals and festivals. These acts of celebration have given rise to a new form of the original concept of entrepreneur as the organiser of musical and artistic events. Again, these new impresarios work with local people, tailoring cultural programmes to meet local preferences and energies. Again, the events are not seen simply as ends in themselves but also as means of raising confidence and as stepping stones to other forms of community activity and engagement.

Not only have community-based social entrepreneurs enabled local people to bring their diverse cultures into the public domain, they have also enabled local people to take 'common ownership' of public spaces. Environmental trusts abound. City farms are no longer fringe activities. Local groups have rescued forgotten buildings and re-established links with industrial heritages that are in danger of disappearing through neglect, or being buried in the foundations of redevelopment schemes.

Social entrepreneurs gain strength from a wide network of alliances. Community action is not—as the words would suggest—only in the community. To 'think global and act local' is simply not enough when the decisions of national and international institutions constrain or proscribe what will or will not work at the community level. Transport, environment, employment, education and trade policies are not distinct, and community leaders and organisations are increasingly networking with those working at national and international policy and advocacy levels. Many community networks, for example, endorsed the emergence of the Real World

Coalition, made up of over 30 UK-based non-government organisations, which published an 'Action Programme for Government' to tackle the problems of poverty, inequality, alienation and environmental degradation (Jacobs 1996).

Alliances are not only made with non-profit organisations but also with organisations from within the business community. Many parts of what were traditionally seen as public-sector activities are now firmly embedded within the commercial sector. From there has emerged a language of social responsibility that at least speaks of its interest to embrace a broader agenda than profit to shareholders. The building and management of relationships of unlikely bedfellows, both between sectors and between different levels of intervention, are often what makes it possible for community-based initiatives to implement effective programmes. These relationships are sustained not by an institutional 'fit' but by the bridging of roles played by key individuals, who identify social entrepreneurs within other organisations—effectively their counterparts—and develop approaches to action that their respective institutions can embrace, or can at least be encouraged to accommodate.

Community-based social entrepreneurs do not start out with all the skills they need. Amidst the wealth of insights gained during the research for this report, one particular strand stood out. The older, more experienced of those consulted had that aura of self-sufficiency gained from extended experience in making things work. The less-experienced people we talked to had that same fiery vision and passion, but too often lacked the knowledge, skills and networks to pull it off.

Some, often older, community-based social entrepreneurs gained their experience within traditional work areas before making the change. Dissatisfied with what they were required to do, or seeing that existing approaches were not meeting need, they changed direction, and chose a rockier path. These older people have many of the classic skills needed to be successful in their chosen enterprise. Often they also bring with them the networks of contacts in public institutions and foundations that make the difference between supported effectiveness and obscurity.

Younger community-based social entrepreneurs, on the other hand, often do not have the professional background of these older leaders. Possibly with an anger born of the experience of constant rejection, they certainly do have the energy, and often the credibility, legitimacy and networks at community level. What they lack, however, are many of the things that others take for granted—an understanding of finances and the pitfalls of grant dependency, or how to build organisations that move beyond informal networks.

Many of the more experienced community-based social entrepreneurs reflected on whether assistance at an earlier stage in their own development would have helped. With a caution rooted within traditions of self-help and a suspicion of the oppressive experience of coping with 'helping institutions', they picked their ways through the possible paths and options. Their overall conclusion was that too many budding community leaders are knocked back by their lack of experience in dealing with the weight of institutional resistance they face. Too many brilliant ideas never reach trial stage because of the inability of inexperienced innovators to develop them to an operational level, and to articulate their strengths to reluctant sources of support. And, finally, too often leaders flounder at an early stage of implementation because of their weak understanding of how to make organisations work.

These perspectives—while not universally held—were common. It was agreed that it would be highly desirable to develop a framework of support sensitive to the needs of community-based social entrepreneurs. This is especially true for those community-based social entrepreneurs who miss out on conventional sources of support because they:

1. Come from the same disadvantaged communities which they seek to empower;

2. Have path-breaking ideas which scare off most sources of support; or

3. Have no track record provable in conventional terms and only partial skills.

It is in the context of this recognition of need that we turn to explore the existing support for such people that is currently available in the UK.

Supporting community-based social entrepreneurs

Within the neighbourhoods where they live, and the communities they seek to serve, and within the organisations for which they work and the projects they run, community-based social entrepreneurs are usually perceived as being self-sufficient and inspirational leaders. They carry the hopes and fears of those who are close to them. They are prized for their independence of mind, their perseverance in the face of adversity and their resilience when they are knocked back. They are often assumed to have inexhaustible well-springs of energy, commitment, ideas and hope.

Community-based social entrepreneurs, and indeed entrepreneurs more generally, have some or many of these characteristics. Indeed, many have all of them for some of the time. But we are ultimately talking about individual people, albeit extraordinary ones. The issues that they deal with are multifaceted; the skills and information base required are beyond the capacity of any single individual no matter how skilled or ingenious. Community-based social entrepreneurs need help.

Entrepreneurs within business, on the other hand, are seen as scarce and precious. They earn often extraordinary profits for themselves and those who venture to risk their capital. Considerable energy is devoted to identifying entrepreneurial potential, and then to developing and exploiting it. The commercial sector has established mechanisms for identifying and investing in entrepreneurs, and for working with them to maximise the chance of their success.

The profiles of community-based social entrepreneurs in the previous section are partial. They offer up the good news, the visions and outcomes of those who have succeeded and a sprinkling of information about the key landmarks towards success. They do not describe the agonies of those who have succeeded, and they do not talk about the many whose initiatives did not survive.

New ventures are under harsh financial pressures. Most of the initiatives launched by community-based social entrepreneurs are to some degree dependent on grant funding from charities and institutions. Although community-based social entrepreneurs are often successful in raising funds and maintaining good relationships with their funders, it is a precarious existence. Many of the organisations founded by such people are stretched to the very limits of their capacities in putting their ideas into practice. Sometimes, usually much later, these organisations settle into a more mature, and somewhat more relaxed, phase, but this is usually once the battle to gain acceptance has been largely won. Meanwhile, successful community leaders need to be able to identify and attract new sources of finance. The more innovative is the idea, the more apparent is the need for innovative sources of funding and support (Zadek 1996).

The Inner City Trust's finances, for example, were put under immense strain when inflation-linked increases in interest rates crippled its cash flow at a time when it lacked a substantial capital base or income stream. The Flax Trust had to contend with independent advisors that incorrectly calculated its financial position at a time when it had not developed its internal financial management skills. The St Paul's Community Project in Balsall Heath has had to live with chronic financial uncertainty throughout its existence.

The ventures initiated by community-based social entrepreneurs can and do fail. They fail for a number of reasons. Some are badly thought through. In some instances, community-based social entrepreneurs lack the necessary experience or have been carried away with the excitement of the venture. Some have not ensured that the necessary control systems are in place. Some have been closed because their financial exposure has increased to such an extent that the institutional backers have withdrawn their support. This happened in the case of the Miles Platting Development Trust in Manchester and Drumchapel Opportunities in Glasgow, both of which were handling large projects with uncertain cash flows. Others have failed because government programmes have changed or local authorities have withdrawn grant support before the venture has achieved financial viability. Others can also lose direction because the entrepreneurs involved, in pursuit of the long-term vision, become embroiled in financial and organisational activities that take them away from their original constituency. In these instances, success can mean that there is an ever-present danger that the later projects may become divorced from their original purpose.

Building pathways towards community-based social entrepreneurship

Participation in community activity needs to be formally recognised and valued and supported. This will require a profound change of culture. Starting at the grassroots level where the greatest potential for change exists, there are many practical support mechanisms that could have a significant impact on the quality of life of individual social entrepreneurs and the people they work with. The path of an individual community-based social entrepreneur often crosses through periods of unemployment, training and education and 'moonlighting' as a social entrepreneur while in employment. It is at these intersections that support can be channelled to potential social entrepreneurs.

There is a need to recognise the contribution made by community-based social entrepreneurs who are unemployed or who are on means-tested benefits. At present, those who are unemployed and actively engaged in community activity face the daunting prospect of running or participating in valuable local initiatives while, at the same time, maintaining their Jobseekers' Allowance status by proving that they are actively seeking employment. In addition, those who are dependent on means-tested benefit are unable to earn above minimum thresholds without having those benefits withdrawn at an almost pound-for-pound level of 'taxation'.

There is a need to create a mechanism that would allow those who are unemployed and are primarily engaged in community activity to 'leapfrog' the Jobseekers' Allowance procedures. The recognition of the concept of 'Active Citizenship' would be an important step in changing the situation. There is a precedent in the arrangements that apply to those people who have a long-term illness that incapacitates them for work. Those people who wish to apply for the incapacity benefit have to meet a number of criteria and those who are accepted are removed from the official unemployment register. In addition, the applicant is able to earn up to £46.50 per week without having his or her benefits withdrawn. A similar approach could be adopted for people engaged in 'active citizenship', although the detail of application would be different.

Thought needs to be given to supporting 'active citizens' entering into part-time or full-time education. The concept of lifetime learning is welcome. But there also needs to be in place a system that does not penalise those 'active citizens' in the community wishing to add to their skill-base and understanding through full- or part-time education. At present, those in receipt of benefit have to run the gauntlet of complex procedures that often pose insurmountable barriers and result in loss of benefits.

Again, there are precedents that could help improve the situation. Individuals who participate in the Training for Work scheme are able to retain their entitlements to benefit while they are on a particular course. A scheme based on similar principles could be devised for 'active citizens' who are undertaking full- or part-time education. This would provide them with the means of consolidating their on-the-ground experience as well as providing a stepping stone to further development.

The role of education in the community and the role of the community within education are areas of immense importance. Primary and secondary schools are important focuses of energy, activity and concern. The school gate is a place for social interaction for parents and many children alike. Secondary schools, sixth-form colleges, colleges of further education and modular university degree courses need to be opened up to the possibilities of community participation.

Educational institutions also need to rethink their approach to meeting the needs of their communities. The local management of schools has enabled local primary and secondary schools to form themselves into clusters in order to meet the needs of their localities in a more responsive way. Others have made a commitment to becoming 'community schools'. Some tertiary educational institutions have established local consortia to serve their areas. Some are developing local partnerships, designed to meet the need for personal development and technical and managerial skills within the community. These educational institutions are reviewing their courses and modules as well as the ability of students to mix and match; some are designing programmes that can be tailored to the needs of the community and within which pathways can be shaped to the needs of individuals.

Many of the activities undertaken by 'active citizens' could be seen as legitimate preparation for work in the formal economy. They are highly service-oriented and involve the development and application of skills that are relevant in other spheres. There is scope, therefore, to extend the National Vocational Qualification (NVQ) accreditation system to include the activities undertaken by 'active citizens' in running community-based initiatives. The experience that they have gained in running meetings, advising and helping neighbours, managing accounts, negotiating with outsiders, resolving disputes, delivering services and other activities could be easily assembled into a portfolio that could be assessed within the criteria of NVQ Levels 1, 2 and 3.

It is essential to provide support to those volunteers in employment who are playing a role in supporting, or may themselves become, community-based social entrepreneurs. It is from this group that, with proper support and encouragement, many of the future generations of community-based social entrepreneurs will emerge. Similarly, it is through this group that many existing community-based social entrepreneurs are supported.

This is an area in which the government needs to take an important lead. There should be a switch of resources and priorities in order to facilitate within the adult population a willingness to participate in rebuilding disadvantaged neighbourhoods and mending the fractures that exist within our own society.

Some companies positively support their staff becoming involved in community activities, as this provides a diversity and sparkle within the company. The Business in the Community's 'Seeing is Believing' programme for senior executives and the Professional Firms' Groups with its Area Focus Regeneration Initiatives are important steps on the way to creating a framework for building a more effective volunteering community, and a more transparent and encouraging pathway for those in employment to embrace the role of social entrepreneur within their own communities.

There is also scope to develop a complementary community volunteers scheme for young people. Already there is a small army of young people who befriend the elderly or those with disability. In addition, many students gain part-time employment looking after the disabled and the terminally ill. The Commission for Social Justice (1994: 361ff.) advocates the concept of a voluntary citizens' service for people aged between 16 and 25. The Labour Party is developing ideas for youth volunteering linked in with the Millennium. The Prince's Trust has also been advocating more volunteering among young adults. Means need to be established that can bring these and other initiatives together.

This, then, is the first raft of public policy proposals that would build a meaningful recognition of the importance and needs of community-based social entrepreneurship:

- The **acceptance of 'active citizenship'** as an alternative to the Jobseekers' Allowance

- The **extension of the principles of the Training for Work scheme to** 'active citizens' seeking to participate in full-time or part-time education

- Making **secondary and tertiary education systems alive to the potential of community action and participation**

- **Establishing courses** specifically targeted to the needs of community-based social entrepreneurs

- Building stronger pathways for volunteers to become and/or support community-based social entrepreneurs

These initiatives would help to establish multiple points of engagement with the community and would help individual and potential community-based social entrepreneurs to move from isolation into the relative mainstream. Engagement would also improve the prospect of community-based social entrepreneurs being effectively advised, counselled and mentored on what for many is a journey of self-discovery as well as a major contribution to our society.

10
the art of mediation
turning practice into policy
co-written with Jutta Blauert

> We are facing new forms of engagement, where unlikely alliances
> bring unexpected returns, where old coalitions prove to be rigid and
> often counter-productive, and where the traditional opposition
> often seems to be saying just what you are saying while meaning
> something altogether different (Zadek and Blauert 1995).

Mediating sustainability

The future of both agriculture and of rural communities in Latin America will
depend on whether existing and emerging policies support or undermine practices
consistent with principles of sustainability. For this reason, rural communities seek
to influence the policies of the state, of commercial organisations, and of international agencies. To this end, rural people and farmers' organisations form alliances with a range of actors, notably non-governmental organisations but also,
increasingly, research institutes, international donors, and the business community.

Alliance building in itself is of course not new. However, today's alliances are
quite distinct from alliances for survival in previous times. History has shown
farmers, particularly subsistence and indigenous farmers in Latin America, that
alliances with 'partners' from centralised political parties or even military regimes
have rarely improved the long-run situation of resource-poor and politically weak
rural families. The impact of structural adjustment policies in Latin America, for
example, may have led to some economic recovery for macro-economic indicators,
but poverty has been exacerbated in the process. In 1994, poverty in Latin American

* Reprinted from Jutta Blauert and Simon Zadek, *Mediating Sustainability: Growing Policy from
the Grassroots* (Kumarian Press, West Hartford, 1998) pp. 1-18. Permission granted by Kumarian
Press, Inc. This piece makes reference to chapters that also appeared in that book.

was higher than in 1980, and rural unemployment has increased alongside the decollectivisation and privatisation of productive lands (Scott 1996).

Today, rural actors are increasingly aiming to strengthen their roles in critical policy formation processes. This assertive agenda is addressed by forming alliances that allow them to develop and apply alternative measurement systems and research methodologies, to form and operationalise new consultative mechanisms, to demand effective adjustments to credit policies and to develop policy-oriented institutions controlled by farmers, rural communities and their supporters.

This book explores ways in which rural communities in Latin America have sought to influence policies affecting their livelihoods and the quality of their natural environment. A selection of experiences from different countries highlights the importance of collaboration between rural communities, producer organisations, NGOs and advisers. The experiences offered map out a potential range of common themes and strategies, providing insights into the means by which *practice* can influence *policy*. While the diversity and complexity of policy formation processes make it difficult to generalise, it is possible to identify patterns that offer lessons that may be taken forward in strengthening initiatives in the future.[1]

The following chapters describe initiatives that seek to distil and articulate knowledge emanating from the *realm of practice* of sustainable agriculture and rural development (SARD) in a manner that can influence the *realm of policy*. The objective is not to analyse the specific changes in policies of governments, donors or NGOs. Rather, we focus on how particular forms of language used to describe practice—and the individuals and organisations that mould and project those language forms—have evolved to support the process of influencing policy.

This process of seeking points of action, of alliance formation, of influencing, and of facilitating and analysing praxis toward the goal of SARD, is the sphere of what we might call *mediation*. This process requires paths or channels. It is these languages, people and organisations that make up the channels through which this influence can be brought to bear. These, then, are what we mean by the *mediators*. Finally, the use of language, the communications media, and new institutional arrangements are the tools that are deployed—by organisations and people as active *agents* of change.

This book is, above all, about mediation between different world-views and interests. However, whereas previously language was one means by which to distinguish these different actors and perspectives, this is now rarely the case. For example, farmers' organisations and multilateral lending organisations often remain, as in the past, antagonistic towards one another. Yet today they organise their arguments around very similar terminology, symbolised best by the common use of the word 'sustainable development' and its ever-widening range of derivatives.[2] Furthermore, these actors are now increasingly talking to each other when political animosity and traditional patterns of racism and other forms of bigotry had in the past limited or prohibited any direct contact. It is not argued, therefore, that there is *one* best or politically correct mediator or organisational type or, indeed, mediation tool.

The newly emerging patterns of communication to which the contributions to this book refer should not be taken to imply that the old problems have disappeared. 'Networking' for marketing and lobbying, using state-of-the-art communications technology still needs to be complemented by the practice of steady, daily listening and learning about the perceptions of other stakeholders, be they scientists, policy-makers or subsistence farmers. Following the argument made by van der Does and Arce (1995) that we can advance more effectively toward the objective of SARD if we learn to be more sophisticated in our reading of project narratives, our argument here is that *mediation* involves a careful listening to 'stories' represented by others, stories that have within the 'development industry' historically been ignored or misheard.

A case can be made for cautious optimism. Public-sector agencies, and even corporate bodies, are increasingly acknowledging, willingly or under duress, the legitimacy of the interests and rights of farmers, rural communities and related actors in agricultural and rural development processes. Yet this acknowledgement does not do away with vested interests, and the power struggles underlying policies formed on the back of 'consultative' processes (Anderson and Cavanagh 1996). Simply communicating more, or using the right 'sustainability' or 'participation' language, is not sufficient. Mediation processes between different conceptions of sustainability should not be confused with consensus, the amelioration of conflict-ing interests, or the alleviation of poverty. The emergence of new or renewed arenas for 'inter-institutional concertation'[3] is occurring at a time when real conflicts of interest are becoming accentuated as a result of macro-economic policies asso-ciated with trade liberalisation, privatisation, and the retreat of the state. Moder-ate—and moderated—mediation is not a substitute for the more familiar forms of confrontational campaigning on social justice, human rights and environmental issues, which certainly remain necessary. The experiences described in this book have occurred within this context, in recognition of, and in response to, the deterioration of the quality of life and opportunities of many rural communities throughout Latin America (Oxfam 1996; Pichón and Uquillas, this book).

Images of globalisation

Agricultural development in Latin America is generally perceived as a problem area in terms of sustainability. Rates of degradation, excessive dependence on oil-based inputs and uncertain or costly credit, coupled with uncompetitive pricing in the international markets, have cost the majority of the region's population dearly over the last 15 years. Rural poverty is on the increase across the region, as is rural outmigration. The social and environmental pitfalls of the green revolution have been widely analysed and documented (e.g. Agudelo and Kaimowitz 1994; Linck 1993; Pichón and Uquillas, this book). Today, a dominant image is of the trans-national company increasingly monopolising profitable rural markets, from basic grains to piggeries and forestry. Rural communities and their supporters consider the current processes governed by liberalisation as one where the continent is being 'eaten up' by market forces that are uncontrollable by all but the strongest in the game of survival from the land.

Yet the 'traditional' alternative to this scenario, the autarchic vision of organic agriculture and small-scale rural production systems, has so far been unable to deliver sustainable livelihoods for the majority or even large numbers of rural dwellers. Off-farm incomes are still (and often increasingly) more attractive in comparison to the low liquidity that much of sustainable small-scale agricultural production implies where markets are weak (see Ruben and Heerink 1996).

'Scaling-out'[4]

For practice to impact policy and to have an effective impact on individual and community-wide livelihoods, vertical interaction is not enough. Linkages need to be established horizontally, and skills in management of resources and markets need to be shared at the regional level: for instance, between farmers' organisations. 'Scaling-up' of impact and activities, as the experiences of social enterprises in the region demonstrate, needs to be coupled with regional alliance-seeking and exchanges between producers. In addition, scaling-up needs to go hand in hand with 'scaling-out', with a greater diversity of forms and a greater depth in quality of participation and engagement between different actors. This book takes as a starting point the view that isolated initiatives at the community level cannot prevent the process of globalisation from undermining both social and ecological systems. For grass-roots initiatives to offer more than temporary relief, they need to influence the broader policies that set the terms on which SARD will, in the longer term, stand or fall.

Limitations on impact of initiatives operating solely within communities are reported from several cases within the participatory technology development sphere (see Guijt, this volume). To enhance effectiveness, it is argued that horizontal and vertical linkages between the community and other actors need to be established and maintained. Local initiatives are, indeed, increasingly making use of the actors at the meso and macro level in sustainable management of local resources, so as to strengthen regionalised and even transnational attempts to achieve social and ecological sustainability. These new approaches to communication and access to data are, therefore, an integral part of a strategic response to the same problematic circumstances. They represent serious attempts to influence the policy agenda and counteract negative globalisation effects in favour of a sustainable development path (see also Engel 1995; Engel and Salomon 1994). Globalisation, furthermore, has taken place in ways and arenas (media, marketing, social justice networks) over which rural organisations can gain some leverage and advantage. Rural organisations can and increasingly do, for example, actively use such trends to their advantage in counteracting international pressures that negatively affect the local SARD agenda.

Changing institutions

Over the last decade, shifts in research and teaching institutions have also raised the prospect of mainstream national and international institutions accepting, or even proactively developing, public policy relevant to the needs of SARD.[5] Sustainable agriculture and rural development has traditionally been associated with two approaches: agricultural production and environmental stewardship—focused on low-external-input agricultural practices—and social production of knowledge and decisions, particularly focused on the principle and practice of participation. These two pillars of SARD are intimately related. Indeed, one of the most important successes of SARD initiatives taken together has been to confirm and legitimise the knowledge of actors such as small-scale farmers in the practice of environmentally appropriate forms of farming. The now quite widespread recognition of the relevance of low-external-input agriculture practices has served to reconfirm that knowledge (see Scoones and Thompson 1994).

In spite of only limited experiences in policy-making conducive to SARD, an extensive experience by the NGO, community-based and research sectors has left seeds for hope and resistance across the wider region (Carroll 1992; Kaimowitz 1995). Increasingly, the same research and development institutions that were in charge of applying and enhancing the green revolution, such as the Consultative Groups on International Agricultural Research (CGIARs), have moved to direct their activities toward the small-farm sector and have moved away from sole-crop-specific research. The maize CGIAR, CIMMYT, in Mexico is a good example, having conducted research on nitrogen-fixing cover crops employed by several of the farmer-to-farmer agricultural and soil conservation programmes in the region. The tropical tuber CGIAR, CIAT, in Colombia has long been undertaking research work with farmers, including studies of participatory methods encouraged by current rural development thinking such as Rapid Rural Appraisal or Participatory Rural Appraisal (RRA/PRA). Supported by new policy drives within the Food and Agriculture Organisation (FAO), the International Fund for Agricultural Development (IFAD) and the CGIAR training centre International Service for National Agricultural Research (ISNAR), these institutions have considerable influence over national agricultural resource centres and teaching institutions. In the end it may well be through these institutions that individual policy-makers learn of new practices and opportunities (FAO 1992, 1994a, 1994b; Scoones and Thompson 1994).

A number of factors, however, have tended to undermine the institutional efforts and resources required to secure the long-term stewardship necessary for effective SARD. Of critical importance is the continuing globalisation of markets, particularly for agricultural products; the associated structural adjustment processes; and the reduced or changed roles of the state accompanied by a rising importance of NGOs. Technology requiring little external or energy-intensive inputs such as many of those rooted in indigenous knowledge systems is an attractive solution in principle, but will not alone withstand the pressures of globalisation. Research focused solely on raising the technical efficiency of small-scale rural production processes is unlikely to be meaningful as a long-term guard to autonomous rural livelihood strategies. Anderson (1996), writing on the experience of a Mexican agricultural university, argues that the need for institutional support to create learning environments for SARD has been recognised by most research and teaching institutions but is still restricted in practice by institutional barriers, among them the reluctance of research councils to fund collegiate participatory research in the agricultural and rural development arena:

> So far, few agricultural research centres have made the policy changes necessary to provide the institutional framework for participatory research. [. . .]
>
> Professional rewards and career structures are not geared to encouraging participatory research and are not tolerant of the requirements for resources and time that such work implies. [. . .]
>
> A challenge faced by [practitioners of participatory action research and those using participatory rural appraisals] is to demonstrate the efficacy of their methodology to policy makers so that further adoption of the methodology might take place. The problem of the time scale of participatory projects from initiation to impact might make this task arduous. Policy makers often work to political deadlines that tend to be short term. Those National Agricultural Research Centres [that are] already operating successful participatory programmes and are aware of the restrictions imposed by economic policies, might facilitate the process of convergence between the interests of government institutions and participant rural communities. Here the advocacy role of participatory researchers is important (Anderson 1994: 10, 13, 21).

The potential role of researchers as mediators through practical engagement and policy advisory functions has become stronger, as failures of the green revolution and technology transfer approaches have become more widely acknowledged.

Institutional opportunities and blockages are also encountered by actors within the public sector. Escalante (1994) reports that, in the case of a Mexican governmental agency funding agricultural technology transfer and production projects, training in participatory learning and planning methods in the 1990s did not guarantee in itself a changed practice on the ground. Training in participatory approaches to working with farmers in itself is no mediating tool, nor does it guarantee a move toward SARD supported by the institution in question. He cites (1994: 6) some institutional and political constraints that echo those facing researchers: institutional and personal investment into participatory practice may not be given by the public sector because 'individuals in charge of relevant departments are motivated to achieve results that will:

- Justify their status

- Demonstrate that they follow government's macro-economic guidelines

- Keep their bargaining power in negotiating their institution's future budgets'

Sustainability derailed?

The language of 'sustainability' evolved in large part from the margin—albeit from politicised intellectuals rather than rural communities themselves (Zadek and Blauert 1995). Sustainability—for the non-conservationist actors—reflects an agenda of social justice within and across current and future generations as well as environmental stewardship, whether as a means, an end, or some combination. In conceptualising sustainability, moreover, there has been a focus on the *inter-relationship* between its social and environmental foundation blocks of rural development strategies, and therefore of an overall socio-ecological approach to understanding development processes. For the current debate in Latin America, sustainability has therefore come to embody an agenda that extends beyond economic viability and environmental regeneration, reaching deeply into the structure of social organisation itself by insisting on the key component of social equity and justice. For many Latin American people, sustainable rural development often represents more a struggle for democratic rights and land rights than an ecological regeneration or conservation. However, Leff argues that

> [t]he environmental issue demands the preservation of the natural base of resources in the interest of a sustainable production. This implies the need to revalue the *ecological conditions of production* and to create the political conditions for a reappropriation of the [peasant farmers'] natural means of production . . . This has been leading to new political strategies for the appropriation and socialisation of nature and has generated new productive practices for a sustainable agriculture (Leff 1996: 38-39; author's translation).

'Sustainability', in this sense, is also on the brink of being moved off this particular track. Often rhetoric is taken over by interest groups effectively repressing the economic organisation of small producers, or else short-term economic and political interests overshadow the interests of the ecological interests of future generations. In these cases, new mechanisms for monitoring policy changes, new institutions and relationships between these, need to be found. A transparency in the evaluation and monitoring processes in the field, and strengthened skills in resource mobilisation, are required to give different actors the legitimacy required to make sustainability a social reality.

Over two decades, the language of sustainability has penetrated the policy discourse and become common currency. At exactly the same time, patterns of production and trade have threatened its attainment. Interpretations of what constituted paths to sustainable development have multiplied to include precisely the same paradigms that had originally been challenged, and to exclude the voices and perspectives that had sought to present those challenges. Transnational corporations and dictatorships alike became the eloquent advocates of 'sustainable economic growth', while the needs of rural communities and environmental systems continued to be ignored and threatened (Korten 1995).

The mainstreaming of the sustainability debate has therefore been a mixed blessing. It *has* opened up new opportunities for influencing those institutions at the heart of the policy-making process. At the same time, it has created an often impenetrable cocktail of linguistic devices and consultative rollercoasters that have absorbed and often weakened the capacity of progressive institutions struggling for meaningful progress: the growing of policy from the grass roots.

The challenge, then, is to find new mechanisms, or to strengthen those that already exist, in order to institutionalise at the level of policy the advances made in *practice* by rural communities and their supporters, collaborators and partners. This is the route from *practice to policy*. It is, to say the least, difficult to travel. However, the practices referred to in this book *do* provide an insight into an ever-growing counter-current to the dominant approach to economic development. They are single experiences or case studies, but have to be set alongside changes in policy-making, organisations and technical expertise which have been described else-where. These practices—organisational, productive, research and methodologi-cal—have emerged from within weaker social groups in internally stratified and often conflictive rural communities. Such communities have traditionally been 'informed' of policy rather than consulted about it. The practices concern small-scale production processes, often with low levels of external inputs to suit the needs and capacities of resource-poor, rural people. Where they relate to the business of markets and distribution, they often highlight the potential of the local or the national. When they concern international markets, they challenge in all cases the rights of large companies to dominate trade and to retain large portions of the overall financial resources generated.

These agendas and perspectives do not enter easily into conventional policy processes. Institutions with the power to influence policy rarely have a form or internal structure that allows for dialogue with, let alone real learning from, those 'below'. This is certainly the case for most public bodies and commercial organi-sations, and it is also the case for many NGOs. The very structure of work and reward has historically constrained such a listening process, and has prevented what is heard from being taken into account. The professions (academic, finance or politi-cal), for example, do not generally reward their members in financial terms and status for communicating with rural people who have few academic qualifications, and often speak the dominant language poorly or incompletely (Chambers 1993; Said 1994). These rural people are usually inhibited in communicating their exten-sive experience in agricultural techniques and processes in a manner that resonates with professional, institutionalised thinking, and they are therefore ignored as a matter of course, even when they are the central subjects of that discourse (Zadek 1993b).

New actors for praxis and mediation

A new set of actors emerged during the late 1980s and early 1990s in Latin America, partly as a response to this pernicious and systematic linguistic confusion. These actors were intent on asserting the core propositions of sustainability in policy fora. These actors saw their task as being able to 'translate' the imperatives of SARD into a language that resonated, and was therefore more effective in influencing the policy debate. Three key sets of institutional actors have taken on this role: NGOs and research and development institutions; public-sector and international funding agencies; and grass-roots organisations, whether as farmer organisations, community-based organisations (CBOs) or community enterprises. In some instances, one point on this institutional triangle sought to influence others, for example, CBOs seeking to influence NGOs. In other cases, coalitions formed among the different types of institutions, such as NGOs and donors working to influence government agencies (for these 'common cause coalitions', see also Biggs and Smith 1995).

However, it was recognised that little could be achieved without shifting the terms on which poorer groups of rural producers themselves worked within the market. A fourth set of actors has therefore entered the fray: the business community itself. This constituency has long been shunned by the development community as essentially part of the problem, despite the fact that the business community has a pervasive impact on every community, and in all likelihood will need to be co-opted into the sustainability agenda if it is to be effectively addressed. A growing and often unhappy acceptance of this fact has meant that there is an explosion of new relationships between private-sector and small-scale rural producer organisations. The aim, however, is to ensure democratic relations guaranteed by associated mechanisms and respect for the needs of rural people (exactly because so much of rural poverty and injustice used to be associated with the commercial sector).

Most policies in the rural sector, designed to change farmers into small or medium-sized entrepreneurs to feed an urban market, were criticised—often for good reason—for destroying the very foundations of rural livelihood systems that had ensured peasant community survival for centuries. Long-term farmers' survival strategies used to be based on customs of exchange labour and consumption arrangements, low reliance on external inputs, and regenerative agricultural practices. These were effectively destroyed in most cases with agricultural modernisation, damaging the production and marketing systems that had assured survival and identity at least on a minimal level (Kaimowitz 1995). Whether this somewhat idealised view of 'rural communities' and their external enemies is correct or not, the dependence of rural people on trade and external relations is undeniable. Modernisation in agriculture, and high-external-input technology may have increased production but have not prevented a rise in rural poverty and rural–urban migration.

Successful and cost-effective implementation of a participatory approach requires the mobilisation of the skills, talents and labour of the rural population. To make this possible, decentralised administrative, fiscal and political systems conducive to the genuine participation of rural people in decision-making, execution and accountability processes are required. Involvement of the private sector is needed in this effort, but partial or full government finance is also required for a small-scale-farmer-oriented strategy to achieve its natural resource management and poverty reduction goals. Public investment in traditional agricultural areas may have high opportunity costs relative to the areas of commercial agriculture where most agricultural growth has occurred. But efficiency trade-offs may be justified in terms of the greater impact on poverty and environmental degradation that can be achieved in traditional areas.

It is along these tracks, many contributions in this book argue, that a 'derailing' of sustainability can be avoided.

Needing mediation

To mediate is to arbitrate, moderate, facilitate, or even to umpire or referee a process of dialogue between parties. Mediation in this sense involves a process of 'coming between' different interests with a view to finding a way forward from what is, or is in danger of becoming, a *cul-de-sac* of conflict or inertia. Beyond this, however, lies a more partisan approach to mediation, which involves a decision to step in, intercede, and help to negotiate a process with an orientation towards particular interests. In its most transparent form, this form of mediation is effectively one of advocacy. In either case—or at any point on the spectrum along which these two extremes lie—a mediation process can work only through the identification of some 'common ground' on which a deal can be struck. Such common ground is more easily arrived at where the different sides have shared values, and discover a language that expresses those values in a way that both can comprehend. Often, however, the identification of common ground requires more than this kind of fortuitous discovery. It requires pressures by one or both sides to shift the values of others, or at least to bring them into line with very different values and interests.

Sustainability has multiple interpretations, each constructed to support a particular agenda, and legitimised through the use of particular ideological and methodological constructs. Mediation in this context is not only a facilitation of dialogue and persuasion between actors with conflicting aims but also between actors who defend themselves by recourse to the cause of sustainable development.

By **mediating sustainability**, therefore, what we mean is the way in which we and others can play a role in channelling the knowledge required to support the informing and influencing of those people involved in policy formation. These people certainly talk of sustainability, but they reflect very different life experiences and interests from those of people working and living at grass-roots level. The challenge then is to be more effective in channelling those grass-roots experiences and facts in a manner that enables policy-makers to understand, believe and act in a sane manner.

This book as a whole suggests that grass-roots or community organisations are by no means the only ones to understand what is most likely to constitute a sustainable development path. However, the objective is acknowledged to be the contribution to a process whereby rural people are able to define and manage their own livelihood system while practising a socially just and environmentally sustainable resource use. To achieve this aim, local world-views, perspectives and interests need to be made visible, or brought forward so that they, alongside insights gained at a more 'macro' level, can be woven into relevant policy.

A key theme throughout this book, then, is communication. Those adopting the role of mediator have sought to improve their effectiveness by developing and applying methodologies that aim to establish acceptable forms of communication— through both language and activities—to provide a bridge between people and institutions from micro and macro spheres. Mediation therefore requires the construction of a common basis—such as indicators agreed by both farmers and policy institutions—which can be used to assess, for example, the effects of a controversial agricultural subsidy programme such as PROCAMPO in Mexico (Gómez *et al.* 1993), or infrastructure development by a social forestry enterprise in Costa Rica. In many instances this involved the development of evaluation systems that could effectively transmit to policy-makers the experiences of rural communities in seeking to implement SARD under such policies, and to expose rural institutions to organisational and technical experiences and advances in different regions. In other cases presented here, this implied a demonstration in and through the market that certain forms of production and trading processes are viable as well as being consistent with the principles of SARD. In all cases, mediation required the development of institutions through which critical messages could be channelled, refined and strengthened. Institutional development, therefore, today constitutes an integral part of a mediation process that aims to contribute to SARD.

In a sense, every institution, and every person or group can potentially be a mediator in this sphere. The contributions to this book do not argue that one organisation or person is *the* mediator for SARD. It is not just down to the NGOs or the experienced lobbyists to take on these roles. Of importance is the *approach*, the way in which, and the direction towards which, mediation takes place. The new environment for testing and designing rural and agricultural development alternatives also points to the need for skilled people who are trusted by all or at least several parties, and can mediate constructively between opposing views. Effective methods or appropriate language adopted by mediators not only send intelligible signals between the parties but also act to highlight both the relevance of their own skills and their overall legitimacy. When researchers make use of standard economic cost–benefit analysis, for example, they send certain signals that validate emerging perspectives to some, while undermining their relevance or accuracy to others. When a non-profit organisation successfully markets a 'fairly traded' product, the effective transmission of its message to commercial traders can be very much greater than a more traditional verbal assertion of the need for justice in trade.

There are many elements required for the effective translation of practical experiences into policy initiatives: for instance, clear conceptual models, an understanding of and ability to manage the necessary switches in language, and an understanding of and ability to cope with professional and institutional paths of policy formation. In addition, an astute analysis of political 'deadlocks' is required, or of the violence hidden behind the language of the negotiation table (as happens in so many cases, from Mexico through Brazil to the lands of the Mapuche) in order to be able to judge when or when not to move forward or to cede points. At every stage there are deals, compromises and decisions to be made. All of these, and many more, are part of the process of 'mediating sustainability'.

Towards optimism

For this cautiously optimistic tale to be realised in practice requires new methods, tools and techniques. While some of these will concern the practicalities of agricultural production processes and rural livelihoods, others concern the more ephemeral needs underlying new communication imperatives that go hand in hand with engagement in negotiations with those who were previously enemies to be confronted, or simply unreachable or unknown (Winter 1995). Methods are also needed that enhance learning processes within each of the sectors involved (e.g. peasant farmers, commercial farmers, policy-makers)—that is, learning related to engagement with new contexts and new 'neighbours'. The example of regional inter-institutional development committees such as those in Bolivia (Péres 1996), the Chilean municipal planning committees, or the Mexican technical forestry committees, support the relevance of bringing different stakeholder groups together in analysing constraints and opportunities for new policies and practices.

Effective mediation towards the new millennium requires several key activities, as the lessons from Latin America and the Caribbean tell us.

Policies and actors in mediation

The spread in Latin America of participatory methods of planning for and evaluating SARD objectives is now being employed in the interest of mediation for locally defined rural development paths as well as to strengthen local or regional economic initiatives. The Andean Planning method used by NGOs such as COMUNIDEC or community-based land use planning in southern Mexico and regional development plans in Bolivia or Argentina are just some examples. The new roles taken on by different institutional actors in this sphere, however, allow new lessons to be drawn. NGOs, public-sector agencies and research institutions participate to mediate, and use the participatory discourse to secure their own involvement in the rural sphere.

Measurement as mediation

Mediation requires a 'conveyor belt' of concise and relevant information. The use of indicators is a highly contested arena, and one where Latin American institutions are contributing much to the macro-level agenda (see MacGillivray and Zadek 1996). But attempts at communication are still not effective enough in designing and *using* indicators with and between different stakeholders: NGOs or grass-roots organisations still largely conceive measurement as a threat of external evaluation. In fact, the 'indicator game' is only too frequently still used as a controlling evaluation instrument by donors and governments alike. Yet measuring is a powerful tool, and locally defined indicators are demanded to complement or replace some of the national-level indicators often holding no meaning for local actors (see Blauert and Quintanar 1997).

Within the SARD arena, indicators have served two purposes. First, indicators allow change to be monitored, along with the relationship between these changes and defined goals or missed objectives (e.g. a community-defined idea of 'sustainability' for their village and immediate surrounding). Second, and clearly closely related to the first, is that indicators can be a means for refining and articulating different perspectives on local as well as global sustainability, thereby offering a critical basis for different perspectives to be compared and related, and providing a clearer sense of the position and performance of each party to negotiations. Indicators are, therefore, potentially both a means of evaluation and a means of mediating between different interests and perspectives: that is, they provide a tool for learning and for communication.

Markets as mediation

SARD is not feasible without economically viable alternatives to approaches that are not socially and environmentally sustainable or attractive. Finding new ways of engaging in the market is increasingly recognised by many rural organisations as a key element of any strategy to strengthen their position not only economically but also politically. Mediation within the new era of international trading blocks—and within this context of initiatives to carve out more equitable and environmentally sound approaches to trade—demands steep learning curves of producers of cash crops and manufactured goods alike. Niche marketing can have an impact on credit and export policies for smallholders which had previously not been thought possible. Local and regional seed banks, as well as genetic resource conservation, may come to be the alternative axes for mediation for subsistence producers in the region.

Organising for mediation

Mediation for SARD may increasingly be a skill of individuals who are able to bridge cultural, professional and language gaps. Yet the rise of farmer organisations in Latin America in the commercial and policy arenas—however limited their power may appear—points to the need for regional approaches to mediation. Without a regional organisation, coffee producers in southern Mexico would not have been able to win a position in the international market (Tiffen and Zadek, this book), nor would Brazilian rubber tappers have been sufficiently strong to negotiate their extractive reserves. The organisational skills of the peasant farmer producer sector are drawing on lessons from the commercial sector. Lobbying NGOs, in turn, are learning quickly to incorporate financial, managerial and negotiating skills in their work, areas that had previously been the prerogative of the private commercial sector.

New strategies, then, require new capacities and capabilities. There is a need for conceptual frameworks, methods, tools and tactics that fit the need to engage, communicate effectively, and ultimately persuade a range of people and institutions that are unfamiliar with, sceptical or downright opposed to the concerns and requirements underlying SARD (Biggs and Smith 1995). Some of these new modes of communication will be oriented towards the traditional sources of policy formation—institutions of the state—particularly those involved in agricultural research and development. However, there is an increased recognition of the need to find means of influencing economic processes through direct interactions with the corporate sector, or through active involvement in markets. In all these cases, there is both the need and the opportunity for institutions of civil society to be innovative in their approaches to self-organisation and alliance-building so that they effectively support these new forms of engagement.

Section III
accounting for change

11
accounting for change
indicators for sustainable development*
co-written with Alex MacGillivray

Mapping the territory

New indicators are being heralded as key tools for moving us along a sustainable development path. The adage 'if you want it to count, count it' has underpinned the drive to construct ever-more detailed mechanisms for measuring environmental, social and economic processes and outcomes, and their relationship.

Is this view common sense, or merely the latest myth? Is this measurement drive going to help deliver sustainable development in the 21st century? Or are the plethora of initiatives to measure sustainability a diversion that does little more than measure what cannot be managed, and ignore what really is valued?

Indicators have long been recognised as effective tools for communicating complex processes, events or trends to a wide audience. The term 'indicator' is drawn from the Latin verb *indicare,* to point out or proclaim. Put simply, it is a device to attract attention, like the pointer on a gauge, or a warning light.

The history of the development and use of indicators is as long and rich as it is complex. In 1928, the League of Nations held an international conference on economic statistics. The first international set of (partial) income figures were published on just 26 countries on the eve of the Second World War, where the need for reliable measures of wartime production led to refinements in methodology. Economic indicators only came fully of age with the standardisation of the system of national accounts (SNA) in 1947 and the widespread adoption of Gross National Product (GNP; later to become Gross Domestic Product, GDP) as the headline indicator of economic progress. It was not until the 1960s that formal research into social indicators was inaugurated. It was sponsored by the US National Aeronautics and Space Administration (NASA). By the mid-1970s social indicators were absorbed into the mainstream of social science, with governments publishing regular social statistics. After a period of inactivity during the 1980s, new ways of measuring development were being addressed by organisations such as the South Commission and the New Economics Foundation. Other key works, most notably the Human Development Index (HDI) were then developed, and remain as an alternative (or complement) to GDP. Environmental indicators have a shorter history, take-off coming in the 1980s, with a series of voluminous 'state of the environment' reports. Initial work concentrated on human pressures on the environment, such as atmospheric emissions of pollutants. Both the run-up to and follow-through to the Earth Summit in 1992 precipitated an enormous effort in the development of international, national and local environmental indicators. As yet, few obvious headline environmental indicators have emerged, although air quality indices, in those countries where they are available, are now routinely reported by the media, along with the weather. By the mid-1990s, attempts to integrate economic, social and environmental indicators were made by the likes of the World Bank, World Resources Institute, and small community-based organisations such as the Jackson Community Council, Inc. in the USA. At the same time, a long history of research on 'quality of life' has led to numerous catch-all approaches.

Seeking the 'good' indicator

Many opinions have been offered as to what makes a 'good' indicator. In most cases, attention has focused on 'technical specifications'. In his pioneering work for NEF, Victor Anderson drew up a comprehensive checklist (see Box 6).

- The indicator, or the information it is calculated from, should be already (or readily) available.
- The indicator must be about something measurable.
- An indicator should be meaningful: it should measure something believed to be important or significant in its own right.
- The indicator should be easy to understand.
- There should only be a short time-lag between the state of affairs referred to and the indicator becoming available.
- The indicator should be based on information which can be used to compare different geographical areas.
- International comparability is desirable.

BOX 6 TECHNICAL DIMENSIONS OF QUALITY

Source: Anderson 1991

However, there is a complex negotiation of interests that needs to be considered when in search of the 'good indicator'. Lord Meghnad Desai of the London School of Economics who has contributed to the Human Development Index, in addressing this problem, concluded that 'if it's worth doing, it's worth doing very crudely indeed!' Given such complex tensions in the negotiation of process, how can we set quality standards for indicators? First of all we need to tackle the basic issue of data.

The data problem

The data problem can be summarised in three areas: lack of data, lack of management, and lack of credibility.

a. The gap, in the **lack of data**, is felt by countries without substantial statistical resources. UNICEF lambasts many governments for what it calls the 'greying of statistics': the failure to keep data on vital issues such as child health up to date. Even in OECD countries, the quality of quite mainstream data leaves much to be desired. What can be done to fill the data gap? A range of 'rapid assessment methods' can be used to build up a picture of performance for Southern countries. The World Resources Institute, for example, is able to compile data on countries remotely for its reports, which is then used by host governments. There can be problems with taking the available data, however. Where there is a lack of existing data, or where the data is out of date, new data gathering exercises are needed, building on locals' traditional qualities of knowledge, memory and courtesy.

b. **Lack of management.** This gap arises when people cannot use the data, which do exist. Information management often lags behind data gathering. Ethiopia provides a familiar story. As the National Conservation Strategy points out: 'there is considerable information, but is scattered in various agencies. It is often not available and often knowledge of its existence is confined to a few people . . . A formal system of information exchange among them does not exist. Neither do documents nor the computerised systems are thus available to decision makers' (Ethiopian National Conservation Strategy 1994).

c. **Lack of credibility.** This gap arises when people suspect information that is disseminated has a political bias. In Ray Bradbury's novel *Fahrenheit 451*, a vision of a world where troublesome information was banned by the government and burned by firemen, the fire chief suggests: 'Cram [the people] full of non-combustible data, chock them so damned full of facts they feel stuffed, but absolutely brilliant with information. Then they'll feel they're thinking, they'll get a sense of motion without moving. And they'll be happy, because facts of that sort don't change. Don't give them any slippery stuff like philosophy or sociology to tie things up with. That way lies melancholy.' The message being: 'good data' can easily suffer from attempts to make them 'non-combustible'.

So what makes a 'good' indicator?

The crucial role of indicators is communication. Good indicators will communicate information that is not only accurate (a.k.a. a cold indicator: e.g. Eurostat's EPI) but also resonant (a.k.a. a hot indicator: e.g. HDI), and a good indicator is one that achieves a judicious balance between the two (warm).

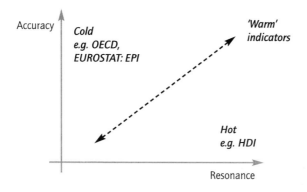

FIGURE 9 THE TEMPERATURE TEST FOR INDICATORS

Source: New Economics Foundation

Using the iconic example of the number of salmon runs in local rivers in Seattle as a way of measuring the quality of life (in this case of the quality of water), two perspectives emerge. First, an indicator can be warm while not being comprehensive. The salmon count, after all, has little or nothing to say about many aspects of sustainable development, such as income inequality or indeed the state of other ecosystems. Second, an indicator can be resonant for one reason and accurate for quite another. People may not consciously be making the connection between salmon runs and water quality or the behaviour of the timber industry.

So a good indicator is neither one that is merely warm, nor even one that is necessarily effective in achieving the intentions of its inventors or users. A good indicator is one that is effective in being resonant about the subject that it sets out to measure. It will inform and influence its intended audience according to its capacity to reveal information about the chosen subject.

Weaving together the strands of sustainable development

Sustainable development is, at the very least, clearly about economy, equity and the environment: the 3Es. The big question for indicators of sustainable development is how to integrate these three critical spheres. This is important for two reasons. The first is that tackling the three separately misses the crucial interlinkages between them. Sustainability is an integrated system, not three distinct categories. The second is that people need indicators that help them understand those inter-linkages. When it comes to decision-making, appropriate indicators can help iden-tify potential synergies, and also inevitable trade-offs.

There are a number of ways in which the weaving of the 3Es is being approached. One approach is the cluster or basket approach that brings together a group of indicators to measure the quality of life of a city or country (indicators include crime and safety, housing, pollution, access to goods and services). However, at scale these baskets (e.g. Eurostat) have both practical as well as credibility prob-lems.

One of the major shortfalls of this approach is that sustainability cannot be understood simply through a compilation of information about its various dimen-sions, however sophisticated the compilation might be. The pursuit of a sustainable development path is in practice about the outcomes of the interaction between its components. This means that measurement must seek to understand and reflect their relationships. This explains the inclination to produce composite indicators—or indices—that seek to capture and integrate elements of sustainability. A good example is the Index for Sustainable Economic Welfare (ISEW) compiled by a number of US and European research organisations (Daly and Cobb 1990). The ISEW was developed as a counterweight to GDP, which fails to measure many of the things in life that make us happy, and equally misses the point when it comes to measuring our effect on the environment. For example, as Robert Kennedy said, 'GNP [as it was termed then] includes the destruction of the redwoods and the death of Lake Superior. It grows with the production of napalm and missiles and nuclear war-heads.'

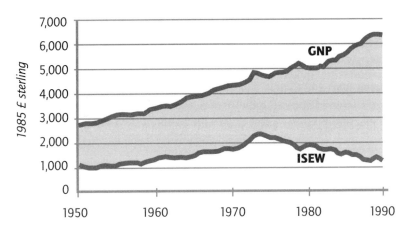

Gross National Product (GNP) does not account for the social and ecological costs of economic activity. The Index of Sustainable Economic Welfare (ISEW) does, and, when these costs are taken into consideration, a very different picture of the health of the economy emerges.

FIGURE 10 GROSS PRODUCTION VERSUS SUSTAINABLE ECONOMIC WELFARE IN THE UK, 1950–90

A key feature of the ISEW is that it allows comparison of a single measure of welfare across time, and therefore enables people to engage in the quality-of-life debate. Composite indices (i.e. the Big Number approach) such as the ISEW have been (quite correctly) criticised for their lack of consistency and coherence by many professional indicator makers. However, GNP equally lumps together incommensurables that in terms of sustainable development may have very different values to those attributed through the market. Thus logging activities in Malaysia will count as a positive contribution to GNP, while in the ISEW it would earn a negative count in terms of the country's path to sustainable development.

Do indicators really work?

Appropriate indicators will be a necessary element of any sustainable development path. Equally, however, the use of such indicators would not guarantee such a path being realised. Indeed, they would not be effective at all without being deeply embedded within the decision-making processes of mainstream institutions, especially within the state and corporate sectors.

In order for indicators to make a real difference, they need to influence the bigger picture; i.e. move more into the mainstream. The real difficulties in moving values, perspectives and approaches into the mainstream, however, reflect the nature of the challenge rather than providing cause for despondency. Just as there is always ample scope for dismay and cynicism, there are causes for celebration. The mainstreaming of the sustainability agenda itself has provided some leverage over key debates and decision-making processes. The UN Commission for Sustainable Development does exist, and continues to promote an agenda for progressive change. The UN's Human Development Report does challenge fundamental assumptions about development through its alternative measures of the progress of nations. The ISEW has resonated strongly with growing concerns about the gap between economic prosperity and the 'quality of life' experienced by citizens of the richest nations on earth.

Indicators do make a difference. They give voice to people's hopes and fears. They provide substance in debates about the real options facing us, and in descriptions of our practical experiences. Without this 'voice' there is no possibility of an evolution of our paths towards one that is environmentally sustainable and socially acceptable.

An agenda for action

In light of the above, we wish to offer a practical agenda for action which, if carried through, could deliver some of the gains from using appropriate indicators of sustainability. Specifically, the proposed agenda is intended to underpin a realisation of the following scenario:

- **National sustainability reporting.** Every nation will provide an annual report of its performance against agreed sustainability targets, and communicate it widely.

- **Local sustainability reporting.** The growing body of experiences in community-based sustainability reporting will be expanded, especially through the production and delivery of high-quality training and awareness-raising.

- **Corporate sustainability reporting.** Companies will begin to report against a wide range of sustainability indicators covering the environment and social spheres, as well as financial performance.

- **Public programme sustainability reporting.** Public programmes—particularly massive ones such as the European Union's Structural Funds—will have integrated appropriate sustainability indicators for both resource allocation and monitoring and evaluation.

Below are a few of the most obvious areas for development:

- **Bridging technical professionalism and participative competence.** The professional indicator-makers should not merely consult with organisations with different perspectives and experiences; they should work actively with them, building strong research alliances, and exploring the nature of grass-roots experiences and expertise.

- **Tracking international footprints.** A key part of the sustainability equation concerns economic activities, particularly trade and consumption, on the social and environmental fortunes of distant communities: i.e. the ecological footprint. However, as yet it has been largely ignored or indeed marginalised from the research agenda and associated resources.

- **Exploring Southern perspectives.** Much of the indicator work to date has been undertaken by Northern organisations. From the initiatives that have taken place in the South, it is clear that Southern perspectives do raise both qualitatively different issues and assert interests that sometimes conflict with Northern concerns. Without these perspectives, the debate will therefore remain incomplete and illegitimate, and policy will ultimately fail for these reasons.

- **Building sustainable business.** Developments in practical measurement tools within the corporate sector are still not taken into account. Yet innovative work on the integration of corporate environmental and social accounting will provide a key pillar for future sustainability indicators.

- **Integrating cultural dimensions of sustainability.** Now is the time to focus on the dimension of cultural diversity of sustainability to ensure that it remains a central part of any debate and decision-making process.

- **Building on the success of local practice.** It is important to build on the practice of indicators at a local level, both to inform the work in other localities, and also to provide lessons for the development of national and international indicators for sustainability.

Indicators that 'make sense' need to make sense to many different people. Most directly, those who are responsible for making important decisions about our future; most critically, those who could influence the basis on which these decisions are taken; ultimately, the citizens and their representatives without whose pressure there will be no reason for meaningful change. An agenda about measurement must therefore be aware of and responsive to these different elements of change. The agenda we have set out is not comprehensive, nor perhaps as aggressive as some would wish. It is, however, ambitious. Our experience suggests that it is feasible in this world, and could make a difference if realised.

12
trading ethics
auditing the market*

> Few trends could so thoroughly undermine the very foundations of our free society as the acceptance by corporate officials of a social responsibility other than to make as much money for their shareholders as possible (Milton Friedman 1962).

> . . . songs, not things, are the principal medium of exchange. Trading in 'things' is the secondary consequence of trading in song (B. Chatwin 1987).

A critical perspective emerging from the 'Earth Summit' at Rio concerned the non-sustainability of the current pattern of trade. Links between 'environmental trade', such as in pollutants, and trade in goods and services were stressed. Equity, seen as a prerequisite to long-term survival, requires that the terms of trade take greater account of human and environmental needs.

Those who argued this viewpoint spoke against the inequitable dimensions of such trade agreements as Maastricht, GATT and NAFTA. Today, however, all of these exist. The industrial world has failed, at least at this broad legislative level, to directly address the matters of equity raised at Rio and elsewhere. Such shortfalls should not, however, minimise the value of other initiatives to establish a trading ethic based on acceptable human rights and environmental needs. Ignoring these developments undermines the insight they offer for the wider debate. It is necessary, in particular, for evolving forms of economic theory to be based on an understanding and integration of these new approaches to trade and ethics.

Poverty of economics

Economics leaves little room to explore the complex texture of ethical behaviour. Few practitioners deviate qualitatively from the subject's tidy approach to ethics, which Sen dubs the paradigm of 'ethical egoism' (Sen 1987). Recent work has main-

* Reprinted from the *Journal of Economic Issues* Volume 28(2) (June 1994) by special permission of the copyright holder, the Association for Evolutionary Economics.

tained a lively debate about the treatment of ethics in economics (Bürgenmeier 1992). However, there remains a dearth of analysis supporting alternatives to the main thrust of economics.

The treatment of ethics within economic theory has become divorced from the ethics of economic research and business ethics (Rothchild 1992). This in turn divorces practice from theory. Recent developments in business ethics, for example, offer a rich source of data on the manner in which complex values influence market behaviour (Adams *et al.* 1991). These developments, however, have not impacted on the discourse on ethics and economic theory. Theoretical work in other disciplines, similarly, has been shunned by economists. Anthropological literature on 'reciprocity'; work on the social psychology of economic behaviour; and the sociological and philosophical literature on needs and entitlements generally remain marginal to mainstream economic discourse. This paper seeks to overcome these shortfalls in the process of evolution of economic theory by offering perspectives from both practice and theory.

Social auditing: the principle

Social auditing is the process of **defining, observing, and reporting measures of the ethical behaviour and social impact of an organisation in relation to its aims and those of its 'stakeholders'**. Stakeholders are people who can affect, or who are affected by the activities of the organisation, or by the set of events under consideration (Zadek and Evans 1993).

Critique of economic behaviour predates the industrial revolution and arguably can be traced to early philosophical texts. More recently, an extensive applied literature has emerged examining the social consequences of particular commercial ventures (Gray *et al.* 1987). Social auditing is, however, different from such previous work.

1. It is comparable to a statutory financial audit in that it involves **external verification, publication of findings**, and is **repeated annually**.

2. It takes *a* **comprehensive, inclusive view** of the scope of market relationships to be accounted for in the social audit.

3. Assessment criteria are **chosen by stakeholders** on the basis of their own agendas and values.

4. It **allows for analysis of behaviour** as well as impact or effect.

This approach therefore straddles two worlds. The first, mirroring the financial audit process, aspires to a form of **secular universality**. The second, a **collage of value statements** on which the organisation is audited, aspires to socialise the audit process itself by allowing for incomparable, group-subjective perspectives.

Social auditing: the practice

The method summarised above was established in order to audit the practices of one particular company. Traidcraft plc, although a business organisation, has objectives that combine the needs of commercial practice with a focus on benefits to stakeholders other than shareholders, as set out in Table 1.

Traidcraft's stakeholders are 100 producer-suppliers from the 'third world', thousands of customers, 100 staff members, 2,000 sales representatives and 4,000 shareholders. Consulting with this diverse, extensive group was a major exercise. Most interesting, perhaps, was the need to identify criteria that each stakeholder group wished to use during the auditing process, which was quite unlike financial or environmental audits. Methods adopted for this purpose included questionnaires, one-to-one and group interviews, and workshops and seminars. The process included visits to producers in the Philippines and elsewhere (Traidcraft 1993; Zadek and Evans 1993).

A range of value statements emerged from this process as the critical bases on which the company's social and ethical performance should be audited, as summarised in Table 1. Particularly important was that many of the values highlighted could not be directly associated with concrete 'economic' behaviour. Criteria for producers, for example, included the level and stability of sales and prices, which could be directly observed and subjected to analysis.

However, producers also asserted the importance of values such as solidarity, shared aims, and the quality of communication, which were more difficult to analyse in anything but qualitative, individual, and group-'subjective' terms. Similarly, the voluntary (sales) representatives worked for the company for a range of reasons which included personal financial gain, wishing to assist producer-suppliers and the communities in which they were based, and a sense of personal empowerment gained through finding a way to act in their own communities.

This complex relationship between values and economic behaviour posed a very real methodological challenge. How could diverse, qualitative criteria be handled within an 'auditing' framework; how could they relate to quantitative market data (e.g. prices for producers, wages for staff, dividends for shareholders, etc.); and how could, or should, these different perceptions and quantifications be aggregated to provide an overall view of the ethical behaviour and social impact of the organisation?

The approach adopted was permissive in allowing a range of cognitive statements from stakeholders to coexist with market data. It was holistic in asserting the interrelationship of its different parts, rather than the potential for aggregation into a single parameter of assessment. This approach generated interesting tensions. Producers participating in the audit, for example, emphasised the importance of 'fair' prices and stable sales income. The data showed that sales to the company for a number of producers consulted had fallen dramatically, and that inflation-adjusted prices for several had also fallen. The direct financial and social impact of this was negative. The producers considered, however, that the company had behaved ethically over the same period. Ethics, they maintained, could not be understood in terms of material and financial flows, but concerned more the matter of why the company had reduced sales and prices, how they had communicated

Stakeholder	Traidcraft's aims	Stakeholders' stated aims
Producers	A just trading system between North and South with regard to fair prices paid to, and stable business with, community-oriented producers	a. Sales value and stability b. Shared aims and solidarity c. Product development d. Communication
Staff	To establish an inclusive community of purpose . . . there should be an open style of management which will encourage the consultation and participation of staff	a. Shared vision and aims b. Material rewards and relativities c. Personal development, participation and communication
Voluntary representatives	To offer . . . a partnership for change, that puts people before profit, and enables them to influence their own communities	a. Supporting fair trade b. Christian vocation c. Financial arrangements d. Personal empowerment
Consumers	To encourage people to change their consumption patterns to take account of issues of social justice and the environment	a. Ethics of producers b. Cost of product c. Environmental aspects
Shareholders	To restore profitability and dividends and to inform and involve shareholders	a. Social return b. Financial return c. Participation/consultation d. Education/learning

TABLE 1 COMPANY AIMS AND VALUES: TRAIDCRAFT AND STAKEHOLDER VIEWS

this, and the extent to which this reduced commercial interest influenced the level of empathy and solidarity maintained between the different organisations and individuals involved. Similar tensions between economic outcomes and perceptions of the ethics of behaviour were found for all of the stakeholder groups.

The full implications of the social audit data cannot be explored here. Of particular interest, however, is that the permissive and polyvocal approach revealed tensions between perceptions of ethics of particular actions and economic behaviour. The translation of changes in material gains from trade into perceptions of the ethics of that trade is particularly complex. Even where a material gain or loss relates directly to stakeholders' interests or values, the perceived ethical consequences may move, qualitatively, in the opposite direction. **This raises the possibility that some forms of 'ethic' are being exchanged in the trading process.**

Unpacking ethical trading

The social audit data indicated 'ethical' influences on the economic behaviour of key stakeholders. What are these 'ethical' aspects on economic behaviour? Are they altruism in the sense of 'the eradication of self-centred desire', or do they reflect the utilitarian proposition of 'vicariously experiencing pleasure in [someone else's] pleasure' (Lutz and Lux 1988: 109)? Should they be interpreted as spiritual advancements in the market or as complex sociological phenomena? The view here is that a definite and exclusive explanation of 'ethical' behaviour arises more through preconceptions and underlying agendas than from unbiased analyses. The perceived need to choose between different world-views reinforces what Vandana Shiva calls 'monoculturalism of the mind', which oppresses the very notion of pluralism in interpretation and practice (Shiva 1993). Only by achieving a pluralism **integral to analysis, rather than merely allowing of difference**, can economics become 'evolutionary' in supporting comparison, combination, innovation and (if necessary) selection between world-views rather than merely between different projections of a single world-view. The implications of this view can be better understood by outlining some differing perspectives that one might be trying to relate or enable to coexist.

1. **Economic utilitarianism.** This world-view reinterprets terms such as empathy and 'fairness' as experiences sought for personal gain. Economic utilitarians see this world-view as compatible with any ethical posture. However, this view has been effectively challenged by numerous writers, who demonstrate that the utilitarian 'economic individual' is unable to extricate itself from the sphere of economy (Sen 1987; Zadek 1993a). Within this world-view, higher prices paid for fairly traded products or reduced dividends are explained by individual utility functions that trade off material and non-material forms of gratification. This world-view has its corollary in the business ethics literature, where 'ethical' behaviour is interpreted as just another marketing posture (Lloyd 1990).

2. **Social psychology of ethics.** Social psychological perspectives also treat ethics as an instrumental form of behaviour. Unlike the utilitarians, however, social psychologists interpret behavioural patterns in terms of social groups analysis rather than as a reflection of individual interests.

    Social psychology offers two possible explanations of 'ethical' behaviour. The first argues that the 'material conditions of consumer society constitute the context within which people work out their identities' (Lunt and Livingstone 1992: 24). This work has focused on a supposed need to 'reconstruct' a sense of personal identity in the context of the growing existential crisis within industrial societies. The second version inverts the previous approach to the relationship between economic behaviour and social identity. Social identity, then, dictates economic behaviour. An extensive literature argues that behavioural patterns can be interpreted in terms of responses to 'in-groups' and 'out-groups' and their respective norms (Tajfel 1978).

Northern stakeholders appear to behave ethically toward people in the South who have little to do with them in terms of social identity (culturally, familial ties, etc.). This 'ethical behaviour' can nonetheless be interpreted from a social-psychological perspective. Northern stakeholders belong largely to well-defined social groups: white, middle-class, a preponderance of women, and a very high incidence of active Christians. Supporting oppressed people in the South from this perspective is certainly one means of reinforcing their sense of belonging to one or more of these social groups. Alternatively, the behaviour of Northern stakeholders can be interpreted as a search to achieve greater meaning in their consumption, investment and working patterns.

3. **Reciprocal ethics.** The anthropological literature offers a third possible approach, particularly its treatment of the issue of reciprocity (Sahlins 1972). Anthropological conceptions of reciprocal 'gift-giving' interpret the ethics of economic behaviour as enabling stability between communities. Marcel Mauss therefore advocates an approach to analysing trade that would establish the **total service** function embodied within the relationship at both the individual and social levels (Mauss 1990).

This world-view supports a further interpretation of the data. Purchasing decisions of 'fairly traded' products, for example, can be understood as including elements of an intent to strengthen the bonds between consumers and producers. This is similar for staff, who have effectively committed an element of their potential earning power to the strengthening of links between them and producer communities. A broader implication of this viewpoint is that it suggests that the social audit process itself needs to be contextualised in the wider pattern of relationships between the relevant communities. Thus, the 'fairness' of trade would need to be interpreted in the context of the overall trading patterns between, say, the South and the North or the particular representative communities.

4. **Transcendent ethics.** The final interpretation diverges from the ego-based perspective of previous approaches. It is possible, although unfashionable, to believe that people can achieve non-self-centred behavioural forms. This belief may be held from many religious and other spiritual perspectives as well as from a humanist viewpoint (Maslow 1954).

This view of ethics is particularly relevant to the audit data since the majority of people directly involved in this company are practising Christians. Thus, Traidcraft's mission statement explicitly refers to the Christian values of selflessness as underpinning its aim to engage in 'fair' trade to benefit economically disadvantaged groups in the South. A considerable proportion of stakeholders, including third-world producers, referred to their religious beliefs and experiences as a prime motive for, and cause of, their involvement in the company's activities.

Spiritual and humanist interpretations of ethics in the economy suggest potential behavioural characteristics that transcend those instrumental forms underpinning utilitarian, social-psychological and anthropological perspectives. While problematic for conventional social critique, there does seem to be a need to at least accept the possible relevance of these interpretations. Not to do so would be to deny *a priori* the perspective of many of the actors that are being analysed.

An ecological view of trading ethics

These outline interpretations suggest that there is no single way to analyse ethical behaviour. This does not suggest the impossibility of establishing *which* competing claim is correct. Rather, it arises from a perspective that there is no reason *why* any one of the explanations should represent the essential truth. A meaningful approach should allow for multiple interpretations of people's perceptions of ethical behaviour. Ethical behaviour could therefore be understood as a combination of self-centred, transcendent and sociological factors. Only by having the facility to handle different world-views simultaneously can a pluralistic perspective prevail. It then becomes possible to understand why different individuals and communities engage in trade and how to encourage certain reasons and approaches.

A pluralistic approach should not imply an ad hoc approach. It should embody a framework that enables multiple perspectives to exist simultaneously and interactively. None of the above approaches fulfils this condition. The utilitarian approach cannot incorporate transcendent or social factors without reducing them to the very numeraire that denies their basic qualities. The social psychological model cannot manage propositions concerning the individual outside of her or his social context. The anthropological spectacles, while aspiring to cultural sensitivity, deny the very spiritual or humanist terms in which ethics may be versed by the communities being considered. Each of these approaches is therefore not only partial but exclusive.

Current discourse on biodiversity offers a path to overcoming this partiality. Shiva argues that monoculturalism underpins a partial and exclusive analysis of the value of complex, interacting biological and social processes (Shiva 1993). What is needed is an approach that offers a systemic analysis of *all* of the resource flows *and* associated social uses, needs and implications. Terms such as ' "productivity", "yield" and "economic value" are defined for the integrated ecosystem and for multi-purpose utilisation' [1993: 21] rather than in relation to the sole purpose of commercial gain.

Figure II illustrates the partial account conventionally taken of the full set of interactions between environmental and social spheres. Factors accounted for are those related to the purpose of commercial exploitation. Thus, while wood, oilseeds, wheat and rice are 'visible' within the dominant language, other 'outputs', such as water and fertiliser, are rendered 'invisible' or unvalued. Figure 12 illustrates the reasons for, and the implications of, elements of the pattern of 'ecological transaction' being marginalised. Shiva argues that this process occurs because only 'monetarised' transactions remain visible. In comparing the 'productivity' of traditional crops and 'green revolution' variants, for example, some inputs and outputs are taken into account, while others are ignored.

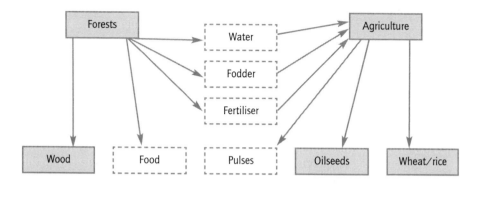

FIGURE 11 DOMINANT KNOWLEDGE AND THE DISAPPEARANCE OF ALTERNATIVES

Source: Adapted from Shiva 1993

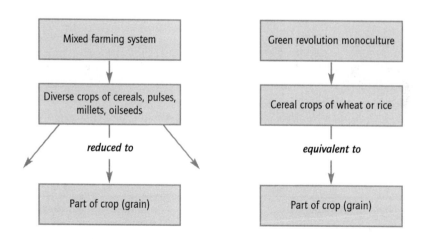

FIGURE 12 HOW THE GREEN REVOLUTION MAKES UNFAIR COMPARISONS

Source: Adapted from Shiva 1993

Marketable outputs are counted as benefits, while non-marketed outputs remain unvalued. In this manner, mixed farming systems are deemed to be relatively inefficient in comparison to 'green revolution'-based farming systems. Time has demonstrated the problematic nature of this approach. Not only have critical positive outputs been ignored, as Shiva points out, but also a range of costs such as the long-term exhaustion of the soil and the wider systemic effects of capital-intensive farming on the environment.

This framework can be used to visualise an approach to 'ethical trading' that allows for multiple intentions and outcomes. The corollaries to Shiva's approach to analysing biodiversity are set out in Figures 13 and 14. Figure 13 suggests some of the components of 'ethical trading' that are unseen or rendered invisible within the analytic processes and interests of mainstream economics. The economist will conventionally 'see' a range of financial and resource flows that allow him to approximate the generalised concepts of producer and consumer surplus. While these two terms can in principle include benefits such as solidarity, they rarely do in practice. The 'pragmatism' of monetarisation allows for these aspects of the trade to be effectively ignored. **The problem revealed in this manner is not merely that the economist's summation is a little too high or low. The problem is more serious, since he actively misinterprets the underlying nature of the transaction** in terms of the intentions of the various parties, in terms of what makes it a stable (or unstable) relationship, and how the relationship is related to the wider pattern of exchange relationships between the same and other individuals, groups and communities.

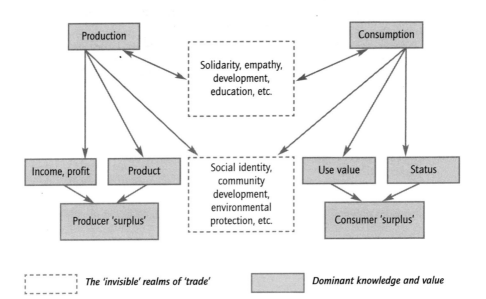

FIGURE 13 DOMINANT KNOWLEDGE AND THE DISAPPEARANCE OF REALITIES

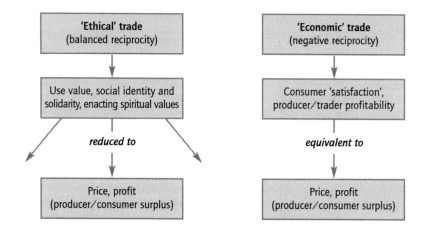

FIGURE 14   HOW ECONOMICS MAKES THE WRONG COMPARISON

Figure 14 strengthens this visualisation, again paralleling Shiva's analysis. The dominant language of the economist perceives and values 'economic trade'—or what Sahlins (1972) dubs 'negative reciprocity'. The valuation focuses on marketable throughputs. What is actually going on, however, is a far more complex transaction—what we have called 'ethical trade'—and what Sahlins calls 'balanced reciprocity'. This trade includes effects that can only be understood by 'seeing' the social texture of the transaction, which may contribute to enhanced solidarity between the trading partners, and/or between one of the traders and third parties and groups. The socialisation of trade also, arguably, is related to what we have called the 'transcendent' aspects of the individuals involved, which may both contribute to the pattern of trade and be influenced as a result. Furthermore (not depicted in the figure), there is the full range of possible environmental effects suggested by Shiva. All these factors need to be taken into account, whether they directly affect the particular exchange, further exchanges between the traders and third parties, or are related to the wider pattern of trade between the communities of which the traders are a part.

Acknowledging ethical trade

The ecological perspective offers a possible framework for understanding the ethical dimensions of economic behaviour. Even at this broad level, it offers conclusions relevant to economic theory.

- **Ethical trade exists as a counterpoint to conventional economic views of trade**. Analysis of the ethics of trade reveals the complexity of valuations, social interactions and broader systemic implications of trading relationships.

- **Ethical trade is polymorphous and can only be understood through a polyvocal approach.** Attempts to reduce the pattern to a singular basis will marginalise relevant perspectives and will reinforce the dominant language underpinning associated power structures.

An appreciation that every exchange of goods and services involves an engagement of a range of social and environmental values is the critical perspective offered here. That there is an engagement is not a matter of choice. To take a view that trade is concerned essentially with self-gratification is narrow, inaccurate and potentially destructive toward others and ultimately oneself. The choice lies in the decision to reveal and acknowledge those values and to actively engage in decisions regarding the values that one wishes to be represented and enacted through one's economic behaviour. The challenge is to support this process in the language that we evolve to describe the sphere of economy. The social audit data, and the short analysis offered of this data, is a contribution to this process.

beyond fourth-
generation evaluation*

Essentials of fourth generation

When Guba and Lincoln published *Fourth Generation Evaluation* in 1989, they provided a coherent voice to the concerns of many people involved in evaluation processes. It was time, they argued, to recognise the limitations of current evaluation methods which understood the task as being to 'discover the truth'. It was necessary instead to give form to the complex hermeneutic process that evaluation should be, or maybe already is.

Guba and Lincoln define three historical generations of approaches to evaluation. The 'first generation', they argued, was basically about measurement. The role of the evaluator was therefore that of **measurer**, and was required to have the expertise to apply the relevant measurement instruments. The 'second generation' of evaluation introduced objectives into the analysis to enable factual outcomes identified by the measurement paradigm to be described against the intentions of the events. The evaluator in this context therefore added the additional task of **describer** to the measurement role. The 'third generation' of evaluation was to acknowledge the need for the evaluator to make certain judgements on the basis of the available data in the light of predetermined aims. The evaluator therefore became **judge** in addition to the existing roles of measurer and describer.

All of these conceptions of the meaning and operation of evaluation processes understood the core characteristic of good evaluation as being for a **neutral outsider** to reach a decision as to what 'actually' happened in relation to what 'was wanted'. Guba and Lincoln argued that there were a number of serious limitations to the perspectives on evaluation offered by all of these three generations. They all failed to appreciate, in particular:

- The **real power relations** existing and pressuring the evaluator within the evaluation process. These power structures not only affected the relationships between those being evaluated but also limited the practical ability of the evaluator to be a neutral outsider.

- The **plurality of value bases** existing simultaneously within the evaluation process, as well as multiple interests, agendas and perceptions; and the consequential need to accept and cope with multiple perspectives within the evaluation process that are not mediated by resort to the assertion of facts but to the mediation of perspectives.

Further developments in evaluation methodology, a 'fourth generation', were therefore seen by Guba and Lincoln as needed to take account of these facets of actual evaluation process. They defined fourth-generation evaluation as a **hermeneutic dialectic negotiation**, where the evaluator is both a **facilitator** that elicits the views of different stakeholders, and a **mediator** in bringing the stakeholders to a level of consensus as to what happened in the past, and what should happen in the future. The fourth-generation evaluator does not therefore seek to identify 'facts' but rather to highlight and mediate between different views rooted in different interests and world-views. Similarly, the fourth-generation evaluator does not seek to determine a solution but rather encourages the various stakeholders towards an agreement.

Certain key principles need to be adhered to in order to be able to effectively undertake fourth-generation evaluation, according to Guba and Lincoln:

- That the **evaluator accepts the limitations of the previous three generations of evaluation**, and therefore understands and identifies with the new approach

- That all of the stakeholders must also **accept the limitations of a positivist approach**

- That **the evaluator must adopt a constructionist** approach. This operationalises the perspective that no assertion of truth exists independently of a particular set of values, and that this is just fine so long as one realises it and treats all information on that basis. Thus, the evaluator spends most of her or his time eliciting and mediating between constructions of the issues and events under review from different stakeholders.

- That the **process is responsive** in that the aims of the processes being evaluated, the goals and approaches used to evaluate these processes, and the descriptions of the processes themselves, are all determined by stakeholders, and therefore take multiple forms.

The evaluation double-bind

Fourth-generation evaluation offers insights into the shortcomings of conventional approaches to evaluation processes. Guba and Lincoln's work represents a serious attempt to establish an alternate methodology that allows for multiple world-views, value bases and perspectives on the events selected for review. Whether this alternate approach is 'new', or is a rationalisation of what evaluators are in practice doing anyway, is an interesting question. Evaluators often find themselves making 'third-generation' judgements based on questionable 'hard' data, leaning instead on superbly articulated viewpoints. As one senior official in the World Bank argued recently, 'we are an institution that makes very heavy use of tabulated data in justifying our decisions, but we base our decisions on qualitative arguments that can only be understood by analysing text and oral exchange'.

This gap between stated criteria and practical decision-making processes is not at all unusual. Every evaluator knows too well that there is often a vast chasm between the documented rationalisation of decisions and the real reasons people choose one path over another. The difficulty for both the evaluated and evaluator lies in the ubiquitous 'emperor's clothing' double-bind. Those being evaluated do not wish to disclose the real basis for decision-making, since this would undermine credibility and power rooted in a personal and institutionalised professional persona. The position of the typical bureaucrat, manager or economist would be undermined, as McCloskey points out, were it revealed that substantive decisions were made, say, on the basis of intuition, hearsay or defensiveness (McCloskey 1986). The evaluator, similarly, does not wish to reveal the real basis for decision-making. It is necessary for the status of the evaluator to be sustained through being seen as a sort of secular 'revelator', who brings unspecified expertise to bear despite her or his relative ignorance of the situation. Not to have this status would bring uncomfortable challenges to the evaluators' viewpoints, and would undermine the authority of their conclusions.

Thus, this symbiotic deception perpetuated by the evaluated and the evaluator underpins a basis for **non-disclosure of the fact** of fourth-generation evaluation. There are a few rare cases of explicit fourth-generation evaluation, usually within relatively safe areas for the stakeholders involved, particularly the sponsoring stakeholder group. More recently, for example, the New Economics Foundation has developed and applied an approach to social auditing of commercial and non-governmental organisations that replicates many of the key principles of fourth-generation evaluation (Shared Earth 1994; Traidcraft 1993; Zadek and Evans 1993). A similar approach that also adheres to many of the principles of fourth-generation evaluation is the work of the Copenhagen Business School in the area of ethical accounting statements (Pruzan and Thyssen 1990). The area of **participatory research** developed and applied mainly in the context of rural development projects in the 'third world' has also implicitly taken on many of the principles of fourth-generation evaluation (Chambers 1993).

This view that Guba and Lincoln have *identified* an existing but unrevealed process rather than *invented* a new way of carrying out evaluations does not in any way undermine or lessen the significance of their contribution. However, it does provide a basis for reinterpreting elements of what and how they have argued their case. By attempting to create an alternate paradigm, Guba and Lincoln potentially fall foul of their own argument. 'Fourth-generation evaluation', as a counterpoint to 'conventional evaluation', is in danger of constituting a renewed basis for maintaining the invisibility of what people are actually doing, rather than a basis for its validation. In presenting the hermeneutic process as the opposite of what is being carried out by evaluators everywhere, there is a real danger of reinforcing the appearance of exclusivity of apparent opposites in approach.

Given the underlying tenets of fourth-generation evaluation, particularly the need to disclose the interests of the evaluator, it is worth speculating on why Guba and Lincoln have taken this approach. They argue that they are convinced that 'the positivists' will never be convinced by fourth-generation evaluation. The book, for this reason, is not even intended for 'them'. This perspective is surprising in the light of their methodological position that all views are part of conversations that form the basis of mediated understanding, decisions, solutions and directions. There may also be professional or other institutional reasons for Guba and Lincoln's interest in 'creating a new paradigm', rather than embedding views within existing practice. New paradigms bring status and other rewards to its investors, as well as creating more notice and possibly effect. This is of course not a criticism. There is nothing inherently unacceptable within the terms of fourth-generation evaluation, including of course the interests of its creators.

The reasons for the construction of would-be new paradigms are important to understand in order to accurately interpret the underlying patterns of methodological change that their adoption imply. From this perspective, it would have been interesting for Guba and Lincoln to apply their invention to the processes of their own formulations and conversations.

Questioning the foundations

Fourth-generation evaluation suffers from several shortcomings that left unchallenged undermine the value of the method from both theoretical and practical viewpoints. These shortcomings are arguably rooted in Guba and Lincoln's decision to assert a paradigmatic shift through their insights. This assertion on their part has forced them along the path of dualism of supposed opposites, and has acted to marginalise or make invisible existing practice that is close to, but far more subtle than, the processes that they describe. There are two particular shortcomings that are highlighted below.

a. **Preconceptions of preconditions.** Guba and Lincoln assert that it is only through a hermeneutic process that effective mediation between different interests and insights becomes possible. To assert the search for 'a truth' can damage mediation processes, particularly in an apparently zero-sum game situation, or where stakeholders have radically differing worldviews as well as interests. Guba and Lincoln then set out what they consider to be the preconditions for such a 'productive hermeneutic dialectical negotiation', which include: the need for all parties to work from a position of integrity; a willingness of all stakeholders to share power; a willingness of all stakeholders to change; and a willingness of all stakeholders to reconsider their value positions (1989: 149-50).

There are several problems with these conditions. The most obvious is that these conditions, while desirable, are unlikely to pertain except in the rarest of cases. Groups with relative power rarely want to share it on any meaningful basis in practice, even those who say or actually think that they do. Similarly, very few people fulfil the condition of integrity, if by that is meant that there are no significant hidden agendas. The danger, then, of Guba and Lincoln's severe conditions are that they marginalise fourth-generation evaluation from practical processes, rendering it little more than a fascinating curiosum. Secondly, the hermeneutic dialectic process proposed by Guba and Lincoln would arguably not be necessary if these conditions *did* actually prevail. That is not to say that there is no place for a process to increase mutual understanding between the most angelic of people. Rather, it is to miss the point that the hermeneutic process is necessarily political, which in itself implies that Guba and Lincoln's preconditions do not hold. That is, fourth-generation evaluation has potential value as an *emancipatory* process primarily because these preconditions do not prevail in our society. In this sense, Guba and Lincoln *undervalue* their own insight by imposing these preconditions.

b. **Mediation for action**. The manner in which Guba and Lincoln construct their argument for fourth-generation evaluation is in itself an interesting example of the very polarisation process that they themselves are criticising. Fourth-generation evaluation is posited in this process as an *alternative* to a positivist approach. A different and potentially more useful interpretation is that the critical responsive and constructivist elements of the approach constitute *one aspect* of an appropriate evaluation process. In particular, without incorporating an understanding of a mediated solution that is essentially deemed a 'consensual truth' by the stakeholders, *consequential actions* become almost impossible to determine. It is therefore entirely possible for different stakeholders to define diverse interpretations of a particular event. However, for a consequential action to arise from the evaluation process requires ultimately that a 'fact' be determined through this process that forms the basis for agreement and further action.

If there is to be no further action, this final stage is not necessary. However, Guba and Lincoln themselves stress that evaluation is integral to a continual process, rather than an *ex post* approach that presupposes the end of the critical process. In this sense, then, a hermeneutic process is one that creates a form of truth which Habermas would call consensual or 'democratic rationality' (Rasmussen 1990). Critical here is that this democratic rationality is not seen as merely the point at which *some* consensus was reached. The closer to a fully ethical or democratic discourse the hermeneutic process is, the more does the resolution constitute a core form of rationality or truth.

Constructs revisited

These shortfalls in Guba and Lincoln's exposition of fourth-generation evaluation indicate that some adjustments are needed to operationalise the approach within a world of prevailing power relations and entrenched interests. Practical evaluation procedures requires a 'cut' at some point that allows a move from the hermeneutic dialectic negotiation process to action.

This section suggests some simple conceptual amendments to fourth-generation evaluation. The basic approach adopted is to reinterpret the underlying features of fourth-generation evaluation as necessary but not sufficient components of an effective evaluation process. Moreover, it is suggested that elements of conventional interpretations of evaluation processes, i.e. a positivist approach, be reintroduced, albeit in a particular form and context.

a. **Constructivist–positivist axis.** The first of the two constructs required are the constructivist and the positivist axis of an evaluation process. In the previous section it has been suggested that it is necessary for *both* to be present in an effective evaluation process, the first to seek meaning and the second to decide on action. Here, then, 'positivism' is not understood as a rejection of the hermeneutic process but as a landing point of that process. This is not merely a word play. While there may be an intellectual appreciation of the subjectivity of any perspective, our practical experience is informed by a *sense* of a positivist reality. There is an existential need, it might be argued, for us to maintain this posture in order to attain any sense of stability in our lives. Thus, a hermeneutic process may at one level be a never-ending ongoing process, but **in practice we understand it as a process of moving from one realised reality to another.** The need for a positivist outcome to the process, however temporary, is crucial. Thus, the two polarities depicted in Figure 15 need to be understood as interacting phenomena, rather than (as Guba and Lincoln would have them) as excluding opposites.

Constructivist   Positivist

FIGURE 15 THE BASIC CONSTRUCT

b. **Action–mediation axis.** Another aspect of the perspective offered here can be understood along another axis, from mediation to action, as depicted in Figure 16. Guba and Lincoln point out that the mediation process is a necessary feature of effective evaluation. However, mediation alone is insufficient to ensure a meaningful outcome. An action or set of actions needs to arise for the process to have had meaning. This requires that at some point the mediation process comes to an end, for whatever

Action   Mediation

FIGURE 16   THE SECOND CONSTRUCT

reason and for however temporary a period. While this is similar to the point made above, it is not the same. Whereas the positivist–constructivist axis offers two different modes of *understanding*, the action–mediation axis offers two different forms of *behaviour*.

Relating the constructs

These two axes are clearly not independent of each other, either in meaning or in their functional relationships. Each state of being or understanding has a particular set of tensions with each form of behaviour. What, for example, is the form of understanding most needed for effective mediation? As Guba and Lincoln point out, it is necessary for the participants to engage in what they call the constructionist mode of understanding. Thus, as the double-ended arrow in Figure 17a suggests, the higher the level of constructionist stance achieved, the greater the possibility for mediation across different world-views, values, interests and perspectives. The lower the level of hermeneutic dialectics achieved, the more difficult will be the mediation process. The mirror of this relationship is shown in Figure 17b, which suggests an inverse relationship between the level of positivist stance adopted, and the quality and extent of possible mediation achieved.

There is a similar set of relationships suggested between the other two poles of the two constructs. Figure 17c suggests that the greater the level of constructionism achieved *alone*, the more difficult it is to reach agreement on a course of action. This may at first seem counter-intuitive, since it suggests that the more the various stakeholders understand each other, the more difficult it becomes to determine a course of action. This is, however, not quite what is being suggested. While understanding may be a necessary condition for consensus, it does not alone offer an effective recipe for action. Hence the oft-quoted view that groups rooted in highly consensual decision-making processes find it very difficult to forge a clear and decisive direction, particular where substantive conflicts of viewpoint and interests are involved. This is not to offer a justification for dictatorial approaches to decision-making. It suggests, rather, that it is necessary to move beyond understanding through mediation in order to choose from a menu of possible actions. The mirror image of this hypothesis is presented in Figure 17d, where a strongly positivist approach to understanding a situation tends to allow for more directional decisions to be taken, however unjust or inappropriate they may be.

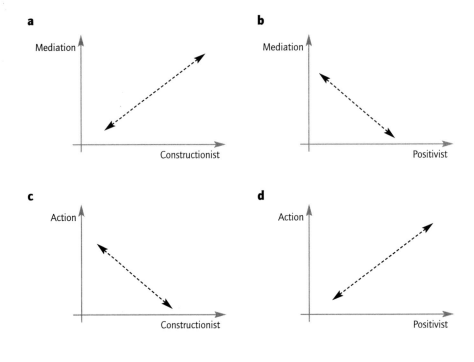

FIGURE 17 RELATING THE CONSTRUCTS

It must be stressed that the suggested direction of the relationships are not necessary or always unilinear in the way described. Rather, it is being suggested only that they constitute the dominant tendencies of the relationships in question. Thus, there will clearly be times when the opposite relationships hold, or that the actual shapes of the curves are complex.

Process cycles revisited

The relationships between the two sets of constructs outlined above can be interpreted in one further way. Each in effect represents *one part* of the cycle of an evaluation process, thus proceeding from a set of actions that have taken place in the past. Firstly would come the constructionist phase. This would be broadly along the lines set out by Guba and Lincoln, although without the preconditions they have suggested. On the basis of the evaluator's/facilitator's ability to elicit a collage of different perspectives, it is then possible to engage in a mediation process between the different stakeholders. At some point it becomes necessary to determine a set of 'consensual facts', the so-called positivist stance. This agreement on 'what happened and why' allows a set of actions to be chosen for the future, which at some stage allows for the evaluation process to begin again.

This process cycle is described in Figure 18. Each of the four quadrants reproduces one of the relationships summarised in Figure 17, with a double-ended arrow to indicate the dominant direction of the relationship for each pair of poles. The curved arrows outside of the circle indicate the direction of the evaluation process. To reiterate the main point here, fourth-generation evaluation focuses on the top right-hand quadrant and to a lesser degree the bottom right-hand quadrant. The 'enemy without' that they identify—the positivist paradigm—is reflected in the two left-hand quadrants. The difference is that, by making this latter paradigm the 'ally within', it is recognised that a positivist stance is *needed* to choose subsequent actions, rather than it being a contradiction of the earlier stages in the process.

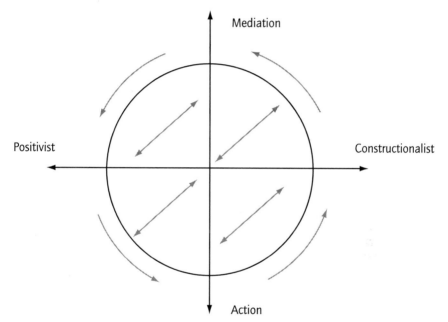

FIGURE 18 THE PROCESS CYCLE

Interpreting the process

A notable feature of the process cycle is that the relational arrows provide some guidance with regard to *qualitative* aspects of the process cycle. So, for example, it suggests that a failure to achieve a high level of hermeneutic dialectic (i.e. constructionist) will lead to a difficult (low level of) mediation. At the same time, the top left-hand quadrant suggests that a low level of mediation is associated with a high positivist stance. That is, low levels of mediation allow for the dominant powers within the evaluation process to assert a strong claim for the universalisation of their particular views. This high positivist stance in turn makes it easier to determine a course of action, essentially because the interests and perspectives of the less-powerful stakeholders have effectively been marginalised from the process. This particular sequence is summarised in Figure 19 through the A1–D1 sequence.

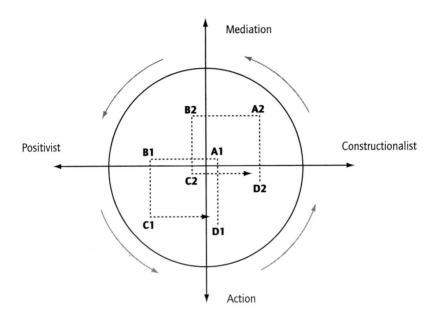

FIGURE 19 INTERPRETING THE PROCESS

Alternative paths can also be identified, such as the A2–D2 sequence. In this case, a high level of hermeneutic dialectic is achieved, placing the first stage of the path at A2. This allows for a high level and quality of mediation to be attained. In this case, however, it did not prove possible to build on this mediation process to reach a clear decision about what facts will be taken to be of dominant importance, i.e. the key 'facts'. The results of this are that only a very low level of action is defined and enacted.

It is not possible or correct, it must be stressed, to interpret high and low levels achieved as being necessarily good or bad. There are many occasions where a rapid decision is required to enable a radical action to take place to avoid disaster of some kind, whether it be choosing a path to turn a ship away from the rocks, or making a decision regarding a possible investment in a rapidly changing market. Arguably, in such cases, high levels of mediation are not useful or even possible. The statement 'we are heading for the rocks' is one that needs to be taken in a positivist vein very quickly to allow action to be taken. Decisions are made rapidly by the person given or taking space and power, and the others merely hope that the right decision is taken, or that their interests are being taken adequately into account. In other cases, of course, high levels of mediation are more desirable, and more possible given the time available. This might particularly be the case where long-term processes are involved, with varied and highly distributed implications and insights across the different stakeholders. Statements such as 'Should we build this major dam?' would tend to necessitate a higher level of constructionism and mediation within the evaluation process, with caution about the positivist and action elements of the cycle. Then the question of what transpires has far more to do with the relative power structures within the evaluation process, and the skills and agenda of the evaluator/facilitator.

Concluding comments

Fourth-generation evaluation is clearly a powerful critique of conventional interpretations of evaluation processes. It is successful in this sense in dispelling the myths and dusty self-images regarding the neutrality of evaluations, and the power of the professional evaluator. Guba and Lincoln's exposition of fourth-generation evaluation is not, however, without problems. Their strict preconditions and polarisation of conventional approaches endangers the practical application of their proposed method, and its internal consistency.

The adjustments suggested in this chapter offer a mediated settlement between the supposedly opposing camps in a typically hermeneutic fashion. Each represents different interpretations of the event of an evaluation process. Each interpretation in turn is more or less relevant to different stages in the evaluation process, rather than each being resolutely exclusive. The suggested model for interpreting the relationship between both approaches is intended to have a practical function, as well as constituting a theoretical exploration. It is possible to use the process cycle for analysing the course of evaluation processes along and between the two sets of poles. In this way, it is possible to take a view as to the appropriateness of the process in relation to the issues being considered, the differential powers, interests and perspectives engaged in the process, and any other impositions on the evaluation process due, for example, to time constraints.

14
social labels as
a tool for ethical trade*
co-written with Sanjiv Lingayah and Maya Forstater

Consumers increasingly want to buy products produced under conditions where minimum standards of human rights for workers in global supply chains are achieved. Consumers are confused about what products are more ethical than others and in what ways. Companies are not clear how best to move 'ethical consumerism' from its current negative focus to one that embraces 'positive choice'. Civil institutions are reluctant to endorse products and companies without being absolutely sure that agreed standards are being met. Governments and international institutions are unsure as to what interventions are feasible let alone effective.

Social labelling is increasingly being used or considered as a tool for more effectively communicating about 'ethical trade'. Labelling can provide information and can act as an incentive to improve the social and environmental impact of production and trade. Existing social labels have focused particularly on labour standards in global supply chains, sometimes based around one specific issue such as child labour.

> **Social labels** are words and symbols associated with products or organisations, which seek to influence the economic decisions of one set of stakeholders by describing the impact of a business process on another group of stakeholders.

There is serious concern about the quality and effect of social labels as a tool for communicating 'good practice'. Doubts exist whether companies will fulfil the terms of adopted codes, and how best to monitor and verify claimed performances. There is a lack of understanding as to how public bodies could or should intervene through this route in support of ethical trade. There are doubts that social labels actually work in encouraging consumers to reward companies in the marketplace, and a recognition of the need to see them as part of a wider process of civil- and public-sector action.

> **❝** By the time you have breakfast, you have depended on half the world. **❞**
>
> *Martin Luther King*

---

* The *Social Labels: Tools for Ethical Trade—Executive Summary* was the object of a contract between the European Commission and the New Economics Foundation, London. First published by the Office for Official Publications of the European Communities. © European Communities, 1998.

Responsibility for the information and views set out therein lies entirely with the authors.

The European Commission has decided to explore these developments, and has commissioned the New Economics Foundation to clarify issues in order to enable an objective appreciation of social labelling, and thus provide a working basis for future discussions.

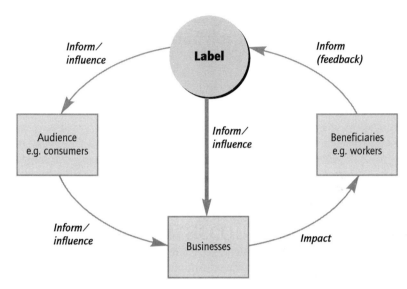

FIGURE 20 HOW DO LABELS WORK?

How do social labels work?

Social labels operate through both 'window' and 'mirror' effects. The most obvious fact is that they inform the consumer about how the product was or was not produced—the 'window' effect. Less obvious perhaps, but equally if not more important, is their function as a 'mirror' for the consumer in securing the benefits of self-expression and positive social identity. In economic terms, they change consumption patterns by shifting consumers' balance of costs and benefits of finding, buying and using goods and services. As one study by the National Consumer Council concluded, 'use of "green" detergents and cleaning products was almost a credential for judging environmental awareness'.

> ⁶ In the factory we make cosmetics, in the store we sell hope. ⁹
> *Charles Revlon*

Social labels impact directly on participating producers, and indirectly by influencing the behaviour of non-participating companies and

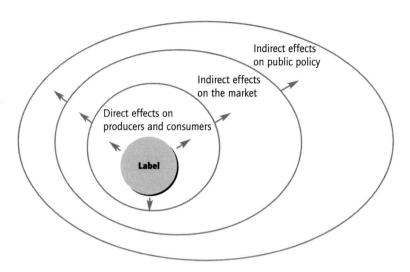

FIGURE 21 DIRECT AND INDIRECT EFFECTS

shifting or reinforcing public policy. Fair-trade labels, for example, directly benefit a relatively small number of producers, but have influenced the development of 'ethical trade' in the mainstream business community.

Impact	Explanation	Conditions
Positive	Label provides market leverage to improve standards in the supply chain	Label's standards are higher than current practice, *and* Labels succeed in conferring market advantage
No impact	Label makes no difference to producers/workers	Label standards do not exceed current practice, *or* Label is ignored, *or* Label is not financially viable
Negative	Label has negative effect on participating producers/workers	Label leads to lower standards not covered by criteria, e.g. minimum wage may be offset by forced overtime, *or* Beneficiaries displaced, e.g. child labour from inspected factories, *or* Label leads to fall in market share (e.g. if it undermines consumer confidence through scares or confusion), *or* Compliance with criteria is an unmanageable burden

TABLE 2 HOW LABELS CAN IMPACT ON PRODUCERS

Social labels in action

Several characteristics of labels determine their effectiveness: relevance, clarity, trust, accessibility, accuracy, financial and legal viability, and impact, as set out in Table 3.

Relevance	Is the issue important to the *consumers* and intended *beneficiaries*?
Clarity	Do *consumers* understand the label?
Trust	Do *consumers*, *businesses* and *beneficiaries* believe in the legitimacy of the label and the way in which it operates?
Accessibility	Can *consumers* buy labelled products? Can willing *businesses* participate in the initiative?
Accuracy	Can *businesses* participating in the initiative be assured that the label's claims are verified?
Financial viability	Is the label consistent with the financial goals of participating *businesses*? Does it add additional assurance to that contained in the brand? Are *consumers* able to afford labelled products?
Legal viability	Will participating *businesses* be acting within national and international regulations?
Impact	Does the labelling initiative have a 'positive' effect on *beneficiaries*? Do these outweigh potential negative side effects?

TABLE 3 CHARACTERISTICS OF AN EFFECTIVE LABEL

The effectiveness of labels also depends on the broader institutional framework within which they operate, including: structure and governance; standards; monitoring; and marketing. For example, a labelling initiative will be more effective if it is associated with organisations that the public, or non-governmental organisations (NGOs) and other opinion leaders trust, such as the Fairtrade Foundation label in the UK, or the sustainable forest label offered by the multi-constituency-governed Forest Stewardship Council.

> **'** Our best social label is our brand label. **'**
> *Alan Christie, Levi Strauss*

Five different categories of social labels have been identified.

- **Self-declared:** e.g. The Co-operative Wholesale Society '99' Tea; corporate brands backed by codes of conduct
- **Industry body:** e.g. British Toy and Hobby Association

FIGURE 22 OPERATIONAL CHARACTERISTICS

- **Partnership:** e.g. FIFA/International Confederation of Free Trades Unions; 'No Sweat' label, USA; Forest Stewardship Council; and SA8000

- NGO-**led:** e.g. Clean Clothes Campaign; Max Havelaar; Fairtrade Mark; Transfair; and Eco-Ok, Abrinq

- **Official:** e.g. US 'Trend Setters' list; Kaleen; Investors in People

Civil action and social labels

The research has highlighted that social labels **are more effective when they are linked to strong public feelings and underlying civil action**. Civil activism, for example co-ordinated through the work of NGOs, acts as a form of awareness raising and marketing for labels. The Max Havelaar labelling initiative, for example, invested heavily in promotion of the label using classic channels of civil society: public media exposure, mouth-to-mouth promotion, mobilisation of support groups, as well as more traditional commercials in newspapers, magazines, radio and television, etc. This process of civil mobilisation has yielded the result that 89% of Dutch consumers have heard of Max Havelaar. This compares well with the EU Eco-label—which has had little associated civil action and has only an 11–12% consumer recognition in the UK. This finding is critical in understanding the relevance of labels, and provides fertile ground for understanding their basis of effectiveness. The research, including both detailed case-study work and a survey of labelling organisations, also confirms that partnership-based labelling initiatives score best against the effectiveness criteria. This has strong implications for the role of public policy. In particular it emphasises the need for public policy, which fosters civil-society involvement in labelling.

- Bought and consumed by the general public
- Identifiable products, i.e. branded
- Products strongly associated with social identity, e.g. clothing
- Products not competing solely on price
- Products that are simple to trace

BOX 7 FOR WHICH PRODUCTS DOES LABELLING WORK BEST?

Opportunities and limitations

Our assessment of relative successes and failures in the area of social labelling allows us to summarise what opportunities are offered through the use of this market-based tool, and what are its main limitations, as summarised in Table 4.

Characteristic	Opportunity	Limitation
The incentive for ethical purchasing comes from independent civil processes.	Social labels provide a way of translating concern into positive action.	Without these civil processes social labels are unlikely to be effective.
Social labels reduce the cost to consumers of finding an ethical product.	Labels can ease the take-up of labelled products.	Social labels can also increase 'costs' in terms of price or choice.
Labels can form part of self and group identity for consumers.	Products can be labelled on this basis, particularly for those products concerned with identity and lifestyle (e.g. clothing, branded goods).	Social labels are unlikely to work well on generic products and products, which are heavily price-competitive.
Social labels require significant resources—both to set them up and to promote and monitor them.	Social labelling initiatives are able to attract start-up and ongoing funding from a variety of sources.	Social labels may rely on external funding to avoid higher prices to consumers.
Social labels have emerged around 'hot' issues.	Social labels are likely to be most attractive where the issues and products are carefully targeted and backed up by campaigning and education.	Social labels do not provide a blanket solution for all products and all issues related to trade and labour standards.

TABLE 4 OPPORTUNITIES AND LIMITATIONS OF SOCIAL LABELS

Public policy options

The question for policy-makers in this area is what public interventions, if any, can help to make social labels more effective? In answering this question we have considered:

- Likely future scenarios in relation to which decisions will need to be made
- Types of public policy interventions
- Most appropriate interventions for each scenario considered

As a part of this, we have considered which interventions would be consistent with prevailing public policy and international agreements, and whether the likely benefits would warrant the costs involved in making such interventions.

Scenarios are futures that can be created. There is a particular role in this for public institutions responsible for formulating, recommending and implementing public policy. Public bodies need to decide which of the three (or some other) scenarios appears most attractive, and what interventions would lead us down that path. Of course, developments may follow all three routes simultaneously.

Ethical brands. Companies respond to consumer pressure mainly by promoting their own brands as social labels, and adopting supporting codes of conduct and independent monitoring.

Partnership labels. Civil partnerships promote independent social labels backed by agreed labour standards and approaches to monitoring and verification.

Multilateral labels. International organisations underpinned by governments develop multi-sector international labels, independent of, but in some cases coinciding with, civil movements.

BOX 8   POSTCARDS FROM 2003

There are a wide range of possible interventions that might be made, ranging at the 'lighter' end of the spectrum from informing and educating, to more extensive intervention involving changing fiscal arrangements through to a publicly supported social label more akin to the EU Eco-label. The policy options outlined below become progressively more formalised and 'interventionist'.

- **Increasing support for education and awareness raising around labour conditions, trade and consumption issues.** This research has made it quite clear that the 'civil movement' element behind social labels is critical to their success. It would be possible to support the broad area by increased funding of awareness programmes involving civil organisations in the North and in the South.

- **Sponsorship of annual awards for companies demonstrating good and best practice in the social area.** Awards could be given for both demonstrable positive social impact, and also for best practice in social labelling and other approaches to consumer information.

- **Facilitate the development of new partnerships.** Multi-stakeholder initiatives such as the Ethical Trading Initiative and a similar process being initiated elsewhere are seeking to define standards in this area. There are calls for these initiatives to operate or be consistently linked at a European or trans-Atlantic level.

- **Develop pan-European standards in social labelling** by playing an active part in agreeing, and possibly endorsing, labels that had achieved agreed standards of integrity and transparency. This would support the development of credible private labels.

- **Use of public procurement** in promoting and supporting appropriately labelled products. This strategy has been used by local government and parastatal organisations in promoting child-friendly, sweatshop-free and environmentally friendly labelling. It is, however, vulnerable to challenge under World Trade Organisation (WTO) regulations.

- **Use of fiscal incentives** to reward socially responsible purchasing. One approach might be for the government to explore how best to use a variable tax policy to secure consumer interest through essentially offering price discounts based on demonstrated corporate performance, linked to consumer-oriented social labels.

- **Establish a European social label.** Clearly there are attractions to a more comprehensive approach to standardisation. However, the research indicates that the most effective labels are associated with specific civil-society movements, which encourage buy-in from key stakeholders such as consumers, producers and retailers.

These policy options have been rated in terms of significance against each of the three scenarios. The most hands-off education role is most crucial in promoting the development of 'ethical brands' and labels, but dialogue facilitation will be critical in developing effective and independent monitoring. Promoting dialogue and the formation of standards are the most important interventions in assisting the development of partnership labels.

It is clearly possible through a range of initiatives to reduce the cost and increase the benefits of ethical trade. A portfolio approach to supporting ethical trade is preferable to public policy focused solely or indeed at all on the development of a social label. This view is strengthened in the light of the ambiguity in WTO regulations towards private labels. In particular, it is cost-effective for public policy to be focused on the development of the civil framework providing the fertile ground for labelling and other initiatives, through education and dialogue promotion. Private social labels can also be supported through the use of awards and the orientation of public procurement towards ethical trade. These types of interventions will go a considerable way to enhancing the impact of social labels. To them can be added fiscal support and a process standard as the legal framework set through the WTO begins to be clarified.

> ❝ To live means to buy, to buy means to have power, to have power means to have duties. ❞
> *National Consumer League motto, 19th century*

Conclusion

In conclusion, social labels are among a number of devices that can help to deliver positive social change through the market. Existing experience and the evidence from environmental labelling suggests that labels can make positive impacts, by increasing returns to beneficiary groups and by triggering changes in the behaviour of consumers, retailers and brand companies. Social labels are deserving of EC support, in particular of fostering civil-society understanding of the issues, which they address. With this foundation in place, further efforts to promote improvements in social impacts are more likely to succeed.

• We say 'yes' to work, 'no' to exploitation, 'yes' to work, 'no' to abuses, 'yes' to work, 'no' to social exclusion. •

Ana Maria Catin Torrentes, Movement of Working Children and Adolescents

15
accounting works
a comparative review of contemporary approaches to social and ethical accounting*
*co-written with **Peter Raynard***

Major changes throughout the 1980s has meant a delegation by the state to commercial and private, non-profit organisations, in key social and economic spheres. This shift has created a need for accounting practices that assess the social impact and ethical behaviour of such organisations, as well as their financial and environmental performance. This chapter, by examining three contemporary social and ethical accounting systems, explains how far down the road in accounting we are for such change. It concludes that 'social auditing' techniques are currently the most theoretically well-rooted, comprehensive and practical, in that they give voice to those affected by the organisation, strengthen the organisation's strategic management procedures, and make the organisation both more transparent and accountable.

A new moral mandate

Of the many changes that took place in the 1980s, the most important has arguably been the systematic transfer of the moral mandate that for decades had been almost the sole preserve of the state to commercial and private non-profit organisations. This transfer happened in many shapes and guises, including the privatisation of previously nationalised industries, the dismantling of legislation that had historically preserved labour rights, the relentless process of international trade liberalisation and the retreat of many aspects of the welfare state. These patterns of change have all allowed greater freedom for commercial organisations to determine their

---

* First published in *Accounting Forum* Volume 19 (2/3) (September–December 1995). © 1995 University of South Australia.

own moral or social stances and for the non-profits to take up the moral mantle in advocacy and service provision.

It did not take long for this new situation to generate a complex and problematic relationship between institutional survival and success, and moral rhetoric and aims. The corporate sector discovered that their social activities could underpin effective advertising, as well as often providing staff with productive insights into other parts of the economy (Goyder 1987). The non-profits discovered increasingly graphic ways of depicting social misery as a route to fundraising (Hancock 1989). Both sectors, albeit in different ways, found themselves balanced on a publicly declared moral tightrope.

The verification problem

This mixture of socially responsible activities and public relations hype created, in short, a verification problem. Financial performance could be reasonably well verified within established statutory frameworks. Verification of environmental performance was rapidly becoming an established procedure, albeit through best practice and benchmarking rather than through statutory force. Some aspects of social performance assessment were reasonably well understood and accepted, such as in relation to equal opportunities legislation, corporate gift-giving, secondments and customer service.

The broader dimensions of social performance remain, however, outside of the statutory realm. Indeed, not only do most of the many claims of social performance remain unverified, they are often quite unverifiable given the types of information that the organisations concerned are generating regarding their own activities. The recent experience of the fierce debate about the ethics of the international body care company Body Shop International illustrated the problem very clearly. Because all parties to the debate presented little more than anecdotes, there was no real clarity as to what The Body Shop's activities actually were.

The recent Body Shop experience highlights two key issues. The first is that it should be expected that there will be an increasing number of challenges to the moral rhetoric of those organisations claiming to have aims and practices that go beyond the struggle for profit or institutional survival: 'The high moral tone taken by the Body Shop has exposed it as a target for scrutiny'.[1]

The double edge of re-acknowledging the moral responsibilities of all institutions—including business—is that these responsibilities will become entangled in the cut and thrust of survival. The second, therefore, is that there is a paramount need for clear verification procedures. The work of organisations such as the New Consumer (in the UK) and the Council for Economic Priorities (in the USA), has contributed to the evolution of such procedures (Adams et al. 1991). However, verification of practices in relation to social aims remains under-developed, particularly for larger organisations with extended, complex patterns of activities and influences.

Social and ethical accounting: a comparative overview

Social and ethical accounting can be, and has been in practice, undertaken in many different ways. Comparison is not straightforward, since the circumstances of different accounting processes are often critical in determining both the design and the practice. It can be problematic to compare two approaches that have evolved through application to very different types of organisation, whether in terms of size, ownership and control, pattern of aims or activities. At a very simple level, the matter of equal opportunities for staff may involve radically different issues for organisations of different sizes, at different stages of their life-cycles, with different levels of financial and time surpluses, and in different cultures. In an organisation where social accounting has been carried out, the relationship, for example, between its core Christian values and the secular societal norms of equal opportunities has raised many issues, which cannot be resolved easily or compared with the situation of other organisations (Traidcraft 1994).

With this qualification in mind, we have constructed a cautious comparison of three approaches to social and ethical accounting. The three have been chosen on the grounds that they all have been thrown against the litmus test of practical application, represent (to the authors) broadly sound approaches and are likely to be at the core of approaches adopted in the future.

With the limits to comparison in mind and the rationale for selection, the three approaches compared below are:

1. **Social auditing:** broadly the system developed by the New Economics Foundation and Traidcraft plc, and now being used in adapted form by The Body Shop plc, Happy Computers, Shared Earth, several non-governmental organisations (NGOs) and the New Economics Foundation itself (NEF 1994; Pearce 1993; Shared Earth 1994; Traidcraft 1994)

2. **Ethical accounting statement:** system developed at the Copenhagen Business School, adopted first by SBN Bank and now in use in a range of companies and socially oriented organisations in Denmark and Norway (Pruzan and Thyssen 1990; SBN Bank 1993)

3. **Social assessment:** system developed in the USA with the company Ben & Jerry's (Ben & Jerry's 1993)

Table 5 offers an outline comparison of the approach taken by each of these three methods to nine critical features of social and ethical accounting. The table suggests a number of strong similarities between the three methods. First, they all start from a position that the key to the process is to give voice to a wide range of stakeholders. None of the approaches in this sense restricts the scope of stakeholder consultation through design, although operational differences can create variations in the practical scope of consultation. Second, they all involve a commitment to a regular accounting cycle, which has in practice meant an annual cycle. There is nothing within the accounting process that makes an annual cycle particularly significant. Rather, the annual cycle has tended to arise through a deliberate synchronisation with financial and environmental reporting cycles, as well as annual reports (in the

Social and ethical accounting			
Principle	Social audit	Ethical accounting statement	Social assessment
Multiple-stakeholder perspective	Yes	Yes	Yes
Comprehensive[a]	Yes	Yes	No
Regular	Yes	Yes	Yes
External benchmarking	Yes[b]	No	No
Target-setting	Yes	Yes	No
Systematic book-keeping	Yes	Yes	No[c]
External verification	Yes	No	Yes
Audit group	Yes	No	No
Publication of accounts	Yes	Yes	Yes

a None of the approaches is comprehensive during any one cycle, since the costs of such an approach would be prohibitive. The difference is that the Ben & Jerry's approach adopts a sampling approach and reports only on that basis, whereas the other two approaches seek to be comprehensive over a number of cycles.

b Partial external benchmarking seems to be possible, although the ethical accounting statement approach views this not to be the case.

c Ben & Jerry's does not aspire to be systematic, whereas the NEF/Traidcraft approach is moving towards a greater systematisation of social book-keeping.

TABLE 5 SOCIAL AND ETHICAL ACCOUNTING: A COMPARISON

case of Ben & Jerry's) and annual general shareholder meetings (in the case of Traidcraft plc). Third, all three approaches involve the publication of the accounts and thus its availability to the stakeholders themselves.

The above table also shows a number of important differences between the three approaches. First, the social audit and ethical accounting statement approaches are notably different from the social assessment approach in being comprehensive and systematic. Also, the construction of a social assessment does not, as the opening comments in their 1993 social assessment stressed (as part of their Annual Report), involve a systematic accounting process:

> the company [Ben & Jerry's] does not as yet maintain or have available the complete records that would allow a social audit to be accomplished on a timely basis (Ben & Jerry's Annual Report, 1993).

An external person, who the company feels has the relevant expertise and ability to carry out an objective assessment of its social performance, is invited to investigate any aspect of the company's activities, and to report on them in a manner that he or she might wish. This relatively ad hoc approach does limit the process in that it is impossible for a systematic account of the organisation's activities to be constructed, particularly when the organisation is large and geographically dispersed. It follows from this that the social assessment does not lead the organisation to establishing a systematic approach to social book-keeping, which is an evolving but important feature of the other two approaches.

A second significant difference between the three methods concerns their approach to benchmarking. The ethical accounting statement approach rejects any external benchmarking, arguing that this form of comparability is largely meaningless. A rigorous approach to assessing the changing pattern of different stakeholder group perspectives *over time* is instead the focus of this benchmarking process.[2] The social assessment similarly does not involve any systematic external benchmarking, although (unlike the ethical accounting statement) there is nothing inherent within the approach that prevents external comparisons to be made. The social audit approach both allows for and encourages external benchmarking. However, the external benchmarking is in general restricted to the third level of value constructs, 'societal aims', as discussed below. This allows for external benchmarking against aims for which there are generally accepted indicators.

The third significant difference concerns the matter of target-setting. The social assessment approach does not in general lead to explicit, publicly declared, target-setting. This reflects a view of it primarily as a reporting tool: 'accounting' in its most basic sense. The social audit and ethical accounting statement approaches, on the other hand, both involve target-setting. Target-setting under social auditing takes place outside of the formal accounting and auditing process. The organisation itself sets targets that subsequently appear in the proceeding social audit. These targets often arise in practice from dialogue that takes place with stakeholders within the social auditing process. The ethical accounting statement approach, on the other hand, involves target-setting as a formally integrated part of the accounting cycle. Once the formal accounting for the previous year has been completed, the organisation brings together 'dialogue circles' comprising members and representatives of each stakeholder group. The dialogue circles are responsible for making recommendations for the adoption of targets to the senior managers of the organisation concerned.

In this sense, then, the social auditing and ethical accounting statement approaches are not only accounting tools in the traditional sense of reporting past behaviour. Nor are they only an accountability tool, in the sense of giving practical leverage to stakeholder groups through the provision of information. They are in addition practical strategic planning and management tools. In this latter role, the two approaches are particularly relevant to those organisations that have explicit non-financial objectives, and can be of critical use for those organisations that can only survive in the long run if these objectives are addressed adequately.

The final significant difference considered here concerns the matter of external verification. In this critical area, it is necessary to distinguish a number of differences and their possible reasons. First, the social assessment and the social audit both involve external verification, whereas the ethical accounting statement does not. Interestingly, when this difference was discussed at a meeting of some of the principal architects of the various approaches, it came as some surprise to most that the veracity of the main example of ethical accounting, the annual statement produced (without external verification) by SBN Bank, had never been challenged.[3] To those working elsewhere in Europe, this seemed quite inconceivable. The view expressed by those involved in its production argued that the relative smallness, homogeneity and strong sense of 'moral economy' in Denmark and Scandinavia as a whole was central in explaining why unverified accounts could go unchallenged in this manner.

The social assessment and social audit approaches are both externally verified, but in very different ways. The social audit approach to verification is discussed in more detail below, but, in brief, places considerable stress on ensuring multiple levels of verification, each involving both an auditor and stakeholders themselves. The social assessment, on the other hand, has a far more individualistic approach to external verification. It is the responsibility of the one 'distinguished person' to investigate the organisation, write the social assessment and in this sense validate it as an objective statement about the organisation's social impact.

Focus on social auditing

The more recent history of social and ethical accounting has seen rapid developments in both methods and applications. This section explores in more detail the method underlying one of the three approaches outlined in the comparative section above, 'social auditing'.

Social auditing is 'a means of assessing the social impact and ethical behaviour of an organisation or set of activities in relation to its aims and those of its stakeholders . . . Stakeholders are individuals and groups who are affected by, or can affect, the activities under review' (Zadek 1994: 632-33). Social auditing has a number of particular characteristics, some of which have been outlined above. The following description, however, offers both more detail on key features of social auditing and highlights its underlying principles.

Polyvocal

The approach is based on the views and accounts of all stakeholders, as well as the mission statement and wider interests of the organisation concerned. Furthermore, social auditing does not seek to judge the relative relevance of these different views, many of which in practice can offer very different accounts and judgements of the same set of events. Rather, it seeks to report these different viewpoints and where possible to conceptualise them with other information in a manner that allows the audience to come to a view as to how to deal with the various perspectives. In the Traidcraft social audit for 1993, for example, it was reported that a significant number of staff considered that the lower-paid levels they were receiving were too little in relation to the organisation's 'fair trade' declarations. At the same time, the quantitative data showed that these staff were being paid roughly the same as people working in other trading organisations doing similar work. These two views were conflicting, but not incompatible. Traidcraft's staff considered that comparability was an inadequate basis for setting wages for an organisation with a declared social policy such as Traidcraft's. The role of the social audit was not to decide on this matter, or even judge whether one or other of the views should be omitted from the published audit. The role of the social audit, rather, was to show the different viewpoints in as clear a manner as possible to enable all of the stakeholders, particularly the staff (including management) and the board, to understand the issues being raised and the root of the different existing perspectives.

Social auditing in this sense follows a broadly constructionist approach to accounting, as, for example, set out in Guba and Lincoln's *Fourth Generation Evaluation* (1989). To avoid this approach to 'accounting receptivity' degenerating into an unmanageable soup of values, aims and measures of performance, social auditing practice has been moving towards a three-tier categorisation of values (see Figure 23):[4]

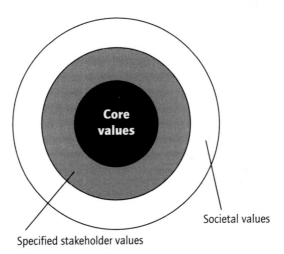

Core values

Societal values

Specified stakeholder values

FIGURE 23 POLYVOCAL: A THREE-TIER APPROACH

- **Core values** of the organisation, generally reflected in its mission statements. These would include, for example, trading relationships, attitudes towards staff, forms of corporate involvement in community activities and, of course, the need for financial viability and in some cases surpluses and dividends.

- **Specific stakeholder aims**, which are those that are identified during the consultation process with identified stakeholder groups. This would generally include staff and for commercial organisations often some combination of suppliers, customers and the wider community in which the organisations are active. For non-governmental organisations (NGOs), stakeholder groups can include funders, policy-makers, collaborators and beneficiaries, as well as staff and volunteers.

- **Societal aims,** which are those 'benchmark' concerns established in the societies in which the organisation is active. This might include, for example, social norms made explicit through statutory means, such as in equal opportunities legislation. However, important social norms are often not made explicit or statutory. In these situations, these norms are often in practice voiced through specific stakeholder perspectives.

Multi-directional accounting

The three-tier approach outlined in Figure 23 requires a complex consultation process. In particular, accounting needs to take place in several directions at the same time (see Figure 24). Staff of an organisation, for example, would be consulted

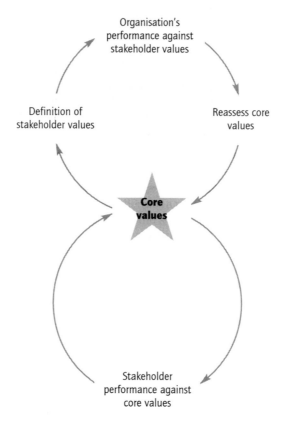

FIGURE 24 MULTI-DIRECTIONAL ACCOUNTING

as stakeholders. From this perspective, they would be able to highlight their own values and interests and to construct indicators to measure the organisation's performance on that basis. The same staff, on the other hand, would be subject to a performance assessment themselves in order to judge the organisation's performance against its core values or the values declared by other stakeholders. This complexity, it should be stressed, is not simply a 'feature' of the accounting procedure. Rather, it is a formalisation of the very complexity of values, aims and two-way accountability that in practice exist within organisations (and indeed societies in general).

Comprehensive

The approach supports and encourages comprehensive assessments of an organisation's social impact and ethical behaviour. It is critical that this principle is upheld to avoid any exclusion (deliberate or otherwise) of reporting of one or other aspect of the organisation's activities. There has been interest shown by some organisations, for example, in applying social auditing to one part of their activities, such as their 'community work'. While there certainly would be value in understanding the impact of such activities in themselves, such an approach would endanger the integrity of the social audit approach more generally, and therefore has been resisted to date.

Often, however, those practical considerations make it impossible for every aspect to be dealt with during each accounting cycle. It would be impossible or certainly prohibitively costly, for example, for The Body Shop to consult fully with every one of its suppliers, franchisees and staff every single year. For this reason, the auditor's report (see below) each year makes recommendations as to on what areas the organisation should focus its accounting in the coming cycles.

Comparative

The issue of comparability has been one of the most contentious issues with which the social auditing method has had to grapple (as well as other social and ethical accounting approaches). On the one hand is the difficulty of comparing social and ethical effects across different situations, as the previous section highlighted. On the other hand was a recognition of the need to provide some basis for contextualising social accounts for them to have any meaning. The need for meaning ultimately meant comparison of one kind or another. Thus, the issue is *how* rather than *whether* to maximise the level of meaning through enabling comparison. This is a very different standpoint than that taken by, for example, the proponents of the ethical accounting statement and social statement approaches, which explicitly reject comparison with other organisations.

Externally validated

The principle of external verification is central to social auditing, as it is with classical evaluation. However, the classical approach to external validation is fraught with difficulties. The 'evaluator', for example, typically has an impositional role. In the case of NGOs, for instance, the evaluator often acts on behalf of donors and therefore tends to restrict the scope of the assessment to the interests of these parties. A further difficulty is how the external assessor can retain her or his 'objectivity'. The more they invest in understanding what is going on, the less objective they become, and yet to remain outside of the process involves the maintenance of a high level of ignorance.

The social audit process has attempted to deal with these issues through a two-stage approach to external validation. In the first instance, an external person—the auditor—develops and agrees a methodology with the organisation and stakeholders, and monitors the preparation of the social accounts. The social accounts are prepared by the organisation, however, rather than the auditor. During this process, the auditor is expected to become compromised to some degree in order to get close enough to the organisation to understand what is going on. This is acknowledged and accepted rather than hidden from view. Thus, to verify the accounts further, the auditor establishes an audit group, which considers the social accounts by interrogating the auditor and the organisation during a single session once the draft accounts have been prepared. The audit group includes people who can represent the interests of the key stakeholder groups involved and have expertise in issues related to the particular organisation's activities; for example, the New Economics Foundation's audit group consisted of people from different areas of the NGO community, such as Intermediate Technology, the Environment Council and the World Development Movement. It is through this latter dialogue that the values and concerns of the stakeholders are once again secured within the accounting process. It is centrally these values that create meaning for the accounts, rather than a professionalised (in the sense of 'devalued') accounting process.

Disclosure

The results must be disclosed to the stakeholders, as well as other possible groups. Thus, unlike traditional evaluations, the social audit is in the public domain. This is critical, since it is largely through public disclosure that the interests of diverse stakeholders are made effective. The significance of this stage of the social audit process cannot be overestimated. With financial audits, it is the fact of full disclosure that allows shareholders and other interested parties to assess the performance of the organisation and to decide whether to pressurise the organisation to change its practices, to purchase or to sell shares. The publication of social audits fulfils a similar purpose in the social domain. The revelation, for example, that a company has not traded according to its declared ethical principles or has acted against the values and interests of other stakeholders offers the opportunity for stakeholders to bring pressure on the organisation to change its practices, or at least to amend its declared principles in line with its practice.

Conclusion

Social auditing is an approach, not a solution. It allows organisations to move towards new forms of accountability without major shifts in ownership and organisation form. It allows for an evolutionary process of taking stakeholder interests more directly into account and having to report on activities according to their interests. Finally, through the information thrown up by social auditing and its open publication, it can be effective in reorienting the organisation's activities towards stakeholder interests.

16
adding values
the economics of
sustainable business*

co-written with Chris Tuppen

Economics and sustainability

Economic development is undoubtedly a prerequisite for sustainable development, especially for poorer nations and disadvantaged communities whose well-being is dependent on increased access to resources for both consumption and investment. But economic growth does not always deliver the levels of environmental security and distribution of income and wealth that are consistent with the underlying tenets of sustainable development. This implies a need to understand economic impacts and their relationship to sustainable development.

This is not always easy. What, for example, are the effects of investment in a new plant, or a shift of product procurement from local to international sources? These are not only economic but also social and environmental. In fact, the social and environmental effects arise largely through the economic effects. Therefore, there is a real need to be able to measure and effectively communicate the impact of specific activities on the economy, alongside their effects on people's lives and the natural environment.

But what exactly is economics?

The study of economics is traditionally about how people use scarce resources (land, labour, capital goods such as machinery, knowledge, etc.) to satisfy society's many wants. Scarcity of resources means that we have to make choices between

---

*   This chapter is a summary of the report 'Adding Values', first published as BT Occasional Paper 4. © 2000 BT Group plc, London.

competing wants, individually and collectively. Economics is about why and how those choices are made, and to what effect.

This traditional view of economics is useful, but can all too easily miss some issues that need to be confronted head-on in any serious inquiry into economics as it relates to sustainable development.

- **Economics and the environment.** Economics is concerned with how human and natural resources are used in pursuit of human welfare, both today and in the future. The problem is that, if a natural benefit is perceived to be free, such as fresh air, traditional economics gives it zero value. In addition, economic activities that destroy the environment or exploit natural resources, as well as the cost of cleaning up pollution, all count positively towards Gross Domestic Product (GDP). So our current measures of economics can include the wrong things, include the right things in perverse ways, or exclude the right things altogether.

- **Economics and society.** Similarly, since economics is about how people allocate resources in pursuit of human welfare, it is clearly not separate from the social dimension of sustainable development. Economics is rather another way of looking at decisions and events that also have social outcomes.

The economic dimension therefore lies entirely within the social, since it is about what individuals and societies do in allocating and managing scarce resources to satisfy human wants. The economic dimension also lies within the environmental, since the social system is nested within, and is thus a subset of, the ecological system. We can therefore usefully think of economic activities as being about the *means* rather than the *ends*. They are the means by which society transforms environmental resources, and the capacities and competencies of people and other species, into processes of production, distribution and consumption that enhance or detract from human (social) welfare.

Economics is no more or less than the process through which humans create social and environmental outcomes.

Economics counts—but who's counting what?

Strongly influenced by, and often reinforcing, voters' perception of the importance of their material standard of living, governments have historically identified their success in terms of measures of economic performance, such as GDP. Decades of such investment in increasingly accurate measures of the economy have, however, failed to establish agreed approaches to capture either all aspects of economic processes, or their social and environmental consequences.

> GNP measures neither our wit nor our courage, neither our wisdom nor our learning, neither our compassion nor our devotion to country. It measures everything, in short, except that which makes life worthwhile (Robert F. Kennedy).[1]

The **economics of business** has generally been taken to be synonymous with financial performance. However, the economic and financial are simply not equivalent. The financial concerns the market valuation of transactions that pass through a company's books. The economic, on the other hand, extends beyond the boundaries of the single organisation and takes into account activities in, and outcomes for, societies at large.

Of course, financial measures can capture elements of economic performance, at least in principle, if the actual financial price of all goods and services were equivalent to their full economic price (with all its social and environmental costs included). This incorporation (or, in economics jargon, **internalisation**) does not, however, exist in practice. Significant positive and negative 'externalities' (i.e. costs and benefits not taken into account) remain, so that financial data does not accurately reflect the economic, and therefore also the social and environmental, outcomes.

Company accounting

The financial accounts of a company in their current form miss much of what is important in economic terms. In fact there are no contemporary examples of companies adopting a systematic approach to accounting for, and reporting, their economic performance, let alone building it explicitly into transparent decision-making processes and linking it to social and environmental outcomes. There are, however, cases that illustrate the innovative use of financial data. South African Breweries, for example, reports on the distribution of the financial value it creates across its different stakeholders. This at least highlights some of the pathways along which there are economic impacts.

Even leading-edge companies that have publicly embraced the principle of 'triple bottom line' reporting have focused their economic reporting on an ad hoc bundle of performance measures covering profit and growth, dividends and shareholders return, tax, competition and investments.

Without clarifying the broader economics (as opposed to only the financials) of business, we cannot fully understand its contribution, or otherwise, to sustainable development.

Measuring the economics in sustainability

The economic impact of a business depends particularly on three things:

1. The nature of its goods and services, why and how they are consumed, and to what effect;

2. How it produces and distributes them, and;

3. Its significance in influencing the markets and societies right along its supply, operating and delivery chains.

Measuring and managing the economics of business is clearly important if companies are serious about aligning their strategies to the imperatives of sustainable development. In addition, measuring and communicating the economic footprint of business and how this in turn creates social and environmental outcomes is a prerequisite for companies wishing to engage in a meaningful long-term dialogue with key stakeholders.

But how can we capture these effects? How do we then interpret them within the context of sustainable development and what indicators might we use?

We propose that the starting point is identifying the principal domains of impact on the one hand and the main pathways of origination on the other.

Domains of impact

The domains of impact are the three primary parameters that together can be used to describe the nature of a company's interaction with the wider economy. They cover the level of influence (from direct to indirect), the scale (from micro to macro) and the geography (from local to global).

Direct to indirect

A company's most direct contribution to wealth creation is through employing people's competencies in creating goods and services and investing in new plant and equipment. Indirect impacts arise where a company's operations affect the economic activities and performance of others, both individuals and organisations. For example, where companies are inefficient or are able to levy high prices because of a monopoly position, the performance of other parts of the economies with which they operate may suffer.

Micro to macro

Whatever the scale of the business, all companies affect certain individuals and other businesses; these are micro-economic effects, which can be both direct and indirect. Large companies may also have an identifiable effect on macro-economic indicators such as a country's exchange rate, balance of payments, level of inflation and so on. Where this is the case the macro effects will be part of the company's indirect economic impact.

Local to global

A company's economic effect will differ depending on the geographical measurement framework. A decision, for example, by a bank to relocate a call centre away from the UK to the Republic of Ireland may well have negative economic effects on the former economy and positive ones on the latter. If the 'accounting entity' is Europe, on the other hand, there may be significant efficiency gains from the relocation that, on balance, benefit Europe as a whole.

Impact pathways

Impact pathways describe the sources of company connections with the wider economy, and for each pathway an evaluation can be made against each of the three domains.

Profit

Profitability is clearly a measure of business performance, and so also provides one indicator of the viability of the business in generating economic as well as financial wealth. A company that is not financially viable ceases to exist and contributes nothing. However, profitability is less helpful as a more specific measure of economic performance. For example, a business may be very profitable by behaving monopolistically, which in turn may have a negative economic effect in terms of both resource-use efficiency and overall human welfare (because, for example, consumer choice may be limited or prices artificially high).

Profitability is therefore a precondition for successful economic performance, but the fact that profits are being made, or even that taxes are being paid, does not tell us whether the company's economic impact is positive or negative.

Indicators: profits

- Indicator A: the level of profit achieved, measured in terms of what the company considers to be a 'reasonable' level of profitability

- Indicator B: total amount paid in dividend as a share of total financial value added

- Indicator C: geographical location of profits earned and amounts remitted across national boundaries

- Indicator D: the level of taxes paid, in which countries, and their levels as a proportion of country-specific and global profits

Investment and technology development

The economic impact of a company's investment portfolio can be broken down into several parts: primary effects (which derive from investment in people and equipment); secondary effects (for example, where skills may be developed); and tertiary effects (which are longer-term and stretch across geographical borders). For some companies, though, investment is not a major element of their economic impact. A typical non-manufacturing sportswear company will impact on Asian economies more through the volume and longevity of its orders. For other companies, however, their level of investment is a major source of economic impact, particularly in the areas of transport, utilities and telecommunications. Finally, technological development is a critical element of some investments. This is central to bringing about improvements in the efficient allocation and use of resources (both human and natural). Still, one must be careful not to assume that all technological innovations support sustainable development.

Indicators: investment

- Indicator A: the level of total investment broken down into broad categories such as fixed capital investment (e.g. plant and equipment), investment in knowledge (e.g. research and development, new products and processes) and acquisitions

Goods and services

The production of goods and services by businesses may have significant economic effects: (a) through individual use; e.g. smoking of cigarettes, which contribute to poor health and feed through to a series of negative economic effects, notably healthcare costs; (b) through business use; goods and services supplied by one company (e.g. telecommunications) will be used directly by other businesses in ways that will affect their financial performance and thereby contribute to broader collective economic outcomes.

Indicators: goods and services

- Indicator A: an evaluation, quantified wherever possible, of the externalised economic effects caused by the aggregation of many individual uses of the company's goods and services

- Indicator B: an evaluation, quantified wherever possible, of the contribution the company makes to the wider economy through the widespread application of its goods and services

Employment

The level of employment is often used as an indicator of a company's economic contribution, along with the wages and salaries paid in the process. There are, however, limits to the usefulness of such top-line indicators, as they don't account for the efficiency of employees, for example. It is goods and services produced, the efficiency of their production and their relevance in terms of needs, that are the true economic indicators. Since there is no obvious or easy way to capture this with direct measures, it is proposed here to use (despite its limitations) wages and salaries, as a measure of the implied productivity of those who earn such income and the secondary effects of the manner in which incomes are spent.

Indicators: employment

- Indicator A: the market value of people's productive capabilities measured by the number of employees, the annual wage and salaries bill, and the share of total financial value-added that accrues to employees, all broken down by geographic region

Human capital and knowledge development

On international stock exchanges many of today's most highly valued companies are those that have significant intangible assets. Such assets reflect value in knowledge, intellectual property, brand and reputation. It is in these virtual asset areas that tomorrow's economic value will be realised and where a consideration of the relationship of that economic value to sustainability will become increasingly important.

Indicator: human capital and knowledge

- Indicator A: the amount spent on training, broken down by the main training areas

- Indicator B: the breakdown of intangible assets: e.g. the value of brand, reputation, etc.

- Indicator C: company policy on the protection of intellectual property rights and technology transfer, especially with respect to new innovations that deliver significant social or environmental benefits

Outsourcing and procurement

The direct economic impact of procurement is clearly dependent on the amount of a company's direct spend in its supply chain. Beyond this, the longer-term economic effects of outsourcing and procurement depend on its impact on the development of people's technical skills, capacities to mobilise other business activities and the wider social and political environment. In general, the longer-term and more stable the business relationships embodied in supply chains, and the less mobile they are geographically, the more they influence the economic circumstances of specific communities and nations.

Indicators: outsourcing and procurement

- Indicator A: financial spend on outsourcing and procurement. The important issue here is to specify where the spend is being made (most likely by country or region), on what and over what time-frame

Public policy and practice: compliance and advocacy

All businesses should act within the law and operate within the terms of their operating licences. But that is not to say that they necessarily agree with the law or their regulator. This is why many companies seek to, and in practice do, influence public policy, individually in the case of large companies and collectively through chambers of commerce and trade associations for smaller enterprises. The position companies take on such matters are mainly based on considerations of their future profitability. However, there is little doubt that the influence business exerts over public policy can also have extensive economic effects.

Indicators: public policy

- Indicator A: the level of financial contributions made to political parties plus the disclosure of any other means of winning political support

- Indicator B: the company should state its position on relevant public policy issues and the routes through which it seeks to influence governments, including the membership of associations, clubs and other groups that lobby on its behalf

Community economies

One final pathway along which a company can have an economic impact is where it seeks *intentionally* to effect economic change for the social and environmental good, in addition to financial reasons. For example, leading companies are increasingly joining the struggle against social exclusion. In this case the traditional corporate community investment (CCI) element of company activity is focused on work, which seeks to rebuild the capacity of distressed communities to provide an enabling economic and social environment. Generally termed 'corporate social responsibility' or 'corporate citizenship', a wider role has developed that often involves the development of working partnerships with non-business organisations such as government departments and civil-society organisations. Where such partnerships extend into core business activities, there can be economic benefits to both the company and to the local community.

Indicator: community

- Indicator A: financial value of grants and contributions in kind (including volunteering) specifically targeted at community economic regeneration

- Indicator B: partnerships with core company activities (not the CCI department) that lead to activities that deliver community economic benefits

Accepting the challenge

Businesses that wish to align their strategy, operations and communications with some or all of the principles of sustainable development—for whatever reasons—will need to be able to understand, manage and communicate how their economic impacts link to social and environmental outcomes. This need will be particularly marked for those corporations that have the most significant economic impacts.

Effective management and communication requires, above all, the ability to measure economic impact within an analytical framework, which allows for robust, practical and commonly agreed interpretations. This chapter has sought to provide the beginnings of such a framework. Two principal sets of considerations—domains of impact and impact pathways—have been proposed. A number of possible economic indicators, which align with existing social and environmental indicators already used by many businesses in their social and environmental public reports, have also been suggested.

Sustainable development is about thinking holistically and the economic dimension is the one that most closely links the environmental to the social within the context of the company's business activities. In that sense it is an important key, but we must also recognise that, for the very reason that it moves to the very core of a company's *raison d'être*, it may need the most care in advancing.

In the context of sustainable development, it is impossible to consider the economic dimension in isolation from the social or the environmental, or, indeed, vice versa. So perhaps the time is coming when companies should cease compartmentalising the economic, the social and the environmental, in favour of new and innovative ways of reporting their 'joined-up' contributions to a more sustainable society.

17
impacts of reporting
the role of social and sustainability reporting in organisational transformation*

co-written with Catherine Rubbens, Philip Monaghan and Elena Bonfiglioni

'We hardly get any feedback on our report that we send out to thousands of people every year. We wonder if our stakeholders actually read it.'

'Our report clarifies misconceptions around our industry. It will inform those who wish to learn more about us on how we put our values into practice.'

'The activities we report on result from embedding corporate responsibility into our values, policies and practices.'

'We produce a report because we seek continuous transformation of our business practices. Communicating with our stakeholders pushes us to improve our policies, management systems and metrics.'

For over three decades many companies have put tremendous effort into the improvement of transparency, communication and accountability practices in the field of sustainability. For most companies, social and sustainability reports have been the preferred channel to their key stakeholders. Some have long reporting histories, with beginnings in the field of health, safety and environmental reporting; while others have produced their first sustainability or 'triple bottom line' report or are considering producing one in the near future. In parallel to business efforts to disclose such information, a wide variety of initiatives have been developed by 'professional' stakeholders to try and influence the direction that reporting will take.

---

* This chapter is a summary of the full report, 'Impacts of Reporting'. © 2002 CSR Europe, Brussels; and AccountAbility, London.

However, as the number of reports produced by the business community continues to increase, it has been accompanied by growing concern about their value for both companies and their stakeholders. Such reservations have been accentuated by growing associated costs and a surge of reporting standards, guidelines and awards. These initiatives, together with the activities of leading companies, have effectively enhanced the scope and technical quality of public reports. The question remains, however: what is the impact of reporting on stakeholder perceptions and actions, and ultimately on business behaviour, performance and outcomes?

This study by CSR Europe in association with AccountAbility aims to identify ways to assist companies in their efforts towards effective public reporting. Unlike many initiatives today, this is not an investigation into 'what' or 'how' to report. Rather, this study focuses on addressing the underlying question of **what kind of reporting makes a real difference** to what people think, and how they behave, both inside and outside of the business community? Most important is the fact that the research results and future suggestions within this study are based on the wealth of reporting experiences described by company practitioners.

The study is designed to encourage and enable effective reporting among companies as well as the many institutions that are involved in this wide field. First and foremost, it must be relevant to those companies that are actually reporting, or intending to do so in the future. In addition, it should resonate with those stakeholders who see public reporting as a means to achieving other ends, and so want to understand how best to maximise the effectiveness of reporting. Finally, the study should also enrich discussions among European institutions and national governments on creating an enabling environment for effective social and sustainability reporting.

This study is the first stage of a long-term collaboration between CSR Europe and AccountAbility to explore and advance the impacts of reporting. The research to date has been exploratory and intended to stimulate debate rather than propose definitive solutions. Specifically, the research has focused on extensive discussions within the business community. This has included several meetings of a business task force convened to guide and comment on the work and was complemented by a thorough analysis of examples of successful and innovative reporting practices.

To capture the needs of business people best, the research involved an interview programme covering 11 companies from a variety of sectors and different geographical regions of operation. The participating companies in the interview process were BT, Danone, Ford, McDonald's Restaurants, Manpower, Nike, Novozymes, Procter & Gamble, Royal Dutch/Shell, Unilever and Volkswagen. The 32 interviews involved discussions with representatives from a range of departments such as Sustainability and Environmental Management, Corporate Affairs, Purchasing, Investor Relations, and Human Resources—with the intention of mapping communication and accountability pathways within each company. This approach was supported by a preliminary review of relevant academic literature and discussions within a broad constituency of international experts.

Charting the field of impact: working hypotheses

The working approach adopted was to stimulate debate and discussion through the formulation of six interconnected 'hypotheses' about the impacts of reporting. These are outlined below, together with a summary that captures the common ground of responses given during the company interviews.

1. **Social and sustainability reporting must be placed in a broader context in order to fully understand its impacts.**

   New demands of investors, geographical and cultural variations, and the specific circumstances of individual companies all influence the impact of reporting. However, employee and customer relations are seen as the key motivators of companies in reporting.

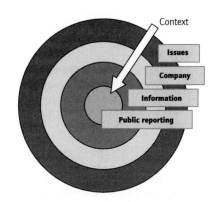

2. **Pressure, strategy and values are key drivers behind social and sustainability reporting. Over time, after an initial 'pressure-driven phase', companies will move towards an 'integrated approach'.**[1]

   Reporting is increasingly seen as integral to enabling engagement with stakeholders in understanding and shaping corporate long-term business strategy. For many companies, however, reporting may have a shorter-term objective of reputation management.

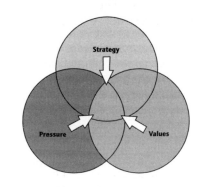

3. **Companies report on social and sustainability issues in order to change internal and external perceptions. Though stakeholder perceptions can be measured, the resulting change in stakeholder behaviour is more difficult to assess.**

   Companies often use conventional employee and

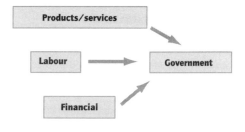

customer surveys to assess stakeholder perceptions, as well as non-traditional means such as NGO dialogue and socially responsible investment indices. In most instances, however, companies do not have a clear measure of the impact of reporting alone on stakeholder perceptions and behaviour.

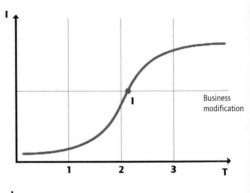

4. **The impact of reporting depends on its 'visibility', which diminishes over time, as well as its technical quality, which improves with time.**

Increasing the technical quality of reporting enhances its impact as a communication and management tool. Technical improvements enhance the internal visibility of reports, but external visibility and impact tend to diminish over time unless aligned to the newsworthiness of a broader corporate communication strategy.

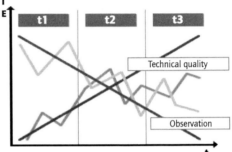

5. **The internal impact of reporting is dependent on shifts in stakeholder perceptions, but will be constrained beyond a critical point unless organisational culture and business systems change.**

Reporting (including stakeholder responses to it) was seen to stimulate internal dialogue that can create significant changes in decision-making and strategy. Companies recognised the potential for this effect to be limited over time, but had not in the main experienced it in relation to social and sustainability reporting.

While it is difficult to attribute change in business behaviour and performance to reporting alone,

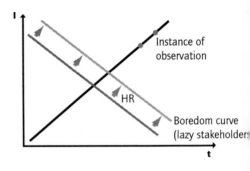

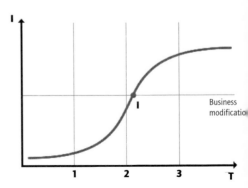

the process of reporting in itself (as well as stakeholder responses to it) can act as a stimulus for internal dialogue that affects big change in terms of decision-making and strategy.

6. **Effective reporting requires communications with external stakeholders to be targeted through different 'pathways'.**
Companies use a range of communication channels to optimise effectiveness, including hard copy reports and the Internet due to the web being 'anywhere, anytime' (and relatively cheap). However, they tend not to assess the costs and benefits of their choices in cash terms as it is hard to measure intangible impacts such as reputation.

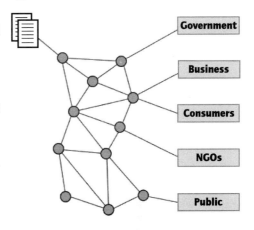

Reporting rationale: what makes it count

Drawing on the results of the case-study interviews and meetings with companies and desk research, some key elements can be elicited that should inform and shape further discussion and analysis on how to enhance the impacts of reporting.

- **The 'transformational' understanding of reporting is more valuable than the 'classical'.** There are two fundamentally different views about the impact of reporting. The 'classical' view holds that public reporting on past experience has an impact only if it changes the perceptions of the report's readers, primarily external stakeholders. If stakeholders change their behaviour as a result of such changed perceptions, this in turn might impact on business decisions, activities and outcomes. The 'transformational' view goes one step further because it drives changes within a company. It holds that the process of reporting, including the very commitment to report itself, can impact on business decisions and outcomes. Such changes would not necessarily occur as a result of changes in stakeholder perceptions, although such perceptions may provide the drivers for reporting.

- **Innovation in stakeholder engagement is key to success.** To more effectively engage with different stakeholders, companies need to be responsive and creative in the way they choose to communicate with different individuals and groups. Different people have variable levels of awareness, interest and information need. Some stakeholders such as mainstream investors express limited enthusiasm for corporate responsibility data. Business could proactively seek their views on how to more appropriately balance communications on social and sustainability issues with financial information. In targeting audiences in this way it should also be appreciated that 'segmenting' combinations of communication channels needs to consider usability, access and different levels of awareness, interest and information needs. It is also important to ensure that a 'segmented' or tailored approach to communication should cater to usability, access and different levels of awareness. Despite the Internet's lower costs and greater coverage, not everybody has the technical capacity to utilise it or simply prefer not to, and would be more receptive and responsive to the paper version or other forms of communication.

- **Assurance increases the effectiveness of reporting by enhancing management systems.** Assurance of trustworthiness of what companies publish in public reports is relevant in building stakeholders' trust, which in turn will tend to support the development of their perceptions about, and affect their decisions that impact on, the company. Effective assurance processes foster internal learning, skills development and more effective decision-making supported by stronger/strengthening management systems. The combined external and internal effects of assurance confirm its importance in influencing the impact of reporting.

A tool for transformation

A decade of learning through experimentation, and efforts to clarify how to provide social and sustainability reporting, present the business community and other stakeholders with a double opportunity: first, to evaluate the conditions that ensure that social and sustainability reporting can make a real difference; second, working together to build an enabling environment for transformation, where public reporting can take its place as one productive tool for enhancing overall business performance.

Despite the current lack of full understanding around certain aspects of the impacts of social and sustainability reporting, many companies consider it valuable to themselves and their stakeholders. One suggestion is that companies, in cooperation with other key stakeholders, reflect on a more holistic process of stakeholder communication and engagement, and identify ways through which reporting can be better linked to their communication and management tools and systems.

Based on the research summarised in this report, CSR Europe and AccountAbility have identified **five key areas** for further research and investigation on impacts of social and sustainability reporting. We invite the business community, together with its partners, to reflect on the relevance and appropriateness of these research avenues and to engage in pursuing them:

1. **Context matters.** Identification of how context-specific factors influence the impacts of reporting, including an analysis of the differences across geographical regions, sectors, and types of organisation.

2. **A 360° perspective of stakeholder communication.** Consideration of both companies and their stakeholders as participants in a 'full' transformation process. This would help them determine effective, proactive and responsive communication approaches. A full impact assessment of stakeholder engagement would include a 360° analysis involving interviews with both businesses and representatives of key stakeholders, and also how the issue of assurance should be approached.

3. **Reporting as a driver for change in business practices.** Establishing the connection between reporting, management practices and governance, including impacts on business partners such as suppliers. Key considerations for this work should be assurance and risk. It would also build on existing academic research concerning the link between shareholder value and accounting for intangible assets such as reputation and intellectual capital.

4. **Materiality and boundaries.** Analysis into the identification, selection and coverage of stakeholder issues in reports. This would help management decide how best to balance what is relevant for them and what is relevant for their stakeholders, and also how the issue of assurance should be approached.

5. **Future of reporting.** Closely linked with academic research on the value of the firm, as well as analysing internal and external factors that are likely to affect reporting contents, coverage and format in the future. It would extrapolate conclusions from different scenarios around stakeholder information needs, communications strategies and regulatory frameworks.

The role of stakeholders

All stakeholders have a collective role to play in fostering the positive impacts of reporting, and enhancing the transparency, effectiveness and efficiency of corporate communication in the field of corporate responsibility. A stronger exchange of information and education among key partners will be of great value on this journey.

As partners in this project, CSR Europe and AccountAbility welcome the opportunity to share the outcomes of this 'Impacts of reporting' study with reference partners at the European, national and global levels including the European Institutions, the Global Reporting Initiative (GRI), the Global Compact, OECD, Siri Group, Eurosif, and other organisations.

- At the **European level**, we look forward to contributing to the work of the European Multi-stakeholder Forum on Corporate Social Responsibility

(CSR EMS Forum),[2] initiated by the European Commission. The CSR EMS Forum is expected to be a key platform for stakeholders to have a constructive dialogue and explore learning opportunities around the key theme of transparency and corporate responsibility practices and tools. We hope to interact with the members of the CSR EMS Forum, and encourage it to go beyond traditional discussions on 'how to report' and 'what to report on' by placing more emphasis on questions such as 'what are the impacts of reporting?'

- With regard to **public policy**, we welcome the European Commission's facilitating role in providing fora for debate, such as the CSR EMS Forum. We also welcome the Commission's commitment in its communication on sustainable development to produce its own sustainability report by 2004. This clearly indicates that the transformational change reached through enhanced transparency does not only concern multinational enterprises but also investors, charities and public-sector organisations.

- **Standard-setting organisations** such as GRI and the International Organisation for Standardisation (ISO) could contribute to ensuring that reporting to stakeholders is part of a wider process, both internally and externally. They could help foster those initiatives that encourage beyond reporting in isolation. Approaches focused on business risk-related reporting to investors could be nurtured and drawn from. The same is true for approaches to social and sustainability-related assurance frameworks, such as the broad-based AA1000 Assurance Standard as well as auditing systems focused on specific areas of concern such as labour standards and the environment.

- The **financial community** is key to providing a foundation for the commonly shared goal of increased transparency and more effective corporate reporting. Thus, they need to send clearer signals to business on how their investment decisions and activities are affected by information disclosure in the field of corporate responsibility. Ultimately, this would clarify the link between corporate responsibility practices and investors' evaluation of good management practices and long-term business success.

- An improved understanding of the impacts of reporting will enhance the effectiveness of reporting as an instrument to improve business practices and outcomes. The **academic community** could be instrumental in promoting knowledge and improving the dialogue between practitioners, policy-makers and researchers. We welcome the European Commission's support for initiatives that promote research on social and sustainability reporting and transparency—in the context of the Commission's newly launched Sixth Framework Programme. We hope that business schools and universities working together in networks such as the European Academy of Business in Society and the European Association of Universities will lead the way in these efforts.

18
redefining
materiality
making reporting
more relevant*

co-written with Mira Merme

The answer to the question of how to define 'materiality' is being sought by companies and their stakeholders alike. Understanding what is material is core to many aspects of corporate governance and accountability, notably the basis on which boards of directors, investors and other interested stakeholders make decisions that drive business performance and outcomes.

Where reporting and assurance are required or desired, the importance of a redefinition of 'materiality' is particularly crucial (AccountAbility 2003a). The current emphasis on reporting as a key 'corporate responsibility' accountability mechanism raises the stakes in making *effective* reporting of fundamental importance. If stakeholders don't think that the information is relevant, it just won't count. Unfortunately, evidence suggests that current 'sustainability reporting' leaves much to be desired in this regard (AccountAbility/CSR Europe 2002). The challenge is to disclose information on social and environmental performance that is material to business performance, whether directly or because its stakeholders care and will in the future make their caring count.

Current definitions of materiality, and their practical interpretation, are not up to the task of guiding companies in the identification of the growing range of non-financial factors relevant to business success. As a result, and in advance of regulatory changes, materiality is being redefined on the ground, through pressures on business from wider civil society, precedents established by company practice and, increasingly, regulation. Associated with this redefinition are a new generation of instruments that offer alternative frameworks. The Dow Jones Sustainability Index, for example, establishes materiality in terms of best-in-class performers in managing social and environmental factors that drive financial performance. The Operating and Financial Review (OFR) of the proposed UK Company Law, similarly, frames non-financial disclosure firmly within a 'business

---

performance' model, while allowing (at this stage) considerable latitude in inter-preting what this can, and cannot, cover. The Global Reporting Initiative Guidelines focus mainly on what is important to society, but less on what is material in any particular situation, although the GRI's sector guidelines will enhance sector-based materiality. AccountAbility's AA1000 Assurance Standard is rooted in a specific defi-nition of materiality, concerning whether 'the reporting organisation has included in the public report adequate information about its sustainable performance for its stakeholders to be able to make informed judgments, decisions and actions'.

A host of initiatives are actively contributing to this process of redefining mate-riality in practice and policy (Zadek and Merme 2004),[1] including AccountAbility and the World Economic Forum's initiative 'Mainstreaming Responsible Invest-ment' (Zadek and Merme 2004). Beyond these 'sustainability' initiatives, the far more extensive changes taking place in corporate governance and practice are also reshaping the interpretation of materiality, for example the US Sarbanes–Oxley Act 2002, the current revisions to UK Company Law and Stock Exchange Listing regula-tions,[2] as well as the major legislative changes in the European Union with the harmonisation of banking, listing and company law (Merme 2003), the new listing requirements in the Johannesburg Stock Exchange, and other major changes impacting disclosure in the financial markets such as the French Vienot II[3] reforms and German corporate governance reforms.[4]

AccountAbility's own contribution to this debate, policy formation and practice has been to develop a set of proposals for how companies can in practice system-atically work with an extended definition of materiality. These proposals build on the work underpinning the AA1000 Assurance Standard, and also the richness underlying for example, the GRI Guidelines, SIGMA and other initiatives.

At the core of the proposal is a **five-part test** (see Figure 25) in determining what is material, and so what to disclose, summarised below.

1. Test one covers the traditional **direct short-term financial impacts** of sustainability performance, i.e. where they appear as significant items on profit and loss and/or balance sheets; 'carbon emissions' is a good example of this.

2. Aspects of **policy-based performance** where agreed policy positions of a strategic nature exist, irrespective of short-term financial consequences. This test seeks to pressure companies to disclose and effectively manage aspects of performance associated with declared policies, such as social and environmental aspects increasingly included in companies' core busi-ness principles.

3. **Peer-based norms** can be determined where a company's peers are deem-ing and disclosing issues and aspects of performance to be material. An example is food companies disclosing information on the use of GMOs in food products because enough consumers have made it known that GMO-free product was a basis of their purchasing decisions. Were one particular food company to deem this issue to be immaterial, then under this test they would have to explain why they considered themselves to be different from their market peers.

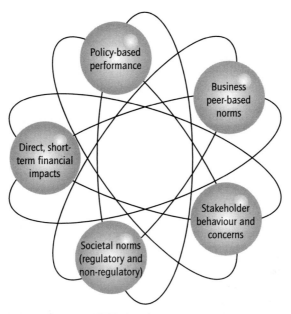

FIGURE 25 FIVE-PART MATERIALITY TEST

4. **Stakeholder behaviour and concerns** are relevant to corporations where there is reasonable evidence that their stakeholders' (such as employees, clients, suppliers and communities) perspectives on the company are likely to impact on their decisions and behaviour. Important here is that stakeholders' views alone are not sufficient to be deemed material—it is behavioural change that makes it material. For example, it is one thing to say that people care whether Marks & Spencer's deals fairly with workers in their global supply chains, but it is quite another to argue that they care enough to act on these concerns in their roles as investors, employees, customers or regulators.

5. The fifth and final test is the consideration of **societal norms**. Beyond regulation, the test would include aspects of performance that are likely to become regulated in the future. In the mid-1990s, for example, the application of this element would have shown the likely advent of anti-corruption legislation emerging on the back of the OECD agreement on foreign corrupt practices. A further element would include emerging norms within the investment community with regard to their own responsibilities. The Association of British Insurers' (ABI) risk reporting guidelines would be a case in point. Finally, international developments might reflect strong indications of emerging societal norms, such as the UN Global Compact's principles.

The five-stage test and related process proposals provide a coherent and consistent approach to redefining materiality that is appropriate not only for 'sustainability reporting' but in a number of crucial related aspects of metrics and disclosure, including both internal and external assurance and risk reporting, stock exchange listing requirements, corporate governance assessments, credit status ratings (e.g. Fitch), and public procurement criteria.

Crucially, the proposals offer a careful balance by extending the interpretation of materiality, while also offering a framework for application that guides company directors and assurance providers more effectively than many existing approaches. Viewed through the eyes of company directors, their concern is often that of the likelihood of litigation over disclosure that is seen to misrepresent the truth. Regulation such as the Sarbanes–Oxley and UK Company Law all broaden the potential for such litigation, and company directors are calling for more guidance to ensure that they have taken 'reasonable care' in their deliberations on disclosure since there is rarely a legal 'safe harbour' available.

In summary, the main advantages of these proposals are:

- **Bridging interests:** links narrow financial and broader 'sustainability' interests into one methodology

- **Evolving practice:** enables companies to evolve capacity over time to assess and manage material factors

- **Compatible with current legislation:** underpins and reinforces legal realignment of materiality and fiduciary duty (e.g. company law)

- **Integrative with future legislation:** does not inhibit the process of legislation yet is compatible with voluntary standards

- **Director guidance and protection:** gives company directors measure of legal protection ('reasonable care')

- **Enhance voluntary 'responsibility' standards:** particularly GRI Guidelines and other 'broadband' reporting standards

- **Assurability:** provides clear basis for assurance (internal and external) of process for determining materiality (and consistent with AA1000 Assurance Standard)

It is of crucial importance that materiality is defined appropriately in order to make social, environmental and economic metrics useful in the process of decision-making. This is true for internal and external decisions, made by those interested in narrow financial interests as well as those concerned with companies' broader performance. Public policy has an opportunity to make a significant change in the way in which risk is identified and disclosed, and how information is reported. By so doing it can significantly improve stakeholder perceptions of the financial and business community. For tomorrow's corporate sustainability reporting to be effective, and so to survive, requires that it communicates information that is 'material' to stakeholders in their efforts to make coherent decisions and take planned and timely actions relevant to their interests.

Section IV
the civil corporation

19
looking back
from 2050*

Looking back from today, it is hard to believe how we got from our late-20th-century economy to the way things are today. Then was the time when corporations were still free-standing economic islands, like the isolated geographic communities of earlier centuries. It was the time of the 'brand wars', and when shareholders were still the main driver of corporate performance. Clear boundaries still existed between business, the state and civil society.

Imagine living at the end of the last millennium. There was unparalleled prosperity for some. World consumption was worth $22 trillion, mainly feeding the frivolous habits of just one billion out of the planet's 6 billion people. The world's 225 richest individuals held a combined wealth of over US$1 trillion, equal to the annual income of the world's poorest 2.5 billion people. Nearly one in three of the world's workforce was unemployed, and 840 million people went hungry each day.

The corporate community still played a relatively small role compared to today. Only 51 of the 100 largest 'economies' in the world were corporations. The top 200 corporations had sales equivalent to only one-quarter of the world's total economic activity. Just think: 75% of the world's economic activity lay outside of the real economy, in what today is little more than the 'hobby economy'.

It is easy to see with hindsight the signs of the changes that have swept through our lives in the last half a century. During that early stage of 'glocalisation', corporations were already dispersing their functions into market webs through franchising and outsourcing. The sources of value-added and profit were already rooted in supply management rather than production, and in brand rather than product. Technological developments in the areas of computing and communications had vastly reinforced this tendency to disperse corporate functions, although they had not really yet transformed the personal domain into the 'hot-homes' we experience today.

It was the first era of the truly global civil society, although it was seen to be separate from the corporate community. Civil groups, which previously focused on narrow, local or perhaps national agendas, increasingly found voice at international levels. They took advantage of exactly the same set of technological and organisational shifts, and increasingly played a role of challenging the globalised brands

* First published in the *European Review of Business Ethics* 8.3 (July 1999). © Blackwell Publishing, Oxford.

by a technique called 'ethical intermediation', a practice as odd as the convention of the time to trade currencies. For a period they were the main civilising force of production and trade, with the decline in the role of both nation-states and the traditional protectors of the weak, such as trade unions.

The term 'stakeholder corporation' took root in this period. At its heart, the term referred to the idea of companies building trust and integrity into their key relationships. Managers were largely bewildered by this notion, since the connection between people's needs and corporate interests had been virtually severed over the preceding century. There was a colourful but largely fruitless debate as to whether this was a business or an ethical strategy. The more visionary leaders saw that a value-led approach to business offered a way of increasing the profitability of increasingly complex webs of suppliers, franchisees and customers. We have seen that these companies have been most adept at taking advantage of technological, regulatory and other changes that we have experienced through the first half of this century.

We can barely imagine today the terrain of that time. It marked the turning point for the nation-state and its various supernational creations, none of which seemed able to cope with the chaotic systems that make or break environmental and social gains and losses. Hardly any wonder that it was all such a mess really. They saw the economy as somehow separate from the rest of society. Even the most progressive thinking understood the world as comprising the social, the environmental and the economic. Today this seems as peculiar to us as the view, from an earlier epoch, that the sun went around the earth must have seemed to them.

It is hard to conceive of this as the forerunner of the great agreement of 2009, which gave us today's Framework for the New Economy (WBCSD 2009).

New communication patterns emerged during that disturbing but fertile period. Communication patterns for day-to-day business, and those needed for stakeholder accountability, imploded into each other. Companies realised that what made suppliers effective was identical to what motivated them in their family life. What secured a long-term client was a level of shared values that extended well beyond narrow notions of business–place relationships.

Social and ethical accounting and auditing developed into a core and essential element of business success. What started as an imitation of financial reporting evolved into an ongoing process of dialogue that gave all stakeholders unparalleled access to company information and to each other. Real-time social reporting became the norm, with stakeholders able to access the underlying social accounts and electronic tools in analysing aspects of companies' behaviour relevant to their own particular interests (AccountAbility 2001).

Companies began to resemble what they are today: 'value-based webs' that bring stakeholders into productive networks with each other.

So what happened to the brands? Well, by the early part of this century, branding had become the dominant source of financial value in virtually all supply chains. New environmental and social standards, backed by legislation, had encouraged markets to consolidate down to one or two corporations and a small number of brands. Unbranded products were almost non-existent, and in some countries illegal (under the 2005 anti-dumping agreement that emerged from the Millennium Round of the World Trade Organisation negotiations).

Up to the 2020s, brands referred to products owned by one company. The 'Swoosh' sign for sports goods and services used to be owned by a company called Nike, the 'Oyster' sign for energy by a company called Shell, the 'O' sign for information technology was actually the brand for a small subsidiary company called Origin, and so on.

The wave of mergers that took place in the late 2020s—what became known as the 'final wave'—completed the process of turning the dominant brands into generic names. Competition became internalised within the value-webs. There was just no place to distinguish between different brands of shoe, since there were no footloose consumers. The only issue for the consumer was which value-webs they belonged to and so would of course buy from.

But of course to understand this shift one has to trace the biggest change of all: the collapse of the specialist shareholder. It is hard to imagine just what was going on at the end of the last century, and here is not the place to try to describe it in depth. Shareholders drove the imperative for short-term profitability because of managers' fears of takeover bids driving them out of their positions if dividends were too low. This was the norm, although shareholders knew little or nothing about the business itself. Indeed, the proportion of invested funds coming from equity was in any case tiny, because major corporations increasingly invested using internally generated funds. Here was a case of the tail wagging the dog.

The global financial meltdown of 2009 changed all this. It was the so-called 'grey dollar' that finally tipped the applecart. By then, over 65% of the equity of the world's major companies was owned indirectly by about 400 million people over 60 years old, with most of the rest owned by people investing for their future old age. Competition for pensions had led to increasingly flexible withdrawal terms, and the bankruptcy of several major financial institutions in 2007 precipitated a global financial pandemic, with old and young alike trying to withdraw their accumulated pension savings.

Virtually every major financial institution faced bankruptcy. Governments watched helplessly, tied by the so-called 'Brown Regime' dating to 2003 which had made it illegal for them to intervene in the financial markets (WTO 2003).

Eventually, a group of 150 of the world's largest corporations came together through the World Business Council for Sustained Development to purchase the bulk of these financial institutions. Governments sanctioned this backward integration as the only hope of avoiding a gigantic economic and human calamity. In effect, these corporations had retrieved their equity (at a knock-down price), and neutralised the world's stock markets.

One further major change followed on the heels of this extraordinary development, which in its early stages became known as 'rented' or 'stakeholder' equity. Picking up on what had been seen as eccentric ideas from Australia in the early 1990s, corporations realised that the value of stakeholder relationships could be enhanced by renting equity to those who wanted to contribute to the business process, whether as producer, trader, communicator or consumer. This, then, became a powerful underpinning for the second-generation stakeholder corporations, which in turn evolved into internally branded value-webs.

Just one final point about that period: key shakers and movers at that time were preoccupied with the purpose of business. Some considered that progress required that business broaden its purpose to one that embraced social and environmental as well as financial aims. Some people wanting companies to behave better argued the 'long-term business case' for being more inclusive. Others argued that corporations had to be got rid of for economic democracy and social equity to be achieved.

The emergence of value-webs rooted in stakeholder equity was at the time welcomed by some as the means of addressing the needs of the marginalised within a global capitalist system. And, to be fair, it has helped a great deal, bringing people in the business chain more closely together, and so creating conditions for reducing inequities between them. The purpose of these value-webs has shifted to include wider interests of its members.

But, as we know, the facts of poverty, social inequality and environmental degradation still exist. There are wealthy and impoverished value-webs. There was a moment in time in 2009 when the big corporates still had real economic and political power. They were a force for change, for better or worse. But today such consolidated power no longer exists. No one seriously believes today that any single group of institutions are in a position to mould the global chaotics. We have achieved the localised order dreamed of by 20th-century utopians, but at what cost?

Looking back from today, 1 January 2050, much has happened over the last half a century. Many problems still exist—including poverty, inequality and conflict. Many of the radical aspirations of the last century have been long abandoned, often with sadness and pain. Some of what we once were sure were to be immutable gains turned out to be short-lived virtues, notably the 19th-century liberal model of representative, electoral democracy. The price of stability and reasonable equity, for those within the high-values webs, has certainly been high.

But what most strikes me looking back was the role of fantasy, or perhaps its lack. Imagine what was in the minds of the citizens of 50 years ago. Those with the power to make change dissipated their energies in despair and nihilism, disguised as a hedonistic consumerism. In this state, things were as they were because they were, for better or worse.

The incredible changes that have since happened did not really take place through visionary purpose, although history reports a few such people. Change seems to have been made up of half-baked solutions to unexpected crises. Some of us are fortunate because of how these crises have been resolved, but by no means all. This realisation challenges us not to relive the despair of our 20th-century ancestors, and not to rely on coincidence and luck. It challenges us to mould a practice of tomorrow based on today's utopia.

20

can corporations be civil? *

Many of Britain's best-known companies are already redefining the traditional roles of the corporation. They are recognising that every customer is part of the community and that social responsibility is not an optional extra.

Rt. Hon. Tony Blair MP, British Prime Minister[1]

If business is so powerful, and is now doing so much good, why is so much wrong in the world?

Oded Grajew, President, Instituto Ethos[2]

The role of business in society is this century's most important and contentious public policy issue. Business is increasingly moulding societal values and norms, and defining public policy and practice, as well as being the dominant route through which economic and financial wealth is created. How business is done will underpin how future local and global communities address social and environmental visions and imperatives. This is true whatever one believes to be critical in creating a just and sustainable world. Economic welfare, peace and security, global warming, human and animal welfare—just to name a few—are and will continue to be deeply informed by business in practice.

* This is Chapter 1 of the book *The Civil Corporation: The New Economy of Corporate Citizenship*. © 2001 Earthscan Publications, London. This piece makes reference to chapters that also appeared in that book.

Our views of business today hang in the balance. On the one hand, business is in the limelight of increasingly concerned public scrutiny. The popular media carries daily fresh allegations of its misdemeanours. An outpouring of books, pamphlets, films and conferences challenge and debate their social and environmental performance. Grass-roots, anti-corporate demonstrations adorn the streets outside city offices, and regularly surround meetings of the world's leaders and major international institutions. On the other hand, recent years have seen the emergence of the philosophy and practice of 'corporate citizenship'. Corporations have sought under this umbrella to gain broader trust and legitimacy through visibly enhancing their non-financial performance. Today, the focus is shifting from philanthropy to the impact of core business activities across the broad spectrum of social, environmental and economic dimensions represented by the vision of sustainable development.

Surprisingly little has been said about where this critical debate and practice might lead us in the future. Activists leading the assault on corporate power and influence have in the main remained entrenched in their negative critique. Few have mapped out credible alternatives for generating and distributing sufficient economic wealth to provide a decent quality of life for a growing world population. Similarly, few corporate citizenship advocates have addressed the challenge as to whether or how such approaches are likely to deliver adequate social and environmental gains to reverse the underlying pattern of growing levels of poverty, inequality and environmental insecurity.

In addressing the *why*, the *how* and the *so what* of corporate citizenship, this book seeks to establish what should and can realistically be expected from the business community in addressing the imperatives and aspirations underpinning sustainable development. Secondly, it addresses whether and how these expectations can in practice be realised. It seeks to achieve this by exploring:

- Contemporary forms of corporate citizenship emerging from the dynamics of the New Economy

- New patterns of civil governance underlying emerging partnerships between business, governments and private non-profit organisations

- The scope for engagement, learning and advocacy that corporations have in maximising their contribution to sustainable development

- Under what conditions corporate citizenship can play a significant role in addressing the darkest sides of unsustainable development

Global balance sheet

Much has happened in the last century. As a species we have become taller, faster and stronger. We have learned how to dominate our natural environment—and to appreciate its ability to strike back. We have experienced terrifying excesses of nationalism and racism—and matched this with expressions of universal values such as those underpinning the vision of the United Nations. Democracy, at least the elective version, came into its own in the 20th century, building from the revolutions of the 19th century to South Africa's liberation struggle.

But the most pervasive outcome of the last hundred years has been the incredible growth of economic wealth and the associated level of material consumption. Certainly, the industrial revolution marked the onset of a rapid acceleration in the income and wealth of a small but significant minority in Europe and North America. But it was during the last century that this acceleration took on quantum proportions. The global economy at the turn of the millennium was driven by annual expenditure on consumption of almost US\$30 trillion, a doubling in just 25 short years (UNDP 1998). By the turn of the 20th century, a billion or so people were experiencing extraordinary material standards of living. Average incomes across this group rose at least sixfold between 1900 and 2000.[3]

Economic growth has unquestionably delivered real gains. Few could quibble about the improvements in most of the better-known indicators of human development, such as personal health, literacy and longevity for enormous numbers of people. As the United Nations Human Development Report in 1999 concluded:

> people in many countries live a much longer and healthier life than just two decades ago. In 31 of the 174 countries included in the Human Development Index (HDI), life expectancy has increased by more than a fifth since 1975 . . . Between 1975 and 1997 most countries made substantial progress in human development, reducing their shortfall from the maximum possible value of the HDI. Of the 79 countries for which HDI trends between 1975 and 1997 are available, 54 made up more than 20% of their shortfall, 31 more than 30 per cent and 19 more than 40 per cent (UNDP 1999: 129-30).

The United Nations *Human Development Report 2000*, similarly, highlights that:

> The achievement of human potential reached unprecedented heights in the 20th century . . . Worldwide, 46 countries, with more than a billion people, have achieved high human development . . . In developing countries during the past three decades, life expectancy increased by 10 years . . . adult literacy increased by half . . . and the infant mortality rate declined by more than two fifths (UNDP 2000: 4).

Well-documented facts are equally clear on the negative side of the equation. Nearly one in three of the world's workforce is unemployed (Lewnhak 1997), 1.2 billion people live on less than US\$1 a day (UNDP 2000: 4), and 840 million people go hungry each day (UNDP 2000: 4). The world's 225 richest individuals have a combined wealth of over US\$1 trillion, equal to the annual income of the world's poorest 47%—2.5 billion people. A further 100 million in the developed world are relatively impoverished.

Over the same period, the state of the natural environment has worsened. The climate has noticeably changed, half the world's original forest cover has disappeared, and overall the Earth's ecosystems are degrading at about 3% a year (Zadek and Tuppen 2000: 2). The growth in consumption has been underpinned by a mushrooming in the use of natural resources, and in the levels of waste and emissions; a quintupling of fossil fuel use since 1950; and a doubling of the use of fresh water since 1960. As the ecologist and writer Paul Hawken poetically notes about the United States economy, 'For every 100 pounds of product we manufacture . . . we create at least 3,200 pounds of waste' (Hawken 1997).

Consumption patterns of the materially well-off have taken on proportions that would be comic if they were not equally tragic. The United Nations points out that Europe and the US spend almost US$13 billion annually on perfume, and almost US$18 billion on pet food; Europeans annually spend more than US$50 billion on cigarettes, and Japanese business runs up an annual entertainment account of almost US$35 billion (UNDP 1998). Against this must be compared the profile of consumption of the typical household in a developing country, where about 80% goes on buying basic foodstuff. Equally it compares with the estimated annual cost of only US$40 billion, according to the UN, that it would take to achieve universal access to all basic services, such as basic education, water and sanitation (UNDP 1998).

Confusing causalities

Facts abound, but what do they mean? Is the heady consumption of wealthier citizens a constraining factor to development for others—the zero-sum view that the wealth of the few condemns many to poverty? Or is such profligate consumption the salvation of those currently in poverty? Many argue, after all, that what is needed is for those without enough to emulate, catch up and join the party. Sakiko Furkado-Parr, Director of the UN Human Development Office, captures perhaps the middle path between these views when she argues that:

> It is not a matter of more or less consumption. I cannot agree with the hair-shirt view that less consumption will make the world a better place. The issue is what kind of consumption—of ensuring that consumption is not environmentally destructive, and that it challenges poverty and inequality.[4]

Such diversity of opinion feeds through, naturally, to contested views about the role of economic growth in promoting human development and environmental security. As the UN, among many, reminds us:

> **The link between economic prosperity and human development is neither automatic nor obvious.** Two countries with similar income per capita can have very different HDI values; countries with similar HDI values can have very different income levels. Of the 174 countries, 92 rank higher on the HDI than on Gross Domestic Product (GDP) per capita (Purchasing Power Parity—PPP$), suggesting that these countries have been effective in converting income into human development. But for 77 countries the HDI rank is lower than the GDP per capita (PPP$) rank. These countries have been less successful in translating economic prosperity into better lives for people.[5]

Our understanding of what-causes-what is not obviously enhanced through increased volumes of data. The economically wealthiest countries certainly offer up the most comprehensive data imaginable, but the results continue to confound us. Economic competitiveness, we are often told, is the foundation of long-term societal success. But we know, equally, that economic competitiveness does not always yield the promised social dividends. For example, the Republic of Ireland, US and UK figure in the top ten competitive nations, according to Jeffrey Sachs and the World Economic Forum (Sachs *et al.* 1999: 15). But this efficient club of three turns out to be the same group identified by the UN as having the highest levels of poverty and inequality among industrialised nations.

> Among the 17 industrialised countries included in the HPI-2 [measure of human poverty], Sweden has the lowest human poverty, with 7 per cent followed by the Netherlands and Germany, with 8.3 per cent and 10.4 per cent. The industrialised countries with the highest poverty according to the HPI-2 are the United States (16.5 per cent), Ireland (15.3 per cent) and the United Kingdom (15.1 per cent) (UNDP 1999: 131).

Tramline debate

The most confusing facts of all concern the contested contributions of business, particularly the corporate community, to the positive and negative sides of last century's overall accounts. The corporate community is vast and rapidly growing. Of the 100 largest 'economies' in the world today, 51 are corporations (Anderson and Cavanagh 1996). The top 200 corporations have sales equivalent to one-quarter of the world's total economic activity (quoted in Wheeler and Sillanpää 1997). General Motors has annual sales equivalent to the GDP of Denmark, and the annual sales of Sears Roebuck's is comparable to the total annual income of over 100 million Bangladeshis (Utting 2000: 5). There has been a twelvefold increase in world trade since 1945, dominated by a small number of global corporations. This trade now accounts for about 20% of measured, global economic income. The 1990s witnessed a massive growth in the pattern of international capital flows to developing countries. In 1990, public sources accounted for more than half of the international money flowing to developing countries. By 1995, 77% came from private sources (World Bank 1997). The volume of foreign direct investment nearly quadrupled over the same period, jumping to US$96 billion by 1995 (taken from Zarsky 1999). Foreign direct investment has increased by 27% in just one year, 1997 (UNCTAD 1998, quoted in WDM 1998).

With so large a footprint, one might expect that corporations' contribution to the global accounts would be utterly obvious. Far from it. Indeed, the facts have underpinned a largely polarised debate about the contribution of the corporate community. Facts abound, but they seem inadequate to the task of building a common view as to whether corporations are at the leading edge of positive change, or irreducibly part of the problem. This polarisation is plain to see in the veritable outpouring of publications about the future of the corporation, backed by conferences, workshops, Internet-based debates, counselling-based 'confrontations', and every other possible form of interaction. Every possible statistic, anecdote and mystical vision has been fashioned to demonstrate that corporations are good, bad or just plain ugly.

Debate on the future roles of the corporation is guaranteed to bring out people's most extreme and often bunkered views. The tramline nature of the debate is in a way not surprising. Stories are written for specific audiences, even those that make ample use of facts. They need to be understood in terms of how they seek to persuade and influence. This is certainly true in the area of corporate citizenship. Some people's words and deeds are meat and bread to corporate audiences, but stick in the throats of those who campaign against the World Trade Organisation (WTO) or Monsanto. Similarly, the views of those who target the would-be activist as audience are in the main dismissed by those charged with the practical challenges of navigating these corporations into the future.

Paul Hawken and Amory and L. Hunter Lovins describe this debate as being made up of the pro-marketers ('blues'), the believers in socialism ('reds'), and those who see the world in terms of ecosystems ('greens'). They encourage us to become 'whites'—essentially synthesists who do not 'entirely oppose or agree with any of the other three views, and are optimistic in adopting a path of "integration, reform, respect, and reliance"' (Hawken *et al.* 1999: 311-12). Hawken and the Lovinses are astute in the caricatures they paint. But it is not clear that the 'rational way' must be for the 'whites' to lead the charge of real change, as they suggest. The paths of those with opposing views about the corporate community do of course cross and at times even converge. Increasingly, innovative partnerships and processes are generated at these unlikely intersections. However, these interactions have also stimulated new generations of opponents, often disappointed and embittered by their sense of a lack of real progress in addressing underlying social and environmental challenges. The increasingly vehement public demonstrations against the WTO, the World Bank and the many other symbols of the so-called Washington Consensus (Broad and Cavanagh 1999), more than anything reveal the accumulated frustration following a decade of tentative engagement. Lynda Yanz, co-organiser of the Canadian-based Label Behind the Label coalition sums up this frustration:

> The view 'from the ground' on codes is so very different from what it looks like when you're zooming in from the international angle. The worlds are so different . . . Almost every group we're working with has a different beef with one or more of the Northern-based campaigns or initiatives we're working with.[6]

Oded Grajew, a Brazilian businessman and President of Brazil's leading business association for social responsibility, Instituto Ethos, similarly and even more starkly summed up the underlying confusion and frustration in a question tabled at the annual conference of the business network, Business for Social Responsibility:

> If business is so powerful, and is now doing so much good, why is so much wrong?[7]

Debate about the corporate community brings out in people the worst of either evangelical optimism or narrow cynicism. And there is no shortage of fuel to feed either habit. There are ample cases of corporate misconduct with bad and sometimes catastrophic social or environmental consequences. When yet *another* case of under-aged workers is uncovered in Nike's supply chains, it only serves for many to reinforce a deep sense of cynical anger and frustration. Similarly, there are many examples where corporations *have* 'done the right thing'. With hundreds of high-profile branded corporations and tens of thousands of less-known multinationals, there is more than ample scope for digging up and exhibiting examples that seek to 'prove' one view or the other.

The tramline character of the debate is therefore understandable. It is unsurprising that polarities are hard to overcome when people have such different world-views, experiences and information, and often an undisclosed cocktail of anger and disappointment, confusion, or just simple ignorance. Objectively, the stakes are high, and historical outcomes have for many been less than satisfactory. It is foolish to dismiss what appears to the 'balanced observer' as extremism of one sort or another that merely needs to be 'flushed from the system' for rationality to prevail. The confrontational features of the current debate cannot be eroded by a 'middle path' that neither appreciates nor engages a fuller spectrum of views and interests. Neither can they be marginalised by repeated demonstration, however convincing, that some companies can indeed behave in better ways in increasingly competitive markets. No side will emerge victorious by either inductive or deductive proof that there is 'only one way to go'. A deeper analysis is needed that will deliver on three fronts. First, the myths about corporate behaviour—both good and bad—need to be revealed and dismissed. Second is the need to identify the varied and often opposing possible pathways that this implies for corporate social and environmental performance and impact. Third is the need to make a considered judgement of what can be expected from different strategies, and in all honesty what cannot.

The new economy of corporate citizenship

Corporate citizenship has emerged in its contemporary forms within the context of the emerging New Economy. The New Economy embraces far more than its exotic variants of (now largely defunct) dot.coms, and extends beyond the communities of wealthy over-consumers and business-2-business Internet relationships. It is, as the 'first great philosopher of cyberspace', Manuel Castells, points out, a social revolution that implies radical changes in the nature of the institutions of the state and business, and redefines the roles of the citizen, both individually and collectively (Castells 1996–2000). The New Economy is characterised by the acceleration of every aspect of social life; the collapse of geographical distance as a basis for defining and sustaining difference; and the growing significance of knowledge and innovation as the primary source of business competition and economic value. As such, the New Economy impacts on the livelihoods of Mexican and Indian farmers, just as it shifts the terms on which wealthy New Yorkers consume to secure their self-esteem.

Corporate citizenship is about business taking greater account of its social and environmental—as well as its financial—footprints. The last decade has certainly witnessed a renaissance in corporate citizenship. However, it would be foolish to assume that this has been underpinned by a widespread moral Damascus or evolution in human consciousness. Although individuals' values, vision and moral commitments are often enabling factors, corporate citizenship as an institutional phenomenon is essentially an outcrop of the New Economy. Success in the New Economy is as much about a corporation's ability to build a sense of shared values with key stakeholders as it is about the technical quality of products and services. Corporations that achieve this will extract the maximum premium for their branded, lifestyle products, get the best employees on terms that secure their committed labour to the business, and most effectively offset criticisms from increasingly globalised networks of non-governmental organisations (NGOs). Accounting for broader society and environmental outcomes *from this perspective* is merely another way of expressing Milton Friedman's proposition that corporations will and should focus on maximising financial performance, if necessary by engaging more effectively with stakeholders that can make or break the business.

Understanding corporate citizenship as emerging from underlying structural shifts in the economy does not, unfortunately, mean that the New Economy *necessarily* creates good companies. Corporate citizenship is not the same as *good* corporate citizenship. Taking stakeholders into account does not automatically translate into 'doing good things' for people and the planet. Just as the New Economy opens opportunities for business to strengthen their competitive position by positively addressing social and environmental aspects of their performance, so too does it offer ample scope for businesses to externalise social and environmental costs. Economic globalisation offers profitable pathways for businesses to behave unethically, to drive down labour standards, to minimise their tax contributions, and to exert undue influence over governments anxious to attract their investments. Different stakeholders, after all, have very different 'social' interests. The need must therefore be to identify and enhance the drivers of corporations' more progressive engagement in the vision of sustainable development.

The civil corporation

The aspiration of sustainable development leads many to talk of the need to create 'sustainable business'. While understandable, this imaginative leap creates more confusion than good. Social, environmental and economic gains and losses arising from particular business processes cannot simply be added up. We do not know, for example, whether an additional four weeks of employee training, minus a dozen or so trees, plus a ton of profit add up to more or less sustainable development. We cannot in all honesty predict the contribution of energy and other resource-intensive corporations to the cause of sustainable development, given the complexity of their direct and indirect impacts over time. In fact, we do not and *cannot* know enough about the system to understand in this way the relationship between the activities of one organisation and the whole.

There is little point in blaming pigs for not being able to fly. Similarly, there is little point in condemning an organisation for something beyond its scope of control. There are some things that particular companies can help to solve, and others that they cannot. Microsoft did not, after all, invent computers, and can hardly be entirely blamed for their costs or congratulated for their many benefits. Similarly, there is little point in blaming Nestlé for the impact on the South African economy for a collapse in gold prices, South African Breweries for the level of HIV/AIDS across the African continent, or Credit Swiss First Boston for the state of Britain's railways. Judging and ultimately guiding corporate performance requires an examination of whether a business is doing what it can do given its range of external options and internal competencies. Internally, this concerns the formal, explicit policies and processes, organisation cultures and values, and patterns of leadership. Externally, this is a question of the multitude of business drivers, from direct, short-term market pressures through to longer-term strategic challenges.

A business's contribution to sustainable development therefore needs to be understood in terms of its viable options and what it makes of them. Internal and external factors together create a spectrum of possibilities at any point in time—or degrees of freedom—that defines a corporation's practical scope for making decisions between viable choices. Whether and how a corporation acts within its degrees of freedom must be the test of responsibility, and indeed the basis on which management decisions are framed. These are the fundamentals of the *civil corporation*, which is understood here as one that takes full advantage of opportunities for learning and action in building social and environmental objectives into its core business by effectively developing its internal values and competencies. This should be the basis for our expectations of business, as well as how strategy is conceived and developed, to address the aspirations and challenges underlying sustainable development.

Civil governance

The emergence of NGOs acting as **civil regulators** of corporations through public campaigning and other forms of pressure is one of the notable features of the last decade. More than any other body of institutions, NGOs have driven the process of popular education and political and economic mobilisation around social and environmental issues. As with the corporate community, NGOs' increased visibility and influence is itself a manifestation of the New Economy, which brings with it associated opportunities and risks. In their civil regulatory role, NGOs have engaged with increasing intimacy with their target, the corporate community. In so doing, they have increased their knowledge of the business process and how to influence it through personal relationships, the development of management and accountability tools, and by otherwise impacting directly on the markets within which business operates.

This increased level of intimacy has, however, also provided a basis through which business has been able to penetrate more deeply into the NGO community.

This in turn has provided them with leverage over future NGO activities, and indeed the shape of future generations of NGOs. In so doing, they are increasingly influencing, and sometimes effectively undermining, new challenges and opportunities emerging from the NGO community. At the same time, some are thereby deepening their knowledge of civil-society processes as a basis for enhancing their ability to respond positively to social and environmental challenges in commercially viable ways. In practice both tendencies are, and will continue to be, in play—the balance depending on many factors. It is significant, however, that the continued effectiveness of NGOs in challenging business behaviour will not be secured through seeking to sustain their separation from the corporate community. Rather, the shift from a challenge-based phase of civil regulation into more intimate, binding relationships between NGOs and corporations will necessitate a more complex set of strategies and tactics on the part of NGOs for their effectiveness as a driver for progressive change to be sustained.

It is in this context that civil partnerships have emerged as a vehicle through which new frameworks of rules have been negotiated within which the corporate community might operate in a more legitimate and, hopefully, progressive manner. Civil partnerships are far more than a 'more effective form of delivery'. They are evolving, organic governance structures and processes that go beyond elements of the cut-and-thrust forms of civil regulation into more institutionalised rule-based frameworks. Some of these frameworks may and do eventually find their way onto the statute books of national governments or international institutions. This can in some instances be with the active blessing of elements of the corporate community seeking for example to level the competitive floor or to re-externalise costs into strengthened public-sector institutions. Other rule frameworks, however, will remain outside of the statutory realm, overseen by increasingly sophisticated partnership arrangements. Corporate codes of conduct created through and overseen by multi-sector partnerships are an early manifestation of these developments. More generally, companies are increasingly seeking to stabilise their commitments and risks by nurturing partnerships that involve human rights and development NGOs.

This is the essence of the new civil governance, which lies at the heart of the new economy of corporate citizenship. It comprises processes through which rules are built around and within markets in relation to which corporations find themselves subject. These rules are negotiated and overseen by a spectrum of institutional arrangements and processes ranging from public scrutiny and debate through to partnerships and the more traditional statutory structures. These different elements have certainly always existed in some form. What is new is that there is no longer a de facto (or for many even an aspirational) pecking order that places statutory rules as higher, more legitimate, or more effective governance instruments. Furthermore, there is no longer a presumption that different rule systems will be stable, well bounded, or even consistent with each other. The new civil governance is most of all marked by an acceptance of partial and temporary rule systems co-existing in often dynamic relationship, overseen by diverse players and institutional arrangements with complex and often unstable bases of legitimacy and effectiveness.

Civil navigation

The civil corporation needs to understand what nuts and bolts will help it identify 'best thinking' from the often confused reality of divergent, contested views. It will need to be able to assess and influence their degrees of freedom within what are generally high-risk, complex, dynamic market environments. Perhaps most of all, they need to be able to manage their relationships with key stakeholders in ways that support learning and change without unnecessarily risking commercial disaster that would bring misfortune to many of these stakeholders.

There are no magic bullets that will create civil corporations. There are no standard systems that substitute for real-life, messy solutions made up of cocktails of unusual leadership, coincidence and luck, and really hard work. But the effective systematisation of such cocktails is, nevertheless, a critical ingredient of longer-term success, both in developmental and commercial terms. Many systems aimed at aligning core business strategies and processes with elements of social and environmental aims and outcomes have emerged in the last ten years. Equally prolific has been the outpouring of books and reports either advocating their development and use, highlighting their irrelevance, or predicting their imminent demise. For most, and most of all for business, it is all rather confusing, and indeed increasingly irritating. In fairness it must be said that 'it is early days', which both explains and in a sense justifies the rich chaos. After all, it is barely 15 years since environmental management systems were taken (and so developed) seriously by mainstream business. However, these 'early days' are taking their toll in terms of rising concerns and cynicism by stakeholders both external to, and within, the corporate community.

There is a need for tools that enable corporations to be civil across the practical dimensions of, for example, information and knowledge management; engagement, dialogue and communication; decision-making and governance; and performance assessment. This is not a matter of starting with a clean sheet of paper and starting the design process all over again. Existing tools for organisational learning provide many elements of the kit that is needed. At the same time, this is not a matter of pursuing a cut-and-paste approach. There is a need to go back to basics to understand what are the possible uses of existing tools, and what adjustments need to be made to their design and operation. There are, furthermore, notable gaps where new tools need to be developed or at least existing ones substantially upgraded.

The application of best thinking to the development of tools is itself a dynamic process in every sense of the word. Our understanding of sustainable development itself changes over time. What is a priority today may not be the most critical issue in a decade, or even tomorrow. The manner in which priorities are made will also change, both for societies and for corporations. Child labour is not a new phenomenon, for example, and yet is today a far more critical issue for global corporations than it was just a few years ago. Similarly, the rights of indigenous people to set the terms of access to natural resources has become far more significant for oil and mining companies than ever before. Today, the notion of a global living wage may seem implausible. In years to come it could well be the reality for workers and business alike.

It is too early to say which standards, guidelines, systems, procedures and practices will turn out to make most sense for any one company, let alone for the wider business community, and society at large. It is unclear, for example, as to whether the more daunting Natural Step will prevail over the pragmatic ISO 14000 series, or whether the labour code and monitoring standard SA8000 will prove to do the job as compared to alternative approaches that embrace wider dialogue and engagement. How this will all, moreover, fit into tools such as the Balanced Scorecard or Total Quality Management is entirely unclear. Indeed, we do not know if these tools will even survive the coming years. And it is in any case a complete mystery how such approaches—all designed for relatively stable manufacturing systems—will fare in the New Economy where the social and environmental footprints of dominant corporations are less clearly defined.

Effective civil navigation lies at the heart of making the most out of the opportunities afforded by the New Economy of corporate citizenship for enhancing social and environmental benefits and minimising associated costs. This is true for individual corporations, but is also the case for the system as a whole. The trick, however, is not to place all one's bets on a particular approach. Better at this stage is to look for the underlying principles needed to guide the evolution of appropriate approaches in the future. This is the aim of the book's third and final section, which identifies and explores the fundamental principles underlying four particular dimensions of corporate behaviour:

1. Setting boundaries of learning, accountability and responsiveness

2. Building engagement that forms the basis for learning.

3. Creating measures that validate and make knowledge effective, and so forms the basis for decision-making and actions

4. Institutionalising trust in ways that create a virtuous circle of practice and further engagement with stakeholders

Is being civil enough?

Corporations can be civil. But can they and will they be civil enough? Can even the most enlightened business improve its social and environmental performance sufficiently to reach universally accepted standards while remaining a viable business? It would be fair to say that not a single major corporation has achieved this to date across the bulk of its social and environmental footprint. Even if some could achieve this by virtue of their visionary leadership and powerful market position, would they remain worthy but isolated examples within what is otherwise a swamp of poor social and environmental performers? Finally and most importantly, will all these developments add up to a coherent response to the question of what roles good corporate citizenship will play in addressing the really big social and environmental challenges of both today's and tomorrow's world.

The cases drawn on throughout this book highlight just how much individual corporations acting alone can achieve. But these cases, and the accompanying analysis, also suggests that even the strongest and most progressive corporations, acting alone, will rarely be able to sustain *significantly* enhanced social and environmental performance for extended periods of time. Another way of looking at this is that, if such corporations are not emulated by their competitors, it either means that the corporation has failed to achieve any competitive advantage through its good practices, or that its competitive advantage exists only within a restricted market niche that has high barriers to entry and does not threaten the broader market (and so will not have extended impact). From this perspective, corporate citizenship based on leadership practices that are not institutionalised beyond the individual corporation are unlikely to make a major contribution to achieving a sustainable development path.

On the other hand, corporate citizenship *can* become a significant route for overcoming global poverty, inequality and environmental insecurity. This requires that it evolves to a point where business becomes active in promoting and institutionalising new global governance frameworks that effectively secure civil market behaviour, globally. Leading civil corporations will therefore be those that go beyond getting their own house in order, and actively engage in promoting governance frameworks that enable the wider business community to address, effectively and without contradiction, the aspirations underpinning sustainable development.

ethical trade
futures*

Mapping the territory

Over the past decade there has been a surge in the development and implementation of corporate codes of conduct covering labour and environmental standards in global supply chains.[1] These developments have been welcomed from many quarters as offering real opportunities for increasing corporate transparency and improving social, environmental and arguably overall business performance. For others, it represents a problematic distraction from the underlying changes in global trade, investment and economic power.

Ethical trade concerns the matter of labour standards in global supply chains. The term is used in the UK, and to some degree elsewhere. However, not surprisingly, it was not possible to look at this in isolation of other macro variables, notably:

- The emergence and meaning of 'corporate responsibility', and in particular its links (or lack thereof) to issues of governance and accountability;
- The remarkable shifts in the position and power of multinational corporations;
- The associated overall architecture of global institutions and regulations; and
- The role of the state in these contexts.

BOX 9 WHAT IS ETHICAL TRADE?

The principal driver of this process has been the evolving interactions between business and other parts of civil society, in particular the non-profit organisations (NGOs) working around development, human rights, and the environment. It has been the ability of the NGO movement to translate political advocacy into market

*   This chapter is a summary of the report 'Ethical Trade Futures'. © 2000 New Economics Foundation, London.

pressures that has opened new pathways for change to take place. Much of this pressure has comprised an actual, or the threat of a, negative consumer, and, to a limited degree, investor responses to branded companies and products. NGOs have been able to create an actual or threat of potential business cost associated with the appearance of unethical behaviour, as simply summarised in Figure 26.[2]

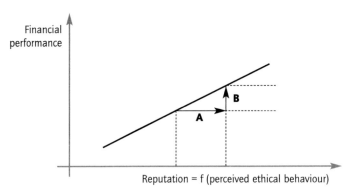

FIGURE 26   CIVIL REGULATION IN ACTION: THE THEORY

Source: Zadek and Forstater 1999

This relationship reflects two coinciding patterns:

- The growing importance of corporate reputation as an element of market value

- The increasing willingness of consumers to reward and penalise companies for perceived ethical behaviour

The growing importance of NGOs has created a complex and volatile set of relationships between business, NGOs, the trade union movement, governments and multilateral institutions. The NGO movement seeks to inform, influence and reflect the interests of key stakeholder groups. However, at the same time it does not represent these stakeholders in any traditional structural sense (e.g. through membership, elections, or ownership). Governments and trade unions, on the other hand, do have more traditional representational structures and processes, and yet in many ways find themselves following rather than leading in this area.

The difficulties of this institutional terrain are further exacerbated when the dynamics between the North and the South are taken into account. A stronger Southern voice is gradually emerging in the debate. However, this voice is fragmented. In particular the differences are apparent between Southern government, NGOs, trade unions and business:

- **Governments** in the main are opposed to any 'creeping development' of non-tariff trade barriers in the form of social screening of products traded internationally.

- NGOs are seeking to strengthen their role in both directly engaging with companies, and maintaining a strong advocacy position, and hence are concerned at the appearance of a growing alliance between Northern NGOs and companies.

- **Trade unions** are seeking to consolidate and extend their historical role in supporting workers' rights worldwide. Yet there is concern as to whether unions are really able to be effective in a rapidly shifting environment.

- **Businesses** are seeking to develop their position in global supply chains, and are responsive to the shifting needs of their branded clients in the North while in the main being opposed to any toughening of the regulatory regime or trade union involvement.

Confusing times

The early to middle phase of development of most innovations is characterised by a profusion of conflicting standards, institutions and processes. A clear example of this has been the emergence of environmental auditing over the past decade; another example is the profusion of eco-labels that has confused consumers and undermined their confidence in 'wanting to buy green' (Zadek *et al.* 1998b).

The area of supply chain labour standards has now moved beyond the point of small-scale, leadership-based experimentation, such as we saw with the earlier work of companies such as Levi-Strauss. There is now a take-off in interest and willingness to adopt codes and moves towards implementation.

This point of take-off is characterised by maximum confusion.

- Companies are not sure what to do.

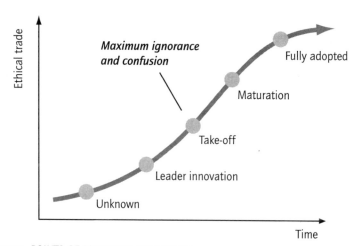

FIGURE 27 POINTS OF MAXIMUM CONFUSION

- Non-profits are not sure what to ask for.

- Service providers such as consultants and auditors are not sure what to provide.

- Governments are struggling to understand what their roles should be.

This is in part an acceptable 'pain threshold' that needs to be passed through to achieve a mature framework. This threshold is however not fixed; it can become so high that the innovation fails, as with the case of much of the eco-labelling that developed in the 1980s (Zadek *et al.* 1998b). Alternatively, building collaborative institutions in order to carry key stakeholders can lower it.

Distinguishing success from failure

It is true that innovations almost always go through such a confusing, rocky path. It is certainly not the case, however, that they all eventually 'win through'. This is particularly relevant when it comes to ethical trade. What appears to some to be 'progress' appears to others as 'failure'. Does a new monitoring report by Reebok represent 'good but not good enough', or does it 'mark another weakening of resolve of those who play ball' (HIS 1999). Is the 'Global Alliance for Workers and Communities' involving Nike, Mattel, the World Bank and the International Youth Foundation a progressive innovation or a cynical ploy (Zadek 1999)?

> **‹** None of the agencies or foundations, so far established, are perfect. They all present one or more problems. First, there is the proliferation of codes. Secondly, delaying tactics on the part of different partners can hinder the tackling of the real problem: exploitation. So too may too much experimentation. Some may be weakened by unscrupulous auditors. Others are unrepresentative shell operations. There is a real danger of one agency being played off against another. Finally, unless care is taken, some companies may abandon suppliers who are not in compliance rather than working for improvement. **›**
>
> *Neil Kearney, Secretary General of the International Textile and Leather Garment Workers' Federation*
>
> Source: Zadek 1999

When representatives from US business and the international trade union movement agree with each other that labour standards are a matter for the ILO, is this an extraordinary development to be applauded, or a perverse end-game of a failed approach?[3] When the accountants KPMG launch a worldwide 'integrity and verification service', is this a sign that the non-profits have successfully created a 'market for change', or is this the first sign that the professionalisation path will not deliver the goods (AccountAbility 1999)?

So how can one tell what is success and failure? The answer lies in part in distinguishing very different visions on the part of the various actors.

- For some, the aim is essentially about economic welfare improvements: how can the situation of workers be materially improved given the prevailing and evolving global production process?

- For others, it is exactly these structural parameters that are targeted as needing root-and-branch change. Economic welfare improvements from this perspective remain important, but institutional issues underpin assessments of effectiveness: for example, the effect of codes of conduct on the strength of independent trade unions.

People and institutions with these varied perspectives and visions do indeed sit together and discuss matters such as health and safety standards. But it is small wonder that they find it hard to reach agreement.

> ❝ When I look at what is going on in this area, it is damned hard to tell whether the fact that it is happening is a mark of success or failure. ❞
>
> *Anon*

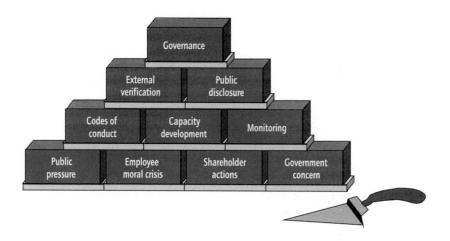

FIGURE 28 ISSUE EVOLUTION

Future conditional

These different visions for change underpin variations in how we see the future, or at least our options for creating futures. For some, a positive future is one where the business community has rebuilt itself to take greater account of the social and environmental dimensions of sustainability (Elkington 1997). For others, a global economy dominated by multinationals can be neither just nor sustainable (see e.g. Korten 1999). Most people in practice live between these world-views—engaged in the practice of incremental improvements while questioning and often doubting the underlying premises of such an approach.

> " Workers must be able to use their own capacity to struggle. A code alone is not enough. "
>
> Sandra Ramos, Movimiento de Mujeres Empleadas y Desempleadas, Nicaragua
>
> Source: Green 1999

Our **discussions with many people working in the area of ethical trade revealed enormous concern on all sides.** Many business people doubt the robustness of current thinking and approaches to ethical trade, whether in terms of its cost, its social impact, or its long-term viability in a business context. Ironically, perhaps, many people from civil-society institutions have concerns about ethical trade for exactly the same reasons.

Ethical trade is characterised by high levels of diversity, complexity and rapid, dynamic change, fraught institutional processes, and ultimately very high stakes in terms of commercial as well as social and environmental interests and impacts. In this context, strategic as well as tactical thinking and behaviour is important on the part of each constituency, as well as where relevant together. Unfortunately, although understandably, most planning is tactical at best, and often very short-term at that. There is intensive and often very exciting and dynamic activity combined with much confusion, and in the main little longer-term thinking.

This, then, is the context.

The scenarios

The scenarios were developed as part of an experimental process to see whether and how such an approach could inform us in understanding and working more effectively in this field. It followed earlier stages of work, including detailed research involving extensive dialogue with some key players. The scenarios therefore benefited from a foundation of information about initiatives and perspectives on ethical trade from a range of actors, as illustrated in Box 10.[4]

- Amnesty Business Group
- Apparel Industry Partnership
- Asia Monitor Research Centre
- Bangladesh Child Rights Forum
- Business for Social Responsibility
- Canadian Council for International Development
- Clean Clothes Campaign
- Council of Economic Priorities (and CEP Accreditation Agency)
- Ethical Trade Initiative
- European Commission
- Global Exchange
- Global Reporting Initiative
- Human Rights Watch
- Institute for Social and Ethical AccountAbility
- Interfaith Center for Corporate Responsibility
- Label Behind the Label
- Maquiladora Health and Safety Support Network
- New Economics Foundation
- Social Venture Network
- Tjopet Njak Dien Women Foundation
- Verité

BOX 10 MAPPING THE CONVERSATION

Many different possible 'ethical trade futures' emerged from the consultation and associated research. Some were more or less smooth extrapolations from the present—others involved environmental and human catastrophes that put ethical trade in a very different light.

In selecting which scenarios to present, we were informed by an interest in identifying:

- The dominant patterns of change

- What appeared *likely* futures based on these patterns rather than what the participants might consider to be *desirable* futures

- The core or essence of these likely futures, rather than their inevitable complexity

On the basis of these criteria, three basic ethical trade futures were identified that captured and grouped what seemed to be the essential elements.[5]

Oasis

Labour standards improve in a sustained manner only for workers in the narrow pipelines that feed high-value brand products to socially conscious, high-income consumers.

Socially conscious consumers would remain a small proportion of the growing consumer market, and so would those workers benefiting from improved conditions arising as a result of consumer-linked ethical pressures. There would be only a minor spill-over effect on other global supply chains, largely where they were inextricably linked—technically or institutionally—to those where labour benefited from consumer pressure. The high-profile nature of this form of ethical trade and other factors would undermine attempts to meaningfully strengthen national and international labour regulation and its enforcement. Leading NGOs and labour organisations become embedded within these ghettoised processes, and so in effect marginalise attempts to strengthen the position of the majority of workers left outside and subject to far poorer conditions.

Desert

Labour standards do not improve significantly for workers in global supply chains as a result of civil pressure, and at the same time these attempts effectively undermine pressure to strengthen and enforce relevant regulation.

Increasing economic insecurity gradually undermines the will of citizens with market and political power to pressure for improved labour standards. Leading companies recognise this trend and backtrack from commitments made in codes and elsewhere. Civil organisations withdraw from collaborative initiatives, as a lack of progress becomes evident. This reduction in effective ethical pressure is reinforced by the increased significance of markets in societies where civil pressure is severely constrained. One possible outcome of this failure is that renewed focused pressure on governments by civil-society organisations to regulate is more effective having marginalised the confusing and unproductive element of 'corporate ethics'.

Mecca

Labour standards in global and subsequently national supply chains would improve over time in a sustained manner partly through the pressure of a growing international 'ethical trade' movement that includes leading companies as well as civil-society organisations and governments.

Socially conscious consumers, investors and ultimately voters would become an increasingly significant force in moulding the practices of leading companies, both directly and through pressure on governments to strengthen and enforce relevant regulation. Leading companies would effectively become complicit in fashioning new market values that reward ethical behaviour. These companies would in turn pressure governments to enforce regulations that ensure that they are not undercut by companies offering low-value brands underpinned by cost advantages derived from lower social and environmental standards.

Seeing the whole

These scenarios can also be seen as alternate pathways, each of which is briefly described below and summarised in Figure 29.

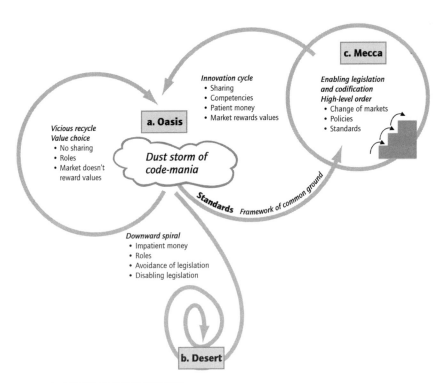

FIGURE 29 ACCOUNTABILITY FUTURES

- **Oasis**. This is what best describes our current situation. A significant but small group of companies have taken up the challenge of aligning their business strategy and operations to the imperatives of, and opportunities associated with, sustainable development. This group, together with some NGOs and governments, are pushing for positive social and environmental change in the context of business needs and performance. However, the bulk of the business community, and many parts of civil society, are either not aware of the possibilities of being part of this process or have actively chosen not to engage. The oasis is not bad in itself, but it certainly is not an attractive option to get stuck there, since this would allow leading, progressive companies to co-exist with a wider, more destructive environment (**vicious recycle**).

- **Desert**. There is the possibility that over time the desert will encroach on the oasis that has been created. This encroachment could happen for many reasons, including short-termism in the financial community and public cynicism, with the result that responsible corporate behaviour is neither recognised nor rewarded. Along this pathway, therefore, there is an erosion of the 'win–win' areas that when they exist allow businesses in a competitive environment to move along a sustainable development path. This is the most negative vision that sees even leading companies driven downwards over time as their attempts to shift their strategies and practices are squeezed out by market pressures (**downward spiral**).

- **Mecca**. Mecca is not an endpoint but a pathway of positive change. Leading companies achieve competitive advantage by evolving innovative and effective business strategies that deliver greater social and environmental accountability, and associated behaviour and outcomes. Their success encourages other companies to move in similar or, at least, compatible directions.

  This is the most positive vision in that it enables leading companies to be joined by others in exploring, taking full advantage of and further developing the competitive advantage of adopting business strategies appropriate in terms of sustainable development (**innovation cycle**).

Underlying dynamics

A number of underlying dynamics have been identified: essentially strong patterns underlying what is happening today which could evolve in two or more significantly different ways. In presenting these below, we recognise that there are certainly other dynamic pathways, and also that what we have described represents acknowledged simplifications.

Civil and public regulation

Civil regulation is the process whereby civil society creates organic patterns of pressure on business and/or the state to achieve societal goals that are not being delivered through public regulation. The notion of civil regulation breaks down the unhelpful binary of public regulation and voluntary action that has characterised much of the debate about corporate codes of conduct and associated tools and processes. Corporate responses in the field of social and environmental spheres are almost never 'voluntary' in that they are responses to external pressure. To understand corporate behaviour therefore requires that we understand the nature of these structural drivers and specific triggers better.

Pressure from civil organisations is one of a number of factors that lead some companies to adopt codes of conduct and other elements of a growing package of commitments and activities which:

a. Shift company practice to some degree with some potential gains for some stakeholders, e.g. labour in supply chains;

b. Improve company reputations and secure them somewhat against civil critiques; and

c. Secure and even build their longer-term business relationship with key stakeholders, notably customers.

The evidence suggests that civil regulation is effective in shifting some corporate practices, such as in the cases of Nike and Shell.

Linked to this is the view that companies that respond positively to civil action strengthen their business position (Zadek and Chapman 1998). In the first instance this is largely a matter of defensive positioning, of securing the brand; however, more and more it is part of a process of strengthening competencies and processes with an ethical dimension.

From this perspective, civil action can have the perhaps ironic effect of consolidating the economic success and associated political power of leading multinationals. Indeed, one argument is that effective civil action actually *requires* relatively monopolistic markets in order to be able to lever change in the market through brand attacks.

There is then a perhaps unexpected symbiotic relationship between civil-society institutions seeking to erode corporate power and to shift their practices and impacts, and some of the very leading multinationals they challenge from this perspective. This in turn raises major issues as to the long-term accountability of civil-society institutions to their stated constituencies as they move towards an ever-deepening engagement with the business community and governments.

It is in this context that increasing corporate power over government, and in particular over the regulation-setting process, needs to be considered.

a. In some instances, companies will use their increasing influence to offset the likelihood of constraining public regulation.

b. In other instances, leadership companies 'voluntarily' adopting new standards will push government to regulate in order to offset any potential cost disadvantage they have incurred in being early adopters of 'voluntary' standards.

This pathway and its associated pivot points are basic drivers in creating the different scenarios presented. The 'Desert' scenario arises through the inability or unwillingness of NGOs to sustain stakeholder pressure on companies that translates into financial bottom-line effects—whether actual or threatened. Similarly, the 'Oasis' scenario is driven in particular by a combination of NGOs' inability to extend the effectiveness of their pressure beyond a small portion of the market, and potentially a process of co-option of major NGO brands. This could lead to their active participation in restricting the damage to their corporate partners that could potentially be inflicted by more radical civil-society groups frustrated with the limited scope of success through NGO–business partnerships.

Government and corporate relationships

The second underlying dynamic considers the relationship between government and corporations, with a particular focus at the policy formation level.

The first level concerns the degree to which governments act in the interests of their country's citizens in relation to multinational activities, when enacting public policy measures. This clearly concerns the degree to which they have clarity of purpose, and is an even greater issue for ethical trade when one moves to the international level, to include such bodies as the World Trade Organisation.

The next level concerns the degrees and ways in which governments are responsive to different pressures, and their relationship. Here the implied relationship between civil-society organisations and multinationals seemed particularly important in the following possible senses:

- The degrees to which civil-society organisations are able to effectively pressure governments to act directly: for example, through mobilising public support

- The degree to which civil-society organisations are able to effectively pressure governments to act by creating leverage through particular multinationals. An example here has been the shift in the UK government's position on genetically modified organisms (GMOs), in response to the policies of UK supermarkets

This underlying dynamic generated by far the greatest debate during discussions and workshops. The predominant view was of government being responsive to civil and business pressure in the formation of public policy and practice, rather than asserting its own programme to secure minimum labour standards in global supply chains. From this perspective, the route to effective legislation would often require that leading business on balance acquiesced because it was in their interest (the argument at the heart of the 'Mecca' scenario). Alternatively, this pathway leads more directly to the 'Desert' scenario if governments yield directly to civil-society pressure despite resistance from leading businesses. In this situation labour standards might be enhanced despite, or perhaps exactly because, the ineffective and distracting 'ethical' stance of business has been marginalised in favour of a renewed interest in a compliance-based regime.

Community values and economic power

This third pathway concerns the potentials and limitations of mobilising communities in pursuit of economic resilience and influence.

The debate about corporate power is intimately linked to the matter of the place of 'community' in the future. This debate usually moves between the following positions:

- At one end is 'radical localisation'—essentially arguing that economic processes need to be broken back down to a level where they are controllable at the community level, by which is normally (although not always) meant a geographically defined community of people.

- A second version of this is that local communities are able to develop sufficient economic strength to redefine the 'contract' between the community and the global economic systems, particularly multinationals.

- A third version argues that 'community values' are far less robust. If and when communities do develop local economic networks with significant 'retained economic value', multinationals will develop products and processes that will intervene and absorb part or all of this economic value.

The strength of communities is not always worked through as a key issue in the area of ethical trade, where it is more conventional to focus on the ability of labour organisations to negotiate for improved labour standards. The dilemma perhaps here is that if organisations based in one particular area become more adept at negotiating for better labour standards, the area will become vulnerable to the mobility of capital. Without strong community-based economies, the penetration of global supply chains into the community becomes more complete, and the community has less leverage because of a lack of alternative livelihoods.

This underlying dynamic relates to all three pathway scenarios. First, without strong community economies, there is a reduced ability to mobilise civil-society processes around the actual production sites in the supply chain. Second is the view that community mobilisation is an essential counterpoint to the potential co-option of professionalised NGOs set out in the 'Oasis' scenario in their relationships with the business community.

Invisible traders

This fourth underlying dynamic concerns the relationship between those companies and elements of the production and trading chains that are in the 'ethical' spotlight, and those that evade it.

Experience in pressuring companies to address environmental concerns shows that, despite a growing positive record of some leadership corporations, many more companies evade both civil pressure and public regulation and remain broadly speaking unreconstructed 'environmental destructors'. This is the case despite often dominant market leaders making significant progress. This implies that market leaders in business terms are not always capable of (or perhaps interested in) driving the rest of the market.

A further version of the 'invisibility' or perhaps better 'un-get-at-ability' of many parts of the global economy is the potential for 'ethical' initiatives to more tightly bind the spheres of production and trade in which the higher-profile companies engage. The clearest example of this is probably the possible 'consolidating' effect that codes of conduct will have on supply chains. In this context, the dilemma becomes that people might be systematically excluded from working in and gaining an income from the global economy.

A further dimension of this might be the impact of the growing importance of multinationals with their roots outside of the West, and the shift of principal markets away from the West to other parts of the world. Here the issue is not so much the 'culture' of multinationals, but whether they are as accessible to civil pressure if their headquarters are, for example, in countries where effective civil action is far more constrained due in particular to the form of government and underlying political system.

This underlying dynamic suggests that without finding ways to pressure these 'invisible traders', the ability of civil-society institutions to sustain pressure for change is likely to deteriorate. A growing level of 'invisible trade' in particular will tend to deliver the second pathway scenario, 'Desert', and a renewed thrust towards public regulation.

Complex purpose

The final and in some ways most contentious underlying dynamic concerns the conditions under which companies develop a more complex array of purposes, of which only one is to secure financial success.

The growing consolidation of key resources, production processes and markets is giving increasing power to an ever-smaller number of multinationals. This development, taken together with civil pressures, is influencing the internal sociology of corporations. New people are being brought in from parts of civil society, social and environmental issues are increasingly being explored at a strategic rather than a purely 'public affairs' level, and chief executives and senior managers are increasingly being asked to play roles in diverse aspects of public policy and practice.

In this context, companies are expressing 'new values' and aims that cover human rights, environmental issues and, more broadly, 'sustainable development'. These 'new values and aims' can be and are being interpreted in two broad ways:

a. As **instrumental** in that they contribute to financial success, whether through rhetoric, practice, or more likely some combination of the two

b. As **fundamental** in that business leaders are seeking (or being encouraged) to play an increasing role in the governance of our societies and are using the strength of their corporations to do exactly that

Whether a company is pursuing narrow business interests or has a more complex set of interests including those one might consider 'civil' (doing 'good') cannot be easily determined by looking at behaviour or outcomes. A 'good' outcome for workers can be interpreted as resulting from the company acting in its best business interests, as we see in such varied cases as The Body Shop and Nike. Outcomes do not give a good indication of intentions. An exploration and view of the integrity and values of specific individuals has quite different but equally problematic aspects. It is certainly true that the values of leaders do count in what companies do. However, companies are certainly more than the expression of particular leaders at particular times.

The suggestion here is that there is an underlying factor facing any company—namely the **degrees of freedom** it has given actual and future possible competitive position. Specifically:

a. Where there are few or no degrees of freedom in the sense that the **market is highly competitive**, even 'honest intentions' have to be expressed in terms that align with and strengthen a company's competitive position.

b. The second possible route is that the company has significant degrees of freedom in the sense that the company has a **sufficiently strong position** to enable them to take 'ethical' actions, which do not contribute or even in places may detract from their competitive position.

c. A third possible route combines elements of the first two in suggesting that companies that lead in their markets see an increasingly politicised role for themselves in sustaining business success.

This underlying dynamic is once again relevant across all three pathway scenarios. The 'Mecca' scenario requires that leading brand companies are able to drive their respective markets, at least in the first instance prior to enabling legislation that obliges the rest of the market to follow suit. This in turn requires that they are relatively dominant and able to invest in shifting the underlying ethos of these markets. In this situation they are more likely to push for regulation that reduces their competitors' position to compete on the basis of lower social and environmental standards. At the same time, the increased economic power of a small number of multinationals also creates the conditions for the 'Oasis' scenario. Here, symbiotic relationships between leading NGOs and these companies seem more possible exactly because the latter are able to express their broader interests and points of engagement in social and economic change.

Strategic insights

The perspectives contained in the pathway scenarios and underlying dynamics are simplifications of what are in reality more complex and differentiated processes across sectors, companies, countries, and over time. Yet they do hopefully provide food for thought in developing strategy and tactics, whether as an NGO, or indeed as a company, trade union or government. The focus in this section, however, is on the possible strategic implications of the proceeding analysis for civil-society institutions, and specifically for NGOs.

Building monopolies

A key proposition in the analysis is that civil-society pressure may well positively influence corporate behaviour but may also actively (if somewhat thoughtlessly) assist in the consolidation of market power by leading multinationals. This may aid in—or at least be part of the process of—achieving certain 'ethical' gains. However, there are possible downsides, certainly in the eyes of many civil-society organisations. Most significant is that the growing influence of a small number of growing multinationals may do little to develop, and might undermine, the evolution of more democratic societies. Real freedom may diminish which, as Nobel prize-winning economist Amartya Sen points out, is at the core of meaningful development (Sen 1999). The potential downsides need to be set against possible gains that might include:

- Making it easier to shift the basis on which business is done across an entire market, which would be more difficult in a market with many more or less equal players. This consolidation is particularly useful if there are significant numbers of 'invisible traders'.

- Leveraging public regulation that is in the relative interests of the lead business players, and possibly to the relative disadvantage of smaller would-be competitors.

Red-lined worlds

Red-lining is the term used to describe the practice of financial institutions to demarcate communities as 'no go' areas because of their perceived high-risk and low associated returns. One possibility raised in the pathway scenarios is of a red-lined world where global supply chains producing high-value, high-brand goods are red-lined from the rest of the global economy. This would create a labour force within its walls that experiences a relatively high quality of life, and an increasingly impoverished majority outside the chains.

In this situation, it would become far more difficult to mobilise civil action against companies, especially as they grow more sophisticated at communicating to stakeholders with market power the relatively good situation of people directly in the chains or associated communities. This is described in the pathway scenarios as the 'vicious recycle', where the Oasis survives, but leaves outside swathes of populations living in a degenerating natural and social environment.

Civil society observed

The growing significance of civil regulation as a market driver has led directly to the creation of new cadres of professionals working in and for business to assist them in understanding, engaging with and, where necessary and possible, neutralising, civil-society institutions and processes. Civil society is today observed ever more closely, and in many ways is more intimately understood than ever before by those institutions lying outside of it. The more civil-society processes penetrate the corporate community, the more rapidly does the former become known by the latter.

The implications of this are potentially profound:

• Increasing integration of front-line, high-branded NGOs into (often implicit and unspoken) alliances with their corporate challenge-partners is virtually inevitable. It is just a matter of when, how and to what effect.

• Emerging, radicalised civil-society processes will have decreasing time and space to effectively mobilise into resilient institutions before being penetrated directly or indirectly by the corporate community through engaging dialogue and active financial and other support.

State as facilitator

The state is not withering away, as some would claim. However, its self-image and role in society is changing, probably irrevocably. Central to this change is an acceptance by virtually all governments of the basic rules of the global economy. This includes:

a. Highly mobile capital, albeit increasingly regulated to avoid volatility

b. Relatively open trading borders except where significant domestic interests in politically and/or economically strong countries prevail, notably the USA and Europe but increasingly also China

c. An economic playing field that constrains the emergence of serious challengers to either the main paradigm or the largest corporate interests within it

The state does respond to pressure, but at the moment apparently only to the degree that these underlying premises are left intact, or that policy oriented towards deeper change has the prior support of leading businesses.

This is an unappetising perspective for most civil-society institutions, which in the main see the state as the critical refuge and advocate of the democratic process. The scenarios and pathways are posited within this perspective of the state not as a normative view but as one that seems to paint the most likely picture for the coming period. From this perspective, the degree of leverage on the state and the public regulatory process becomes in practice a function of 'credible threat' rather than common cause. Furthermore, access for civil-society institutions to state processes is increasingly predicated on their willingness to engage with the business community.

Critical strategy

Ethical trade futures is intended as a contribution to the work of many people and institutions working in the field of corporate governance and accountability. It is self-consciously *not* a strategic planning exercise, which would require in particular a more intensive constituency building process. The offering of strategic insights in the previous section does provide some possible directions for strategic planning and actions, but still in a fairly open-ended manner.

This final section takes the plunge in suggesting what are the strategic implications of the arguments presented in this chapter. Once again, it focuses on the possible implications for civil-society processes and institutions.

Full-spectrum alliances

There is an urgent need to strengthen alliances between civil-society organisations working at different points on the spectrum from challenge-based corporate campaigning through to strategies involving deep engagement.

Funding challenge-based campaigning

Sustaining effective, challenge-based campaigning is central to the continued evolution and effectiveness of civil regulation, as well as being a key element in promoting appropriate public regulation and its enforcement. Continued and indeed strengthened funding is essential to this end. There is, however, considerable evidence of a collapse in funding available for this purpose. Foundations and the better-endowed NGOs are directing resources towards initiatives focused on engagement strategies. There is a need to inform and educate institutional funding sources about the creative and necessary dynamic between engagement and challenge-based work.

Learning from practice

It is essential that civil-society institutions learn from practice, and formulate strategy and initiatives from that learning. Learning among this community of individuals, processes and organisations can be extremely rich, and the organic characteristics of civil society lend themselves to non-linear learning and application. Civil-society institutions need to mobilise more effective learning processes that deepen knowledge of ethical trade and associated fields of action.

Building 'second-generation' capacity

It is important that civil-society institutions emerge that have an understanding of the pros and cons of engagement strategies with the business community, and yet with sufficient autonomy from existing initiatives to be able to both offer objective critiques and to design and form the next generation of interactions with business.

Building civil accountability

Many civil-society institutions will be undermined in the coming period unless new and effective approaches are built to strengthen their transparency, accountability and legitimacy. This possibility arises in part because of the general increase in visibility and influence of civil-society institutions, which results in an increased interest in their activities and effectiveness.

22

conversations with disbelievers

persuading companies to
address social challenges*

co-written with John Weiser

We present here the 'disbeliever's scorecard': a tool we designed to help people understand why sceptics disbelieve evidence, and how to present the evidence so that it is most persuasive.

We start by looking at why some managers do choose to increase their community engagement (CE) activities, to understand what drives their decisions. If we can understand the drivers that compelled some managers to increase CE activities, we can better understand how and why other managers might be persuaded. We also note the dynamics of the change process, and the impact of increasing CE on the company's ability to innovate.

We then look at the rationales that managers have put forward for disbelieving or ignoring the evidence. We present a scorecard based on these rationales that you can use to understand the likely objections to the data presented, and to present the evidence in a more favourable light.

Why managers increase CE activities

In order to understand what would be persuasive to sceptical managers, we surveyed over 100 case examples of businesses that did increase their CE activities. There were a wide range of reasons and rationales for increased CE. While some are specific to a particular company, we were able to identify three primary drivers:

- **Pressure**: a short-term need to respond to external pressures such as regulation or advocacy groups

* This chapter is a summary of the report 'Conversations with Disbelievers'. © 2000 Brody•Weiser•Burns for The Ford Foundation, New York.

- **Values**: an expression of core values in the company

- **Strategy**: CE supports or enhances a key long-term business strategy

These three drivers are not mutually exclusive. Rather, they interact with one another, causing shifts over time. Companies that increase CE activities initially because of pressure, for example, often find there is a business strategy rationale that develops over time. Values may also shift, depending on the depth to which CE causes changes in the organisation's activities and culture (Zadek *et al.* 1997).

Interacting drivers for increasing CE

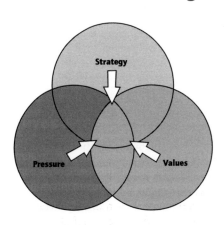

In reviewing the case studies, we also noted that innovation plays an important role. Companies under pressure from one or more of these drivers feel a strong need to act and respond. But often, when a company experiences a need to respond to drivers pushing it to increase its CE, it does not have the skills and competencies it needs to succeed. In most of the cases we examined in which companies dramatically and successfully expanded their CE activities in response to drivers, they experimented and innovated as they figured out how to compete effectively and profitably under these new circumstances.

Why managers disbelieve

While there are many companies that have increased their CE activities, there are many more that have not done so. In order to understand why, we talked to 'disbelievers'—managers who are sceptical about the benefits of CE. At the heart of most conversations with disbelievers is a debate over the quality of the evidence. Most disbelievers dismiss the data showing significant business benefits. Often, we heard comments such as 'Yes, but they would say that, wouldn't they?' and 'No one in their right mind would believe those numbers'. In order to respond effectively to the dismissal of data, it is important to understand why the data is dismissed, and how to respond to the different reasons for dismissal.

In our conversations with disbelievers, we teased out four principal reasons why disbelievers dismiss data. These reasons are described below. In each case we describe the general reason, and highlight the main types of data to which it applies. For each category, we note which types of evidence are more persuasive or less persuasive.

1. Information type

This paper provides many types of evidence in support of the case that CE delivers business benefits, ranging from people's opinions to data on the impact of CE on business functions and finances. Generally, the disbeliever argues that only evidence about the impact on business functions and finances is really credible.

The least credible data, for most disbelievers, is data about **opinion**. The disbeliever, for example, dismisses the many public opinion surveys confirming that a high proportion of consumers say that they would switch their purchasing to buy products made in ethical ways by ethical companies. 'They would hardly say anything else,' the disbeliever retorts, 'since one is asking them if they are ethical. The facts are that consumers buy the products they want at the cheapest price and rarely look at its ethical credentials.' The one exception to note here regarding the importance of opinion data is that disbelievers can be quite persuaded by the candid opinion of their peers.

Disbelievers are usually more convinced by data about **action** than about opinion. For example, it is more persuasive to show examples where people actually did purchase products because the producing company is deemed ethical than it is to show a survey where people said they would. Disbelievers' confidence in such data is, however, limited by the fact that cause and effect can be hard to demonstrate. Did Nike footwear sales fall, for example, because of allegations of use of child labour, or because Nike did not keep pace with fashion?

Data about effects on **business processes and finances** are the most convincing. When CE can be shown to have an impact on a business process that a disbeliever thinks is critically important to success, he or she is most likely to be persuaded. Disbelievers are likely to be engaged by the evidence, for example, that volunteering increases employee morale, when they are already convinced that employee morale is directly linked to financial performance. It is particularly helpful if CE can be shown to have an effect on the finances of the company. Where cause and effect is straightforward, this is the best way to catch the attention of even the most ingrained sceptic. For example, there are numerous studies that demonstrate that cause-related marketing can increase sales, and some studies actually set out the net financial gains through such marketing.

It can be quite difficult to show a direct link between CE and increases in financial results. For example, Shell International's financial performance is currently excellent, but no one has been able to demonstrate statistically that this has anything to do with its considerable investment in corporate citizenship. But that doesn't mean that sceptics can't be persuaded. Businesses spends billions of dollars each year on important activities, such as advertising and training, even though there is very little evidence showing a direct link between those expenditures and specific increases in the bottom line. The critical issue is to show the link between those activities and improvements in business processes and functions that the sceptic views as key to attaining future profitability.

2. Relevance

Relevance is perhaps the most important foundation on which the disbeliever can challenge the data. This combines several possible elements, including accuracy, materiality and applicability.

a. **Accuracy** is about whether the data is correctly describing what it purports to. This can be an arithmetical issue (were the numbers added up correctly?), or a statistical issue (was the equation that draws conclusions about cause and effect correctly specified?). It also can be a representative issue when it comes to qualitative data (do the quotes really reflect what the body of people felt?).

Disbelievers have good reason for their scepticism. Wood and Jones, in a careful review of the data and cases brought forward by advocates, show that many of them, unfortunately, are seriously flawed. They noted that the studies as a group presented inconsistent measures of corporate social responsibility, and that many of the studies were lacking in methodological rigour and were therefore of uncertain validity, reliability and generalisability (Wood and Jones 1995).

Because it is nearly impossible for disbelievers to review the evidence in detail, they tend to rely on the reputation of the organisation as a proxy for whether the data is accurate. For example, a statement such as 'CE practices of the following type have been shown to reduce turnover by 9.3% in entry-level positions in customer service organisations' would be much more likely to be accepted as accurate if it came from a highly reputable human resources consulting firm than if it came from a small non-profit advocacy group.

b. **Materiality** is about whether the business effects being described were material in the case or cases in point. This may be a statistical issue of whether the size of the positive effect being recorded is significant. Alternatively, it may be a judgement call as to whether the effects are worthwhile. Volunteerism may increase morale, but is it the type of morale-booster that does in practice feed through to real financial benefits? A further variant of this concerns value-for-money, or what has elsewhere been described as 'efficiency'. Cause-related marketing may indeed increase sales, but is it more or less than if the funds had been spent on other marketing approaches?

The disbeliever is least likely to be persuaded if the evidence presented leads him or her to think that increased CE will not create a large enough effect to matter, or that it will create a large enough effect, but at far too large a cost. The greater the benefit, and the lower the cost, the more interested the disbeliever is likely to become. However, there is a 'Catch 22': if the evidence presented claims too great a benefit at too low a cost, the disbeliever may scoff—'if it were that good, why isn't everyone already doing it?'

c. **Applicability** is about whether the experience being described is applicable to the company or situation in which the disbeliever lives and works.

'Just because it worked someplace else, how do I know it will work for me?' There is often good reason for being sceptical about applicability. For example, there is little doubt that BP enhanced its image in the eyes of opinion leaders concerned with the environment by leaving the Global Climate Coalition. But managers at General Motors would be right if they were sceptical that this then proved that General Motors would make the same gains if it did the same thing. It is not directly applicable, partly because it would not be the 'first out' (as was BP), partly because it is in a different industry, and partly because it is a US- rather than a UK-based company. Similarly, it is unclear as to whether Ben & Jerry's positive social image will be retained under the new Unilever ownership even if they have exactly the same programmes in operation. Most significant perhaps is that the benefits gained through CE by high-profile consumer brands do not necessarily translate to similar gains for lesser-known companies, particularly if they are essentially business-to-business operations.

Clearly, the least credible evidence comes from situations that are enormously different from those faced by the disbeliever, and the most credible evidence comes from peers facing the same situations as the believer.

3. Source

People believe people, not data.

This should be an 'old adage', at least for this area, because it is just so true. Disbelievers who dismiss data from opinion surveys find themselves lapping it up when a respected colleague or competitor finds it to be of value. Financial data collected by business networks takes on a mystical relevance even where similar data produced by academics has been rejected as 'pie in the sky'.

Most managers have a 'hierarchy of belief'. They are most likely to believe information coming from their peers; after their peers, they are most likely to believe well-respected consultants or vendors; after that, they listen to their trade associations. Information from most academics, foundations, advocacy groups and much of the media is generally ignored. (Of course, there are exceptions, in that some academics have attained the status of 'business guru', and some business media such as the *Wall Street Journal* and the *Financial Times* are generally held in high regard.)

Managers are also deeply suspicious of information that comes from companies such as Ben & Jerry's, which they regard as being 'outside the mainstream'. Since much of the information that proponents bring forward comes from these sources, it is often dismissed without careful review (Eisen 2000).

The best way to convince a corporate disbeliever is to bring them face to face with a business person who can claim to have tried CE and found that it 'really does work'. Often the stories will be anecdotal, and the business advocate and disbeliever will cheerfully agree that most quantitative data is nonsense and that 'real hands-on experience' is the only way to distinguish fact from fiction.

Of course, there is not always a compliant business person at hand during a conversation with disbelievers. In these situations, the best one can do is to seek credibility by knowing what other business people have said, and by bonding with the disbelievers by acknowledging the problems with data sources and methodology. Evangelists make bad advocates when faced with sceptics. Gain the disbeliever's trust by being *more* sceptical than them.

4. Underlying attitudes

Evidence that is brought forward to support increased CE may be accepted or rejected because of underlying attitudes. Weak evidence may be embraced because it supports an underlying attitude. Even the strongest evidence may be rejected because it runs foul of deeply held beliefs or political agendas. For example, managers very often want to increase CE, but don't yet have a rationale that is acceptable in the company. In this case, the business argument *enables* rather than *motivates* them to act. The managers need to be able to rationalise their actions using business rather than, say, moral or ethical arguments. But what often energises them to do something is precisely that undercurrent of caring and ambition to make a wider societal contribution, and maybe being acknowledged for just that.

There is, unfortunately, a dark side to this tale. Just as people will use the business argument to provide support for their caring, they will use it to avoid engaging with difficult challenges. A recent report on how to get more disabled people into the workplace described surveys of managers who revealed a strong distaste for and indeed anger against disabled people masquerading under the guise of 'it's just too expensive to help'. Rational arguments and convincing data may be insufficient alone to shift deep-rooted bigotry based on ignorance and fear. In such situations, it is often only direct experience that opens the possibility of a change in attitudes and in turn behaviour, whether it be of disabled people or unemployed youths (Zadek and Scott-Parker 2000).

Rules of engagement

People disbelieve for a host of reasons. We have outlined here some of the key ones. Convincing business people is not a matter of evading their scepticism. What is critical is to demonstrate that CE improves their ability to meet their *existing* objectives. The key is to show not only that it can generate black on the bottom line but that it does so in strategically important areas of business performance.

There is no single way to handle the extraordinary diversity of conversations with disbelievers. However, a few rules of engagement do come to mind that might help CE advocates to better navigate their way through such conversations making the best use of data and patterns of argument.

a. **Know who you are talking to.** Spend as much time as possible listening to what they do in the business, who they have to persuade, and what are likely to be the key objections facing them.

b. **Be an insider.** Even if you know little about the business, be sure that you come armed with insider examples of other companies. Don't let the disbeliever think or say 'this person understands nothing about business'.

c. **Be sceptical first.** Following from this, be sceptical about the data, and so build trust in the disbeliever that you know your subject, and do not take her or him for a fool.

d. **Help solve their problems, not yours.** Be clear about whether they really are sceptical, or whether they are rehearsing an argument to be had with others. In either case, consider yourself a resource, helping the person to marshal the arguments. Everyone likes a free consultant (if they are good).

e. **Never evangelise.** It seems so obvious to say, but we do forget that most people are put off by evangelical arguments, particularly when it is linked to a sense that it will be followed by a request that involves resource and some risk.

To convince a disbeliever, you have to be able to think, feel and communicate like one (or indeed like many different ones). This section aims to help you in this task. We have used the key findings in this chapter to create the 'Disbeliever's Scorecard', which is essentially a list of the main reasons why 'data failure' occurs when in conversation with disbelievers. Its use allows you to predict and effectively handle the complex twists and turns that can and do happen in conversations with disbelievers.

Stock price and financial performance						
Score	1 Low	2	3	4	5 High	Notes
Information type						
Relevance						
Source						
Attitudes						

TABLE 6 DISBELIEVER'S SCORECARD

In this scorecard, '1' is the lowest score—the least persuasive evidence; '5' is the highest score—the most persuasive evidence. We will use the Disbeliever's Scorecard at the end of sections within the various chapters to present some thoughts about how persuasive the data presented in that section is.

Try out the Disbeliever's Scorecard for yourself. As you go through this paper, note in the margin what are the main challenges that would be lobbied against each piece of data that we offer in support of CE. You will quickly see the patterns and internalise the lessons. Hopefully you will also discover new elements that can usefully be added to the scorecard, and so improve your ability over time to navigate critical conversations to an effective conclusion.

23
accountability
and governance*
co-written with Malcolm McIntosh

Interesting times

The corporate community has grown remarkably in recent decades. Some 60,000–70,000 multinational corporations operate in today's global economy, with an additional 200,000–300,000 nationally and regionally based subsidiaries. The largest of these mega-institutions are large indeed. General Motors, for example, has annual sales equivalent to the gross domestic product (GDP) of Denmark (Utting 2000). And size counts. Global corporations deeply penetrate the political economy both of developing countries and of super-powers (Zadek 2001b). Their investments underpin the capital base of many emerging economies, and their donations are essential to ever more costly political campaigns.

Many commentators argue that our collective destinies are framed by the future of the corporate community and that this is not a matter of choice. 'Disengagement' from globalisation, and the role in this of the corporate community, although politically attractive in the 1970s, is no longer a serious option for nations, communities or even individuals. We are in this together, like it or not, as Castells and subsequently many others have pointed out (Castells 1996–2000: II; Mulgan 1998). This fact variously underpins a call to revolutionary arms, augurs a recipe for despair or elicits distressing levels of managerial smugness. Although understandable, both individually and collectively, they represent a sadly limiting set of foundations for forging strategy and practice in ensuring that the business community is very much part of the solution in addressing social, environmental and economic challenges.

This is the broad context within which the decision was made to prepare a special issue of *The Journal of Corporate Citizenship* on 'Corporate Transparency,

* First published as the Editorial in *The Journal of Corporate Citizenship* Issue 8 (Winter 2002). © 2002 Greenleaf Publishing, Sheffield. This piece makes reference to articles that also appeared in that issue.

Accountability and Governance'. The trigger was, however, more specific to the events surrounding the Enron debacle and its (still emerging) aftermath. In our call for papers, we sought to relate the broad and specific contexts as follows:

> Since Enron applied for receivership, issues of transparency, accountability and honesty have risen to the top of the public agenda. But will these developments add force to, or in fact diminish, focus on the wider aspects of accountability underpinning corporate citizenship, just as the actions to prevent a further 'Asian financial crisis' did little to focus the world on social and environmental issues in the region? Will the call for greater financial transparency, and the associated shake-up in the financial accountancy profession, advance the cause of overall accountability? Or will these developments in practice reinforce corporate conservatism that reduces the potential for citizenship-based innovations? Do the events surrounding the case of Enron shift our thinking about what is the preferred balance between voluntary and statutory approaches to securing appropriate levels and forms of corporate accountability and in general the role of public policy and practice?

Spectrums and perspectives

The papers in this issue provide valuable points of reference along a spectrum that runs from classical perspectives on corporate governance as it relates to financial performance, through to broader views of both the mechanisms of corporate governance and the relevant aspects of performance.

Starting at the former end, the papers by Gerde, Silva and White and by Stanwick and Stanwick explore a related set of hypotheses concerning how classical elements of corporate governance impact on (particularly financial) performance. Focus in both papers is placed on characteristics of the board, board directors and the various audit functions. Gerde *et al.* offer a thoughtful review of key theoretical perspectives, thereby making explicit the hypothetical underpinnings of some of the classical assumptions linking governance and performance. Understandably, given its classical premises, the paper concludes that the core governance parameter of 'independence' should underpin improved performance. The paper by Stanwick and Stanwick also covers some of the theoretical territory, building a set of propositions concerning good governance that include independence but also covering aspects of board 'performance' and shareholder accountability. Using a publicly available data-set, Stanwick and Stanwick then offer the results of empirical tests of their hypotheses. Once again, the tests suggest a correlation between corporate financial performance and board independence, competences and shareholder accountability.

Papers by Puri and Borok and by Betit take the debate into different territory in exploring the implications of extending the scope of accountability to focus on employees as well as shareholders. Both papers offer a combination of descriptive, analytic and normative perspectives. Puri and Borok reject the pure shareholder accountability model, arguing that the rights and responsibilities afforded share-holders do not amount to 'ownership'. Having also rejected the pure stakeholder model as being too complex in terms of implied governance and accountability arrangements, drawing on Enron as a case in point, Puri and Borok embrace a hybrid that privileges employees as well as shareholders as the stakeholders with the greatest stake and associated potential risks and rewards. Also moving beyond the purely organisational aspects of corporate governance, this paper draws on the US and Canadian context in teasing out in broad terms some of the regulatory impli-cations of adopting an extended (albeit limited) model of corporate governance and accountability. Betit's paper takes the exploration of employee accountability through its focus on the US-based, employee-owned Carris Companies. The only paper based largely around one case study, it explores the historical transition of the company, its primary philosophical and demonstrative influences (e.g. the Mondragon Co-operatives) and the resonances of its underlying approach with emerging thinking on broader-based, open-book, dialogue-based governance mod-els (Zadek 2001a).

Swift and Dando's paper continues the extension beyond classical corporate gov-ernance rooted in shareholder accountability models. Drawing on the history of one particular standard, the AA1000 accountability framework and the more recent AA1000 Series Assurance Standard, the authors argue that some of the key challenges in managing complex, stakeholder-based approaches to governance and account-ability can be supported by emerging best practice in 'social and sustainability auditing'. Although acknowledging the complexities and challenges in avoiding the dangers of managerial co-option of stakeholder-based performance models, the authors take an upbeat view on the possibilities of best practice and related stan-dards closing the expectations gap created by inadequate assurance to date.

Puri and Borok's, Betit's, and Swift and Dando's papers encourage us to stretch beyond classical theory and case material to face some of the broader questions of the role of the broader rule framework in guiding both purpose and outcomes. The two final papers, by Sullivan, and by Clark and Demirag, both raise the need for sig-nificant shifts in the overarching framework of norms of corporate governance, whether 'voluntary' or regulatory. Sullivan, stressing specific lessons associated with the Enron case as well as the broader dimensions of corporate accountability, usefully unpacks the all-too-often binary dialogue on 'self-regulation versus statute'. Although rightly highlighting the apparent limitations of the former, he acknowledges the problems with a focus on statutory compliance. He offers, rather, a view of the potential of being able to draw on both regimes in a carefully time-sequenced manner to ensure graduated, orderly take-up en route to new statutes establishing minimum governance and performance floors. Clark and Demirag are even more bullish in exploring fallout from Enron on corporate governance and accountability. They highlight short-term shifts in US corporate practice and associ-ated changes in US regulations that have been pushed through in direct response to cases such as Enron and WorldCom. Moving beyond this, however, they predict far deeper changes, extending internationally throughout the accountancy profession but also more broadly into the heartland of business regulation.

Accountability pathways

There is certainly a wealth of material and insights provided by these seven articles, both individually and collectively. Drawing from these, and taking account of other thinking emerging on these topics, we can identify a number of themes that are likely to be key aspects of tomorrow's pathways towards enhanced corporate governance, accountability and transparency.

Extended accountable entities

One of the greatest challenges today is not only the broadening of the scope of governance and accountability (e.g. human rights) but also the extension of the accountable entity. In recent years this has been mainly about extending accountability along the supply chain (e.g. labour standards and food source traceability). In the coming years, the accountable entity will extend further to embrace particular partnerships between businesses, public bodies and civil-society organisations, particularly in light of the future mainstreaming of such partnerships signalled at the Johannesburg World Summit on Sustainable Development (Zadek *et al.* 2002). This in turn will shine light on the governance and accountability of these partners of business, as well as that of the partnership in itself.

Multi-stakeholder governance

There seems little doubt that business will be under increasing pressure to demonstrably develop and apply competences and approaches that enable them to effectively handle complex decision-making that factors in the perspectives, interests and influence of multiple stakeholder groups. In the near future, corporate governance and accountability will increasingly be judged on this basis, whether framed by a 'multipurpose' model of business responsibilities or by a more reductionist model that incorporates these de facto realities into risk-related and opportunity-related shareholder interests.

Assurance and reporting

The combination of events associated with companies such as Enron, and significant practice and standards-based innovations in sustainability reporting and assurance (e.g. the Global Reporting Initiative and AccountAbility's AA1000 Series Assurance Standard), will shift the basis on which assurance and reporting is done globally (AccountAbility 2002). A further driver will be a growing concern that many aspects of enhanced disclosure (e.g. non-financial) are not providing the expected accountability gains. Needed and expected will be major methodological breakthroughs that will both strengthen robustness and extend scope. As important, however, will be an opening-up of the assurance professions in terms of the basis on which they can continue to do business.

Ownership

Corporate accountability and governance will be deeply impacted by emerging alternative ownership models on the back of the lows as well as the highs of two decades of privatisation and by new rules for incorporation. Some of these new models will be rooted in the mainstreaming of 'responsible investment' through mainstream financial institutions. Others are likely to emerge from more fundamental shifts in the range of legal vehicles for incorporation that factor in the imperatives and potential performance gains from institutionalising aspects of multi-stakeholder approaches.

Regulation

Regulation will almost certainly lag emerging new practices by leadership companies that embrace the more complex environment and approaches. This will partly reflect the fact that what is good for leadership companies is not always good for the rump of the business community. Partly emerging from this fact, lags will reflect the 'negotiation' complications in forging new regulations where diverse interests are at stake, between business and its external stakeholders, and between different parts of the business community (e.g. large and small). It seems likely that there will be increasing amounts of regulation sensitised to multi-stakeholder perspectives, whether established in an orderly fashion such as the development of the new UK company law, or in a more disorderly fashion, such as through campaign-led litigation such as that witnessed in California against Nike, and emerging legal battles in relation, for example, to pharmaceuticals, food and finance.

Concluding remarks

It is actually somewhat difficult to justify the prefix 'corporate' to the term 'accountability and governance'. This is not just semantics. The scale of the corporate community, both individually and collectively, its impact, its evolving purpose and its growing interconnectedness with and impact on public and private public-interest institutions all reduce the practical relevance of the distinction between corporate and societal governance.

In this light, one might speculate that the coming years may witness the gradual dissolution of 'corporate' (i.e. business) governance and accountability as a distinct work area and discipline by academics, lawyers or indeed (and perhaps most difficult to imagine) of social activists. What might take its place is work on how best to understand the relationship between and make effective different spheres of governance and accountability throughout society. This will relate as much to distinguishing power relations between the state and the individual, and between the state, corporations and civil society. These spheres will partly be differentiated by their technical governance approaches and targets and topics of application. Beyond this, however, they are likely to operate under quite different jurisdictions.

Some of these may indeed be geographic and specifically sovereign, allowing existing institutions to underpin negotiations as to how best to join up differing approaches. But many more are likely to be driven by multi-stakeholder processes and institutions—what today are often called 'global policy networks', made up of state and non-state actors (Edwards and Zadek 2003). This in turn means that the mechanisms and frameworks that they develop and advocate will stand or fall not only on the basis of their technical quality but also on the basis of the legitimacy of these new institutional formations (i.e. their own governance and accountability). Strange? Indeed. Likely? Yes, although only time will reveal just how far these predictions might be on the mark. Significant? Enormously so. One thing certain is that the topic of 'corporate governance, accountability and transparency' is out of its shaded box, historically overseen by learned and powerful interests and professions. The importance of the corporate community in forming our futures has made 'good governance, accountability and transparency' a public good in itself, which will without doubt have the effect of throwing it into the cut and thrust of public debate well beyond any memories of Enron and its immediate fallout.

24
reflections on corporate responsibility after 9/11[*]

It is widely predicted by self-styled progressive internationalists that the ghastly destruction of the World Trade Center, the quintessential symbol of global capitalism, will bring with it a realisation that 'business as usual' is both morally bankrupt and, critically, no longer feasible. A radical reappraisal of globalisation, and in particular of the role of the US and the corporate community, may be one potential silver lining to the otherwise dark events of last autumn.

So how is the business community responding to the world since September 11th? In particular, how have those corporations responded that have in recent years identified themselves with the movement to make business more responsible? Indeed, what is the future of 'corporate social responsibility' (CSR) in a new century already beset with worrying signs of conflict and extremes?

The Institute of Social and Ethical AccountAbility set out to explore these questions, especially the last, in an event hosted by Cable & Wireless in London in early December 2001. Attending were representatives of such diverse organisations as Amnesty International, British Airways, the European Commission, KPMG and Oxfam, with many of the doyens of the world's corporate responsibility movement leading the discussion.[1]

The refreshingly frank debate raised real concerns as to the future course of corporate responsibility as a means of addressing major social and environmental challenges. Even the most inveterate inside players were vocal in challenging the adequacy of progress made to date. Such challenges are undoubtedly good news. Like all movements in their early stages, the field of corporate responsibility has been dogged by over-idealism, evangelism and a lack of serious self-critique. What the debate revealed was that its leading advocates are now able and willing to tussle, more publicly, with the tough questions. In so doing, we are set for a new round of insights both about the short-term corporate response to September 11th and more generally about possible futures for corporate responsibility. Below are some of the key perspectives that emerged from the AccountAbility event.

Frustration and disempowerment

September 11th has starkly revealed what many already knew: that there is enormous anger and frustration across the world at how globalisation is playing itself out. It was notable that contributors from outside the North Atlantic community highlighted the considerable support around the world for the view that the attack on the World Trade Center was understandable, although unacceptable. Public opinion surveys, for example in Brazil and South Africa, revealed support for the view that the US and the global business community need to understand the implications of the despair that communities feel in the face of globalisation. Such views are indicative that for many this is not a 'Muslim issue', but one that reflects the facts of how globalising business and US foreign policy are undermining and disempowering people and communities.

That does not, the participants stressed, mean that global business was responsible for September 11th. But it does mean that corporations are an integral element of an economic and associated political environment that creates unacceptable outcomes for many, many people, and ultimately for us all.

Corporations and public debate

The corporate community has been almost entirely absent from serious public debate about what the events of September 11th mean for the future. One obvious reason is the perceived need to show unquestioning solidarity in condemning any and all groups dubbed terrorists and their supporters. Another is that most businesses—and so most corporate leaders—have been painfully focused on just trying to survive in what is for many the roughest economic climate for over two decades.

A further, less obvious reason is that even the most out-there corporate leaders, who are used to opining on all manner of issues, have been humbled by the enormity of the possible implications of recent events, and are honestly recognising that they don't know how best to address them. It was refreshing, if ironic, to see civil society and business leaders together struggling to understand the practical implications of the current situation with few of the normal pretences that 'the answer is obvious . . . if only you would understand me'. The acknowledgement of a common set of challenges that require joint action was really grounded: a hopeful sign for the future.

Kicking the tyres of the
corporate responsibility movement

The current political and economic turmoil seems to have presented the first real test of the embeddedness of many corporations' approaches to social and environmental responsibility.

For those mainly engaged in short-term reputation management, there has been a welcome relief as the anti-globalisation movement has been driven into at least temporary recess. Indeed, many of the short-term drivers for CSR have weakened as the media's appetite for corporate social and environmental misdemeanours has diminished (with the notable exception of Enron), the labour market has loosened, and consumers rediscover their primary interest in price (if, indeed, most of them ever lost it). Add to this the financial belt-tightening within businesses, and the scene is set for a shake-out.

On the other hand, there has been a notable robustness in approaches to corporate responsibility on the part of those companies that are most advanced in aligning their long-term business strategy to enhanced social and environmental performance. It is becoming painfully clear that accountability processes that are not part of an organisation's underlying success model are unlikely to survive tough times, a salutary lesson for NGOs as much as the business community.

Raising the bar

The September 11th events have highlighted the need for those advocating corporate responsibility to honestly face the challenge of what can and cannot be achieved through its current forms. In so far as poverty and inequality have some bearing on those events, the participants at AccountAbility's seminar were united in agreeing that corporate responsibility will have to go a lot further than the isolated good practices of individual companies if it is to make a serious contribution in the future. Many highlighted the need for leadership companies to step forward and join (rather than resist) the critical public debate about globalisation. They should also work more closely with public bodies and civil-society organisations to explore what international frameworks would support companies committed to enhancing their social and environmental performance as part of their core business process and long-term strategy, and force companies that are not to reach agreed minimum standards. Again it was stressed that corporate leaders should avoid the inclination to conclude that the correct public policy response is simply 'more of the same' globalisation.

Don't predict the future, create it

It is really far too early to tell what the longer-term effects of the events of September 11th will be. But then the real challenge is not to predict the future, but to create it.

The event and its fallout to date creates the potential for both positive and negative change. For corporate responsibility to count (positively) in this larger macro-landscape requires that it evolves beyond its current forms—what I have called elsewhere 'third-generation corporate citizenship' (Zadek 2001b). Ultimately, any serious notion of responsible business will have to address the question of what business's appropriate purpose is, and seek to establish the global governance mechanisms to ensure that these purposes are effectively met.

The events of September 11th will test the foundations of corporate responsibility. Bits of what many of us have worked to create over the last decade will undoubtedly fail the test, revealed at best as being of marginal significance and at worst as part of the problem. But the shake-out in the field will strengthen the resolve of those who are serious about business making a real contribution, and encourage them to set themselves apart from, and bring pressure to bear on, those who are currently along for the ride.

This will certainly challenge the current Big-Tent approach, which argues that it is better to have the half-serious part of the business community in the team. On balance, it is probably time to mark out real difference, and the dynamic debate at AccountAbility's event did suggest that the corporate responsibility movement is perhaps now ready for this challenge.

Section V
partnership alchemy

25
partnership
futures*

August 2002, winter in Jo'burg. An estimated 60,000 people packed their bags in order to join in the World Summit on Sustainable Development. Among them were many of us who had vowed forever to avoid the hubris, the financial and environmental costs and, so often, the disappointment associated with such mega-summits. Yet here we were again, shipping bodies and souls across the planet for a few short days in an effort to talk our way through and out of the pervasive and daunting social and environmental challenges facing us.

Difficult and challenging, perhaps. But this gathering was far more than the cynics' picture of a modern-day, Babylonian folly. Its antecedents in Monterrey, Beijing, Copenhagen and Rio, just to name a few, all played crucially important roles in driving forward progressive agendas. More than anything, mega-summits generate change by ushering in new players and processes onto the world stage. These players and processes are validated through a new framing of the nature of challenges, lessons from the past, and reasons why and how things can be different in the future.

In this light, it is easy to see that Jo'burg was more than anything about partnerships. Much of the event, whatever topic was being addressed, sought to validate (or challenge) the legitimacy and potential contribution that the business community could play, working in partnership with public bodies and civil-society organisations. The Summit's silver bullet and *bête noire* were those partnerships created from businesses' choice, whether for market-related, fiscal or statutory reasons, to address social, economic and environmental aims as part of its day-to-day practice and underlying success model.

It is an exciting and also a somewhat eerie moment when a movement comes of age. What was considered absurd, naïve, or just plain silly becomes 'the obvious'. What seemed unlikely or impossible becomes normal, and rapidly passé. Scant resources skimmed from innocent budgets turn into billion-dollar, often one-eyed programmes. What passed as experiments become the 'real thing', as did earlier generations of pre-packaged development solutions.

* First published in *Partnership Matters: Current Issues in Cross Sector Collaborations*. © 2003 Cross Sector Partnership Initiative, Cambridge.

Where are we going?

But the rules of the game change in this transition from the margin to the mainstream. Notably, open season can be and is legitimately declared on business partnerships for development. Criticism is no longer purely a matter for civil activists, as it falls within the ambit of the professionals who know most about private–public partnerships and the business community. The core evaluative question posed by these knowledgeable inquirers shifts in this transition from 'did something good happen?' to 'was it really worth it?'

Most of all, however, come the searching questions about scale and accountability.

Take first the crucial issue of scale. Can partnerships and corporate responsibility contribute sufficiently to addressing development goals for it to warrant its honoured place at the table and associated public patronage and resources? Is our picture of effective development a million blossoms blooming, each one a stand-alone partnership creating business and societal value, profit and environmental security? For many of course the vision is less chaotic, more aligned to the role of the state as rule-maker rather than marriage partner. For this group, scaling up partnerships through replication merely reproduces the problem of under-regulated business and markets, or at best delivers loads of little gains without addressing the underlying systemic problems.

Another option on the matter of scale is that the partnerships are more than the sum of their parts, but not through unwieldy regulation. AccountAbility and The Copenhagen Centre (2003) have recently argued in *Responsible Competitiveness: Corporate Responsible Clusters in Action* that potential development impacts of partnership and corporate responsibility practices will not be forthcoming unless they are integrated into national economic competitiveness strategies and practices. The arguments presented are particularly relevant to the situation of most developing countries, whose economies are often highly dependent on resource- and cost-based export competitiveness. Partnerships and corporate responsibility approaches that are not aligned to new forms of economic competitiveness might undermine, the research argues, development by pushing yet more financial value to the brand end of the value chain, or by favouring global corporations over smaller, indigenous businesses. On the positive side, the work offers examples of how corporate responsibility can enhance economic competitiveness.

On the second issue of accountability, it is noteworthy that focus has to date been on the potential for 'bluewash', that commercial interests can pervert development aims, outcomes and institutions. But a report produced by this author and published by Business for Social Responsibility, *Working with Multilaterals* (Zadek 2002), highlights the dangers of ignoring pervasive accountability shortfalls within public-sector and civil-society partners, as well as real deficits in our understanding of how to build effective partnership accountability. Looking to the future, it argues that multi-stakeholder partnerships will only remain legitimate and serve to deliver business and development benefits if their basis of accountability, including that of each of its participants, is clarified and greatly improved. More generally, the mainstreaming of partnerships forces us away from the view and practice that accountability can be vested in the good intentions, commitment and leadership quality of their creators. At best this is true for the vanguard, but scaling-up requires a reliance on more explicit, replicable forms of accountability. This is all the more so where partnerships become a, if not *the*, key pathway for routing both public funds and private investments, shifting the emphasis from 'new social partnerships' to public–private partnerships as means of delivering public service through private means.

Is this the future?

It is all too easy to post 'health warnings' about partnerships. Much more difficult is to usefully imagine the longer term. Forget for a second our near-sighted view on the Summit, for many framed by sadness and weary cynicism. Try another perspective, looking back on the recent events in Jo'burg from the year 2020. From such a standpoint, the 18 years following the Summit would be facts at your fingertips, allowing you to judge the Summit by its more durable significance, rather than its momentary importance.

Looking back from 2020, it was obvious that the Summit's real outcome was to open the floodgates to public–private partnerships as a primary development vehicle. Testimony to this outcome was the multitude of operational partnerships created in the first years following the Summit. These early partnerships were, of course, a mixed bag. Following the World Bank-facilitated 'Business Partnership for Development' initiative, some directly helped real people in real situations, particularly the ones that utilised the operational infrastructure of the business community. Others unfortunately followed quite different pathways, commercialising and reducing the availability of 'public goods' such as water and healthcare, wasting public and private money, and draining the energies of communities, activists and the more enlightened business leaders.

In the years following the Summit, the arguments about whether to have partnerships with business for development waned. As in the wider debate on globalisation, the ideological question of *whether* became subsumed by the policy questions of *to what effect*. This development was not really about technical or managerial issues, although literature and consultants abounded on these micro-level challenges. It concerned the more profound, related issues of accountability and scale.

Our recent history, you will all no doubt recall, went like this. Five 'development decades' preceding the Summit had shown that incremental change was just not enough—it left most people standing still or, all too often, worse off than when they started. Credibility of the partnership approach therefore depended on it achieving a (positive) 'development discontinuity', a demonstrable leap in social and environmental gains. In seeking to achieve this, tens of thousands of partnerships were created, rapidly becoming the entry condition for accessing public funds for development. Beyond this, many of the partnerships that made most impact moved rapidly away from voluntary associations to become contract-based commercial arrangements, largely exporting the experience in Europe and elsewhere of public service delivery through public–private partnerships operating with income-based public payments.

Achieving scale meant bigger, not only more. Ever-larger and more-ambitious partnerships were created, involving the world's largest corporations joined at the hip with under-resourced governments, multilaterals and civil-society partners. Global partnerships became complex, multi-billion-dollar enterprises with staff and offices sprawling across the continents. These partnerships became, generally with the best will in the world, laws unto themselves, accountable to everyone through 'stakeholder engagement', and so to no one in particular.

Most partnerships, particularly the larger ones, suffered the same fate as their public-sector predecessors. Personal, political and commercial interests replaced innovation based on social entrepreneurship. Cultures of low performance set in, driven by the high transaction costs endemic to partnerships, a lack of focus and, increasingly, straightforward corruption. Public demand for greater accountability shifted their focus from business to partnerships, and from partnerships to their constituent partners, notably public bodies and civil-society organisations. Calls for greater statutory regulation moved beyond business transparency and foreign direct liability as the first cycle of lawsuits emerged targeted at partnerships over their alleged misdemeanours. Partnerships began to appear as contingent liabilities rather than assets on company balance sheets. Gradually, the partnership approach suffered the same ignominious fate as its antecedent, easy-win 'silver bullets' for development.

Or this . . . ?

But of course none of this has really happened. The history of partnerships over the next two decades is waiting to be invented, by us. Build your own scenario, hopefully one less miserable, less predictable and with better development outcomes. A preferred pathway from the Summit would be based on a recognition by the advocates and architects of tomorrow's partnerships that effective development requires meaningful accountability. This would mean a greater emphasis on the terms on which business behaviour is pro-development, and a little less on the possibilities for business voluntarily contributing to development. It would mean considering how best to balance innovative leadership, partnerships and regulation in creating more inclusive and equitable markets, rather than how best to build partnerships mainly to manage risk and reputation.

In this scenario, the Summit would set the stage for building effective approaches to partnership accountability. This could start in two places. First would be to extend current work on corporate disclosure to embrace partnerships, particularly emerging standards for reporting (Global Reporting Initiative Guidelines) and related assurance (AA1000 Assurance Standard). Second would be to promote a clearer sense of what is good partnership governance. This would require a hard look at accountability issues for each partner (including, but not just, business) as it relates to the collective partnership endeavour, as well as for the partnership itself.

Partnerships involving business could make a real contribution to development. Taking this possibility seriously means honesty, leadership and innovation in facing the matter of their accountability. Without this, partnerships for development will go the same way as other 'unaccountability initiatives', not only deemed illegitimate but ultimately ineffective. With robust and credible accountability at their core, on the other hand, partnerships could establish their legitimate place in an effective development process.

26
partnership
alchemy
engagement, innovation
and governance*

New challenges to old problems

Businesses, communities and individuals are learning to live with the realities of the New Economy, characterised in terms of economic globalisation, technological transformation, demographic change and political transition. The forces of privatisation, market liberalisation and electronic communication have meant a massive transfer of assets and attention to the private sector, and a radical reorientation of the role of the state. These new realities are creating unprecedented opportunities for many citizens, but increased insecurity and inequality for others. In almost every country, it is possible to find cosmopolitan pockets of growing affluence, high technology, world-class social services and increased economic competitiveness, existing side by side with areas of rising unemployment, inadequate skills, low incomes, poor housing, family breakdown, crime, ethnic conflict and environmental deterioration.

The widening gap between those who are beneficiaries of change and those who are excluded from its benefits poses a fundamental threat to the project of economic and political modernisation that countries at all levels of development are pursuing. Bridging this gap has therefore become a central goal for policy-makers, whether in government or leaders in business, trade unions and the community.

* First published in in J. Andriof and M. McIntosh (eds.), *Perspectives on Corporate Citizenship*. © 2001 Greenleaf Publishing, Sheffield. It draws from the publication 'Partnership Alchemy: New Social Partnerships in Europe', which was co-authored with Jane Nelson and supported and published by The Copenhagen Centre.

Partnership times

Traditional roles are under threat. Governments often seem impotent in the face of the economic and social forces that their predecessors have helped to create. The labour movement appears stunned by the collapse of its power base of organised labour, and disturbed by the emerging influence of other civil-society actors. These other actors—the eclectic blend of non-governmental organisations (NGOs)—are unprepared for power and remain unable to effectively handle the politics of engagement rather than marginalised resistance. And then there is the business community. As the era's most powerful constituency, this community—particularly its largest, transnational members—has been thrust into the limelight of public policy debate and practice.

There is growing recognition of this shifting balance of power between the state, the market and civil society. Familiar configurations of power are being replaced by more complex and fluid patterns of interactions, transitory alliances, and long-term relationships between the key institutional actors and individual citizens. We have entered the 'era of the partnership'.

There are many kinds of partnership. Companies come together to drill for oil or to share airline codes. They also join forces to lobby for or against legislation, and often work continuously with trade unions to ensure a productive and profitable business environment. NGOs join forces to campaign for new legislation to secure environmental improvements, and to influence corporate governance. Equally they work closely with business and government in mobilising resources to battle disease and poverty. Governments join with each other to fight wars, provide humanitarian aid, and to make laws. Equally, governments join with business in bringing private finance to public projects, and to inject public finance into private business.

There are many forms of 'new social partnerships' which involve institutions from different sectors of the community (business, government, civil society) that come together in addressing common purposes that involve the realisation of both social and commercial ends. The Copenhagen Centre has defined these new social partnerships as:

> People and organisations from some combination of public, business and civil constituencies who engage in voluntary, mutually beneficial, inno-vative relationships to address common societal aims through combining their resources and competencies (Nelson and Zadek 2000).

These new social partnerships are often marked out as distinct from other forms of partnerships. IBM outsources its catering because it does not see this as a core competency that it has or wishes to develop. The United Nations spends upwards of $4 billion in purchasing goods and services from business, often through complex, long-term relationships. The French utilities giant Suez Lyonnaise des Eaux engages with Brazilian community groups to design a mechanism of delivering water to low-income areas in a commercially viable and politically sensitive manner because it recognises its lack of competencies in realising this challenge. The British retail chain Sainsbury's works with other companies, NGOs, labour organisations and the UK government through the Ethical Trading Initiative on the issue of labour stan-dards in global supply chains because it recognises the potential gains from differ-ent competencies, shared learning, and distinct reputations and credibility.

These partnership cases appear different because the former are familiar and the latter are novel, innovative and experimental. However, there is an underlying pattern that links the unfamiliar with the traditional. They are similar in that the actors are **consciously seeking opportunities that enable relationship blends that allow them to lever the maximum effectiveness and value of their own (perceived) core competencies and capacities.** The implications of this similarity are that an analysis of their rationale and process can usefully draw on existing language and insights into how and why individuals and institutions collaborate.

That does not mean, however, that they are the same. Certainly the latter differs from the former in that they involve actors that embrace non-commercial interests, and this means that social goals are explicit in the partnership process. Indeed, this difference has complex ramifications that go beyond the simple fact of non-commercial interests and actors. Centrally it raises basic governance questions. At a micro level, it introduces a significant ambiguity into the matter of the purpose of business, which raises basic issues concerning, for example, the fiduciary duties and competencies of directors. At meso and macro levels, it poses the challenge of how social policy in its broadest sense is to be defined in the future if it will increasingly require a complementary business case to be in place for it to be effectively implemented.

Describing partnerships

Numerous frameworks have been developed in recent years in search of the best way to look at partnerships, particularly new social partnerships. Most of them embody a broadly similar set of underlying categories or building blocks. Some of these were drawn together during the research undertaken for the report *Partnership Alchemy* (Nelson and Zadek 2000), and included:

a. **Context**, with a focus on general drivers and specific triggers

b. **Purpose**, collective and specific, and their evolution over time

c. **Participants**, in terms of organisations and individuals and their respective roles and relationships

d. **Organisation**, legal form, structure, governance, etc.

e. **Outcomes**, both actual and expected

How partnerships work is constantly flagged as the key to understanding whether and to what extent they work. Partnerships are, after all, **not a thing, but a process**. The *Partnership Alchemy* study identified a number of dynamic pathways that were consistently raised in various forms in different studies as being critical determinants of effectiveness and efficiency.[1]

a. Acknowledgement by all the participants as to what **drivers and triggers** have brought individuals and organisations to the table and an ability to understand and reappraise on an ongoing basis the **shifting context** and its influence on the partnership

b. Clarity and openness about individual expectations and agendas, with mutual agreement on a **common purpose and agenda**; in short: synergy between desired participant benefits and societal benefits.

c. Mutual agreement on the **scope and complexity** of the partnership's intended locations and levels of action, variety of functions, range of desired outcomes and time-scales

d. An individual or institution(s) capable of playing a **leadership** role, acting as inspirer, mediator and/or facilitator between the partnership participants, and in many cases between the partnership and its ultimate beneficiaries

e. Understanding the **resources, skills and capacities** that are needed to meet the partnership's objectives and how to optimise both the quality and quantity of resources, skills and capacities that each partner brings to the initiative

f. Appropriate **organisational and legal structure** to meet the common objectives of the partnership

g. **Transparency, representation and accountability** both within the partnership and externally

h. **Communication** strategies and systems, which facilitate clarity of language, ensure regular dialogue and feedback, provide forums for problem-solving and conflict resolution, generate a shared vision and celebrate success

i. Methodologies for **measurement** and **evaluation** of partnership processes and outcomes against common and individual agendas

j. Flexibility and willingness to allow **adaptation** of the partnership's purpose, participants or process in response to evaluation or changes in the external context

Analysing partnerships

It is critically important to move beyond the broad descriptors provided above to defining in analytic terms the dynamic elements of partnerships.[2] Once again, many approaches have been proposed. Below are a few of the key parameters that would need to appear in any assessment and illustrations of how they figure in different analytic models.

Building enablers

The Business Excellence Model (BEM), created by the European Foundation for Quality Management, is used by many companies, particularly in Europe, and an increasing number of not-for-profit organisations. The BEM has traditionally been a nine-segment analysis of enablers of business performance and spheres of performance. Business in the Community (BITC) in the UK has used the BEM as the assessment basis for its prestigious annual Awards for Excellence for partnerships with community and business involvement. Some of the boxes are badly under-specified, in particular the 'Impact on society' box. But the underlying idea of enablers and results is helpful in framing our understanding of how partnerships work.

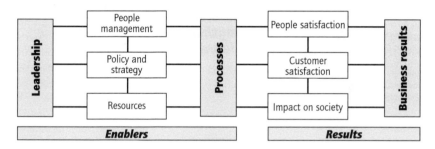

FIGURE 30   THE BUSINESS EXCELLENCE MODEL

Innovation

The UK-based *Innovation through Partnership* (ITP)[3] initiative has built on the BEM in exploring the innovation effects of partnerships. This has involved the following propositions and methodological actions:

1. The core proposition is that potential benefits from partnerships are often longer-term and indirect, and that most partners (including business) are not able to recognise and realise these potential benefits.

2. That many of the benefits are usefully understood as developments in the capacities of people and organisations, both those directly involved in the partnership (impacts) and in others in the wider community of businesses, civil-society and public-sector organisations (outcomes).

3. That one way to capture this is to turn the 'enablers' in the BEM into 'results' as well as enablers.

ITP's proposition and approach therefore seeks to capture the learning, knowledge and innovation effects, as summarised in Figure 31.

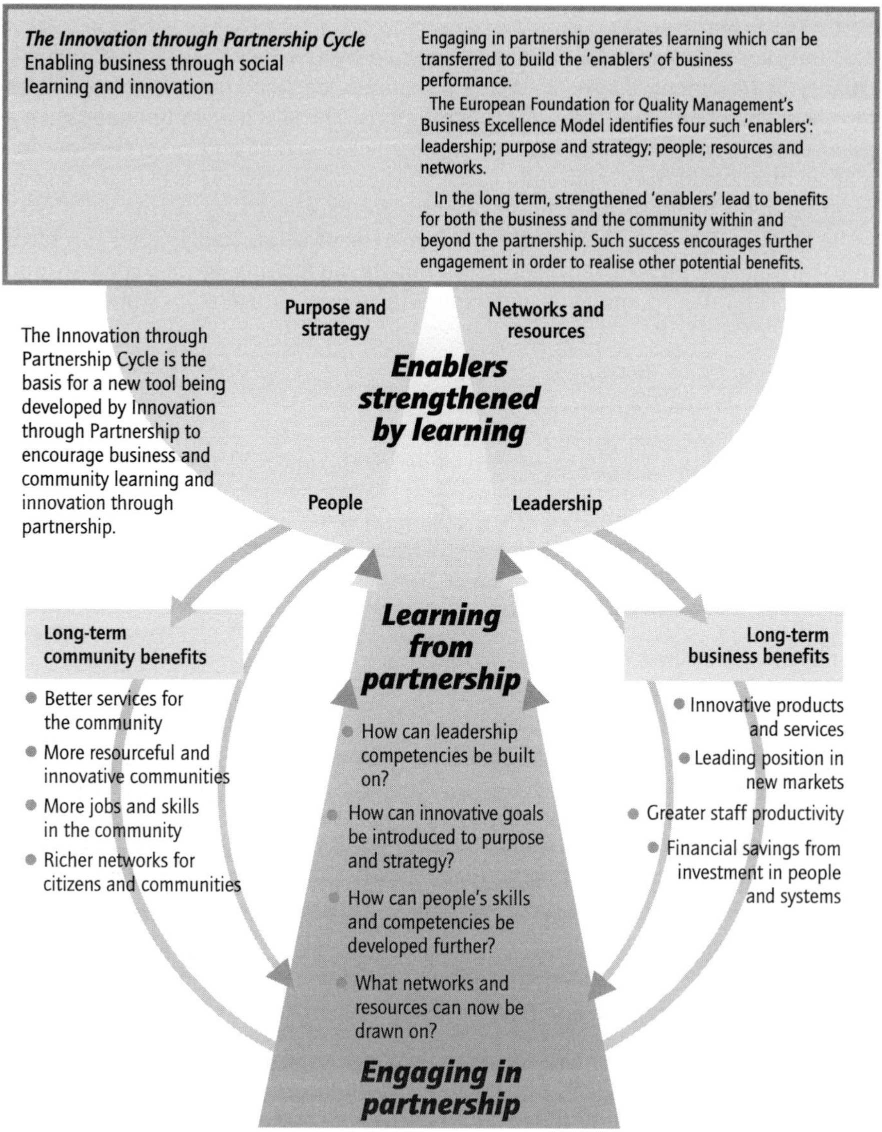

The Innovation through Partnership Cycle
Enabling business through social learning and innovation

Engaging in partnership generates learning which can be transferred to build the 'enablers' of business performance.

The European Foundation for Quality Management's Business Excellence Model identifies four such 'enablers': leadership; purpose and strategy; people; resources and networks.

In the long term, strengthened 'enablers' lead to benefits for both the business and the community within and beyond the partnership. Such success encourages further engagement in order to realise other potential benefits.

The Innovation through Partnership Cycle is the basis for a new tool being developed by Innovation through Partnership to encourage business and community learning and innovation through partnership.

Purpose and strategy

Networks and resources

Enablers strengthened by learning

People

Leadership

Learning from partnership

Long-term community benefits

- Better services for the community
- More resourceful and innovative communities
- More jobs and skills in the community
- Richer networks for citizens and communities

- How can leadership competencies be built on?
- How can innovative goals be introduced to purpose and strategy?
- How can people's skills and competencies be developed further?
- What networks and resources can now be drawn on?

Long-term business benefits

- Innovative products and services
- Leading position in new markets
- Greater staff productivity
- Financial savings from investment in people and systems

Engaging in partnership

FIGURE 31 THE INNOVATION THROUGH PARTNERSHIP INITIATIVE

Source: AccountAbility 2000

Knowledge

Innovation does appear to be a critical dimension, and it is the learning and knowledge effects that can translate this into longer-term change within the organisations involved and indeed others. This suggests the need for some way of thinking about learning and knowledge. Knowledge management is a hip subject at the moment, with all manner of models being promoted as *the* way to look at the subject. One of the first ones out there in the business community was developed by Skandia in Sweden, the Intellectual Capital Model. This is set out schematically below for illustrative purposes.

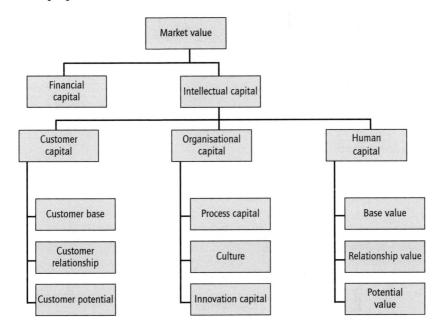

FIGURE 32 THE INTELLECTUAL CAPITAL MODEL

Accountability

One of the most contentious dimensions of partnerships concerns the matter of accountability. New social partnerships are portrayed as having public interests as well as commercial and other institutional interests, and yet rarely have a clearly defined mechanism for ensuring stakeholder accountability. All too often the issue of accountability pervades the debate about partnerships, even to the extent of crowding out substantive issues such as social and environmental impact.

Developments in social accounting are beginning to offer up basic frameworks that allow accountability to be framed, managed and assessed where traditional structures such as voting, ownership and classical approaches to public accountability are not alone appropriate or possible. The Institute for Social and Ethical AccountAbility, for example, has developed the AA1000 standard, which is rooted in a model of systematic stakeholder dialogue, as a means of creating measures and testing policy and practice.

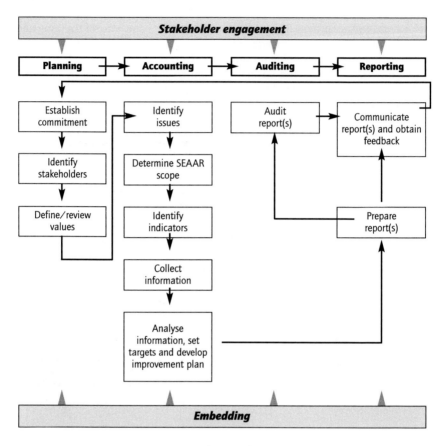

FIGURE 33 ACCOUNTABILITY MANAGEMENT (AA1000)

Strategy

Businesses of course do not measure and manage only financials, even in the crudest case of this being their only real interest. In recent years, non-financials have increasingly emerged in leading-edge planning, management and assessment tools. A very good example of this is the Balanced Scorecard (BSC). Even the classic BSC builds in qualitative perspectives, including the views of some stakeholders, and the linkage to the whole learning side of the equation of business development.

There are an increasing number of companies trying to build social and environmental elements into their BSC. This is not necessarily difficult in principle, as Figure 33 shows. Although it does not solve all sorts of issues, what it does do is to build the analytic framework into an existing and much-used (at least within business) strategy tool, which may have value in itself.

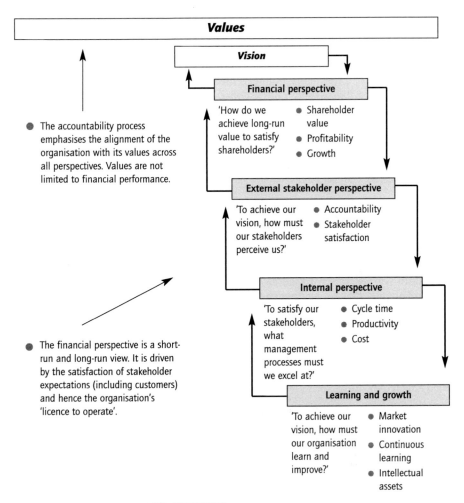

FIGURE 34 ADJUSTED BALANCED SCORECARD

Source: Prepared by Lisa Curtis from Renaissance Worldwide as part of her presentation at the annual AccountAbility conference

Effectiveness

There is an extraordinary mythology about the way companies work out the 'business case' for doing things. The adage 'if you can't measure it, you can't manage it' has been taken literally to mean that business always does financial sums to work out whether to do things (the 'super-rationale' model). Without wishing to caricature the point, this is very often not the case. The cost–benefit of building a factory is often subjected to financial analysis, but the vast majority of business decisions are not (check out the value of Internet stocks, for example).

The most-favoured measures have changed over the years. In the 1970s, earnings per share and price-equity multiples emerged as lead indicators of financial performance, whereas the 1990s saw the emergence of economic value added (EVA) as a favoured formula (Ampuero *et al.* 1999). It must be said that the emerging evidence regarding the use of hard-core financial measures such as EVA is of patchy usefulness. Although EVA can in theory be cascaded down the organisation, it is in practice poorly understood and applied at the level of the business unit. Furthermore, EVA is an outcome measure and therefore cannot usefully drive organisation behaviour. As Marcos Ampuero and his colleagues conclude:

> EVA must exist within a larger universe—a universe that often includes non-financial measures (Ampuero *et al.* 1999: 48).

A business case is therefore constructed differently depending on what type of investment is being considered. At the simplest level, the larger and lumpier the investment, the more pressure is there to produce data in support of its likely financial benefits. The smaller and less risky the investment to the business as a whole, the less precise will be the associated financial predictions. But precision has little to do with accuracy. Research into the financial consequences of major mergers and acquisitions shows that the predicted financial results rarely materialise. Indeed, one need look no further than the current explosion of investments in Internet companies to realise that projections of likely financial returns is based as much on the alchemy of intuition, judgement, perhaps prejudice and habit, or just plain old copying, as it is on the scientific calculus of cost–benefit analysis.

Now turn to partnerships. At the end of the day, what would be great would be to be able to say things like:

a. 'The partnership was not worth it for one group but it was for another group'; or even

b. 'It is not going to be worthwhile, so let's forget it'; or, best of all,

c. 'This sort of partnership will (not) be worth it to these types of partners under these sorts of situations.'

In its crudest form, this is a holy grail wish-list. But this does not mean that the questions cannot be answered. The (relatively) easiest cases are where the costs and benefits principally accrue to the actual people and organisations involved. In these instances, a solid stakeholder dialogue-based planning and assessment approach will deliver the most effective ways in which to gather data, plan, manage and assess whether the bottom line is red or black. This makes the whole issue of stakeholder accountability and inclusion very central and points towards the use of methods such as AA1000 to systematise dialogue. Similarly, it points towards the use of process models such as the Business Excellence Model in order to ensure that the various categories of enablers and outcomes are being clearly identified and explored.

It is where both costs and benefits are indirect and longer term that the difficulties arise to assess the net outcome to different parties. The most obvious cases of these might be:

a. Where the business unit actually participating in the partnership incurs the (business-related) costs but the business as a whole or indeed the wider business community derives most of the benefits

b. Similarly for civil-society and public-sector organisations where the wider community of organisation derive most of the gain through, for example, replication of the approach (or its abandonment if it does not seem to work)

This is the externalities problem. It may often be the positive externalities (i.e. things that happen outside of the sphere of the partnership itself) that actually make the partnership worthwhile. For business it may be a product innovation, new approaches to marketing, training and leadership. Often it may involve gains that accrue to the business (or indeed the sector) as a whole and yet are 'paid for' through the efforts of one or a few business units. For civil-society and public-sector organisations it may be a way of addressing deeply rooted human rights or other problems that can then be used elsewhere.

It is in these more complex areas that some of the other elements of methods and tools described above may come into use. The Partnership Scorecard being developed through *Innovation through Partnership* may be helpful, as would be taking into account leading-edge work on knowledge management and social learning. Similarly, the use of a suitably adjusted Balanced Scorecard might be useful in more effective predicting, realising, and making most use out of potential benefits right across an organisation, sector or community.

Adding it up

The aspects described above can be grouped into three broad spheres:

a. Direct development impacts and institutional benefits

b. Learning, indirect and strategic effects

c. Cost–benefit

The first sphere—**direct development impacts and institutional benefits**—is the one we know best. It addresses the question, 'What happened within the narrow bounds of the partnership?' Here we find that the traditional project assessment tools are helpful: the LogFrame, participative assessment techniques, etc. These tools have several decades of the best thinking from the development and other communities. There is no need to reinvent and rename this thinking, and there is also no need to be overly restrictive in defining which technique to use since they will vary between contexts and over time.

The second sphere—**learning, indirect and strategic effects**—is much more tricky and yet is probably where a great deal of the potential value of partnerships in practice lies. This sphere concerns:

a. Evolution in the **networks** within which the organisation operates, which both reflects and reinforces the shift in knowledge and learning (actual and potential) and the overall capacity to act differently in the future

b. Specifically the shifts in **knowledge** within the partners and elsewhere as to 'how things can be done'

c. Innovation in the partners' **governance and organisational capacity**: for example, the enablers such as policies, procedures and incentives

d. As a specific and critical sub-set of the above, how has the pattern of **leadership** within the partner organisation's changed, and how does this reflect and impact on their values orientation and focus?

e. Specifically, how the partners individually and collectively evolve their understanding and practice of their **accountability** to key stakeholders

f. How this translates into **strategic** implications for partners and how this is modelled in their decision-making processes beyond the partnership

The classical tools used to assess development projects are not so helpful here. The business community is very focused on the more effective management and measurement of learning and knowledge, so that the tools on offer from this neck of the woods offer considerable potential (as the previous section hopefully illustrates).

The third and final sphere—the **cost–benefit piece**—asks the holy-grail question, 'Was it worth it and could it have been more effectively and efficiently achieved in some other way?' The earlier discussion highlighted the complexity of the business case even as it relates to purely commercially oriented investments. But that does not mean that the business case is not alive and kicking. High-level strategic business decisions are made with much qualitative and quantitative data, but the key is that they are made by the right people at the right time. The essence of the Balanced Scorecard, for example, is not precision, but materiality, linkage and usability by senior managers who are accustomed to applying their knowledge in relative information vacuums. Similarly, the good programme officer of a development agency will know far more about the cost–benefit relationship of an initiative than he or she is able to express in a simple, quantitative model.

What this suggests is that achieving the highest-quality cost–benefit analysis requires that the best available information is delivered to the preferred decision-making points in the partnership and partnership organisations where the best knowledge, skills and experience can be applied to the matter. What this may mean in turn is that the partnership framework should be 'attachable' to existing strategy tools that are already part of key processes involving the right people, rather than seeking to reproduce this essentially qualitative process with mechanical calculus.

Partnership-based governance

There is a shift taking place in our understanding and practice of governance, underpinned in part by the emergence of new social partnerships. Traditional reliance on structured representation and the rule of law is giving way to a more fluid pattern of participation. This is characterised by communication-based forms of accountability and partnership-based forms of governance.

These shifts in the structure, process and scope of governance emerge from deeply rooted changes in the global economy and associated shifts in organisational, technological and political processes. These changes are still in their early stages and will continue to impact on governance as they evolve.

New social partnerships are a core element of this process—both influencing it and in turn being driven by it. At the local level, the partnership approach is increasingly embedded in designing and implementing public interest programmes and policies. At national and international levels, there has been a sharp growth in the active participation of business and civil-society organisations in policy formulation. This has ranged from the development of voluntary guidelines and codes of conduct, to regulatory design. Just as business and civil-society organisations are having a growing influence on public policy and public service delivery, companies are increasingly extending their own corporate strategies beyond statutory compliance in response to the views of consumers and civil-society organisations. Similarly, although with perhaps less visibility, the business community is taking a more active role in the evolution of policy and practice within civil-society organisations. In part, this is a result of greater interaction, trust and intimacy between these two groups and in part due to shifts in conditionality of funding, particularly in public contracts for infrastructure development, service delivery and management.

Governance structures are changing fundamentally at all levels of society—locally, nationally and globally. The way this transition develops will have critical implications for the ability of communities and countries to address the challenges of economic competitiveness, social cohesion and sustainable development.

With these changes come a range of dilemmas associated with these new forms of partnership. In particular:

a. Will **citizen participation be enhanced or undermined** by the growth in governance forms embodied in these new social partnerships? Can the capacity of civil-society institutions be developed to enable them to play an effective role in these new forms of governance? How will these institutions evolve to ensure that they remain representative and indeed strengthen their degree of citizen representation?

b. What are the **implications for the state**? It is not accurate to assert a 'reduced' role and yet it is clear that the state's structure of intervention is going through a radical transformation. Can the institutions of government rise to the challenge of handling increasingly complex, cross-sectoral relationships through the development of a more diversified, responsive culture and more integrated approaches to working? Can the growing and more explicit roles of business be balanced with the continued need for governments to regulate business activities?

c. Will the **business community engage in broader societal processes** with combined social and financial purposes? Can business develop its values to support a new understanding of how social and environmental responsibility and accountability can form the foundations for both long-term market competitiveness and contributing to meeting social aims?

The emerging forms of governance therefore present both a potential threat to participative democracy and a real opportunity to strengthen meaningful citizen involvement in decision-making and service delivery. The challenge is to ensure a form of 'civil governance' which effectively manages human affairs while enabling citizens to take an active role in designing the policies, institutions and programmes that shape the quality of their own lives. New social partnerships need to be measured against this yardstick in determining their underlying contribution to societal improvement, as well as measuring their specific tangible outputs and outcomes.

Linked to this, the future of new social partnerships depends critically on whether they prove capable of delivering societal benefits that cannot be achieved more effectively through other means. To be effective they will need to demonstrate clear added value at the:

a. Local level in building sustainable livelihoods and improving quality of life, in ways that actively and practically engage local communities and beneficiary groups; and

b. Strategic level in helping national and international government bodies to create an enabling environment for more proactive and innovative approaches to addressing socioeconomic problems.

New social partnerships *can* be effective at both the local and strategic level, but will not *necessarily* be so. The conditions under which they can be successful have been highlighted above, as have been the pitfalls and dangers that partnerships represent in terms of micro-level effectiveness and meso- and macro-level aspects of societal governance. The challenge is to make it more likely that the positive dynamics will prevail.

27
endearing myths, enduring truths
partnerships between
business, civil-society
organisations and government*
co-written with the Business Partners for Development team

Business Partners for Development (BPD) was established to study, support and promote strategic examples of partnerships involving business, civil society and government working together in and for communities around the world.

BPD's core purpose has been to explore the proposition that such tri-sector partnerships:

- Provide development and business benefits

- Can be much more widely used throughout the world

- Can be scaled up to national and regional levels

BPD in action

BPD has been a project-based **learning initiative**. Its engagement in, and support and development of, specific partnerships has intended to serve the dual purposes of:

- **Promoting** their effectiveness

- **Learning and communicating** what role different sectors in society can play in a collaborative approach to sustainable development

From 1998 to the present, more than 120 companies, civil-society organisations and government agencies have participated in 30 different 'focus projects' and programmes in 20 countries. These activities were selected by the four 'BPD Clusters' (Global Partnership for Youth Development; Global Road Safety Partnership; Natural Resources Cluster; and Water and Sanitation Cluster). The clusters were chosen partly based on themes (youth development and road safety). Each cluster's activities have been managed through its secretariat, housed within the non-governmental organisation (NGO) that helped convene that cluster.

The age of partnerships

Risks and opportunities in many developing and transition countries have become more complex, volatile and extreme. Efficiently overcoming risks, building new bases of legitimacy, and taking advantage of latent opportunities are often beyond the reach of individual organisations. Increasingly, the preferred route is to 'stretch' competencies and capacities by linking the technical specialisations, networks and resources of diverse organisations.

Tri-sector partnerships, involving business, civil-society organisations and government agencies, are among the more complex partnerships. They pose particular challenges because they seek to draw together often very diverse interests, perspectives and organisational cultures. However, they also offer significant potential gains if this diversity can be effectively focused and operationalised.

BPD's diverse experience

BPD partnerships are not well-defined development projects that begin and end at the will of one organisation. The 30 projects were selected because of their diversity. They are at very different stages of development, and have two different types of relationships with BPD:

- **Partnerships formed through BPD.** These range from the work of the Global Road Safety Partnership—which involved setting up an entirely new NGO, called 'GRSP Ghana', to secure the effective transfer of internationally available information and knowledge to Ghanaian organisations—through to the work of the Global Youth Development Programme, which facilitates the creation of the 'Out of School Youth Project' in the Philippines, involving the Ayala Foundation, the Children and Youth Foundation in the Philippines, the International Youth Foundation, and the World Bank.

- **Ongoing partnerships drawn into and enhanced through BPD.** The partnership in Dakar, Senegal, between SONES (the public water department), Senegalese des Eaux (a private water operator), ENDA (an international NGO), and local communities was established some years before

BPD. BPD has sought to contribute to its effectiveness on the ground, while learning from its experience. The tri-sector partnership focused around the BP-operated site in Casanare, Colombia, also builds on earlier tri-sector initiatives in the region, involving community organisations and local and regional public authorities.

Why organisations engage in partnerships

BPD partnerships have focused on solving complex and historically intractable social issues. Indeed, BPD's experience highlights that tri-sector partnerships are often turned to as an option precisely because other approaches have been tried and have failed.

Beyond this general reason, organisations turn to partnership-based solutions for widely differing reasons—especially when they come from different sectors with distinct mandates and diverse organisational orientations, cultures, patterns of accountability and histories.

The growing power and influence of business in shaping the future makes it particularly important to understand both how BPD has engaged businesses in partnerships for development and their reasons for such engagement. BPD's experience highlights five distinct categories of tangible, direct business benefits from partnership:

- **Risk management**. Although a potential benefit for all businesses in partnerships, BPD experience revealed that the management of risk associated with, for example, civil disruption of business activities, is particularly relevant to the extractive and water and sanitation industries due to their long-term time-horizons and the large scale of their fixed investments.

- **Expectations management**. The management of stakeholder expectations, internal as well as external, is a key rationale for business engagement in partnerships. This partly has the underlying aim of managing risk but, beyond that, it also aims to enhance stakeholders' contributions to project success. This is particularly relevant for businesses with large-scale fixed investments, those managing sensitive resources, those operating in relatively poor communities, and those with national and global, as well as local stakeholder management requirements.

- **Market development**. Market development as a rationale for partnership engagement is most relevant for those corporations needing to promote sales in the countries where the partnerships are based, although there is clearly also a public relations dimension linked to international marketing and sales. Through the partnership, businesses are able to strengthen their overall relationships with potential customers, particularly with public-sector bodies responsible for procurement. This has proved to be especially relevant for corporations involved in youth development and road safety partnerships and, to a lesser degree, with water and sanitation partnerships.

- **Legal and contract compliance**. Meeting legal contractual obligations is relevant to all businesses. BPD experience highlights the particular importance of this factor for customer-related contract compliance, which concerns businesses involved in the water and sanitation sector. To a lesser degree, it is also relevant for extractive industries where contract compliance covers aspects of community engagement and development.

- **Business process and productivity**. Some partnerships have a direct impact on production and other operational processes, including customer outreach. Process and productivity gains in BPD were most relevant for the water and sanitation and natural resources-related partnerships generally. These benefits are also being sought in some partnerships in the other two clusters, such as the youth-related Global Alliance for Workers and Communities where supply-chain productivity gains are expected to result from improvements in workers' competencies and overall morale.

The powerful business drivers underpinning tri-sector partnerships do not reduce the importance of social and ethical values in encouraging greater business engagement on social and environmental issues. Such values are generally personalised, rooted in the commitment of a chief executive, or in champions elsewhere in the organisation. However, the effectiveness of these drivers is at risk if they undermine a company's financial performance and will tend to prosper if shown to enhance it. On the other hand, business engagement for purely financial reasons is often seen by other partners as superficial and short-term, which may lead to a less-than-successful experience resulting from a failure to gain the trust of key stakeholders. In practice, it is therefore usually a blend of values-based and business drivers that underpin effective business engagement in these issues.

Learning beyond the wave

International experimentation over recent years in partnerships has given rise to an emerging body of advice, tools and techniques to aid partnership makers and participants. However, much of this remains based on limited practical experience, often drawn from a single case or a few examples, and only a small part is based on tri-sector partnership experience. BPD's breadth and depth therefore provides a unique opportunity to draw broader lessons about partnerships to inform future policy and practice.

As in any innovation wave, only a few core lessons will prove to be robust enough to inform partnerships in the future. BPD's core mission has been to 'learn by doing' and to communicate these lasting lessons. However, such lessons need to be useful as well as true. Lessons such as 'partnerships are hard' or 'commitment is an essential ingredient of successful partnerships' are certainly true, but their general and obvious nature mean that they do little to improve practice.

Useful truths about partnerships are those that are:

- **Durable**, beyond the current fashionable wave

- **Quality-oriented**, in offering ways to enhance the capacity to deliver desired development outcomes in replicable and scalable ways

These truths are enduring, not because they hold true in every conceivable situation, but because the available evidence suggests that they will stand the test of time.

The remainder of this document summarises and illustrates in brief the most important enduring truths that have emerged at this preliminary stage of BPD's learning, and in so doing seeks to dispel some of the current wave's most endearing myths

Endearing myths, enduring truths . . .

1. Ensuring that the partnership contains the right mix of partners

Partnership design needs to take account of the pattern of potential costs and benefits. For example, the greater the variation and dispersal of potential beneficiaries, the more important the role of public bodies in actively building programmes, as pure market mechanisms or localised collaboration cannot be relied on to meet agreed objectives. In general, therefore, the more diffused the potential costs and benefits, the broader the participation will have to be.

Recognising this, the Global Road Safety Partnership and the Global Partnership for Youth Development have focused on building partnerships at the international and national, rather than site-specific, levels. Road safety—like youth development—is typically under-provided through pure market mechanisms because its widely dispersed benefits make it an unattractive commercial proposition. Having a significant impact on accident rates requires broad public policies and programmes, such as education and the enforcement of suitable regulation, in addition to location-specific road safety initiatives. However, development programmes to address issues such as road safety are also typically under-provided by governments because of institutional weaknesses in grappling with such cross-cutting issues. This is particularly evident where responsibility is dispersed among a number of government agencies and resources are limited. This helps us to understand why public bodies are attracted by tri-sector partnerships as a means of addressing these broad-based development programmes and goals.

This argument is further supported by BPD experience in the Natural Resources Cluster where site- and locality-specific partnerships have been used to mitigate investment risk and the negative social impacts of oil, gas and mining operations. Such partnerships can bring significant net benefits to the company, employees and surrounding communities. In these instances, higher-level regional and national initiatives may not be necessary to achieve development and business benefits, as the primary beneficiaries are the business and local community.

2. Partners' aims as partnership drivers

It is critically important to establish each partner's individual aims and to design the partnership activities to ensure that these are sufficiently realised. If the partnership does not meet these individual aims through its activities, it will be difficult to secure the partner's continued involvement. For example, securing the engagement of the business partner in joint activities will be easiest where these activities, in practice, assist the business in meeting its contractual obligations, in identifying marketing opportunities, or in managing risks and expectations related to specific sites and contracts.

These conditions have proved to be more explicit for the partnerships in the Natural Resources Cluster and the Water and Sanitation Cluster. Konkola Copper Mine plc's commitment to a partnership that aims to develop and implement a local business development programme in the Zambian copper belt fulfils its contractual obligation established at the time of privatisation, thereby helping to offset social risks associated with community tensions and dislocation arising through retrenchment.

Similarly, the partnership of the Water and Sanitation Services South Africa (a subsidiary of Ondeo, formerly Suez Lyonnaise des Eaux) with an NGO, the Mvula Trust, was formed with the common aim of improving sustainable water and sanitation services to poorer communities in Northern Province and Eastern Cape in South Africa. This common aim of the Build, Operate, Train, and Transfer (BOTT) Programme of the Department of Water Affairs and Forestry certainly frames the partnership's joint activities. However, these activities are possible because they also enable each partner to address its specific interests. For those businesses involved in the consortium formed as a result of the partnership, this meant finding appropriate, sustainable and cost-effective ways to comply with their contractual obligations to service poor communities and strengthen their bidding position for future contracts in South Africa and elsewhere. The joint activities also enable the Mvula Trust to enhance the quality of the intervention to ensure sustainable availability of water and sanitation services to poorer communities.

3. Process method key to operational success

The Global Road Safety Partnership's approach to partnership development has been to leverage the personal reputations and expertise of international, senior road safety specialists, particularly in convening national road safety networks in the early stages of operationalising partnerships. The Global Partnership for Youth Development's approach to partnership development has also relied heavily on the engagement of key individuals during the formative stages of the partnerships, drawing particularly on the patronage of national figures with prestige and influence as an aid to partnership convening and resource mobilisation.

The approach to partnership development taken in the Natural Resources Cluster, on the other hand, involved from the outset a more formal process, structured around the principle of building collective commitments to undertake activities through a shared work plan, underpinned by the identification and mutual recognition of both partner-specific and common interests. Individuals' competencies as facilitators and brokers were certainly relevant, but face-to-face (unfacilitated) consensus-building was at times equally, if not more, important.

4. Fractured contexts can enhance partnership potential

In 1991 Placer Dome de Venezuela entered into a joint venture with Corporation Venezolana de Guayana, of the government of Venezuela, to commercially develop gold deposits at a site in Bolivar State, south-eastern Venezuela. The joint venture, 'Mineras Las Cristinas' (MINCA), operating in the face of a rapidly declining international gold market, suspended construction in July 1999. The suspension meant that community expectations of a socioeconomic improvement programme could no longer be met by the company. MINCA therefore faced the possibility of confrontation with the local community and their potential invasion of the concession. It was in this context that a tri-sector partnership was formed and has delivered real benefits to both the community and the business: for example, in the provision of local health services.

Similarly, BPXC in Casanare, Colombia, is a joint venture of BP Oil, Triton Energy and TFE with the national oil organisation ECOPETROL. The region is subject to the civil conflicts that exist throughout much of the country, endangering the site, infrastructure and personnel. Government inefficiencies and corruption have restricted the flow of oil-related royalties to benefit the region's communities. Use of a tri-sector partnership model of social engagement is seen by BP as one important way to improve its licence to operate by influencing the flow and allocation of royalty revenues according to the community's interests.

The context of the partnership in Kwa Zulu Natal Province, South Africa, between the municipalities of Durban and Pietermaritzburg, Vivendi Water, the Mvula Trust, Umgeni Water and the Water Research Commission includes a climate of incredibly high expectations on the part of the communities involved. For poor communities, water has been at the centre of a heated debate about service levels, cost recovery and other issues in a time of dramatically expanded municipal jurisdictions and their mandate. Within this context, the urgency to explore innovative partnerships clearly increases in order to resolve operational challenges.

5. International dimensions provide key experience and leverage

Partnerships involving global corporations, international agencies and governments operate at several levels at the same time. In some instances, these tiers are formally structured. The 'Partnership for Careers in Agriculture for Thai Youth', for example, operates at international, national and local levels. The international players include the IYF and Shell International, the latter advocating the activities to its Thai business unit, and providing financial resources. The national level, essentially where convening and strategy development takes place, involves Shell Thai and several national companies, various government departments, and the IYF's Thai partner, NCYD, where the practical activity takes place in working with youth. These different levels can be mutually reinforcing and so directly enhance the partnership's performance. However, there can also be tensions between the different levels as diverse interests become apparent, even within the same organisation. Whether formally structured or informally operating at different levels, this highlights the need to manage partnerships vertically as well as horizontally, particularly when large and complex international organisations are involved.

Receptivity and capacity of key organisations is a critical ingredient in realising partnership potential. Corporations such as BP, Rio Tinto, Vivendi and Ondeo have highlighted the need for a 'participatory and responsible' approach to handling social and environmental issues. They see this as a key competitive advantage in securing contracts, managing reputation and attracting, retaining and motivating key staff. The need for this approach is further accentuated in a climate where accessing finance increasingly comes with complex conditions attached, particularly where public financial institutions such as the International Finance Corporation have a role to play. Corporate headquarters therefore encourage partnerships involving their business units, subsidiaries and in joint ventures, both as a means of addressing situation-specific issues and as a means of enhancing the corporation's overall attractiveness to sources of finance and contracts. Businesses positioning themselves in this way are building multi-country experience in working across sectors, and can bring much-needed partnership capacity drawn from experience gained elsewhere.

6. Evolving partnerships

Partnerships change over time, and sometimes dramatically so. The life-cycle of many tri-sector partnerships begins with a less-diverse set of engaged organisations. Aguas de Cartagena was created as a joint venture between the Municipality of Cartagena and the Spanish water utility Aguas de Barcelona in 1994. The contract was conceived exclusively as a joint venture between the municipality and the business partner. At that initial stage, there were no contractual specifications regarding service to poorer communities. This changed as a result of the political imperatives of the municipality, the corporate culture of Aguas de Barcelona, and a World Bank loan to the municipality, signed in early 2000, to support the development of water and sanitation infrastructure in Cartagena. This loan was made conditional in part on the existing partners engaging with community groups to determine how best to extend the municipal water supply in the locality. This in turn led to the formation of a tri-sector partnership involving NGOs that have moved in and out, and community-based organisations that have steadily gained credibility within the partnership.

The evolution of organisational engagement can go beyond the partnership's direct formal participants. The Global Alliance for Workers and Communities (GA) was from the outset formally a tri-sector partnership, involving the International Youth Foundation, Nike Corporation, Mattel Inc. and the World Bank. However, the critical relationship within the partnership was between Nike and the IYF, highlighting the importance of understanding which partners, in practice, exert the most influence and to what effect. Following its inception in 1999, the GA has evolved further and is now beginning to engage with the international trade union movement, other key civil-society organisations involved in the labour area, and the International Labour Organisation (ILO). What this example reveals is that, in many partnerships, key relationships exist, both within and outside formal boundaries, and that these change over time. Indeed in the case of the GA, its very success depends on such developments.

7. Direct partnership costs and benefits

The initial motivation for many large companies to enter into tri-sector partnerships is often negative—reacting to pressures from a range of external stakeholders. But, in the course of implementation, the BPD focus projects are providing more evidence that tri-sector partnerships can and do generate direct business benefits, alongside enhanced development impact. In partnership with local NGOs, community institutions and the district authorities, the project sponsor for the Sarshatali coal mining project in West Bengal, India—ICML/CESC—has implemented a range of income-restoration and trust-building measures in the area of mine impact. In addition, four government departments—health, welfare, agriculture and infrastructure—are now active in the area, each sharing with ICML the cost of wider community development and collaborating voluntarily with local NGOs (ASHA and Suchetana) and village committees to ensure relevance to local need. These tri-sector partnership arrangements have reversed what a year ago were rising levels of local dissatisfaction with the mining project, have helped ICML gain the confidence to begin construction work, and are helping to secure sustainable benefits for the local population—independent of whether the project eventually proceeds. However, the partnership's direct net financial benefits to date to CESC Ltd have been estimated at US$280,000, made up mainly of cost savings in achieving the following:

- Information and knowledge acquisition
- Trust-building measures and community development
- Road construction

Aguas Argentinas has formed a variety of partnerships with city authorities, the regulator, local NGOs and community groups to explore how best to deliver water and sanitation services more effectively to poor communities in Buenos Aires, Argentina. Although not quantified, there have been significant net business benefits. These include converting fraudulent users into customers in terms of reduced 'leakage', vandalism and other security issues.

Direct development benefits also accrue through partnership and can sit comfortably alongside the business benefit. In the case of Buenos Aires, the latest available figures (July 2000) indicate that water services have been extended to 1.2 million poor people and sewerage services to 0.3 million poor people in part as a result of the partnership approach. About 60% of these connections were funded by the operator's regular expansion programme, while the balance has been funded through tax credit agreements and other innovative institutional arrangements underpinned by a combination of public and private funds, and by community contributions.

8. Extended partnership benefits

Broader, longer-term benefits can arise through the partnership's positive impact on partner competencies. These in turn enhance their ability to engage elsewhere in beneficial activities—including other partnerships. Such competencies have developed as a result of the Sarshatali coal mining project.

- **Good governance:** improved ability of, and confidence in, the ability of local government to be effective and visible in carrying out its civic duties

- **Attitudinal change:** greater receptiveness of businesses and government agencies to NGO-generated knowledge and NGO-led community engagement

- **Expertise:** growth in expertise of all parties, notably the NGOs involved, to mobilise and focus community participation towards tri-sector programme development and implementation

The potential for extending benefits beyond the individual partnership is particularly enhanced where the international partners seek to systematically build learning across their operations. Ondeo is keen to share learning from its experience of using partnership mechanisms to meet the needs of the urban poor across its operations globally. To facilitate this, the company has created a unit in its Paris offices to co-ordinate and facilitate the cross-fertilisation of such learning and ideas among the different Ondeo concessions and contract areas.

Conclusions

Many of the initiatives developed or supported by BPD would not have been cost-effective or even feasible if they had not been built as partnerships. The success, for example, of the Sarshatali coal mining project in India, the Global Alliance for Workers and Communities, the Global Road Safety Programme in Ghana, or the Build, Operate, Train and Transfer water and sanitation project in the Eastern Cape and Northern Province of South Africa all relied heavily on enhanced relationships formed between participating organisations to mobilise and create synergies between needed competencies and resources.

But the uniqueness of BPD's overall experience has not been in imposing tri-sector partnerships. After all, the water and sanitation partnership in Port-au-Prince in Haiti involves an international NGO, GRET, working with a state-owned utility. The Global Alliance for Workers and Communities has little more than nominal public-sector involvement, and indeed has to date progressed with scant engagement with the labour movement. The road safety initiatives in Vietnam and Costa Rica have had little real civil-society engagement to date, and the NGO engaged in the road safety partnership in Ghana was actually created by the Global Road Safety Partnership. Almost all of the water and sanitation partnerships are tri-sector, but the main corporate partners are also experimenting in other approaches to contract compliance that are rooted in legal, technological and pricing innovations, rather than partnership-related ones. Only the Natural Resources Cluster partnerships have been exclusively tri-sector, but even here there were several that did not get off the ground, and one that was abandoned midstream.

BPD's tri-sector partnership approach has been permissive rather than prescriptive. It has created the possibilities for institutional innovation in addressing both individual and common organisational goals, rather than seeking to impose a 'one size fits all' model across extraordinarily diverse situations and challenges. This way of appreciating a 'tri-sector partnership' approach appears, from the evidence to date, to be effective in that:

- It actively encourages innovative approaches to addressing social and environmental issues as well as business challenges and opportunities.

- It opens people's minds to the possibility of breaking down historical barriers and forming working relationships between key organisations spread across different parts of the local, national and international community.

- It engages people and methods that are attuned to building unusual, complex, and often difficult partnerships.

On this basis, BPD's experience clearly demonstrates that this tri-sector partnership approach can deliver the resources, competencies, legitimacy and, critically, the will, energy and focus to succeed, where institutions and sectors working alone have previously failed.

Summary

Aspect	Endearing myth	Enduring truth
Ensuring that the partnership contains the right mix of partners	Successful partnerships are those where partnering organisations share an interest in addressing common goals.	Successful partnerships include the right combination of organisations to secure the necessary institutional mandates and delivery mechanisms to achieve the partnership's objectives and activities.
Partner's aims as partnership drivers	Successful partnerships are primarily shaped around a common or shared long-term vision or aim.	Successful partnerships are those shaped around common or shared activities that first and foremost deliver against the individual aims of each partner, particularly where these have been legitimised within the partnership.
Process method key to operational success	Individual champions are the key to successful partnerships, all the more so when diverse organisations are involved with very different aims and world-views.	Methods for building partnerships are relatively interchangeable during their initial stages but, as the partnership is operationalised, structured methodologies become relatively more effective than approaches dependent on individual champions.

Aspect	Endearing myth	Enduring truth
Fractured contexts can enhance partnership potential	Partnership potential is greatest when the context ensures that partners are most receptive to, and knowledgeable of, each other.	Potential benefits from partnerships are often greatest where social, economic and political uncertainties have historically constrained co-operation (although, if the historical grievances are too great, this can also prevent the partners from coming together without an initial process of conflict resolution).
International dimensions provide key experience and leverage	Partnership success is dependent on those most directly involved and with most at stake.	Partnership success often depends on individuals and organisations not directly involved that can bring critical experience and financial leverage, a feature of many partnerships involving international business and public-sector agencies.
Evolving partnerships	Stable and clearly bounded partnerships are most likely to be effective.	A partnership's success often depends on its evolution—for example, in its membership and wider relationships—and in some instances even in its purpose.
Direct partnership costs and benefits	Partnership costs are so high as to make them unprofitable for the participating business units.	Focused partnerships often yield net benefits to those organisations directly participating, particularly over the medium and longer term.
Extended partnership benefits	Extending benefits from the partnership requires scaling up or replicating successful partnership experience.	Extended benefits from the partnerships are most likely where there has been growth in participants' own abilities to work across sectors, and where the abilities are recognised and rewarded.

28
working with multilaterals*
co-written with Tanya Schwarz and the staff of Business for Social Responsibility

The partnership imperative

The UN is by far the largest multilateral in terms of size, geographic mandate and scope of activities, including many high-profile bodies such as UNCHR (dealing with human rights), UNHCR (for refugees), UNICEF (for children) and the WHO (dealing with health). Equally high-profile, but more distant, members of the UN family include the International Monetary Fund (IMF), the World Bank and the World Trade Organisation (WTO).

The development challenge is enormous. As a primary engine of economic development, business is a major determinant of social and environmental outcomes. However, businesses' negative social and environmental impacts are not adequately offset by classical statutory mechanisms, particularly in countries where enforcement is weak. Furthermore, the development potential of the expertise and resource embedded within the business community is not fully realised through 'business-as-usual'. The UN has therefore increasingly experimented in new forms of engagement with the business community, particularly the international business community—the 70,000 or so multinational corporations and their many subsidiaries and affiliates. These new forms of engagement extend beyond both the rule-making underlying much of the

> ### The essence of the UN
>
> " The UN Charter's very first Article defines our purposes: resolving disputes by peaceful means; devising cooperative solutions to economic, social, cultural and humanitarian problems; and broadly encouraging behaviour in conformity with the principles of justice and international law. "
>
> *Kofi Annan, UN Secretary General*
>
> Source: Annan 2000: 6

---

* This chapter is a summary of the report 'Working with Multilaterals'. © 2002 Business for Social Responsibility, San Francisco.

UN's work in earlier decades and the classical forms of philanthropy based around the business-as-giver model.

- **Mobilising funds.** Philanthropy remains an important aspect of business–UN partnerships.

- **Voluntary standards.** A key example is the Global Reporting Initiative, established with UNEP and supported by grants from the United Nations Foundation.

- **Policy dialogue.** Often such dialogues are part of initiatives (e.g. UN Global Compact and UNEP Finance Initiative) that can incorporate voluntary standards.

- **Learning and knowledge.** All initiatives of course require a certain amount of learning. But some are designed specifically to promote education, such as Business Partners for Development.

- **Operational delivery.** Increasingly, business engagement involves working with the UN in the actual delivery of goods and services for development: e.g. partnership between UNAIDS and Coca-Cola.

The fact of these new forms of engagement between business and multilaterals make it all the more important to understand their diverse underlying drivers, and the different emerging operational lessons.

Getting started

Collaboration is often painfully difficult even between commercial organisations with similar financial bottom-line interests and comparable competencies and approaches. Businesses are more or less unanimous in their criticism of the UN during partnership start-up periods. There is a universal sense that it takes far too long to get going. Most businesses highlight the apparent confusion of aims, priorities and decision-making within the UN. Several companies were critical of what they perceived as extreme UN adversity to risk. As one business executive commented, 'They were concerned with being co-opted and being perceived as whitewashed. They were blowing us off, but we kept working because we knew we were going to have to do something anyway.'

Several cases highlighted strategies for getting through this initial period with the minimum of difficulties. One business executive with several years' experience in working with the UN reflected on the start-up period: 'You have to be prepared to come to the table with a full set of cards . . . You have to have the head count to be able to do the work . . . once the goals have been set, someone has to be there to make sure they are met. That's sometimes hard to accept.' The most important lesson was summed up by one executive as: 'these partnerships are not between businesses and multilaterals, but between individuals that work within these institutions'.

The presence of champions within multilaterals and businesses is obviously crucial in helping to overcome historical barriers and real differences of interest. Equally, however, there is a need to move beyond a champion-led process if the partnership is to survive beyond the initial entrepreneurial stages.

Accountability dilemmas

The UN's most importance asset is its legitimacy as the independent steward of universal values developed through consensual dialogue between sovereign states over five decades. The dilemma is that the UN's traditional approach to accountability does not necessarily secure independence, nor is it any guarantee for ensuring effectiveness in terms of actual performance. International experience of public–private partnerships more broadly has highlighted the inadequacy of traditional approaches to public accountability once applied to the more complex operating environment of today's public bodies (IPPR 2001). As one UN official commented, 'The bottom line of accountability is making sure no one is going to make a fuss, that there is general buy-in. Beyond that, accountability is driven by personal integrity and ambitions shrouded by institutional aims.'

In practice, accountability of UN agencies engaging in partnerships with business is more often rooted in personal, rather than institutional, forms of accountability. As one executive involved in a commercially significant project noted, 'There is no really formal basis. Accountability happens because we speak at least twice a week.' As another business executive said, 'These are partnerships between people who drag their institutions with them, more or less willingly.'

The issue of accountability in relation to the Global Compact was cited by many of those interviewed as reflecting many of the underlying issues. The basis for the Compact's own accountability is unclear, since it has no transparent governance process, and no line of recourse if it makes decisions that are seen to damage businesses or other related participants. Several interviewees compared it to the Global Sullivan Principles, and argued that the latter had a clearer accountability mechanism, albeit one that was far narrower.

Was it worth it?

Knowing whether a partnership has succeeded or failed is not always so simple, particularly when they are still at their early development stages, or where the outcomes are diffused or contested. There are some clear instances where it is possible to note significant positive business and/or development benefits, and others where views were mixed:

- **Product and market development.** Cisco and the Female Health Company both argue that the direct business benefit certainly warranted the investment in building partnerships with multilaterals.

- **Strategic philanthropy.** Companies involved in the Change for Good initiative and Merck, through the Mectizan Donation Program, considered that reputational and other business gains easily outweighed programme costs.

- **Voluntary standards.** There were diverse views expressed by those companies involved in the Sialkot Partnership, the Global Compact, the Global Mining Initiative, the Global Reporting Initiative, and the UNEP Finance Initiatives. Businesses involved in the Sialkot Partnership were generally of the view that they had achieved the desired reputational gains, but were less confident that the programme had really delivered the desired development results. Similarly, there is widespread support for progress to date of the Global Reporting Initiative and the UNEP Finance Initiative. Doubts were raised, however, as to the effectiveness of the Global Mining Initiative and the Global Compact, although it was pointed out in both cases that it is too early to tell what will be the outcome of these broader initiatives.

Just as there is no 'general' business case for corporate responsibility, there can be no general conclusion as to whether business–multilateral partnerships pay, whether in financial or development terms. The research evidence, supported by evidence from other work, suggests that it *can* pay on both counts if it is done right, there is loads of effort and personal commitment, and not a little luck. This conclusion is of course unsurprising in that it is similar to that for any business investment decision, whether a new product area, new plant or a major rebranding exercise. Partnerships with multilaterals are not profitable initiatives waiting to be discovered. They are potentially rewarding investments, with commensurate risks, waiting to be created.

Analysing risk and return

A major constraint in the evolution of business–multilateral engagement is the difficulty of assessing the risk-reward potential.

- For **multilaterals**, the frustrating slippages experienced by business in the planning and start-up phases often occur precisely because the multilaterals involved have no clear basis for assessing potential risk–reward and, like most bureaucracies, respond to this through prevarication and delay.

- **Business** has more experience in working with risk. But it became apparent during the research that few if any companies are effectively able to calibrate the risk–reward potential of working with multilaterals.

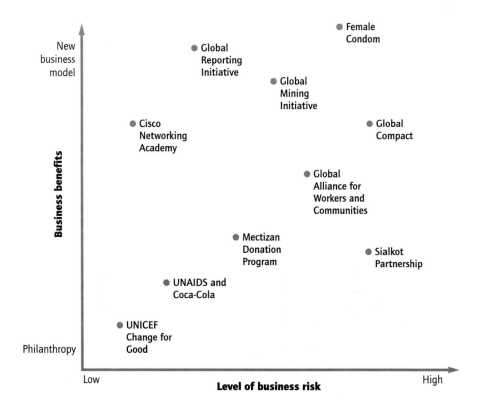

FIGURE 35 RISK AND PROXIMITY TO BUSINESS PERFORMANCE

Risk parameters

There are clearly many factors involved in assessing the risk–reward potential, and no single tool will do the job even with the best possible information. Below we have set out spectrums along which an assessment can be undertaken, with illustrations drawn from the case studies.

- **Short- versus longer-term benefits.** Initiatives such as the Global Compact and the Global Reporting Initiative offer the prospect of long- rather than short-term business benefits: for example, by enhancing a company's overall reputation. Other types of engagement, such as the UNAIDS/Female Health Company alliance offer the prospect of short-term business benefits through direct product sales. Compliance-based initiatives such as the Sialkot Partnership may also offer short-term business gain through reduced risk of, or actual damage to, the brand.

- **Direct and indirect.** Business gains to corporate participants in the Global Mining Initiative are largely indirect in being associated with an overall improvement in the reputation of the mining industry. Indirect gains also accrued to the businesses involved in the Sialkot Partnership, the UNEP Finance Initiative and the Global Compact. Increased sales and profitability to Merck for its leadership role in the development of the Mectizan Donation Program are, on the other hand, far more direct.

Businesses and multilaterals need to be able to assess potential risk on an ongoing basis, and to relate that to possible and realised rewards. Most effective would be if partners—potential or ongoing—collaborated in more explicit risk–reward assessments, which would then set the stage for more effective partnership-based risk management and, hopefully, performance. This might involve:

- Development of simple, appropriate **risk assessment and management tools** for use by all partners

- More explicit formulation of partnership accountability structures and processes

- Partnership capacity development for collaborative risk assessment and management

- More systematic reporting on partnership processes and performance

Today's increasing engagement between business and multilaterals is neither a passing fashion nor a pastime reserved for 'special needs' companies. The research clearly indicates that such engagements are both extensive and growing, cutting across sectors, countries and regions, and approaches. Contrary to popular belief, many of these forms of collaboration are alive and well—difficult certainly, but providing tangible benefits to all sides. What will further extend such engagement, and make it increasingly effective, is an honest acknowledgement of some of the current constraints and pitfalls. Of the many that exist, a small number of strategic challenges need to be addressed.

- **Honest analysis and disclosure.** There is little in-depth, serious research published about these engagements, despite the enormous amount of available 'partnership' material. Without some honest accounting for what does and does not work on the ground, it is hard to see how learning can really take place.

- **Risk–return analysis.** Engagement in partnerships needs to be framed within more coherent models that take greater account of the risk–return potential for all parties. Without this, uncalibrated risk will understandably discourage much-needed experimentation and innovation.

- **Accountability.** Notable among these accountability challenges is the need to enormously strengthen accountability in such engagements, for both the business partners, and also crucially for the multilaterals themselves. This requires deep-rooted change in policy and governance frameworks.

- **Future-casting**. Today's experiences of engagements between business and multilaterals need to be understood and judged in the context of likely futures. Although risky and seemingly forward-thinking, today's forms of engagement will be looked back on as uncertain steps towards a future where the traditions that distinguish these types of institutions become almost unrecognisable.

Section VI
responsible competitiveness

29
responsible competitiveness
corporate responsibility clusters in action*

co-written with John Sabapathy, Helle Dossing and Tracey Swift

The scaling-up challenge

The private sector is now recognised as having a key role in delivering sustainable development—through its impacts on the natural environment and social and economic development. And there has been progress, with ample evidence that increasing numbers of companies are integrating social and environmental policies into their business practices. But when is enough 'good enough'? Even with an optimistic view of the growth in corporate responsibility practices, there remains little confidence on the part of the general public in most countries that business is willing to become active in combating social exclusion, poverty and environmental insecurity.

Corporate responsibility is above all else viewed as being about how businesses can 'do well by doing good'. Much attention has focused on developing the 'business case' that provides an economic rationale for companies to invest in improving their environmental and social performance. But there are limits to the 'business case' that are inherent in any particular market constellation. Some of the measures demanded of companies in the name of corporate responsibility are incompatible with current business models and markets. Pharmaceutical companies cannot alone provide affordable drugs to the poor, and footwear companies cannot just decide to pay workers in Mexico or Vietnam a wage comparable to that earned by workers in London or New York. The challenge is not so much to 'find' profitable opportunities in today's markets, as to create markets (in societies) that systematically reward responsible practices.

Corporate responsibility and competitiveness

Scaling up corporate responsibility requires that it be integral to and supportive of, broader sustainable development strategies and policies. Sustainable development depends on the health of the economy and its pattern of social, environmental and economic impacts. Economic health in turn does depend on international competitiveness, which plays a key role in determining a country or region's pace of economic development as well as its social and environmental characteristics.

The mainstreaming of corporate responsibility therefore requires it to be at least consistent with, and preferably mutually reinforced by, national and regional competitiveness strategies. The European Community has acknowledged the potential role that corporate responsibility might play in realising its goal of becoming '**the most competitive knowledge-based economy in the world, capable of sustainable economic growth with more and better jobs and greater social cohesion**'.[1] Similarly for other countries and regions. South Africa's policy of black empowerment is challenged for its impact on the nation's international competitiveness. Vietnam's responses to international criticism about labour standards in its footwear sector are in danger of pricing the country out of this market as manufacturing multinationals shift towards lower-cost parts of the region. But there is really no clear understanding as yet as to how corporate responsibility might be mainstreamed in ways that contribute to national and regional economic competitiveness.

The question is whether corporate responsible practices can play a significant role in driving 'responsible competitiveness', characterised by a positive relationship between national and regional competitiveness and a nation's sustainable development performance. Businesses can compete effectively across the responsibility spectrum, spanning from investment in environmentally friendly technology and raising productivity by improving their employees' work–life balance, through to cutting corners on environment and labour standards and engaging in corrupt relationships with governments.

The relationship between international competitiveness and corporate responsibility is not a simple one. However, our research suggests that corporate responsibility can, *under certain conditions*, stimulate innovation, investment or trade, and so competitiveness.

Understanding competitiveness

❝ To understand competitiveness, the starting point must be the sources of a nation's prosperity. A nation's standard of living is determined by the productivity of its economy, which is measured by the value of goods and services produced per unit of the nation's human, capital, and natural resources. Productivity depends both on the value of a nation's products and services, measured by the prices they can command in open markets, and the efficiency with which they can be produced. True competitiveness, then, is measured by productivity. ❞

Peter Cornelius and Michael Porter, 2002

Source: Cornelius *et al.* 2002

Corporate responsibility clusters

The potential for 'corporate responsibility clusters' has been identified as **creating competitive advantage within one or several sectors arising through interactions between the business community, labour organisations and wider civil society, and the public sector focused on the enhancement of corporate responsibility.** Corporate responsibility clusters come in different shapes, sizes and types with different types of organisation leading their development. Common, however, are their underlying effect on business performance by expanding their ability to learn from diverse, rich sources; grow competencies to translate these learnings into improved business performance; gain support from a growing network of service providers which enables companies to more effectively manage their relationships and reputation; and benefit from an approach to public policy that moulds markets in ways that reward responsible practices. The research has posited four broad types of clusters, each characterised by different dynamics, institutional relationships, and forms of leadership:

- **Challenge clusters** tend to be initiated by civil-society actors. They are characterised by antagonistic relationships between its participants forming at least the initial basis for the development of competitive advantage.

- **Market-making clusters** are often led by one or more companies. They involve remoulding competitive conditions from the inside out, by innovating more sustainable products, services or business processes.

- **Partnership clusters** involve formal, multi-sectoral partnerships supporting competitive advantage.

- **Statutory clusters** involve public policies focused on corporate responsibility standards and practices that support competitive advantage.

These four types of clusters are neither static nor distinct phenomena. They rarely take one form for prolonged periods of time, and often combine several or all of these forms at different stages in their development. There may indeed be a typical sequencing in the development of clusters. Clusters considered often appeared to go from confrontation through market-making, partnership and then statutory forms.

Corporate responsibility clusters draw on, and yet take us beyond, Michael Porter's seminal work on industrial clusters (Porter 1998). Core to the difference is that clusters that form around corporate responsibility practices and outcomes are not only made up of businesses, but include NGOs, labour organisations and a range of different public bodies. Furthermore, while Porter's original thinking on clustering focused on the role of geographic proximity in stimulating innovation, learning and productivity, our research raises the possibility of geographically dispersed clustering, for example, along value chains. Global value chains mean that clusters may in effect extend along international supply chains.

Corporate responsibility clusters throw a different light on the roots of international competitiveness. But their potential is not evenly distributed across sectors, value chains, geography or time. Labour-intensive sectors such as textiles and footwear, for example, might seem obvious sector cluster candidates. However, their current potential is reliant on companies' sense of the commercial importance of the 'ethical concerns' of citizens in key European and North American markets and on how closely these concerns reflect the reality of the workers and communities affected. Pharmaceuticals might have seemed an unlikely cluster candidate just a few years ago, with low retail brand visibility and high-tech supply chains. But the explosive issue of 'access to health' has changed all that, and today there is far greater likelihood that corporate responsibility clustering might arise. Clusters are driven by two dominant factors.

- **The 'legitimacy' effect.** Clustering is most likely to arise where the potential is greatest for making social and environmental aspects of the value-chain of tangible concern to stakeholders who count.

- **The 'productivity' effect.** Clustering is most likely to arise where the potential is greatest for translating social and environmental enhancements in the value chain into labour and resource efficiency, and productivity gains.

Legitimacy and productivity effects that create business advantage are the prerequisites for clustering to arise, but not sufficient. What makes legitimacy and productivity effects relevant to the development of clusters are the ways in which the potential gains can be increased through the synergies arising out of interactions between the companies and with other actors in society. The legitimacy effects, for example, depend to a large extent on the vibrancy of civil-society organisations in raising public attention and responsiveness. At any point in time this may be directed at individual companies or sectors. But, over time, such vibrancy extends beyond, and indeed is enhanced by, the very success of these individual initiatives. Similarly for public bodies and service providers, which develop competencies that can be more widely applied over time, with collective as well as individual effects.

The role of public policy

The challenge in scaling up corporate responsibility is to shape sectors, entire markets, and ultimately the global economy in ways that mean business strategies and practices can be successful *only* if they contribute to, and do not undermine, sustainable development. Regulation clearly has always had a role to play in this regard; and still does. But regulation that undermines national and regional competitiveness will understandably be resisted, both by the business community and communities who have much to gain from economic growth.

The challenge, then, is to shape public policy in ways that deliver responsible business practices and competitiveness. Business benefits from responsible practices are clearly a key ingredient in any such policy. But such benefits are themselves dependent on the evolving shape of markets, as well as being a driving force of such changes. The challenge is not to frame public policy within existing business models, but to nurture the evolution of new ones.

The potential for **corporate responsibility clusters** is by no means conclusive. But the evidence is sufficient to conclude that they might offer a significant route for scaling up corporate responsibility by delivering competitiveness and sustainable development outcomes. In summary, then:

- Scaling up corporate responsibility can be more effectively achieved where it supports, and is supported by, national and regional competitiveness strategies.

- Public policy aiming to scale up corporate responsibility practices should be established within broader competitiveness strategies.

- Competitiveness strategies, similarly, should reflect the potential for corporate responsibility to support 'responsible competitiveness'.

- 'Corporate responsibility clusters' offer a pivotal mechanism for scaling up corporate responsibility practices through their effective integration into national and regional competitiveness strategies.

Public policies aimed at enhancing overall competitiveness or supporting corporate responsibility practices will often be specific to particular sectors, situations or even companies. Furthermore, promoting corporate responsibility clustering has to be in the context of issues such as access to markets, trade barriers and competition policy. In a European context, this general thrust is acknowledged in the European Commission's recent communiqué on 'corporate social responsibility' (EC 2002), and reinforced through the mandate of the Commission's recently established Multi-Stakeholder Forum for CSR (CSR EMS Forum). The same is true beyond Europe. The Doha 'development' round is one where the question of corporate responsibility has already surfaced. Bilateral trade and investment agreements increasingly include issues and aspects concerning labour and environmental standards. Corporate governance codes, and reporting and stock exchange listing requirements—to name a few—are no longer distinct from the issues underlying corporate responsibility, and are seen as key in defining the basis on which nations nurture not only the probity but the competitiveness of their business communities.

Public policies to amplify corporate responsibility practices need to be, and indeed are being, formulated in the context of this complexity, at an international level, and also at regional, national, and even community levels.

- **Refining our understanding of 'responsible competitiveness'.** There is a need to refine our understanding of the potential for 'responsible competitiveness', where national and regional competitiveness strategies enhance, and are supported by, corporate responsibility practices and clusters.

- **National, regional and sector analysis.** There is a need for more detailed empirical studies examining at national, regional and sector levels the links between corporate responsibility and responsible competitiveness, and the role that corporate responsibility clusters might play in strengthening these links.

- **Standards, tools and competitiveness.** There is a need to explore the potential competitiveness impacts of reporting and other standards and tools associated with corporate responsibility practices, and how such impacts can be managed.

- **Responsible competitiveness, winners and losers.** There is a need to understand the potential for winners and losers in scaling up corporate responsibility within a broader competitiveness strategy, particularly the place of small and medium-sized enterprises (SMEs) within such developments.

- **Redefining competitiveness measures.** There is a need to redefine the basis on which national and regional competitiveness is measured to include key aspects of corporate responsibility that, particularly through clustering, can impact on competitiveness.

30
third-generation corporate citizenship
public policy and
business in society*

Business in society

The role of business in society is this century's most important and contentious public policy issue. Business's role goes beyond the creation of economic and financial wealth: today it is increasingly moulding society's values and norms, and defining public policy and practice. How business is done will underpin how future local and global communities address social and environmental visions and imperatives. All the biggest issues we face today are deeply informed by business practice, from global warming and animal welfare to peace and security.

But as a public policy issue, the role of business in society is like an 'elephant in the bedroom'.[1] It is so big and so important that policy-makers often seem in denial that the issue exists at all. Most governments and public agencies accept as the de facto rules of the game the basic tenets of today's global economy, and the role of the corporate community within it. Public policy is increasingly framed in this light, often allowing an accumulation of yesterday's ill-conceived compromise deals to underpin and even justify today's unacceptable social and environmental outcomes. When challenged, governments speak of the limits of their power in the face of liberalised markets, hot capital, and the complexity of global governance. The prevalent view of the 'inevitability of globalisation in its current form' has become as much an excuse for inaction as a description of historical events or possible futures. Not a single government of a major economic power has seriously engaged in debate about the merits of globalisation with the citizens they represent (although the recent interest in French political circles in the so-called 'Tobin Tax'

---

* This is a summary of the report 'Third Generation Corporate Citizenship'. © 2001 Foreign Policy Centre, London.

on international financial transactions is perhaps one indication that times are changing). Such an approach to public policy can at very best get most from the status quo, and at worst threatens to be an outright—and wholly unnecessary—disaster.

The topic of business in society has of course been treated in a more boisterous manner on the streets of Seattle and Genoa. But activists leading the assault on corporate power and influence have in the main remained entrenched in their negative critique, encouraged in part by the lack of serious mainstream debate (Edwards 2000b). Few have mapped out credible alternatives for generating and distributing sufficient economic wealth to provide a decent quality of life for a growing world population. Similarly for those who advocate 'corporate citizenship' as a means of squaring the circle of unfettered trade liberalisation, few have seriously faced up to the challenge of whether corporate citizenship can deliver sufficient social and environmental gains to reverse the underlying pattern of growing poverty, inequality and environmental insecurity. Few within this community have acknowledged with any real urgency the potential bankruptcy of an approach that fails to meet this challenge.

The elephant that is the role of business in society, although visible, remains critically under-exposed in mainstream policy debate and practice.

Generations of corporate citizenship

The scale that corporations have achieved through mergers, acquisitions and the opportunities opened through national and international market liberalisation has transformed them from businesses as 'financially viable producers and purveyors of needed (or at least wanted) goods and services' into vast, complex, 'profit-needing' institutions which, almost coincidentally, deliver goods and services. Extraordinary facts about this historic transformation have been turned into apparently mundane truths. It is today almost passé among opinion leaders to point out that 51 of the 100 largest economies in the world today are corporations, or that the top 200 corporations have sales equivalent to one-quarter of the world's total economic activity. We seem to accept as normal that General Motors has annual sales equivalent to the GDP of Denmark, and the annual sales of Sears Roebuck's is comparable to the total annual income of over 100 million Bangladeshis (Utting 2000).

And size counts. Global corporations deeply penetrate the political economy of both developing countries and superpowers. Their investments underpin the capital base of many emerging economies, and their donations are essential to ever-more-costly political campaigns. These mega-institutions are accused of sapping the means of national governments to represent their citizens' best interests. The effect of this, it is claimed by many intellectuals and civil activists, has been to unleash a competition between the world's communities to cut public spending, privatise public assets, convert often severely curtailed public services into private profit centres, and to draw back from any regulation that constrains business activities, particularly those of the corporate community.

So what has been the response of companies? They *are* responding, whether by virtue of their enlightened leadership, the brute force of actual or expected market pressure, or—most likely—some muddled combination of the two.

The first response from the corporate community is that it is 'doing its job' by creating economic wealth. After all, over three-quarters of international investment in developing countries—the lifeblood of economic growth—comes from private sources, mainly large corporations. Corporations such as Shell International and South African Breweries are increasingly incorporating measures of their economic contribution into their non-financial reports (UNEP/SustainAbility 2000). Such investment and trade can and does at times underpin an economic growth that can alleviate poverty. As the UN Human Development Report points out:

> people in many countries live a much longer and healthier life than just two decades ago. In 31 of the 174 countries included in the HDI [Human Development Index], life expectancy has increased by more than a fifth since 1975 . . . Between 1975 and 1997 most countries made substantial progress in human development, reducing their shortfall from the maximum possible value of the HDI (UNDP 1999: 129-30).

It is this apparent link that underpins the argument of those advocating a trade-liberalised, business-as-usual public policy environment as the most effective means of alleviating poverty and overcoming environmental challenges. Indeed, advocates rightly point out that investment from global corporations can bring with it higher environmental and labour standards than prevailing local conditions (Zarsky 1999).

Anti-corporate views typically undervalue the positive income and wealth gains that can accompany globalisation. Even companies many people love to hate, such as British American Tobacco, are the prime sources of livelihood for many agricultural communities and, in some instances, handle the product that is the main source of export earnings for entire nations. However, a recent study by the Washington-based Centre for Economic and Policy Research, for example, suggests that the economic growth rates of the majority of developing countries, and many human development rates, have worsened during the period of accelerating globalisation (1980–2000) as compared to other periods (Weisbrot et al. 2001). As inequality within developing (and developed) countries and between the North and the South grows, it harms the very consensus for globalisation, which is the licence to operate for all global companies. This is why companies need a more concerted response to the critique of their role as the main actors in the globalisation process.

The second stage of corporate response is corporate citizenship. By 'corporate citizenship' I mean here where businesses have explicit social and/or environmental aims that go beyond what the national or local rule of law requires of them. Of course this can mean many different things, which goes some way to explain the suspicions towards corporate citizenship. Just within one sector, food retailing, Tesco's highly successful programme of donating computers to schools sits uneasily under the same rubric of 'corporate citizenship' as Littlewood's leadership in addressing labour standards in global supply chains, Waitrose's approach to common ownership as part of the John Lewis Partnership, or Iceland's high-profile stance in the market-sensitive campaign against genetically modified organisms.

Indeed, all of these examples are entirely different to the radical ambitions and approaches of parts of the fair-trade movement, such as the innovative Day Chocolate Company and Cafédirect.

Such diversity becomes all the more problematic when it appears present within a single company. The Ford Motor Corporation has sought to take a leadership role within the automobile sector in using the principles of sustainable development to frame its business strategy. But it remains unclear how this squares with alleged racism within the company's facilities at Dagenham, or their approach to the recent revelations over apparent fatal weaknesses in the alchemy of their SUV vehicles and Firestone tires. Certainly, technological developments underwritten by companies such as Ford are likely to dramatically reduce the environmental footprint of tomorrow's vehicles, but how does this square with the continued overall increase in vehicle-related emissions with the rapidly growing number of vehicles sold worldwide (Hawken *et al.* 1999)?

It is therefore useful to unpack the notion of corporate citizenship into discrete elements. One approach outlined below and described elsewhere in more detail is to frame differences in generational terms, each subsequent generation raising the bar on the challenge and aspirations underlying corporate citizenship.[2]

The **first generation** frames the question, '**Can corporations be responsible in ways that do not detract from and may add commercial value to their business?**' For many business communities, philanthropy is simply part of the way business is done. Often, it is part of how senior management and in some instances private owners comply with the needs of their individual leadership roles in their respective societies. This generation also marked the rise of corporate citizenship as a route to defend themselves against the financial pain (and often managers' and employees' personal humiliation) associated with public campaigns following alleged social or environmental misconduct. In both of these cases, citizenship generally involves 'bolt-on' philanthropy unrelated to a company's overall strategies, business processes and footprints.

The answer to the first-generation challenge is a measured 'yes'. Philanthropic costs either yield limited but worthwhile financial benefits such as positive reputational effects or are so low that they don't impact commercial success. Corporate citizenship as an integral element of a communication strategy to combat public criticism was also proving more effective than the alternative, more high-handed denials of culpability or even responsibility adopted by, for example, Nestlé, in its handling of the long-running campaign about baby milk marketing.

The **second generation** of corporate responsibility raises the question, '**Are responsible companies more likely to prosper in the future?**' This question takes the debate beyond the short-term frame of simple cost–benefit analysis and pain alleviation. It poses the challenge of whether corporate citizenship can underpin or at the very least be an integral part of a business's long-term strategy for success.

The response to the second-generation challenge seems to be a qualified 'maybe'. GlaxoSmithKline and other pharmaceutical companies are rapidly finding ways to provide lower-cost access to drugs in commercially marginal markets across Africa; telecommunications companies such as BT and Cisco have launched a multitude of initiatives to overcome the so-called Digital Divide (Zadek and Raynard 2001);

extraction industries such as Rio Tinto, BP and Shell have invested heavily in improving the social and environmental outcomes associated with their site operations; and brands such as Nike and Marks & Spencer have done much to clean up social and environmental performance in their supply chains. This is the emerging heartland of corporate citizenship (Andriof and McIntosh 2001).

Research suggests that companies that take key principles of sustainable development into account in forging and implementing their business strategies consistently outperform the market (Weiser and Zadek 2000). Such results do not mean that 'being good' automatically leads to 'doing well'. But, as Reto Ringger, President of Sustainability Asset Management, the architects of the Dow Jones Sustainability Index, explains, 'companies which are better managed environmentally indicate more sophisticated management throughout the company . . . And good management is the single most important factor in corporate profitability, growth, and future earnings.' Businesses that embrace corporate citizenship effectively deepen their associations with stakeholders. In doing so they build the insight, will and capacity to learn and respond by innovating their processes and products in ways that are likely to enhance their longer-term business strategy and performance.

Corporate citizenship *can* be superficial and inadequate. In its worst form, it can be a conservative safety valve that offsets the pressure for much-needed structural change in markets, in the ways of the business community, and in the role of government. Where I part ways with many of its critics is that such outcomes are not a *sine qua non* of corporate citizenship. Whether corporate citizenship can live up to its potential is a strategic challenge rather than some given truth.

This then brings one to the need for **third-generation** corporate citizenship. The more daunting challenge here is: **'Is corporate citizenship likely to be significant in addressing growing levels of poverty, exclusion, and environmental degradation?'** To what extent, for example, will the responsible behaviour of the world's largest purveyor of alcoholic beverages, Diageo, actually reduce the level of alcoholism and the associated abuse, crime, violence and death? Will the results of Ford embracing sustainable development make a significant difference to the growing environmental and health problems caused by traffic-related pollution?

The simple answer to the third-generation challenge is that current, essentially voluntary, approaches by individual companies to corporate citizenship will *in themselves* not contribute significantly to resolving deeply rooted social and environmental problems. However large companies have become, few if any are individually able to refocus the markets in which they operate towards more sustainable production and distribution of goods and services that meet real needs. If a company such as GAP effectively implemented an agreed labour code of conduct throughout its supply chains, it might *directly* benefit as many as 5 million workers. But this seems limited when set against the 1.2 billion living in absolute poverty. That does not make such voluntary initiatives by individual companies wrong or bad—just limited. This shows how third-generation corporate citizenship will need to involve collective processes that move beyond individual initiatives and seek to forge progressive alliances between business, government and NGOs in raising the global performance bar. Failure to achieve this maturity in corporate citizenship could mean that the wider public policy aims of governments are hampered by businesses that are unwilling to put longer-term business success and overall social progress above short-term profits. Moving to third-generation corporate citizenship will therefore involve broadening our idea of citizenship so that it is not just a commitment to developing communities that benefit companies but also a recognition of the need to respect government's duty to deliver public policy goods.

The stakes are high as the credibility of democratic governments will also be affected by their ability to change the underlying relationship between business and society. The issue is not merely whether there are things that the government can and should do to encourage corporate citizenship. Rather, the challenge is whether the government can find ways to raise the strategic significance of corporate citizenship in addressing social and environmental challenges, both to business as an imperative, and as an enabler of more effective government policy, both nationally and on the global stage. At this level the role of the business community—and so the contribution of corporate citizenship—becomes a matter of governance rather than merely one of operational competencies and capacities.

First generation

Can corporations be responsible in ways that do not detract from, and may add, commercial value to their business?

Second generation

Are more responsible companies likely to prosper in the future?

Third generation

Is corporate citizenship likely to make a significant contribution to addressing the growing levels of poverty, exclusion and environmental degradation?

BOX 11 CORPORATE CITIZENSHIP'S GENERATIONAL CHALLENGES

Source: Zadek 2001a

Public policy and corporate citizenship

The enhanced role of corporate and civil-society actors is often framed as being accompanied by a shrinking role for national governments. We hear of their growing irrelevance in a borderless world. It may indeed be true that national governments are weakened by the increasingly global nature of decisions that need to be made. But these facts do not make governments less important. The need for strong government is all the greater where international public agencies such as the World Trade Organisation (WTO) are accountable to citizens only indirectly through the membership of national governments. This becomes even more significant where international negotiations are increasingly subject to pressures from both the business and non-profit communities, and when these sectors form an increasingly important mechanism for delivering public goods. The more we rely on diverse institutional mechanisms to deliver public goods, the more we need overarching stewardship that democratic and accountable government provides to ensure that it all adds up to the right level delivered in the best way to the right people.

The key message for governments from the demonstrations around the meeting of the WTO in Seattle in late 1999 is not that the street activists were right or wrong in what they were saying, or even in how they said it. It was that the governments that sat around the negotiating table had conclusively failed to establish their claims to legitimacy in many people's minds.

Most governments have failed to rise to the challenge and have seen resistance to globalisation as a problem of communication rather than as a result of genuine concerns about poverty and inequality. Instead of treating those protests about globalisation with barely concealed contempt, political leaders should go out of their way to show how seriously they take these concerns and to demonstrate how governments and companies can make globalisation contribute to poverty alleviation and sustainable development. One part of the response will be to show that governments can secure business's contribution to public policy aims. It is clearly not possible to focus purely on national legislation in enhancing the contribution of business. It is not just that it would lead to an outflow of mobile capital and a diminished competitive position for relatively captive capital that nevertheless faces international competition—it ignores the fact that many of the most creative responses come from within the business sector. At the same time, an approach that merely exhorts business to 'do the right thing' is inadequate since the most that can be expected from this approach is first- or occasionally second-generation responses by a few companies.

Government's task is to develop a policy framework that enables it to enhance the delivery of public goods in the context of a globalising political economy. This will mean going beyond compliance to mobilising the active support of the business community. Partnerships that position corporations purely in the role of commercial provider of public goods and services may in some instances be effective. But even the best scenario will not see this market route as sufficient to enable government to fulfil its mission.

The third generation of corporate citizenship requires that governments, business and non-profit organisations embrace at the very least the following principles and their practical implications:.

a. Government should embrace the underlying **principle of corporate citizenship**—that the purpose of business is more than to make a financial profit, and that business is therefore more broadly accountable to society than its responsibilities to shareholders. From this perspective, the business case is not the *justification* for corporate citizenship, but what *enables* corporations to address their wider purpose. Furthermore, potential financial rewards to corporate citizenship are not so much something existing to discover and take advantage of, so much as a result that needs to be created for corporations to be successful.

This principle takes public policy beyond the view of corporate citizenship underpinned by 'enlightened shareholding' to one that more fully embraces a broadening of the underlying purpose of business. In practice, this broadening purpose is increasingly reflected in the mission statements of some of the world's largest corporations. Governments are beginning to support this in their pronouncements.

Witness Tony Blair's statement that 'Many of Britain's best-known companies are already re-defining the traditional roles of the corporation. They are recognising that every customer is part of the community and that social responsibility is not an optional extra.'[3]

Such leadership statements are certainly supported through, for example, the requirement that pension funds disclose any social and environmental criteria applied to their investments, and the forthcoming guidelines of the Association of British Insurers that will require that UK-listed companies publicly report on their approaches to managing risks associated with social and environmental policies and impacts. However, third-generation corporate citizenship will need to extend beyond the management of risk on behalf of shareholders, just as the visions of governments must extend beyond short-term electoral demands, and those of NGOs must not be determined solely by fundraising imperatives. Governments have a critical role to play in making this possible and necessary, but have failed so far in meeting this challenge. The Company Law Review, for example, while extensive and in many ways progressive, has failed to set the stage for such a broadening of business purpose in that it argues that the responsibility of companies to their broader stakeholder community should be limited to where it serves the interests of their shareholders. Despite this, the European policy debate emerging following the publication of the EU Green Paper on Corporate Social Responsibility offers an important route for promoting a broadening of the purpose of business.[4] In this respect, the UK government has an opportunity to take a leadership role in bringing together the continental European tradition of social partnership with the UK's leading-edge experience of corporate citizenship. This could underpin future European policy initiatives in the field of corporate governance and disclosure requirements.

b. Government should establish the **principle of competitive citizenship** as a core element of its support for British business. Certainly, it helps to sponsor awards for good practice and to document the growing body of company-level evidence of the business case. However, this falls far short of the strategic approach needed to take advantage of the potential for competitive clusters discussed above. Initiatives such as the Dow Jones Sustainability Index and FTSE4Good are highlighting which business sectors are likely to prosper in the future as they realise opportunities associated with social and environmental gains. Government can do much more to support the knowledge infrastructure required for businesses to take advantage of such opportunities, as they are already beginning to do, for example, through the Department of International Development (DFID)'s business responsibility resource centre located at the International Business Leaders Forum.

The effective promotion of an enabling environment for competitive citizenship must, however, extend further than information provision. There are a host of public instruments that need to be refocused to support competitive citizenship. Government should amend the Export Credit Guarantee Department (ECGD) mission statement to include its own development objectives and environmental goals. This will prevent any repeat of experiences such as the Ilisu Dam debacle, particularly if the ECGD is also banned from underwriting projects, which jeopardise the human rights of workers and the local community. Beyond the avoidance of the negative, however, instruments such as ECGD should actively search out and support business propositions that consolidate the reputation of British business for being sensitive and innovative in its approach to dealing with social and environmental issues. More generally, fiscal policy should reflect governments' interpretation of good corporate citizenship, just as it currently provides incentives, and indeed often 'perverse subsidies', for all manner of investments and other activities. Similarly, there is enormous scope for orienting government procurement to such performance criteria. Such an approach would have implications, for example, for the criteria of best value. 'Joined-up thinking' would suggest the need to define them more broadly than narrow efficiency measures and direct cost. There is also a strong case for changing the criteria for the ECGD.

A familiar objection is that such policies would be inconsistent with international agreements, particularly the rules overseen by the World Trade Organisation that seek to prohibit trade restrictions based on the conditions of production of goods and services. For example, under these rules it is problematic and possibly illegal for governments to require some products to be labelled according to the labour conditions prevailing in their production. But these rules are there to be moulded through precedent and, if necessary, changed in pursuit of equitable development. Though achieving an agreement would be fraught with complexity, the government should at least publicly make clear that it is lobbying for a change in the rules. Rules are currently being tested: for example, by the Belgian government, which is seeking to pass national legislation that sets out an approach to voluntary social labelling. Indeed, most European Community governments are currently inclined towards legislative interventions to enhance the competitive gains of corporate citizenship. The UK government could help in consolidating and reinforcing the lead gained by the British business community through voluntary initiatives by promoting appropriate, enabling legislation that prevents this lead being eroded through pure price-based competitive strategies.

It is important that these principles be extended to all international organisations. At an EU level, the government should support the extension of this principle across Europe in the context of the EU Green Paper. This should encourage the European Commission to benchmark the performance of governments in creating an environment conducive to good corporate citizenship. This would publicise the most successful in, for instance, tailoring their corporate taxation regime to social and environmental goals, and force the poor performers to raise their game. The CSR agenda should be pursued internationally through the work of the DFID.

c. Government should embrace the **principle of civil accountability**, which would involve an overhaul of its approach to public accountability in the light of the increasingly intimate relationships being forged between public agencies, non-profit organisations and business. The growth of public–private partnerships in its broadest sense is opening up a democratic deficit, at local, national and international levels. The intention was for the public good to be assured through a combination of regulatory oversight, shared risk and an emphasis on performance contracts based on clear measures of outputs and outcomes. There is little evidence that these safeguards have been as effective as they need to be in ensuring, for example, that public services are really improving and that there are real long-term savings in public funds.

This is not necessarily a sign that public–private partnerships cannot work, or that business is over-exploiting the commercial opportunities opened by these partnerships. As important is that the outdated, inadequate mechanisms for ensuring public accountability make public bodies weak partners in their dealings with business. Public accountability needs to reflect the new reality of public bodies— including local authorities—being increasingly encouraged, empowered and indeed often cajoled to enter into arrangements with parts of the business community. The activities of politicians and civil servants need to be more visible, as must be the basis for their decisions. Service shortfalls and cost overruns associated with privatisation, inadequate regulatory oversight, or inappropriate partnership arrangements need to be published and those responsible held to account. The government needs to review and publish options for revising the accountability of all public– private partnerships.

Account also needs to be taken of the underlying citizenship strategy of potential business partners. On this basis, governments may well continue to offer public contracts across the entire spectrum of the business community, but should seek to restrict 'partnerships' to those relationships formed with businesses that demonstrate common cause in addressing public policy objectives.

A particular aspect of civil accountability concerns the development of a new generation of Generally Applicable Accounting Principles for Sustainability (GAAPS) that embrace social, environmental and economic aspects to enable comparative organisational performance in these spheres to be measured and communicated.

The last decade has seen a rash of exciting experiments by individual companies and alliances such as the Global Reporting Initiative, the Institute of Social and Ethical AccountAbility's AA1000 stakeholder-based process standard,[5] the London Benchmarking Group's community engagement benchmarking standard,[6] and the labour-focused standard embodied within Social Accountability International's SA8000. The UK government is already offering some support to work in this field, such as the SIGMA initiative of the British Standards Institute, Forum for the Future, and the Institute of Social and Ethical AccountAbility.

There is an urgent need to accelerate such work and bring closure in agreeing a basic framework for social, environmental and overall sustainability accounting, auditing and reporting that will underpin tomorrow's GAAPS. Such a standard must conform to best practices and enhance businesses' ability to respond to customers' needs and the needs of investors and the financial community as they seek assurance that their investments are in compliance with emerging social and environmental governance frameworks such as those established by the Association of British Insurers. Ultimately, an effective GAAPS must fulfil the needs emerging as a result of new statutory legislation, such as the social and environmental elements of the Operating and Financial Review of the proposed revised UK Company Law.

Government should make clear its commitment to developing such standards for use throughout the business community, as well as for public agencies and private, non-profit organisations. Practically, it should increase its currently modest support to UK and international initiatives working in this area, focusing not just on management tools (such as SIGMA) but the development of formal accounting, auditing and reporting frameworks such as AA1000 and the GRI. As part of this support, the government should be more active in the wake of the advent of the EU

Green Paper on Corporate Social Responsibility in promoting a European-level approach to these developments. Finally, the government should commit its own operational departments to annual published sustainability reports as a contribution to evolving standards that would also be appropriate for public bodies and partnerships.

d. Finally, the government should embrace the **principle of global accountability**, which acknowledges the need for mechanisms for holding global institutions such as corporations to account, globally. International conventions negotiated, mainly through the United Nations, have long provided an aspirational backbone of universal values, rights and accountability. These conventions have, of course, been agreed between sovereign states, and have historically applied to private institutions and individuals only where rooted in national and regional legislation. The OECD Convention on Foreign Corrupt Practices is a case in point, agreed by OECD governments, and over time incorporated in national legislation in the UK and elsewhere.

International conventions are, however, increasingly impacting directly on the policies and practices of global corporations. The Ethical Trading Initiative is underpinned by a Base Code adopted voluntarily by its corporate members that effectively operationalises the core labour conventions established through the International Labour Organisation. The UN Global Compact has been built around its core principles that are simplified versions of key human rights, environmental and labour-related UN conventions. Today's reality is that leading corporations recognise the need to embrace internationally applicable social and environmental standards.

The dilemma remains, however, that these standards are neither internationally applicable nor enforceable across the corporate community. This creates an uneven playing field for those corporations adopting competitive citizenship strategies, which in turn threatens the viability of these strategies. From this perspective, it is perhaps unsurprising to find Phil Knight, Nike's CEO, arguing in favour of international regulation governing performance disclosure at the time of the launch of the Global Compact: 'We believe in a global system that measures *every* multinational against a core set of universal standards using an independent process of social performance monitoring akin to financial auditing'.[7]

Global accountability for global institutions is the clarion call of many of those most concerned with the role of corporations in the downsides of globalisation. Disagreement on this as a principle certainly exists. However, the real devil lies in the practical question of how best to achieve meaningful accountability without either undermining national sovereignty or the potential for economic development. For example, many governments of countries with export-based development strategies such as China, Brazil and India oppose any social or environmental clauses in international trade arrangements, arguing that such clauses will do more development damage than good by restricting their economic growth. Others have argued for an extension of the rule of law as it exists in Western Europe and North America to cover these regions' corporations' activities elsewhere in the world. This route for building globally enforceable rules of accountability has been set out in a recent paper by the Royal Institute for International Affairs on 'foreign direct liability' (Ward 2001). The basic idea mirrors the case of General Pinochet, arrested in the UK for alleged human rights abuses in Chile. It aims to encourage countries where most global corporations are headquartered to accept more responsibility for regulating the impact of their corporations' overseas activities. Formalising a basis on which corporations can be challenged in public debate for their international performance is another possible route, where compliance is a reputational rather than a statutory matter. The European Parliament's work in building a 'monitoring platform' for labour standards is one such experiment, where corporations are effectively invited to face accusations and give evidence at the European Parliament regarding their approach to labour standards in their global supply chains.

The dilemmas and challenges facing any attempt to extend global accountability should not prevent the government from embracing the principle that seeks to ensure mechanisms of accountability that are commensurate in reach and scope to that of the institutions to which they are to be applied. Leaders in corporate citizenship should, moreover, openly acknowledge this need, as BP did in the case of global warming, many companies did in the lead-up to the OECD Convention on Foreign Corrupt Practices, and as Nike has now done in the case of social auditing in relation to labour standards.

Conclusion

Corporate citizenship in almost any form is to be welcomed, celebrated and encouraged. Sadly, however, most of its current manifestations will not contribute significantly to achieving national and international public policy objectives, particularly those that seek to address the most daunting global challenges of extensive and growing poverty and inequality, and environmental security. The leadership of individual businesses in corporate citizenship will not offset the appearance and reality that the structure of global corporatism has become part of the problem. The current menu of policy options on offer from the mainstream political community will not do the job. Similarly, their alter ego—the radical critique from the streets—currently has little to contribute to the debate. Third-generation corporate citizenship strategy tries to set out a credible framework for moving forward that builds on what is already there and yet seeks to break down some of the more intractable institutional barriers to success.

31

dangerous trading

trade and growth pose a threat to the environment unless care is taken*

co-written with Christian Haas

The expansion of international trade lies at the heart of the mainstream view of how to achieve economic growth. The theory of comparative advantage, still the foundation of the free-trade paradigm, says that it is beneficial for all countries to export goods that they can produce comparatively cheaply. This is put forward as a way to alleviate poverty in less-developed countries, and to bolster the economies of industrialised countries. The route to economic success is seen as a matter of increasing trade liberalisation through reduced national regulations on the terms on which production and trade are carried out, and international legislation to support this deregulation.

This view of 'free trade' as a panacea has been challenged by environmentalists. They argue that unfettered export-oriented development leads to substantial environmental degradation. International competitive advantage is achieved in part through 'externalising'—not adequately costing in—the ecological impact of export-oriented production and trade. According to this view, the type of economic growth engendered by an export-led approach to economic development is problematic; free trade is bad for the environment and stronger environmental protection regulation at national and international levels is needed.

Champions of free trade, on the other hand, hold that it promotes quicker diffusion of environment-friendly technologies and leads to more efficient allocation of resources, which will also be beneficial for the environment. They assert that pre-emptive environmental regulation would prevent national communities from becoming affluent enough to invest in protecting the environment.

* First published in *New Economy*, Summer 1995, pp 142-146. © Blackwell Publishing, Oxford.

Data diversity

Despite the intensity of the debate, the empirical evidence presented by both sides is weak. The effects of trade on the environment cannot be captured by any single perspective, method or set of data. There are many types of environmental effects—from pollution to resource depletion—occurring over different time-scales. These cannot easily be reduced to any simple numeraire to produce a single conclusion.

So is there any evidence of short-term environmental effects arising from the process of trade liberalisation itself? And does economic growth per se—in general associated with an export-oriented development strategy—lead to reductions in pollution over time?

Domestic blight

One worry about trade liberalisation is that it ignores market and government failures prevalent in most countries that encourage environmental degradation in various ways. For instance, the market fails to compensate for ecological effects that arise from economic activity and impact on people who do not gain financially from it.

These effects are often referred to as 'externalities'. They do not have to be negative, but in many cases are. In Malawi, for instance, trade liberalisation lowered export taxes for tobacco and cotton. This has led to a significant expansion of tobacco estates and shrinkage in fallow in the cotton smallholder sector. Tobacco and cotton tend to erode the soil, so the result has been impaired welfare for other farmers and future generations of Malawians. Unaccounted externalities are often exacerbated by the lack of definition or enforcement of property rights. In the Philippines, where there were virtually no well-defined property rights in the hill areas in the 1980s, trade liberalisation gave rise to price changes favouring maize and root crops, both erosive when grown in hilly areas. This encouraged farmers and the urban unemployed to migrate to the open access hill areas to plant these crops. Yet the absence of property rights meant there was little incentive for the new farmers to invest in soil protection. The resulting costs of soil erosion have been estimated at 0.4% of the GDP of the Philippines in 1987.

These examples do not suggest that trade itself is bad. Rather, they highlight the fact that economic growth through crude forms of trade liberalisation leads to negative environmental effects and provides a means by which these effects can be ignored. So long as costs (and benefits) are not counted, they can be ignored. And historically they have been. It is only recently that we have seen the emergence of environmental impact assessment at the micro level, and alternative approaches to national accounting that take environmental pollution and resource depletion seriously. These new tools enable us not only to describe the environmental dimensions of economic processes but also to influence them through a combination of regulation, education and investment in production technologies and consumer products that are kinder to the environment.

Free-trade 'benefits'

Despite this emerging ecological awareness, conventional free-traders still say that the way to deal with the environment is to allow unconstrained economic growth. 'The fear is widespread among environmentalists that free trade increases economic growth and that growth harms the environment. That fear is misplaced. Growth enables governments to tax and raise resources for a variety of objectives, including the abatement of pollution and the general protection of the environment' (Bhagwati 1993). This proposition says not that trade in itself is good—or even neutral—for the environment, but that in economic prosperity lies the security of the environment, and that free trade is the best route to achieving that prosperity.

The argument is flawed. There is scant evidence that economic prosperity is good for the environment; equally, free trade is neither the only nor the optimum route to achieving such prosperity.

The Kuznets curve

The view that economic growth is good for the environment is based on two propositions. First, growth is associated with an increasing share of services and high-technology production, both of which tend to be more environment-friendly than production processes in earlier stages of industrialisation. Second, as individuals become richer they are willing to spend more on non-material goods, such as a cleaner environment. At this point governments can allocate more taxes to establishing and enforcing stronger regulatory frameworks for environmental protection.

The development trajectory implied by this argument can be expressed as an inverted-U curve, which shows how negative environmental outcomes, such as the level of a pollutant, change with income per capita. This is known as the Environmental Kuznets Curve (EKC) because of the formative work of Simon Kuznets. This hypothesis has been tested by several authors for a range of pollution indicators (NEF/WWF 1995). For example, Selden and Song's work (1994) suggests that sulphur dioxide emissions rise up to a per capita income of US$8,900 (1985 dollars), and fall again thereafter.

From this perspective, trade liberalisation that leads to economic growth would be a 'win–win' situation, generating both increased material consumption and environmental improvements. The message of the EKC, then, has been: don't worry about the environmental consequences of economic growth, even if it comes through trade intensification that has short-term environmental costs; indeed, to prevent growth through pre-emptive environmental regulation could hamper economic success and thus restrict environmental protection in the long run.

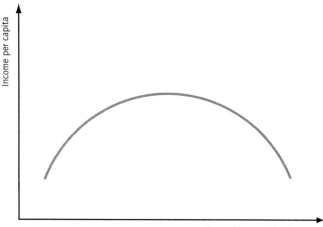

Negative environmental outcome

FIGURE 36 ENVIRONMENTAL KUZNETS CURVE

Different turning points

The significance of this argument—and its use in key policy debates such as the Uruguay Round of GATT—has given rise to investigation of its foundations.

What has become clear is that the shape of the EKC is not the same for all pollution indicators. This is in part a matter of different 'turning points' for different pollutants. For example, as shown in Figure 37, the turning point for cadmium pollution has been estimated at US$11,600 compared to US$1,900 for lead (Grossman and Krueger 1994).

The almost 60% of the world's population living with a per capita income below US$2,000 would have to double their income to reach the estimated turning point for sulphur dioxide at US$4,100. In other cases, income per capita would have to increase five- to tenfold to reach the estimated turning points assuming these points remained stable in the face of such a vast increase of global economic activity.

Studies have produced a wide range of estimated turning points even for the same pollutant. For example, Panayotou (1992) estimated the turning point for sulphur dioxide as US$3,000; Grossman (1993) as US$13,400. This raises serious questions about the empirical robustness of any of the results.

Further, many of the environmental effects of trade and production intensification simply have not been taken into account. Grossman and Krueger (1994) point out that key urban air pollutants, including nitrogen oxides, carbon monoxide and lead, are absent from the sample, as are pollutants that affect the global atmosphere—CFCs, carbon dioxide, methane, nitrous oxide and tropospheric ozone.

Additionally, the most important EKC studies do not consider the effects of trade and production intensification on industrial waste, soil degradation, deforestation and loss of biodiversity. Given these omissions, the proposition of a general EKC is

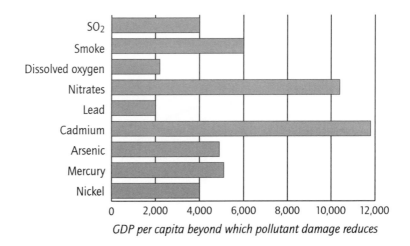

GDP per capita beyond which pollutant damage reduces

FIGURE 37 TURNING POINTS VARY BY POLLUTANT

quite unproven. The evidence in fact suggests that there is a simple linear relationship: as income rises, so does damage.

Shredding the evidence

The argument that growth benefits the environment also requires that the wealth generated is allocated to environmental protection. But it may not be. Research by the Sierra Club on the environmental impact of industrialisation on the northern borders of Mexico in response to the NAFTA suggests not only massive negative effects but a complete unwillingness of national or regional governments to take responsibility for the resultant health hazards.

There is also a growing body of research highlighting the direct negative effects of trade-related intensification of production. Failure to tackle soil erosion, for example, may lead to desertification and hence impair a country's ability to generate agricultural growth. The effects on people's health of some pollutants directly lower their productivity. A study in the USA found that emissions from the burning of leaded gasoline are responsible for high levels of lead in the blood of schoolchildren and a consequent slowdown of their mental development and performance equivalent to the loss of five IQ points (Panayotou 1992).

Policy implications

Although conventional trade liberalisation generates significant and often irreversible environmental damage, it is not proven that increased trade per se must always have such negative effects. The choice is not between trade and the environment but between free trade associated with, at best, short-term economic growth and immediate environmental degradation, and trade within a framework that might foster sustainable development.

It would seem attractive to leave decisions about the degree of environmental protection in the hands of each individual country. However, problems of transboundary and global pollutants suggest there is a need for multilateral environmental agreements. In addition, so long as advantage can be gained through lax national environmental protection, a lack of international agreement on national standards is likely to precipitate less environmental enforcement.

The need, therefore, is to encourage (rather than liberalise) trade within a framework that allows the corporate sector, governments and international bodies to act against market failures to ensure environmental security.

This requires the following steps to be taken:

- The view that economic growth must be achieved before acting to protect the environment must be abandoned; it falls foul of the 'precautionary principle' where major, irreversible negative environmental effects are at stake.

- The environment must be correctly counted—in the national accounts; in relation to the activities of transnational corporations through further developments in environmental and social accounting; and at local levels.

- Environmental legislation must be enacted and enforced where voluntary action in relation to environmental protection is not forthcoming.

- Nations and communities that act to protect the environment should be compensated—financially or through liberalisation that encourages environmentally benign production in poorer countries.

What must be recognised, particularly by the World Trade Organisation and the World Bank, is that trade liberalisation without environmental safeguards will not increase but impede economic growth and welfare in the long run.

32
dealing with and
in the global market
fairer trade in latin america*
co-written with Pauline Tiffen

The last decade has seen the consolidation of a theory and practice of economics that has been loosely, and with ironic accuracy, called 'free trade'. People throughout both the developed and the developing world have forcibly adjusted and made profound efforts to live up to the new conventional wisdom. But, despite the promises of material reward for all, this new economics has meant that most people have to work harder for less immediate reward. However, an economics such as this that recognises need only if it is backed up by purchasing power does not effectively avoid the negative social and environmental consequences of the economic adjustment that have been well documented by many bodies, from the environmental non-governmental organisations (NGOs) to the World Bank.

Although these negative views of the effects of the process of globalisation are correct, far less has been written about the 'openings' afforded by such fundamental change and the new concepts arising from the adjustment process. This chapter aims to outline the efforts of the fair-trade movement, which started in the 1960s. The exponents and champions of this fair trade explicitly espouse and flaunt non-economic values and purposes for trading and seek as a point of fundamental principle to see people as the ends and not the means of economic activity.

What is known about alternative or fair trading?

The fair-trade movement and the alternative trading organisations (ATOs) that are behind it are offering a political concept and practice of a fairer approach to business. ATOs have traded a diverse range of products over almost three decades,

* Adapted from Pauline E. Tiffen and Simon Zadek, 'Dealing with and in the Global Economy: Fairer Trade in Latin America', in Jutta Blauert and Simon Zadek (eds.), *Mediating Sustainability: Growing Policy from the Grassroots* (Kumarian Press, West Hartford, 1998) pp. 163-88. Permission granted by Kumarian Press, Inc.

with for many years a strong emphasis on handicrafts and textiles, and with production based on traditional methods and techniques.

Traditionally, alternative trade in crafts and textiles has been small-scale, with strongly reasoned producer partnerships that have tried to offer opportunities to the most marginal of the rural and urban poor—women, the disabled, those involved in cyclical work (harvests)—against the particularly harsh and unremitting backdrop associated with these sociological groups and occupations in the developing world. Trade in crafts and textiles has also been a springboard for consumer education: about other cultures, wider economic development, world trading regimes, and tariff discrimination issues (for example, the Multi-Fibre Agreement).

From traditionally trading in crafts, the most rapid growth in fair trade in recent years has been in food products, particularly coffee. This growth, built on 20 years' work in building consumer awareness and solidarity, was initially fuelled and accelerated by the Max Havelaar Foundation (MHF) in the Netherlands. In 1998, the MHF established a set of criteria to which conventional companies could adhere and receive an independent mark or seal of approval from the foundation. Among the criteria of fair-trade green coffee, for example, was a floor price paid to producers below which a company using the mark should not fall, regardless of prevailing market price.

The MHF message that viable trade can be underpinned by a fairer deal to the economically weaker partner—the small producer—has found increasing resonance in all industrialised markets. Coffee was a fitting traditional commodity for the movement to work with, in that small-scale peasant family farms are a major global mode of production, making up as much as 15% of world coffee production. Coffee brands on sale in industrialised markets with fair-trade seals have between 2 and 5% of the market share, with the highest percentage penetration in Switzerland. Fairly traded brands have also achieved widespread distribution through conventional outlets (such as supermarkets). This illustrates that the fundamental premise of fair trade is seen by retailers as acceptable to the buying public. This latter perspective suggests that the fair-trade experience in coffee may be pointing the way to a paradigm shift in the marketplace—something not revealed by a conventional statistical analysis of market share, turnover and throughput.

What distinguishes fair trade from other trade?

In general terms, the differences are as follows. At the heart of fair trade is that the primary producers come first, not the product or even the consumer. Local skills, natural resources and context are key. The alternative trader seeks to differentiate and to recast the value of inputs by the different parties in the trading chain, setting out deliberately to maximise the gains from trade that accrue to the Southern suppliers, the weakest links or protagonists in the trading chain, rather than to themselves or to superfluous intermediaries.

Fair trade therefore means in particular a good price to the primary producer. For the fair-trade movement, fairness can and does include many elements apart from price. ATOs know the power and value of information about the market and seek to share this and thereby strengthen the bargaining power of their trading partners relative to other local and international markets. ATOs do not seek exclusive relationships with producers, an approach pursued by many commercial traders to consolidate the producer's dependency on them. ATOs recognise the need for product and organisational development and have provided relevant assistance wherever possible. Marketing has been reformed to mean, in particular, raising awareness of the consumer to social justice and environmental aspects of trade in general, as well as of the brand or product being offered. ATOs frequently involve producers in this process: for example, by voicing their perspectives, concerns and experiences as directly as possible to the consumer.

Does fair trade work?

The fair-trade movement is not homogenous. Some Northern trading companies in the movement are not-for-profit trading offshoots of NGOs working in conventional development co-operation, such as Bridgehead (a division of Oxfam Canada). Others are self-standing trading units, such as the Fair Trade Organisatie in the Netherlands, which also has a producer development arm, Fair Trade Assistance. Some have Christian roots, such as Traidcraft. Twin Trading was established by what was at that time London's regional government, the Greater London Council, and has a sister non-profit charity, TWIN (Third World Information Network).

The Southern trading partners in the movement are also varied. Most have some explicit community orientation, but with many different organisational forms and traditions. Some are co-operatives, such as the Tabora Beekeepers Co-operative in Tanzania; some are community-owned organisations, such as the trading associations of the Ñahñu in Mexico; some are part of the government, such as Tanzania's coffee parastatal, TANICA; others are based on traditional communal arrangements, such as the *ejidos* in Mexico; some are new forms of organisation entirely, based on a mix of modern business and village or indigenous traditions, such as cocoa farmer organisations Kuapa Kokoo in Ghana and El Ceibo in Bolivia.

The heterogeneity of the movement makes it difficult to reach general conclusions of fair trade's effectiveness in offering a good deal to Southern producers. There is no single or commonly agreed-on set of measurable criteria against which the quality of all trade can be assessed. However, there are some agreed-on criteria for particular products and the broad Code of Practice subscribed to by all members of the International Federation of Alternative Trade (IFAT).

Despite the efforts of IFAT and others, however, the effectiveness of fair-trade initiatives is hard to generalise through the prism of single and universally applicable rules. Effectiveness assessments need, for example, to take into account the specifics of the market that is being entered and the supply-side realities and challenges. It is agreed throughout the movement, however, that a fair price is a

1. To trade with concern for social, economic and environmental well-being of marginalised producers in developing countries—this means equitable commercial terms, fair wages and fair prices, not maximising profit at the producers' expense

2. To share information openly, to enable both members and the public to assess social and financial effectiveness

3. To reflect in their own organisational structures a commitment to justice, fair employment, public accountability and progressive work practices

4. To ensure a safe working environment, to provide the opportunity for all individuals to grow and reach their potential, and to ensure humane conditions, appropriate materials and technologies, and good production and work practices

5. To respect and promote development for and responsibility to both people and the natural world

6. To manage resources sustainably and to encourage production in a way that preserves and develops cultural identity

BOX 12 IFAT CODE OF PRACTICE

Source: Based on International Federation of Alternative Trade, *Code of Practice* (Manila: IFAT, 1993)

critical element of fair trade. Indeed, fair trade has entered a terrain of conventional trade and the consuming public; the argument that ATOs pay producers a fair price has become a major plank in the public positioning of fairly traded products. This focus reinforces their simple policy message that the established economic thinking fails adequately to describe production situations, where small-scale producers are forced to extreme levels of exploitation of themselves, and their families.

What constitutes a fair price can be understood in many different ways. Listed below are some of the ways in which actors in the fair-trade movement have discussed and interpreted the meaning of a fair price:

- More than the local price currently available to the producer

- More than the price available from other international traders

- Enough for producers and their families to attain a reasonable or nationally recognised remunerative living standard

- A price that enables the Northern partner to be no more than viable, but not to take a significant profit

- A trading regime that allows Southern producers to earn the same as their Northern trading partners

- Fixed remuneration to all parties involved directly in the chain, reflecting input, skills and risk and not purchasing power or lending power alone— for mutual benefit

A clear perspective as to what constitutes a fair price (and how it is arrived at) is needed by anyone wishing to assess the fairness of any particular trading relationship. To complicate the matter further, the in-depth response to the question 'What is distinctive about fair trade transcends a debate that is only about price?'All fair traders strive for a strategic and qualitative change in the trading process in favour of those who are traditionally the weakest. A floor price or other formula-based approaches give a strong message in a market climate that resists any and all controls or economic instruments (taxes, subsidies, incentives and so forth), but at best it remains only a symbol or emblem of fair trade and its moral and economic objectives.

Fair trade, then, aims to build better livelihoods for the poorest and weakest in the trading chain and to leverage developmental change and longer-term political shifts in their political and economic environment. Trade is the means to this end, and the signs of success might be manifested in a farmers' or artisans' organisation as any or all of the following:

- Greater awareness, the ability to plan and think strategically, and the ability to participate proactively in the marketplace whether locally or internationally

- Greater bargaining power through knowledge, experience and access to infrastructure and inputs in the trading chain (via direct ownership or the ability to negotiate terms from a third party)

- Greater levels and equitable distribution of resources at the community level to invest in human capital for the future, the next generation

Conclusion

Fair trade is a description of an experience and of multiple interlocking efforts by organisations that produce, trade and distribute and that seek to promote and shape the way trade is done in practice. These organisations seek to achieve their aims by tackling a range of both traditional and non-traditional commodities, constantly developing new insights into sustainable production, marketing, and in this way challenging the ideology of free trade, where costs and benefits are narrowly defined and seldom include the wider issues of welfare, mutual benefit, and the common good.

Success beyond the small scale of the current movement will not arise only by adding more fairly traded products to the shopping baskets of consumers around the globe: that is, by simply increasing market share in the traditional sense. Rather, a growing market will mean that the mainstream market players will have to respond increasingly to the demonstration that this trade represents and to the interests of consumers in buying on the basis of broader social and environmental criteria. The original alternative traders have an important role as the 'compass'— the 'true north' for the movement as it expands.

Larger-scale success will depend on other developments, including greater synergy among the various strands of the fair-trade movement and the continuing and honourable uptake of the method and goals by mainstream corporate business.

Quantitative change is, however, required for these forms of qualitative trading and innovation to be converted into effective challenges to the dominant inequitable and environmentally destructive trading patterns.

33

governing the provision of global public goods

the role and legitimacy of non-state actors*

co-written with Michael Edwards

The successful provision of global public goods in the 21st century rests on two complementary tasks. First, increasing the involvement of non-state actors in global governance, because governments will find it increasingly difficult to act alone in designing and implementing effective regimes. Second, ensuring that non-state involvement is structured to avoid the dangers of special-interest politics, because otherwise decisions may favour one group over another or lead to gridlock in the system. These two tasks must be approached together and will require a radical overhaul of the rules of global governance to ensure that state and non-state capacities are combined effectively. Without such an overhaul, global governance is likely to degenerate into the worst of all possible outcomes—as at the 2001 G8 summit in Genoa, Italy, which produced a crippling combination of over-zealous policing, anarchist violence, stalemate in official discussions, and responsible non-state voices drowned out in the general cacophony. The problems in providing global public goods cannot be solved in such an environment. New solutions must be developed.

This chapter shows how these two tasks can be addressed in tandem, a challenge that raises fundamental questions of political theory and democratic practice that take the debate on global public goods into largely uncharted territory. Fundamental to this challenge is the complicated issue of legitimacy: the sense that institutions and the decisions they make must be seen as fair and acceptable to all relevant stakeholders if they are to be effective in changing public and private behaviour. Two dimensions of legitimacy are especially important. The first concerns the

* From *Providing Public Goods*, edited by Inge Kaul *et al.*, copyright 2003 by the United Nations Development Programme. Used by permission of Oxford University Press, Inc.

legitimacy of the international system for negotiating and delivering global public goods. As a result of the current system's perceived failure to achieve results and the appearance of its domination by governments and corporations from industrial countries, its legitimacy is being questioned by those who feel excluded, whether governments or citizen groups. For reasons explored in this chapter, non-state actors are crucial to rebuilding the legitimacy of the international system for global governance. However—and this is the second dimension of the problem—non-state actors are likely to be accepted and effective in this role only if they strengthen their own legitimacy in the eyes of governments, intergovernmental organisations and the general public. Although these two dimensions of legitimacy are closely linked and cannot be resolved in isolation from each other, this chapter focuses on the challenges of legitimacy for non-state actors in the international system.

The rise of non-state actors

In this chapter the term *non-state actor* covers both business and civil society. *Civil society* includes all organisations, networks and associations between the level of the family and the level of the state, except firms. Non-governmental organisations (NGOs), labour unions and business associations form subsets of civil society, but firms are excluded because they are assumed to exist to make and distribute a private profit, while civil-society groups are organised to defend or advance the interests they hold in common. This definition is helpful in clarifying the institutional and legally mandated aims of corporations such as Shell or IBM. But it is less helpful in categorising sections of the business community that exist, at least in part, to generate a social good or advance a collective interest, such as co-operatives, social and community enterprises, and partnerships that combine traditional businesses with public and non-profit actors. Nevertheless, different types of non-state actors have different mandates, interests and characteristics, and these differences make it dangerous to generalise about the role of non-state actors in securing global public goods. Thus, where necessary, this chapter deals separately with businesses and civil-society organisations, and focuses on corporations and NGOs within these general categories.

Civil-society organisations are enjoying an unprecedented upsurge in their profile and—to a lesser extent—their influence over global debates and decision-making (Florini 2000; Edwards and Gaventa 2001; Anheier *et al.* 2001). Although it lacks coherence, the current wave of global citizen action is comparable with, and probably larger than, previous waves in the 1960s and earlier periods. John Cavanagh of the Institute for Policy Studies estimates that more than 49 million people have joined the Hemispheric Social Alliance against the Free Trade Agreement of the Americas,[1] while the US anti-sweatshop movement has chapters in 140 colleges and universities. More than 30,000 international NGOs are active on the world stage, along with about 20,000 transnational civil-society networks—90% of which were formed in the past 30 years, an astonishing growth rate (Edwards 1999, 2000b).

These 'epistemic communities' include associations of local authorities and mayors, federations of community groups such as Shack Dwellers International (Patel *et al.* 2001), global networks of universities, and independent media groups, labour unions and business federations. Successive UN global conferences have provided invaluable opportunities for these groups to mobilise and make connections in an international context that increasingly favours civil society and the national democratic openings that have been such a feature of the post-Cold War world. In particular, developing-country groups such as the Third World Network and Development Alternatives with Women for a New Era (DAWN) are now an established presence on the world stage (Bunch *et al.* 2001). Of course, not all civil-society organisations share the same normative agendas. The international terrorist networks that organised the attacks on the US Pentagon and the World Trade Center on 11 September 2001 are the latest and most visible example of 'uncivil society' at work, but this is an extreme example.

Parallel to the rise of civil-society groups has been the emergence of business as a key player on the global stage. Most visible and significant in the context of any discussion of global public goods are the increased scope and influence of one part of the business community, corporations. Like civil-society organisations, the corporate community has grown remarkably in recent decades. Some 60,000–70,000 multinational corporations operate in today's global economy, and these corporations have an additional 200,000–300,000 nationally and regionally based subsidiaries. The largest multinational corporations are large indeed. Of the world's 100 largest 'economies', 51 are corporations (Anderson and Cavanagh 1996), and the top 200 corporations have sales equal to one-quarter of the world's economic activity (Wheeler and Sillanpää 1997). General Motors has annual sales equivalent to the GDP of Denmark, and the annual sales of Sears Roebuck's are comparable to the annual income of more than 100 million Bangladeshis (Utting 2000). World trade, dominated by a small number of global corporations, has increased by more than 12 times since 1945—and now accounts for about one-fifth of the world's measured economic income. In addition, the 1990s witnessed a huge increase in capital flows to developing countries. In 1990 public sources accounted for more than half of the international resources flowing to developing countries, but by 1995 more than three-quarters came from private sources (World Bank 1997). During the same period, private foreign direct investment in developing countries nearly quadrupled, rising to $96 billion by 1995 (UNCTAD 1998; Zarsky 1999).

Of great significance to debates on global governance has been the increasing political mobilisation of business on the world stage over the past ten years. For example, US and European corporations meet regularly through the Transatlantic Business Dialogue to plan and co-ordinate their lobbying strategies, and throughout 1999 the European Commission met with an Investment Network representing more than 60 leading corporations to establish priorities for a new investment agreement under the World Trade Organisation (Edwards 2000b). According to some estimates, NGOs focused on international development were outnumbered by NGOs representing business interests at the November 2001 World Trade Organisation ministerial meetings in Doha, Qatar—including 26 industry committees advising the US government (Denny 2001). The implications of this trend are considered below.

Non-state actors and global public goods

Securing global public goods increasingly requires co-operation between governments and business, international agencies and civil-society organisations (Kaul *et al.* 1999). The United Nations cannot prevent global warming unless citizens decide that their environment has to be protected from their actions and industry offers them energy-efficient products and services. Likewise, progressive labour regimes will not be viable unless there is buy-in from companies such as Nike and Wal-Mart, and from consumers who are willing to pay higher prices for the goods they produce, procure and sell.

Indeed, civil-society organisations already claim to have established a role for themselves in identifying and lobbying for the increased provision of global public goods, a role that governments and business have been unable or unwilling to fulfil. The landmines campaign (Scott 2001), debt relief (Collins *et al.* 2001), international certification for the diamond trade (Smillie and Gberie 2001) and access to essential medicines are good examples, the last illustrated most recently by the success of South Africa's Treatment Action Campaign in lowering the potential price of HIV/AIDS drugs and by the agreement between the drug company Aventis and the World Health Organisation to provide five years of drugs to African countries to treat sleeping sickness free of charge.[2] Citizen groups were also a significant source of pressure to establish the International Criminal Court in 2000 and to ratify the Kyoto Protocol on climate change in Bonn, Germany, in 2001—the culmination of 20 years of NGO campaigns on the environment.

Many of the most vocal self-identified members of 'global civil society' assert their support for a common goal: to democratise rulemaking and ensure that poor people around the world have more opportunities to benefit from the application of those rules. In reality, however, the interests of citizens—including poor people—are often at odds once one moves beyond the most general call for equity. Trade is the clearest example: for instance, the interests of family farmers in the US Midwest are unlikely to be the same as those of small farmers in Latin America who are trying to gain access to US markets, yet both groups are associated with NGOs and labour unions that lobby for their cause. In this case the global public good at stake is a trading regime that tries to satisfy both sets of interests—a difficult but not impossible task if trade rules are graduated according to circumstance and compensation is provided to the losers. For civil-society groups, however, such differences pose some difficult questions that are taken up below.

The relationship between business and global public goods is complex and multifaceted. At one end of the spectrum, business affects the provision of global public goods through its primary activity of creating and delivering private goods through the market (Zadek 2001c). Most obvious are the positive externalities that may be associated with a general increase in economic wealth. For example, economic prosperity is generally associated with an increase in spending on environmental and social protection, health and education—all of which are or can have indirect impacts on global public goods. As the United Nations Development Programme's *Human Development Report 1999* concludes:

> people in many countries live a much longer and healthier life than just two decades ago. In 31 of the 174 countries included in the HDI [Human Development Index], life expectancy has increased by more than a fifth since 1975 . . . Between 1975 and 1997 most countries made substantial progress in human development, reducing their shortfall from the maximum possible value of the HDI (UNDP 1999: 129-30).

The potential linkage between these improvements and the key role of the corporate community in the globalisation process underpins the argument of those who advocate market liberalisation as the most effective means of enhancing the delivery of global public goods.

But the impact of globalisation and corporations on economic prosperity and human development is contested. The Washington, DC-based Center for Economic and Policy Research recently published a study suggesting that the economic growth rates of most developing countries, as well as many of these countries' human development indicators, worsened during 1980–2000, a period of accelerated globalisation (Weisbrot et al. 2001). Much anecdotal evidence suggests that corporate activities can damage the health of local economies and communities (Korten 1999), exacerbate civil unrest, and contribute to sustaining war—as with the mining companies whose activities have effectively bankrolled the conflicts in Angola, the Democratic Republic of Congo, and elsewhere.[3] Corporations may also try to undermine public policies that enhance the delivery of global public goods. For example, the US government's recent decision not to sign the Kyoto Protocol was undoubtedly rooted in lobbying by the powerful, energy-intensive US business community. Conversely, businesses and business associations are active in lobbying for other forms of global public goods, such as technical standards that need to be harmonised to promote cross-border commerce. Hence the debate about corporate actors and global public goods extends to measuring potential negative impacts as well as positive contributions.

These ambiguities have underpinned the emergence of the philosophy and practice of 'corporate citizenship' (Zadek 2001a), through which corporations have sought to gain broader public trust and legitimacy by enhancing their non-financial performance and wider contributions to society. The focus and scope of corporate citizenship have widened from localised philanthropy to embrace a far broader swath of social, environmental and economic dimensions of corporate performance. In this way businesses are, in effect, adopting policies and practices that explicitly commit them to delivering public goods. For multinational corporations in particular this includes global public goods, such as corporate initiatives to bridge the 'digital divide' (Zadek and Raynard 2001) and code-based voluntary initiatives such as the Forest Stewardship Council, which seeks to preserve and replenish tropical and other forests.

The growing role of non-state actors in the provision of global public goods raises major challenges. There are deeply rooted fears that initiatives such as the UN Global Compact legitimise the increasing influence of corporations on public policy and practice. But there are also concerns about the legitimacy of NGOs that have mobilised against the business community. In this climate it is important to be clear about whether, and under what conditions, increased non-state involvement is desirable.

Non-state actors and the changing shape of global governance

Global market integration, the Internet and the increasing interconnectedness of citizens are gradually eroding the monopoly on power exercised by nation-states in the Westphalian system of international relations. Many scholars have commented on the implications of this shift for global governance and on the move away from 'club' models of decision-making to frameworks built around multi-layered, cross-society dialogue (Ruggie 1983; Edwards 1999; Nye and Donahue 2001). These frameworks are built on the premise that the involvement of non-state actors is a precondition for ensuring institutional plurality and creating viable strategies and programmes. In theory, non-state actors can make two contributions to effective global governance:

- Improving the quality of debate and decision-making by injecting more information, transparency and accountability into the system from a wider range of sources, and making space for unorthodox ideas and 'reality checks' on the effects of policy on the ground. Governments have no monopoly on ideas or expertise.

- Strengthening the legitimacy and effectiveness of decisions and decision-making processes by involving a broader spectrum of those whose support is required to make them work—meaning the public, the media and the business community. Governments can confer authority on decisions but rarely a complete sense of legitimacy, especially in a 'wired' world where information flows much more freely through the media and across the Internet. In this scenario the weight of public or business pressure will be felt much more keenly by decision-makers, wherever they are, and buy-in from non-state actors will be crucial in ensuring that decisions are actually implemented.

Over the past ten years, non-state actors have put these contributions into practice in three ways:

- **Setting new agendas and changing the language of debates**: for example, on debt relief and how to spend the proceeds, where G7 governments have increasingly adopted Jubilee 2000's proposals since a human chain surrounded their summit meeting in Birmingham, England, in 1998 (Collins et al. 2001). Similarly, corporate social responsibility, social auditing and ethical trade have become part of the new language in and through which the role of business and its renegotiated rights and responsibilities are played out (Zadek et al. 1997).

- **Negotiating the details of regimes**: for example, the Ottawa landmines treaty, which was driven through by a global NGO alliance (the International Campaign to Ban Landmines) and a group of middle-power governments led by Canada (Scott 2001). Business is increasingly active in seeking to influence the terms on which global public goods are provided: for example, how best to create a bribery- and corruption-free trading environment through the Organisation for Economic Co-operation and Development (OECD), or to negotiate international labour conventions through the International Labour Organisation (ILO).

- **Monitoring and enforcing global agreements**: for example, certification systems such as the Forest Stewardship Council, or the implementation of measures to combat child labour in Bangladesh and Pakistan, which were negotiated by NGOs, governments and factory owners and backed up by on-site visits and NGO programmes designed to provide alternative sources of income for the families of child workers (Harper 2001).

Each of these roles requires a different form of legitimacy from non-state actors, linked to a particular form of politics. Voicing an opinion is very different from negotiating a treaty, but both are vital to the successful provision of global public goods. At the local and national levels, representative and direct democracy go hand in hand in many societies. But, at the beginning of a new century, the balance between them is changing in favour of non-state actors, driven by rising disaffection with conventional politics, the attractions of direct action (including street protest), and the opportunities for broader participation generated by the macro-level political changes highlighted above. At times of regime transition such as this, the space for non-state actors tends to increase.

Traditionally, the role of representative democracy has been to aggregate private preferences among large numbers of individuals, enabling trade-offs to be made in the interests of society as a whole. This is something that business and civil society cannot do, at least not with the same degree of transparent legitimacy and accountability. The role of direct or participatory democracy has been to generate and shape opinions, ensure that the interests of excluded groups are not ignored, and hold governments accountable for delivering the commitments they make on election day. This is something governments rarely do without sustained public pressure. Effective democracies combine elements of both systems but, when one is sacrificed for the other, problems inevitably arise—the 'dictatorship' of a government elected with a minority of the popular vote in a weak civil society, for example, or the gridlock effect of strong special interests pushing against a weak state.

At the global level this debate is further complicated by the fact that so few elements of a global polity or global political structures exist—for example, the checks and balances provided by the separation of the executive, legislative and judicial branches of government, or the direct links between elected representatives and their constituents that enable the exercise of accountability. As argued below, the absence of these structures exposes non-state involvement to a set of dilemmas. In particular, there is a danger that national, representative processes will be eroded by the relative convenience and easy access of direct global engagement. As one civil-society activist remarked following the street battles that took place around the 1999 World Trade Organisation meeting in Seattle, Washington: 'The question that came to my mind while seeing delegates from mainly developing countries excluded from the talks by protestors—and being sporadically assaulted and intimidated by them—while the US and EU negotiated inside—is when does one group's right to free speech outweigh another's right to free assembly? And when does obstruction of legitimate activity stop being "non-violent"?'[4]

These problems may undermine attempts to secure the provision of global public goods because success depends on mutually reinforcing actions from the local level to the global. A successful campaign at the global level may achieve few concrete results if it is only weakly rooted in local and national politics—especially government policy and regulation, and a sense of ownership among its citizens. Examples include the Ottawa Treaty on Landmines, which has not led to a decrease in mine-laying (Scott 2001); the ineffectiveness of international regulations on labour rights (Harper 2001); and the failure of the global campaign against breast-milk substitutes to eradicate their use in Africa and elsewhere (Chapman 2001). Conversely, successful experiments at the local or national levels may be undermined if they take place outside a global framework, preventing the exploitation of one country's sacrifices by free-riders elsewhere. Climate change is the obvious example. Not every non-state policy position needs to be negotiated along the chain from the local to global level; doing so would suck much of the energy out of global citizen action and lead to lowest-common-denominator consensus. But campaigns divorced from local and national politics will always be vulnerable to co-option by external interests. Despite the gradual erosion of nation-states, states still negotiate the rules of global governance and provide the authority required to implement them. Therefore, reconstructing state authority through democratic means remains a key challenge for the 21st century.

The dilemmas of non-state involvement

None of the contributions listed above will necessarily be realised in every context. The actual outcome of non-state involvement depends on whose voices are represented in debates, how competing interests are reconciled, and whether civic groups and business are effective in playing the roles assigned to them in the evolving international system. History suggests that political pluralism produces effective outcomes when many voices are fairly represented and mechanisms are put in place to arbitrate between them when disagreements arise. But, unless the involvement of non-state actors is managed effectively, the result may be gridlock or chaotic policy-making processes open to manipulation by the loudest and strongest groups—a problem already seen in international negotiations and in the special-interest politics of industrial democracies such as the United States. The reasons are clear:

- The quantity and diversity of businesses and civil-society groups make it impossible for each one to participate equally. 'Global civil society resembles a bazaar, a kaleidoscope of differently sized rooms, twisting alleys and steps leading to obscure places' (Keane 2001: 23), not a body with a common identity or agenda. This produces obvious problems for civic engagement in global governance, but this same diversity protects the public sphere by offering more opportunities for the dispersal and diffusion of power.

- Non-state actors (even if restricted to civil society) may lack a common agenda at the global level because the opinions and interests of different groups do not coincide. Some US NGOs, for example, speak for family farmers (such as the Institute for Agriculture and Trade Policy, headed by Mark Ritchie), and others for agribusiness (such as Truth about Trade, headed by a former president of the American Farm Bureau Federation; Aaronson 2001).[5] These divisions are being replicated at the global level through the emergence of organisations such as International Consumers for Civil Society, which aims to counter the influence of the anti-globalisation movement in debates over the World Trade Organisation (Charnovitz 2000). Similarly, businesses have different models of success that create diverse interests. It makes little sense to equate the interests of Shell and Talisman, for example, merely because both are energy companies that have to make a profit (Shell International 1999). The interests and approach of Rio Tinto today are not the same as Rio Tinto Zinc five or ten years ago, even though it continues to be a global, profit-making mining conglomerate. Wal-Mart's price-minimisation strategy has very different implications for international labour standards than do upmarket brands such as the UK-based food retailer Sainsbury's or the Canada-based clothing manufacturer Hudson Bay (Zadek 2000b).

- Global non-state networks are asymmetrical and often dominated by organisations based in industrial countries, despite the emergence of developing-country networks such as the Third World Network. For example, only 251 of the 1,550 NGOs associated with the UN Department of Public Information come from developing countries, and the ratio of NGOs in consultative status with the UN Economic and Social Council is even lower (Edwards 2000b). Businesses and multinational affiliates based in developing countries have a similarly weak voice in international business networks.

- Accountability is problematic. NGOs have no clear bottom line for results and no single authority to whom they must report on their activities. 'Downward' accountability (to those on whose behalf the NGO is speaking or claiming to speak) is often weaker than 'upward' accountability to the donors who fund the NGO's activities. For business, the financial bottom line and shareholder accountability are relatively clear, but other stake-holders have to struggle to find their voice and adequate sources of accountability (Elkington 1997).

- NGO positions are often criticised as crude and simplistic, poorly researched, and driven by fashion and sensation rather than loyalty to the facts. In reality, many NGO positions are researched with considerable sophisti-cation, but there is always a temptation to trade off rigour for speed and profile in campaigns—as with Jubilee 2000's lack of attention to issues of economic management outside of debt relief, or attacks by some labour unions against forms of child labour in South Asia that turned out to be non-exploitative and essential to household welfare (Harper 2001). Corporate 'intelligence' is similarly weak, despite the vast budgets of multinational corporations and the access they have to the best brains and data. Corporations often do little more than regurgitate outdated thinking about the costs of environmental management, or seem totally unaware of the potential productivity gains that come from treating their employees better. These weaknesses translate into the public policy sphere, where few senior business executives are aware of leading-edge insights into the potential for translating the pursuit of global public goods into viable business propositions (Hawken *et al.* 1999).

- Weak mechanisms are used to arbitrate between non-state interests at the global level and to negotiate levels of consensus above the lowest common denominator. NGOs and business lack an equivalent to the United Nations through which their differences might be resolved or even debated to a conclusion. The result, demonstrated by the NGO declaration to the 2001 World Conference against Racism in Durban, South Africa, is a mixed bag of particularistic views in place of a sense of the negotiated common interest—precisely the outcome that is supposed to emerge from civil society in its role as an arena for public deliberation between competing ideas.

- As noted, NGO advocacy on the global stage is often weakly rooted in local and national politics, especially in classic 'pyramidal' campaigns with centralised control over messages and strategies (Chapman 2001). There is always a temptation to leapfrog over the national arena and go direct to Washington or Brussels, where it is often easier to gain access to senior officials and achieve a response. As Keck and Sikkink (1998) show, international pressure can unlock political gridlock at the national level when it is mobilised effectively, but when this route displaces national political engagement it may erode the domestic coalition building that is essential to sustained policy reform. This is the 'two bites of the cherry' problem, implying that NGOs and business have plenty of opportunities to influence official policy at the national level, but when they lose out they move their arguments to the global arena and undermine positions that have been established by their governments through democratic processes (Charnovitz 2000). On what basis, for example, did business and non-profit organisations create the UK-based Ethical Trading Initiative and the US-based Fair Labor Association, as collusive mechanisms to drive new labour standards down global supply chains, when governments had already decided not to create mandatory international standards (Zadek 2000b)? On what basis is it legitimate for Phil Knight, chief executive officer of Nike, to advocate at the launch of the UN Global Compact that 'we believe in a global system that measures every multinational against a core set of universal standards using an independent process of social performance monitoring akin to financial auditing. This would bring greater clarity to the impact of globalisation and the performance of any one company' (Zadek 2001a: 90).

One can certainly argue that democracy requires individuals and associations to use as many channels as possible to secure their interests, especially if those interests are ignored by people in power or formal citizenship rights are weak. But the problems outlined above raise serious questions about the involvement of non-state actors in global governance. Unless they are explicitly addressed, these problems and questions may erode the benefits that are predicted to flow from non-state participation. At their root are the thorny issues of legitimacy, accountability and connectivity.

Legitimacy, accountability and connectivity among non-state actors

What right do non-state actors have to participate in global governance? Do different types of actors have different rights? And what responsibilities go with those rights? At their root these are questions of legitimacy, a controversial issue that arouses strong reactions. Critics of NGOs usually cite one or more of the following problems to justify their position: NGOs do not formally represent those on whose behalf they claim to speak; they are not accountable for their actions or for the results of the positions they take; their policy positions are often inaccurate and misleading; and they are active only at the global level and have no roots in national politics.

Similar criticisms are made about business, which is accused of exerting undue influence in pursuit of the narrow interests of managers and shareholders. From this perspective the right of business to participate in global governance is challenged on the basis of its institutionalised and often legally dictated disinterest in—and lack of accountability to—the stakeholders who would benefit from the enhanced delivery of global public goods. (After all, most global public goods have distributional effects even if they are in principle non-exclusive.) But what is legitimacy, and how is it claimed?

Legitimacy is generally understood as the right to be and do something in society, a sense that an organisation is lawful, admissible and justified in its chosen course of action or in the global arena, an 'acknowledged right to exert influence in global politics' (Scholte 2001: 97). But there are many ways to validate these claims. The legitimacy of ideas, for example, is very different from the legitimacy of decision-making processes (Brown 2001). Claims to legitimacy can be based on one or more of the following criteria:

- **Representation.** In membership-based bodies, legitimacy is claimed through the normal democratic processes of elections and formal sanctions that ensure an agency is representative of and accountable to its constituents. Labour unions and some NGOs and business associations fall into this category, though whether these processes operate effectively is another matter. If non-state actors claim to represent poor people, they must be specific about which poor people they are representing and how.

In reality, most Northern NGOs are more sophisticated than this and accept that their policy positions are their own, even if substantial consultation has taken place with 'partners' in developing countries.

- **Legal bases.** Businesses, particularly those that are publicly listed, are generally legally obliged to represent the interests of their shareholders. In so doing, however, business also claims that it reflects the needs of consumers, whose interests must be served if shareholders are to be satisfied. Corporate citizenship has extended this argument further, with businesses claiming to act with broader social and environmental interests in mind. Civil-society groups that are not membership-based organisations— and most are not—define their legitimacy primarily according to their compliance with non-profit legislation and regulation in a particular country, and effective oversight by their trustees.

- **Competence.** It is common for non-state actors to claim legitimacy through recognition by other legitimate bodies that they have valuable knowledge and skills to bring to the table. The United Nations, for example, can accord a certain degree of legitimacy to NGOs or businesses when it recognises and accredits them to its Economic and Social Council or Global Compact. In such cases competence is key. No one expects Oxfam, for example, to be perfectly representative of developing-country opinion in order to qualify for accreditation in this sense—only that its proposals on debt and other issues be useful to the debate, rooted in research and experience, and sensitive to the views and aspirations of its developing-country partners. These views can be challenged on the grounds of accuracy, rigour, or simply by those who have a different opinion, but that does not make them illegitimate. The same is true for business: though its competencies may be weak where public policy issues are at stake, it may nevertheless qualify for a seat at the negotiating table by virtue of its expertise or material interest in the issues under discussion (AccountAbility 2000).

- **Moral legitimacy.** Civil-society organisations seem to have touched a chord in the public imagination in voicing concerns about globalisation and the rising influence of corporations. This is evidenced not just in the rise of street protest but in opinion polls as well. A recent poll of 20,000 citizens in G20 nations by Environics International found that only 10% viewed globalisation as 'positive'—and only 1% thought that current global governance structures were satisfactory.[6] Even if civic groups are not formally representative or particularly sophisticated in their critiques, their empathy with large segments of the public awards them a degree of moral legitimacy. The moral legitimacy of business—particularly the corporate community—is a fragile affair. Public opinion surveys around the world repeatedly confirm that business is distrusted when it comes to the public good (ranking together with governments except in the Nordic region, where governments score far higher; Zadek 2001a). Unlike non-profits, brand identification and associated trust among businesses is often built around relationships with other organisations and individuals, such as Nike's link to Michael Jordan (LaFeber 1999) or the growing number of long-term partnerships between businesses, non-profit organisations and state bodies (Nelson and Zadek 2000; Zadek 2001c). However, such trust remains little more than a distant cousin of a more deeply rooted moral legitimacy, despite attempts by leaders in corporate citizenship to attain the moral high ground through substantive investment, change and collaboration with NGOs such as Oxfam, Amnesty International and the World Wildlife Fund (Zadek 2001a).

- **Public benefit.** Many non-state actors, especially NGOs, claim their right to participate in debates by virtue of the fact that they are 'public benefit' or 'public interest' organisations. By definition, many assume civil society to be the defender of the public interest, in opposition to business and corrupt or partisan politicians. When considered analytically, however, the situation is not so clear. Civil society is the arena where the public interest is debated and negotiated, but the organisations that occupy it have different and sometimes conflicting views of what the public interest is, and more especially how to secure it through different combinations of public, private and civic action (Edwards 2000a). There may be a conceptual difference between NGOs that lobby, for example, for gender equity in general and those that lobby for particular groups of women, but in practice it is difficult to categorise NGOs as either special-interest groups or public-interest groups. Similarly, a growing number of corporations claim to have a demonstrable public-interest agenda and argue that they are well placed to deliver it, unlike other non-state actors. This does not mean that NGOs are the same as business, but it does mean that in principle business has a right to argue its case before legislative bodies arbitrate between competing interests when making decisions.

Business and civil-society organisations can answer their critics by facing up to the responsibilities that accompany their right to a voice. This means substantiating the criteria through which they claim legitimacy and being transparent and accountable for their actions. 'NGOs do not have to be member controlled to be legitimate, but they do have to be accountable for their actions if their claims to legitimacy are to be maintained' (Edwards and Hulme 1996: 14). If legitimacy is claimed through representation, non-state actors must be able to show who they represent and how they are held accountable to their constituents. If legitimacy is claimed through expertise, non-state actors must be able to show how their positions have been derived and what depth of rigour has been used. If legitimacy is claimed through the ability to create change on the ground—the business argument—then business must demonstrate that the competencies and will are there in practice, and provide evidence on the ground to show that both have been effectively applied.

In addition, non-state actors can build legitimacy by rooting their global activities in national and local action—for example, by pressurising national governments to represent the full range of public interests in international negotiations, by building dialogues with government that link local, national and global activities, and by developing more democratic ways of deciding on strategies and messages. Jubilee 2000 provides some good examples of these innovations. In Uganda, for example, local NGOs developed a dialogue with the government on options for debt relief, supported by technical assistance from industrial country NGOs such as Oxfam (Collins *et al.* 2001). The results of this dialogue were then incorporated into the international debt campaign. Rede Bancos played a similar role in Brazil, joining forces with the Brazilian Congress to force the World Bank to publish its Country Assistance Strategy and agree to a public debate on the reform of social sector spending (Tussie and Tuozzo 2001). In the United Kingdom the World Development Movement (an NGO) persuaded the Scottish Parliament to hold its first-ever debate on the World Trade Organisation's General Agreement on Trade in Services. These are ways of making global debates more responsive to ordinary citizens and of encouraging citizens to support the action needed to preserve global public goods. A similar example from business is the emergence of Instituto Ethos in Brazil as a significant player in driving through business-led local and national initiatives in response to daunting social and environmental challenges. In South Africa the business community created the New Business Initiative to channel a large, collective, one-time financial donation to support the government's social programmes.

Above all, both enthusiasts and sceptics must be clear about how legitimacy is claimed and avoid conflating the requirements of different criteria, because doing so confuses the debate, makes solutions harder to find, and increases the likelihood that criticisms of legitimacy will be used to exclude rather than structure the involvement of dissenting voices. Any non-state actor is entitled to voice an opinion. This is a basic human right that need only be subject to the minimum amount of regulation required to guard against slander, violence or discrimination. No other legitimacy is required. But negotiating a treaty is a very different matter, and may require detailed rules to preserve genuine democracy in decision-making. In this case, legitimacy through representation is essential. Transnational civil society is far from democratic, and few non-state networks have democratic systems of governance and accountability. Nevertheless, the increasing voice of non-state actors adds essential checks and balances to the international system and helps ensure that excluded views are heard. Problems of legitimacy are not, therefore, a justification for turning back the tide of global citizen action. But they are a challenge to structure such action in ways that combat, rather than accentuate, existing social, economic and political inequalities.

Ways forward: solutions and recommendations

Solutions to the dilemmas of non-state involvement in global governance must reconcile two potentially contradictory imperatives. The first is the need to give structure to the process in order to guard against the potentially distorting effects of those who shout loudest. The huge number and diversity of non-state actors, and the inequalities of voice and resources among them, make rules, standards and protocols essential. The second imperative is the need to ensure that these structures are as light and non-bureaucratic as possible, to avoid eroding the passion, spontaneity and diversity that are the hallmarks of a healthy civil society (including non-violent street protest) and a dynamic business community.

How might principles be put into practice? Given the state of flux in the debate on global public goods, now is not the time for rigid or universal recommendations. Flexibility, innovation, experimentation and learning from experience should be the top priorities, enthusiastically supported by governments and intergovernmental organisations. Some commentators have suggested that new, democratically elected non-state bodies be created to stand alongside intergovernmental structures, such as a Global People's Council to complement the UN General Assembly (Falk and Strauss 1997). The obvious obstacle is the question of representation and of how members would be elected across such a diverse set of constituencies. A number of options exist, including representation from national parliaments, direct elections from subnational constituencies (as in the European Parliament) and elections from non-state bodies that already represent a constituency (such as labour unions, business federations and national NGO umbrella bodies). However, there is little political support for these ideas from governments, who remain unconvinced of the rationale for parallel structures.

A less contentious alternative would be to support a series of non-representative bodies designed to provide a space for debate on particular international institutions or regimes, with participants selected according to expertise or material interest. For example, a World Financial Forum could complement the International Monetary Fund, enabling non-state actors to debate policy and performance every two years, once the dust has settled on particular macroeconomic crises (Edwards 2000b). It is not difficult to envisage something similar on trade for the World Trade Organisation, though in both cases such bodies would need to be given a real job—not just the role of 'talking shop'—and used to bring stakeholders together rather than separate them into the World Economic Forum, World Social Forum and so on. These other gatherings could obviously continue, but they serve a different purpose, not joint decision-making. Such ideas enjoy more political support but lack the resources and will to put them into practice. (The World Trade Organisation's total budget is less than half the World Bank's budget for staff travel.)

Both of these proposals have strengths and weaknesses, but underlying them is a common conclusion: different models should be used for different contexts and purposes. The characteristics of a multi-stakeholder forum designed to resolve a dispute over a particular World Bank loan in Tanzania are different to those of a body designed to develop global policy guidelines on access to affordable medicines for HIV/AIDS. The criteria for non-state involvement would need to vary accordingly. Much more innovation is needed to develop and test such models so that the lessons of experience can be fed back into the international system. There are already many interesting experiments to build on, such as:

- Fully integrated decision-making bodies in place of structures reserved for governments, as long as clear and transparent processes exist to identify non-state actors and their constituencies. The International Labour Organisation shows that this is a possibility, at least in principle.

- Multi-stakeholder bodies that encourage honest debate among governments, business, and civil-society organisations around the same table, without fear of co-option. Many such bodies have already been organised around the implementation of Agenda 21 (Dodds 2001). A solid body of experience exists to guide such efforts and help avoid the problems that can arise—such as the International Labour Organisation's tripartite arrangements for considering labour standards (Hemmati 2001; Enayati and Hemmati 2000; Nelson and Zadek 2000).

- Meetings with non-state actors on particular topics the day before official intergovernmental meetings, as in the committee process used by the Organisation for Economic Co-operation and Development, or the use of the 'Arias formula' to invite NGOs to address the UN Security Council outside its official sessions (Stanley Foundation 2001). Proposals already exist to extend NGO accreditation from the UN Economic and Social Council to the General Assembly for this purpose (United Nations 1999; WFUNA 2000).

- Solicitation of 'alternative reports' from non-state actors to be considered alongside country reports from governments. Some UN treaty bodies already do this (such as the UN Commission on the Rights of the Child). The World Trade Organisation could use the same principle to allow non-state actors to submit *amicus curiae* (friend of the court) briefs to the appellate body (Charnovitz 2000).

- Internal codes of conduct that spell out minimum standards of behaviour, accountability and representation in global non-state networks and coalitions. The UK-based New Economics Foundation has developed a 'Code of Protest' which specifies non-violence as a basic principle, alongside 'remaining curious about perspectives other than our own' and 'focusing on creative action' (that is, what NGOs are for, not just against[7]). Friends of the Earth–Europe has launched a similar set of 'principles for peaceful protest'. NGOs led by the US-based Institute for Agriculture and Trade Policy worked to exchange their accredited places at the 2001 World Trade Organisation ministerial meeting in Qatar with counterparts from developing countries, to ensure greater balance in NGO delegations. CIVICUS and the Hauser Center at Harvard University have produced a 'legitimacy guide' that takes NGOs through the process of establishing their legitimacy (Brown 2001).

- Information and communications technology—such as 'open space' technology and Webcasting—which facilitates discussion and information inputs from large numbers of non-state actors simultaneously or over short periods before an official gathering.

- Publicly accessible policies governing consultations with non-state actors for all international agencies, meetings and conferences.

Overall, there is a pressing need for regular forums at the global level that allow governments, intergovernmental institutions, civil-society groups and business to discuss these innovations and brainstorm new ideas. There is clearly a role for the United Nations here, especially since it has not been a target of the demonstrations that have affected the G7 and the international financial institutions. The United Nations needs to be much more active in using its greater perceived public legitimacy to create opportunities for dialogue around these new 'rules of the road'. The next annual meeting between the United Nations and NGOs provides a good opportunity to host a discussion of this kind. Governments and intergovernmental organisations have the authority—and therefore the responsibility—to create structures that can promote non-state involvement without falling prey to special-interest politics.

Conclusion

Global public goods are arguably the most difficult public goods to provide in adequate, reasonably distributed quantities. Their scale is often daunting, and the large number of actors that need to reach agreement makes global governance a greater challenge than anything attempted before. But, given the price of failure, this challenge cannot be evaded. Environmental security and social stability, to name just two examples, cannot be indefinitely under-provided without threatening the fabric of local and national communities and undermining the viability of businesses, the functioning of public agencies and democratic processes and, ultimately, the lives of millions of people around the world.

In recent years non-state actors have played a growing role in the provision of global public goods, and their influence will continue to increase. The issue is not whether but how best to realise the potential of non-state actors and offset any associated costs. Non-state actors offer enormous resources—in innovation and thought leadership, advocacy, popular mobilisation, financial investment and service delivery. But these resources do not come for free. All non-state actors have institutional interests, ranging from narrow financial interests to broad, ideologically framed agendas for change. These interests may be invidious or even illegal, as with the production and sale of landmines targeted at civilians or the pursuit of sectarian interests using violent or otherwise unacceptable means. For the most part, however, the institutional interests of non-state actors are perfectly legal, legitimate on their own terms, and openly declared and pursued.

In realising the potential of non-state actors, the core challenge is managing diverse interests so that the pursuit of some global public goods—such as the environment, security, health and education—are not achieved at the cost of others—such as the fundamental rights of citizens to speak their minds, associate together and participate in decision-making that affects them. This challenge is particularly pertinent for global public goods because the inability of current governance structures to secure and enforce agreements is most apparent at the global level. Indeed, that inability goes a long way toward explaining why non-state actors have become so significant in the debate about and practice of delivering public goods across as well as within communities.

This is not a time for closure. The challenge of global governance needs to be faced head-on, but solutions will take time to emerge. In the future the very notion of non-state actors may seem outdated and unhelpful, as today's emerging coalitions of businesses, non-profit organisations and public agencies become tomorrow's permanent institutions—blending together the different forms of accountability that have historically separated state, civil society and business. The proposals set out above are part of an emerging discussion about global governance that tries to frame the difficult problems associated with the provision of global public goods. The proposals emphasise the need to strike a balance between developing clear and enforceable rules and encouraging diversity, innovation and the organic evolution of new patterns of governance. As they stand, the proposals reflect (rather than resolve) the tensions between the need to establish globally applicable rules and the need to create frameworks and processes that ensure those rules can be constantly tested and challenged at the local and national levels.

The early years of the 21st century are witnessing a major transformation of world politics. The boundaries between direct and representative democracy and between local, national and global governance are being tested and rearranged. These changes create new opportunities for the provision of global public goods, but we know little about how to manage them without succumbing to the pitfalls of statist inertia or special-interest politics. The question for governments, business and civil society is clear: do they have the courage and imagination to work out new answers in partnership—or only a mind-set that sees a new space to be fought over for power or profit? The stakes are very high.

notes

Introduction: writing by candlelight

1 For an elaboration on the meaning and use of the term 'triple bottom line', see Elkington 1997.
2 See www.accountability.org.uk.
3 See www.globalreporting.org.
4 See www.unglobalcompact.org.

Section I: the economics of utopia

2 The *practice* of Buddhist economics?

1 *The American Journal of Economics and Sociology.*
2 The chapter draws its inspiration from Pryor's two articles; from participating in research on Buddhism and economics sponsored by the New Economics Foundation and the World Wildlife Fund, as part of a wider exploration of the relationship between economics and the five major religions (Batchelor 1992); and finally from my engagement with the Sarvodaya Shramadana Movement in Sri Lanka, one of the world's largest social and economic development organisations informed directly by the social principles of Buddhism.
3 There are of course a great number of 'original texts' in Buddhism, not all of which are entirely compatible with each other. Pryor has focused on texts from the Theravada tradition in Buddhism, as referred to in his 1991 article.
4 The critical intermediary between the individual and the wider society can, of course, be defined in terms of 'local community'. The very fact that there is a perceived difference between the concepts of community and organisation is a matter of considerable interest. Sarvodaya, for example, is often criticised in terms of its performance as an organisation (e.g. low productivity) on bases that would be applauded if it was understood as a community, e.g. supporting the economically unproductive; see the NEF Working Paper on Sarvodaya for further discussion of this (Zadek and Szabo 1993).
5 This collective decision-making arrangement did not extend to the *dasa karmakaras*, the servile labourers, who had no access to political power whatsoever. Furthermore, Chakravarti argues that there are serious shortcomings in the treatment of the women in the Buddha's vision of organisation and social rights, which have largely been carried through to modern treatments of Buddhism (Chakravarti 1992).
6 In a more cynical mood, one might consider the distinction between 'fundamental' and 'helping or hindering' in the light of Keynes's famous saying that 'in the long run we are all dead'. That is to say, whether or not particular forms of social organisation have a 'fundamental' (long-run) effect is unclear, but if particular forms 'help or hinder' (in the short run), that will do just fine.

3 An economics of utopia: democratising scarcity

1 Which requires that a number of conditions hold, such as a large number of participants, perfect market information available to all participants, and ease of entry and exit to and from

the market in question (which in turn requires the assumption of 'non-convexity', i.e. no economies of scale).

2   Subject to a number of conditions, of which most important are a given initial resource distribution and preferences, and incomparable utility functions (de van Graaf 1957; Sen 1982).

3   There are, of course, different views of perfect competition in the economics profession, of which only one is clearly reflected in the text. Donald McCloskey argues, for example, in personal correspondence to the author (9 January 1992), 'In the Good Old Chicago School the competitive system is *not* viewed the way Arrow and Hahn do: namely, as an impossibly remote ideal. It is viewed roughly as how things happen. (Not in the chimerically smooth way that you describe, of course.)'

4   There are exceptions to this, most notable the infamous Cobweb Model which under certain circumstances can produce unstable oscillations in demand and supply. However, this model is a curiosum in economic theory and is not taken seriously as a market likely to prevail in significant circumstances. In addition, the evolving area of ecological and/or evolutionary economics might be seen as further attempts to move away from both the methodological technique and normative idolatry of concepts of equilibrium (Martinez-Alier 1987).

5   There is also the matter of 'welfare optimisation'. However, this is, as Sen argues, dealt with within the relatively narrow confines of 'welfare economics' and remains subsidiary to the main machinery of modern economics that focuses on 'resource efficiency'.

6   This argument is in fact more complex, and more problematic, than it may first appear, since the economy has no 'interest' whatsoever, but is rather an outcome of individual decisions in pursuit of personal self-interest, i.e. the invisible hand. Some economists might therefore argue that resource efficiency is not an assumption but an outcome. At one level this objection would be justified in that it is necessary to enter into the assumptions underlying individual behaviour in order to really understand what are the 'transcendent' aspects of modern economics. At another level, however, resource efficiency is not only an outcome of 'invisible management' but *is* also a basis of judgement of such outcomes. This dual use of 'resource efficiency' as outcome and criterion justifies, we hope, the argument that it does constitute a transcendent aspect of the core model.

7   Transcendence in this sense can also be likened to Gregory Bateson's understanding of the *sacred*. However, whereas Bateson was interested in the underpinning of the *sacred* in that it conveyed meaning *only if* it was not 'rationally' deconstructed into its component parts (e.g. the placebo effect works only if the pill is not revealed as merely the sugared variety), he was not interested directly in considering this in the context of matters of ideology.

8   There are a number of very specific conditions that define this 'state' of being, such as 'commensurability' of options, and the ability to rank them all in order of preference, at least in cardinal terms.

Section II: civil society, power and accountability

7   Civil regulation

1   Non-attributable statement made on anti-GAP campaign listserv.

2   This study is not publicly available, but was undertaken as part of a consultancy by one of the major accountancy companies for a major European blue-chip company.

3   Arguments and cases presented in this and the next chapter have appeared in two publications by the author: Zadek 2000a, and Weiser and Zadek 2000.

4   The idea of lent power was first advanced in a paper prepared for the UN Human Development Report Office, which was subsequently published as Zadek *et al.* 1998a.

5   A group of largely US-based corporations committed to opposing an international agreement on climate control involving business restraints.

6   See Chapter 21, 'Ethical trade futures', for a description of the Mecca pathway concept.

7   See IBFAN 1998 and Nestlé's most recent externally commissioned report, 'Emerging Market Economics 2000'.

8   There are a veritable host of studies covering the link between corporate social and environmental, and financial performance. For a good summary of some of the key ones, see Weiser and Zadek 2000.
9   CSR Europe was formerly the European Business Network for Social Cohesion. The study was carried out by MORI.
10   *The Ethical Investor*, September/October 1998.
11   See note 2.
12   The actual movement of the curves and their shape of course may be more complex or just different. For example, the financial market curves may not swivel but shift upwards over time.
13   See Chapter 21, 'Ethical trade futures', for a description of the Desert pathway concept.

8 Civil governance and accountability: from fear and loathing to social innovation

1   See for example the work of the Global Reporting Initiative and AccountAbility on this.
2   See also on this topic AccountAbility's recent publication, 'Partnership Accountability' (AccountAbility 2003b).

9 Practical people, noble causes

1   The Compact Edition of the *Oxford English Dictionary* reports that the term 'entrepreneur' refers to a 'director or manager of a public musical institution'.
2   *The Guardian*, 9 August 1997.
3   www.ashoka.org.
4   Both Ben & Jerry's and The Body Shop publish annual social audits of their company performance against social and environmental aims: Ben & Jerry's *Social Report* (1995) and The Body Shop International *Social Statement* (1995; summary available at www.think-act-change.com).

10 The art of mediation: turning practice into policy

1   The Study Group did not discuss Sustainable Agriculture and Rural Development (SARD) in the context of large-scale commercial agriculture in the region. This book does not do so either. The reason for this lies as much in the professional background and interests of the contributors and Study Group participants, as in the fact that most SARD initiatives (in practice and policy spheres) are concerned with the small and medium-sized producers and the more fragile rural environments. The Study Group recognised the importance of the large-scale commercial agriculture sector for a long-term success of any SARD strategy that aims to improve environmental aspects of agricultural production, but it was felt that the alternatives to the failures of the green revolution-based agricultural production systems and rural development models have come from the small farming sector. For this reason, and for the eminent validity of analysing a production sector that is central still to the vast majority of the population in the region (whether as urban consumers, migrants, rural dwellers or farmers), this book concentrates on the small farming sector and on the dynamics of organisations of small commercial and subsistence farmers and their farming systems.
2   The term 'sustainability' was until recently voiced predominantly by those wishing to challenge the dominant development model that takes economic growth as the basic indicator of successful progress. 'Sustainable development' in this form was the antithesis of a development model that considered that social and environmental problems would be solved by increasing the size of the economic 'cake'. Today, 'sustainability' is a more explicitly contested term. It is still used to describe a vision of local economies using minimal resources to sustain small communities at modest levels of income and consumption. In addition, however, it is part of a formulation of 'sustainable growth', where it is at best intended as a moderating

pronoun, and more cynically is used to offset potential criticism of the continued dash for economic expansion.

3   Concertation, from the Spanish *concertación*, is the commonly used expression for political negotiation and consensus-seeking between different actors. Originally, this word was used only by public-sector institutions, aided by multilateral funding agencies' language, in seeking the involvement of dissident rural and urban social actors in the proposed policy process. Today, even some NGO sectors accept this word as an expression of the endeavour to find a common purpose and dialogue between different actors in the interest of rural development.

4   With thanks to John Gaventa (Gaventa 1998) for the term, contrasting horizontal 'spread' with 'scaling-up'.

5   SARD is used as a framework for this discussion since it describes more adequately the systemic view of natural resource management and agricultural production and marketing systems: agriculture is set within the sphere of broader rural development, the latter including trading and processing parts of a wider livelihood and policy sphere affecting the life of all rural dwellers, not just the actual agricultural producers.

Section III: accounting for change

15 Accounting works: a comparative review of contemporary approaches to social and ethical accounting

1   *The Independent*, 23 July 1994: 3.

2   A piece of computer software has been developed by the Copenhagen Business School to support the ethical accounting statement process which allows for scaled questionnaire responses to be compared across years.

3   Comments by Peter Pruzan at a meeting of social and ethical accounting practitioners in Dessau, Germany, in July 1994.

4   Particular thanks to David Wheeler and Maria Sillanpää of The Body Shop plc for helping to clarify these different levels.

16 Adding values: the economics of sustainable business

1   Address, University of Kansas, Lawrence, Kansas, 18 March 1968.

17 Impacts of reporting: the role of social and sustainability reporting in organisational transformation

1   This hypothesis and picture is based on and inspired by Zadek *et al.* 1997.

2   The EMS Forum was launched on 16 October 2002, with the objective of providing innovation, transparency and convergence of corporate responsibility practices and instruments by improving knowledge about the relationship between corporate responsibility and sustainable development. The creation of the Forum followed on to the 2001 Green Paper on Corporate Social Responsibility by the European Commission, a subsequent consultation period, experimental round tables and the Commission's July 2002 Communication about the topic. The Forum addresses the key theme of transparency and corporate responsibility practices and tools, through the exchange of experience and best practice. Moreover, the CSR EMS Forum focuses on European approaches while recognising the global dimension.

18 Redefining materiality: making reporting more relevant

1   See the United Nations Environmental Programme Finance Initiative (www.unepfi.net), the Centre for Tomorrow's Company's '21st Century Investment' (www.tomorrowscompany.com)

and Forum for the Future's 'Centre for Sustainable Investment' (www.forumforthefuture.org.uk).

2   The Company Law Review Steering Committee 2002 Modern Company Law for a Competitive Economy Final Report URN 01/942 and URN 01/943 (UK, www.dti.gov.uk).

3   Conseil National du Patronat Français (CNPF) and Association Française des Entreprises Privées (AFEP), *Report of the Committee on Corporate Governance* (Vienot II) (France, 1999).

4   German Panel on Corporate Governance, *Corporate Governance Rules for German Quoted Companies* (Frankfurt, 2000).

Section IV: the civil corporation

20 Can corporations be civil?

1   Social Exclusion Unit, Social Exclusion Unit's Policy Action Team 3 Report, Enterprise and Social Exclusion, United Kingdom Government, London, 1999.

2   Quote drawn from remark made at the annual conference of Business for Social Responsibility in San Francisco in November 1999.

3   *The Economist*, 31 December 1999: 11.

4   Speech at Chatham House, London, 2001.

5   *Ibid.* Emphasis added.

6   Personal correspondence.

7   Business for Social Responsibility's annual conference in San Francisco in November 1999.

21 Ethical trade futures

1   One of the most recent and comprehensive reviews of the field is OECD, *Corporate Codes of Conduct: An Inventory* (TD/TC/WP[98]74/FINAL) OECD Trade Directorate, Paris, 1998.

2   This relationship is discussed more extensively in Zadek and Forstater 1999.

3   European Commission, 2nd EU–US Symposium on Codes of Conduct and International Labour Standards, European Commission DGV: March 1999.

4   We are grateful for the contributions made by people from these organisations. We would re-emphasise that there is no suggestion here that they agree with or endorse the views expressed in this chapter.

5   We are grateful to John Elkington (SustainAbility Ltd), Judith Mullins (General Motors) and Doug Mackay and Mark Wade (Shell) for clarifying and naming these scenarios.

24 Reflections on corporate responsibility after 9/11

1   These included Bob Dunn, Executive Director of US-based Business for Social Responsibility; John Elkington, Chairman of SustainAbility Ltd; Jane Nelson and Robert Davies, Directors of the International Business Leaders Forum; Ed Mayo, Executive Director of the New Economics Foundation; David Logan, Director of the Corporate Citizenship Company; Bradley Googins, Executive Director of Boston College Center for Corporate Citizenship; and Nelmara Arbex from the Brazil-based Ethos Institute

Section V: partnership alchemy

26 Partnership alchemy: engagement, innovation and governance

1   These categories and pathways have been used in a recent report on the role of business in tackling HIV/AIDS [Prince of Wales Business Leaders Forum 2000]).

2   This section draws from an unpublished paper prepared for the Knowledge and Resources Group of the Business Partners in Development (BPD) initiative convened by CIVICUS, the Prince of Wales Business Leaders Forum and the World Bank.

3   Involving the UK Government Department of Trade and Industry, Business in the Community, the Local Futures Group, and the Institute of Social and Ethical AccountAbility.

Section VI: responsible competitiveness

29 Responsible competitiveness: corporate responsibility clusters in action

1   Lisbon Summit, March 2000.

30 Third-generation corporate citizenship: public policy and business in society

1   Thanks to Judy Kuszewski at SustainAbility for showing me the relevance of this metaphor during our Australian conference tour.

2   First described in Zadek 2000b, and then dealt with in more depth in Zadek 2001a.

3   Social Exclusion Unit, Social Exclusion Unit's Policy Action Team 3 Report, Enterprise and Social Exclusion, United Kingdom Government, London, 1999.

4   European Commission, Green Paper: Promoting a European Framework for Corporate Social Responsibility, Comm (2001) 366 Final, EC, Brussels.

5   www.accountability.org.uk

6   www.corporate-citizenship.co.uk/community/lbg.asp

7   www.unglobalcompact.org

33 Governing the provision of global public goods: the role and legitimacy of non-state actors

1   Cox's News Service, 12 April 2001.

2   Guardian Weekly, 10–16 May 2001.

3   One example is the link between war in the Democratic Republic of Congo and the continued mining in key parts of the country of coltan, a critical ingredient in the production of mobile phones (The Guardian, 20 August 2001, G2-3). Similarly, in 2001 corporate lobbyists tried to soften proposals for international certification of the diamond trade (Smillie and Gberie 2001).

4   Excerpted from comments made during a closed online debate, 7 December 1999.

5   Global Knowledge Partnership listserv, 19 December 2000.

6   See www.environics.net/eil (Environics is now GlobeScan).

7   Ed Mayo, openDemocracy Web site (www.openDemocracy.org.uk), 31 July 2001.

bibliography

Aaronson, S. (2001) *Taking Trade to the Streets: The Lost History of Public Efforts to Shape Globalization* (Ann Arbor, MI: University of Michigan Press).

AccountAbility (1999) *AA1000: Overview of Standard, Guidelines, and Tools* (London: ISEA).

—— (2000) *Innovation through Partnership* (London: AccountAbility).

—— (2001) 'A Review of Origin's "Stakeholder-Access Software V2.1" ', *AccountAbility Quarterly* 16.1: 3.

—— (2002) *AA1000 Series Assurance Standard Guiding Principles: Consultation Document* (London: AccountAbility).

—— (2003a) *The State of Sustainability Assurance* (London: AccountAbility).

—— (2003b) 'Partnership Accountability', *AccountAbility Quarterly* 20 (London: AccountAbility).

—— and The Copenhagen Centre (2003) *Responsible Competitiveness: Corporate Responsible Clusters in Action* (Copenhagen: The Copenhagen Centre; London: AccountAbility).

—— and CSR Europe (2002) *Impacts of Reporting: The Role of Social and Sustainability Reporting in Organisational Transformation* (London: AccountAbility).

Adams R., J. Carruthers and S. Hamil (1991) *Changing Corporate Culture: A Guide to Social and Environmental Policy and Practice in Britain's Top Companies* (London: Kogan Page).

Agudelo, A., and D. Kaimowitz (1994) *Las Implicaciones Institucionales y Metodológicas de Promover un Patrón Tecnológico más Sostenible para la Agricultura: Una Reflexión con Base en Dos Casos de Colombia* (San José, Costa Rica, unpublished manuscript).

Ampuero, M., J. Goranson and J. Scott (1999) 'Solving the Measurement Puzzle: How EVA and the Balanced Scorecard Fit Together', in Ernst & Young Centre for Business Innovation, *Measuring Business Performance* (Perspectives on Business Innovation, Issue 2; Cambridge, UK): 45-52.

Anderson, S. (1994) 'Research Centres and Participatory Research: Issues and Implications (Mexico)', paper to the Study Group 'Mediating Sustainability' (London: Institute of Latin American Studies, unpublished manuscript).

—— and J. Cavanagh (1996) *The Top 200: The Rise of Corporate Global Power* (Washington, DC: Institute of Policy Studies).

Anderson, V. (1991) *Alternative Economic Indicators* (London: Routledge).

Andriof, J., and M. McIntosh (eds.) (2001) *Perspectives on Corporate Citizenship* (Sheffield, UK: Greenleaf Publishing).

Anheier, H., M. Glasius and M. Kaldor (eds.) (2001) *Global Civil Society 2001* (Oxford, UK: Oxford University Press).

Annan, K. (2000) *We the Peoples: The Role of the UN in the 21st Century* (New York: United Nations).

Ariyaratne, A.T. (1982) *Collected Works: Volume I* (Sri Lanka: Vishva Lekha, an income-generating project for Sarvodaya Village Development Services).

—— (1985) *Collected Works: Volume III* (Sri Lanka: Vishva Lekha, an income-generating project for Sarvodaya Village Development Services).

—— (1988) *Sarvodaya and the Economy* (Sri Lanka: Vishva Lekha, an income-generating project for Sarvodaya Village Development Services).

Arrow, K. (1972) 'General Economic Equilibrium: Purpose, Analytic Techniques, Collective Choices', in *Les Prix Nobel en 1972* (Stockholm: Nobel Foundation)

Athukorala and Jayasuriya (1991) *Macroeconomic Policies, Crises and Growth in Sri Lanka, 1960–1990* (study undertaken as part of the World Bank Comparative Study 'Macroeconomic Policies, Crisis and Growth in the Long Run', RPO 673-99; Washington, DC: International Bank for Reconstruction and Development).

Batchelor, M., and K. Brown (eds.) (1992) *Buddhism and Ecology* (London: Cassell).

Batchelor, S. (1992) 'The Practice of Generosity: First Steps towards a Buddhist Economics', unpublished paper arising from workshop held at Sharpham Trust, UK, January 1991 and March 1992.

Bateson, G. (1987) *Where Angels Fear* (London: Century Hutchinson, 1989 edn).

Ben & Jerry's (1993) *Annual Report* (Waterbury, VT: Ben & Jerry's).

Bhagwati, J. (1993) 'The Case for Free Trade', *Scientific American*, November 1993.

Biggs, S., and G. Smith (1995) 'Contending Coalitions in Agricultural Research and Development: Challenges for Planning and Management', paper for the conference *Evaluation for a New Century: A Global Perspective*, Canadian Evaluation Association and the American Evaluation Association, 1–5 November 1995, Vancouver, Canada.

Bissio, R. (ed.) (1997) *Social Watch* (Montevideo: Instituto del Tercer Mundo).

Blauert, J., and E. Quintanar (1997) *Seeking Local Indicators: Participatory Stakeholder Evaluation in Farmer-to-Farmer Projects in Southern Mexico* (PLA Notes; International Institute for Environment and Development, March 1997).

Bloch, E. (1938–47) *The Principle of Hope* (trans. N. Plaice, S. Plaice and P. Knight; Oxford, UK: Blackwell, 1986 edn).

The Body Shop (1998) *Values Report* (Littlehampton, UK: The Body Shop).

Bohm, D. (1980) *Wholeness and the Implicate Order* (London: Ark, 1993 edn).

Bovet, S. (1999) 'The Race to Measure Reputation', *PR Week*, 31 May 1999: 14-15.

Bradbury, M. (1983) *Rates of Exchange* (London: Secker & Warburg).

Bradbury, R. (1953) *Fahrenheit 451* (New York: Ballantine Books).

British Airports Authority (1999) *Growing With the Support and Trust of Our Neighbours* (London: BAA).

Broad, R., and J. Cavanagh (1999) 'The Death of the Washington Consensus?', *World Policy Journal* 16.3 (Fall 1999): 79-88.

Brown, L.D (2001) 'Civil Society Legitimacy: A Discussion Guide', in L.D. Brown (ed.), *Practice-Research Engagement and Civil Society in a Globalizing World* (Washington, DC: CIVICUS and Cambridge: Hauser Center on Non-Profit Organizations).

BSR (Business for Social Responsibility) (2002) *Working with Multilaterals* (San Francisco: Business for Social Responsibility).

Bunch, C., with P. Antrobus, S. Frost and N. Reilly (2001) 'International Networking for Women's Human Rights', in M. Edwards and J. Gaventa (eds.), *Global Citizen Action* (Boulder, CO: Lynne Rienner Publishers).

Burgenmeier, B. (1992) *Socio-Economics: An Interdisciplinary Approach* (Dordrecht, Netherlands: Kluwer).

Calva, J.L. (1993) 'Principios Fundamentales de un Modelo de Desarrollo Agropecuario Adecuado para México', in J.L. Calva (ed.), *Alternativas para el Campo Mexicano*. Vol. II (Fontamar: Friedrich Ebert Stiftung; Mexico: UNAM): 185-204.

Carmen, R. (1998) 'Producer Works!', *Development* (Rome: SID) 41.1.

Carroll, T. (1992) *Intermediary NGOs: The Supporting Link in Grassroots Development* (West Hartford, CT: Kumarian Press).

Castells, M. (1996–2000) *The Information Age: Economy, Society, and Culture* (3 vols.; Oxford, UK: Blackwell).

CBI (Confederation of British Industry) (1999) *Global Social Responsibility* (London: CBI).

Chakravarti, U. (1992) 'Buddhism as a Discourse of Dissent? Class and Gender', *Pravada* (Colombo, Sri Lanka: Social Scientists Association) 1.5 (May 1992): 12-18.

Chambers, R. (1989) Editorial introduction: 'Vulnerability, Coping and Policy', *IDS Bulletin* 21: 1-7.

—— (1992) *Rural Appraisal: Rapid, Relaxed and Participatory* (Institute of Development Studies Working Paper, 311; Brighton, UK: IDS).

—— (1993) *Challenging the Professions: Frontiers for Rural Development* (London: IT Publications).

——, A. Pacey and L.A. Thrupp (eds.) (1989) *Farmers First: Farmer Innovation and Agricultural Research* (London: Intermediate Technology Publications).

Chapela, L. (1992) *Buddhist Guidelines on Economic Organisation and Development for Future Tibet: Interviews with His Holiness the XIV Dalai Lama of Tibet and Ven* (unpublished papers; Samdhong Rinpoche).

Chapman, J. (2001) 'What Makes International Campaigns Effective? Lessons from India and Ghana', in M. Edwards and J. Gaventa (eds.), *Global Citizen Action* (Boulder, CO: Lynne Rienner Publishers).

Charnovitz, S. (2000) 'Opening the WTO to Non-governmental Interests', *Fordham International Law Journal* 24.1–2: 173-216.

Chatwin, B. (1987) *Songlines* (London: Picador).

Coleman, J. (1988) 'Social Capital in the Creation of Human Capital', *American Journal of Sociology* 94 (Supplement): 95-120.

Collins, C., Z. Gariyo and A. Burdon (2001) 'Jubilee 2000: Citizen Action across the North–South Divide', in M. Edwards and J. Gaventa (eds.), *Global Citizen Action* (Boulder, CO: Lynne Rienner Publishers).

Commission for Social Justice (1994) *Strategies for Renewal* (Report of the Commission for Social Justice; London: Vintage).

Cone Inc. (1999) *Cone/Roper Cause Related Trends Report: Evolution of Cause Branding^{SM}* (Boston, MA: Cone Inc.).

The Conference Board, Inc. (1999) *Consumer Expectations of the Social Accountability of Business* (New York: The Conference Board).

Cornelius, P., *et al.* (2002) *Global Competitiveness Report* (Geneva: World Economic Forum/Oxford University Press).

Corrigan, P. (1997) *No More Big Brother* (London: The Fabian Society).

The Council on Foundations (1996) *Measuring the Value of Corporate Citizenship* (Washington, DC: The Council on Foundations).

Cowe, R., and S. Williams (2000) *Who Are the Ethical Consumers?* (Manchester, UK: The Co-operative Bank).

Dahrendorf, R. (1968) *Essays in the Theory of Society* (London: Routledge & Kegan Paul).

Daly, H., and J. Cobb (1990) *For the Common Good: Redirecting the Economy towards Community, the Environment and a Sustainable Future* (London: Green Print).

Denny, C. (2001) 'WTO lobbyists keep out the poor', *Guardian Weekly*, 4–10 October 2001.

De van Graaf, J. (1957) *Theoretical Welfare Economics* (Cambridge, UK: Cambridge University Press).

Dodds, F. (2001) 'From the Corridors of Power to the Global Negotiating Table: The NGO Steering Committee of the Commission on Sustainable Development', in M. Edwards and J. Gaventa (eds.), *Global Citizen Action* (Boulder, CO: Lynne Rienner Publishers).

Doyal, L., and I. Gough (1991) *A Theory of Human Need* (London: Macmillan).

Drucker, P. (1994) *Innovation and Entrepreneurship* (London: Heinemann).

Ebihara, M. (1966) 'Interrelation between Buddhism and Social Systems in Cambodian Peasant Culture', in M. Nash (ed.), *Anthropological Studies in Theravada Buddhism* (Southeast Asia Studies; New Haven, CT: Yale University Press).

EC (European Commission) (2002) *Communication from the Commission Concerning Corporate Social Responsibility: A Business Contribution to Sustainable Development* (Com[2002]347 Final; Brussels: EC).

Edwards, M. (1999). *Future Positive: International Cooperation in the 21st Century* (London: Earthscan Publications).

—— (2000a) 'Enthusiasts, Tacticians and Skeptics: The World Bank and Social Capital', *Kettering Review* 18.1: 39-51.

—— (2000b) *NGO Rights and Responsibilities: A New Deal for Global Governance* (London: Foreign Policy Centre).

—— and J. Gaventa (eds.) (2001) *Global Citizen Action* (Boulder, CO: Lynne Rienner Publishers).

—— and D. Hulme (1996) *Beyond the Magic Bullet: NGO Performance and Accountability in the Post-Cold War World* (London: Earthscan Publications; West Hartford, CT: Kumarian Press).

—— and S. Zadek (2003) 'Governing the Provision of Global Public Goods: The Role and Legitimacy of Nonstate Actors', in I. Kaul, P. Conceição, K. Le Goulven and R.U. Mendoza (eds.), *Providing Global Public Goods: Managing Globalization* (New York: Oxford University Press).

Eisen, P. (2000) 'Conversation about Skepticism' (Washington, DC: National Association of Manufacturers, 15 July 2000).

Ekins, P. (1992) *A New World Order: Grassroots Movements for Global Change* (London: Routledge).

—— and M. Max-Neef (1992) *Real-Life Economics: Understanding Wealth-Creation* (London: Routledge).

Elkington, J. (1997) *Cannibals with Forks: The Triple Bottom Line of 21st Century Business* (Oxford, UK: Capstone Publishing).

Emerging Market Economics (2000) *Infant Nutritional Operational Study* (Report for Nestlé; London: Emerging Market Economics).

Enayati, J., and M. Hemmati (2000) *Multi-stakeholder Processes: Examples, Principles and Strategies. Workshop Report* (London: UNED Forum).

Engel, P. (1995) *Facilitation Innovation: An Action-Oriented Approach and Participatory Methodology to Improve Innovative Social Practice in Agriculture* (PhD thesis, Agriculture and Environmental Sciences, Wageningen University, Netherlands).

—— and M. Salomon (1994) 'RAAKS: A Participatory Action-Research Approach to Facilitating Social Learning for Sustainable Development', paper for the International Symposium on Systems-Oriented Research in Agriculture and Rural Development, Montpellier, 21–25 November 1994; also presented at the meeting of the Study Group 'Mediating Sustainability', Wageningen University, Netherlands, 17 November 1994.

Environics International (1999) *Executive Briefing: The Millennium Poll on Corporate Social Responsibility* (Toronto: Environics International Ltd).

Escalante, R. (1994) 'Participation and Economics: Illustrations from Mexico's Agricultural Sector', paper to the Study Group 'Mediating Sustainability', Institute of Latin American Studies, London.

Ethiopian National Conservation Strategy (1994) *National Policy on Natural Resources and the Environment* (Addis Ababa: Ministry of Natural Resources Development and Environmental Protection).

Falk, R., and A. Strauss (1997) 'For a Global People's Assembly', *International Herald Tribune*, 14 November 1997.

FAO (Food and Agriculture Organisation of the United Nations) (1992) *Políticas Agrícolas y Políticas Macroeconómicas en América Latina* (Social and Economic Development Study, 108; Rome: FAO).

—— (1994a) *Sustainable Agriculture and Rural Development. I. Latin America and Asia* (DEEP Series; Rome: FAO, July 1994).

—— (1994b) *Participación Campesina para un Agricultura Sostenible en Países de América Latina* (Participación Popular Series, 7; Rome: FAO).

—— (1997) *Agenda 21 Progress Report* (Rome: FAO).

Fleishman Hillard (1999) *Consumers Demand Companies with a Conscience* (London: Fleishman Hillard Europe).

Florini, A.M. (ed.) (2000) *The Third Force: The Rise of Transnational Civil Society* (Washington, DC: Carnegie Endowment for International Peace; Tokyo: Japan Center for International Exchange).

Ford Motor Company (2000) *Connecting With Society: 1999 Corporate Citizenship Report* (Dearbon, MI: Ford Motor Company).

Friedman, M. (1953) 'The Methodology of Positive Economics', in M. Friedman, *Essays in Positive Economics* (Chicago: University of Chicago Press).

—— (1962) *Capitalism and Freedom* (Chicago: University of Chicago Press).

—— (1970) 'The social responsibility of business is to increase its profits', *New York Times Magazine*, 13 September 1970: 32-33.

Gaventa, J. (1998) 'The Scaling-up and Institutionalisation of PRA: Lessons and Challenges', in J. Blackburn and J. Holland (eds.), *Who Changes? Institutionalising Participation in Development* (London: IT Publications).

Godelier, M. (1966) *Rationality and Irrationality in Economics* (New York: Monthly Review Press, 1972 edn).

Gómez, C., R. Manuel Angel, R. Schwentesius, M. Muñoz Rodríguez *et al.* (1993) *¿Procampo ó Anticampo?* (Reporte de Investigación, 20; Centro de Investigaciones Económicas, Sociales, Universidad Autónoma de Chapingo, Mexico City).

Gorz, A. (1989) *Critique of Economic Reason* (London: Verso).

Goulet, D. (1980) 'Development Experts: The One-Eyed Giants', *World Development* 8.7–8 (July/August 1980): 481-93.

Goyder, G. (1961) *The Responsible Company* (Oxford, UK: Blackwell).

—— (1987) *The Just Enterprise* (London: André Deutsch).

Goyder, M. (1998) *The Living Company* (Aldershot, UK: Gower).

Gray, R. (1993) *Accounting for the Environment* (London: Paul Chapman).

——, D. Owen, and K. Maunders (1987) *Corporate Social Reporting* (Hemel Hempstead, UK: Prentice Hall).

Green, D. (1999) *Ethical Trading Initiative: Southern Consultation* (report for the Ethical Trading Initiative; London: ETI).

Grossman, G. (1993) *Pollution and Growth: What Do We Know?* (Centre for Economic Policy Research Discussion Papers, 848; London: CEPR).

—— and A. Krueger (1994) *Economic Growth and the Environment* (NBER WP 4634; Cambridge, MA: National Bureau of Economic Research).

The Guardian/WWF (1997) *One Thousand Days: A Special Report on How to Live in the New Millennium* (London: The Guardian).

Guba, E.G., and Y.S. Lincoln (1989) *Fourth Generation Evaluation* (London: Sage).

Hahn, F. (1984) *Theoretical Welfare Economics* (Cambridge, UK: Cambridge University Press).

Hancock, G. (1989) *Lords of Poverty: The Power, Prestige, and Corruption of the International Aid Business* (New York: Atlantic Monthly Press).

Harper, C. (2001) 'Do the Facts Matter? NGOs, Research and International Advocacy', in M. Edwards and J. Gaventa (eds.), *Global Citizen Action* (Boulder, CO: Lynne Rienner Publishers).

Hawken, P. (1997) 'Natural Capitalism', *Mother Jones Reprints* (San Francisco), March/April 1997.

——, A. Lovins and L.H. Lovins (1999) *Natural Capitalism: Creating the Next Industrial Revolution* (Boston, MA: Little Brown).

Hayek, F. (1944) *The Road to Serfdom* (Chicago: University of Chicago Press, 1994 edn).

Hemmati, M., with F. Dodds, J. Enayati and J. McHarry (2001) *Multistakeholder Processes: A Methodological Framework* (London: UNED Forum).

HIS (1999) *Peduli Hak: Caring for Rights* (Jakarta: Insan Hitawasana Sejahtera).

HMSO (1999) *Private Service Operators Act* (White Paper; London: HMSO).

Hopkins. M. (1998) *The Planetary Bargain* (London: HarperCollins).

IBFAN (International Baby Food Action Network) (1998) *Breaking the Rules: Stretching the Rules 1998* (Penang: IBFAN).

IPPR (Institute of Public Policy Research) (2001) *Building Better Partnerships: Final Report on the Commission of Private-Public Partnerships* (London: IPPR).

Jacobs, M. (1996) *Politics of the Real World* (London: Earthscan Publications).

Kaimowitz, D. (1995) *El Avance de la Agricultura Sostenible en América Latina* (unpublished manuscript; San José, Costa Rica: Instituto Interamericano de Cooperación para la Agricultura).

Kaul, I., I. Grunberg and M.A. Stern (eds.) (1999) *Global Public Goods: International Cooperation in the 21st Century* (New York: Oxford University Press).

Keane, J. (2001) 'Global Civil Society', in *The Global Civil Society Yearbook* (London: London School of Economics, Center for the Study of Civil Society).

Keck, M., and K. Sikkink (1998) *Activists beyond Borders: Advocacy Networks in International Politics* (Ithaca, NY: Cornell University Press).

Koestler, A. (1971) *The Case of the Midwife Toad* (New York: Random House).

Knight, B. (1994) *The Voluntary Sector in the UK* (London: Centris).

Korten, D. (1995) *When Corporations Rule the World* (London Earthscan Publications; West Hartford, CT: Kumarian Press).

—— (1999) *The Post-Corporate World: Life after Capitalism* (West Hartford, CT: Kumarian Press; San Francisco: Berrett-Koehler).

Koutsoyiannis, A. (1975) *Modern Microeconomics* (London: Macmillan).

Krishnamurti, J. (1972) *The Impossible Question* (Harmondsworth, UK: Penguin, 1982 edn).

LaFeber, W. (1999) *Michael Jordan and the New Global Capitalism* (New York: W.W. Norton).

Lang, T., and C. Hines (1993) *The New Protectionism: Protecting the Future Against Free Trade* (London: Earthscan Publications).

Layard, P., and A. Walters (1978) *Microeconomic Theory* (New York: McGraw–Hill).

Leadbeater, C. (1996) *The Rise of the Social Entrepreneur* (London: Demos).

Leff, E. (1996) 'Ambiente y Democracia: Los Nuevos Actores del Ambientalismo en el Medio Rural Mexicano', in H. de C. Grammont and H. Tejera Gaona (eds.), *Los Nuevos Actores Sociales y Procesos Políticos en el Campo* (Mexico: Plaza y Valdés): 36-63.

Levin, D.M. (1989) *The Listening Self: Personal Growth, Social Change and the Closure of Metaphysics* (London: Routledge).

Levitas, R. (1991) *The Concept of Utopia* (Hemel Hempstead, UK: Phillip Allan).

Lewnhak, H. (1997) in *International Labour Organisation Digest*, January 1997.

Linck, T. (ed.) (1993) *Agriculturas y Campesinados de América Latina: Mutaciones y Recomposiciones* (Mexico: Fondo de Cultura Económica/ORSTOM).

Ling, T. (1980) 'Buddhist Values and Development Policy: A Case Study of Sri Lanka', *World Development* 8.7-8 (July/August 1980): 577-86.

Lloyd, T. (1990) *The Nice Company* (London: Bloomsbury Publishing).

Loy, D., and J. Watts (1998) 'The Religion of Consumption: A Buddhist Perspective', *Development* 41.1.

Lunt, P., and S. Livingstone (1992) *Mass Consumption and Social Identity* (Buckingham, UK: Open University Press).

Lutz, M., and K. Lux (1988) *Humanistic Economics: The New Challenge* (New York: The Bootstrap Press).

MacGillivray, A., and S. Zadek (1996) 'Medir la Sostenibilidad: Revisión Sobre el Arte de Hacer que Funcionen los Indicadores', *Investigación Económica* 61.218 (October–December 1996): 139-76.

Macy, J. (1984) *Dharma and Development* (West Hartford, CT: Kumarian Press).

Mandeville, B. (1714) *The Fable of the Bees* (Oxford, UK: Oxford University Press, 1966 edn).

Martinez-Alier, J. (1987) *Ecological Economics: Energy, Environment and Society* (Oxford, UK: Basil Blackwell, 1990 edn).

Maslow, A. (1954) *Motivation and Personality* (New York: Harper & Row).

Mauss, M. (1950) *The Gift* (London: Routledge, repr. 1990).

Max-Neef, M., with A. Elizalde and M. Hopenhayn (1991) *Human Scale Development: Conception, Application, and Further Reflections* (New York: Apex Press; London: Zed Books [1992]).

McCloskey, D. (1986) *The Rhetoric of Economics* (Madison, WI: University of Wisconsin Press).

Merme, M. (2003) *Study on Legislative and Listings Reviews Relevant to SRI* (Working Paper; London: Just Pensions; www.justpensions.org).

Mulgan, G. (1998) *Connexity: How to Live in a Connected World* (London: Chatto & Windus).

Murphy, D.F., and J. Bendell (1997) *In the Company of Partners: Business, Environmental Groups and Sustainable Development Post-Rio* (Bristol, UK: The Polity Press).

NEF (New Economics Foundation) (1994) *New Economics Foundation Social Audit 1993/94* (London: NEF).

—— (1997a) *Open Trading: Options for Effective Monitoring of Corporate Performance* (NEF/CHR on behalf of the Monitoring and Verification Working Group of the UK-Trade Network of British NGOs; London: NEF).

—— (1997b) *Community Works!* (London: NEF).

——/WWF (1995) *Curves, Tunnels and Trade: Does the Environment Improve Economic Growth?* (Geneva: WWF).

Nelson, J. (1996) *Business as Partners in Development: Creating Wealth for Countries, Companies, and Communities* (London: Prince of Wales Business Leaders Forum).

—— and S. Zadek (2000) *Partnership Alchemy: New Social Partnerships in Europe* (Copenhagen: The Copenhagen Centre; www.copenhagencentre.org).

Nye, J., and J. Donahue (eds.) (2001) *Governance in a Globalizing World* (Washington, DC: Brookings Institution Press).

Olsen, M. (1971) *The Logic of Collective Action: Public Goods and the Theory of Goods (Economic Study)* (Harvard, MA: Harvard University Press, 1996 edn).

Oxfam (1996) *Poverty Report* (Oxford, UK: Oxfam).

Panayotou, T. (1992) 'Empirical Tests and Policy Analysis of Environmental Degradation at Different Stages of Economic Development', mimeo, Harvard University.

Patel, S., J. Bolnick and D. Mitlin (2001) 'Squatting on the Global Highway: Community Exchanges for Urban Transformation', in M. Edwards and J. Gaventa (eds.), *Global Citizen Action* (Boulder, CO: Lynne Rienner Publishers).

Pearce, J. (1993) *At the Heart of the Community Enterprise* (London: Calouste Gulbenkian Foundation).

Perera J., M. Charika and J. Leela (1992) *A People's Movement under Siege* (Colombo, Sri Lanka: Sarvodaya Publications).

Péres, J.A. (1996) 'Reforms, Actors and Popular Participation in Contemporary Bolivia', paper for the Study Group, 'Mediating Sustainability', Wageningen, rev. version.

Placer Dome, Inc. (2000) *Ensuring Our Future: Sustainability Report 1999* (Vancouver: Placer Dome; www.placerdome.com).

Porter, M. (1998) *The Competitive Advantage of Nations* (Basingstoke, UK: Macmillan).

Prince of Wales Business Leaders Forum (2000) *The Response to HIV/AIDS: Impact and Lessons Learnt* (London: PWBLF).

Pruzan, P., and O. Thyssen (1990) 'Conflict and Consensus: Ethics as a Shared Value Horizon for Strategic Planning', *Human Systems Development* 9: 134-52.

Pryor, F. (1990) 'A Buddhist Economic System: In Principle', *American Journal of Economics and Sociology* 49.3 (July 1990): 339-49.

—— (1991) 'A Buddhist Economic System: In Practice', *American Journal of Economics and Sociology* 50.1 (January 1991): 17-32.

Rasmussen, D.M. (1990) *Reading Habermas* (Cambridge, MA: Blackwell).

Reynolds, F., and R. Clifford (1980) 'Sangha, Society and the Struggle for National Identity: Burma and Thailand', in F. Reynolds and T. Ludwig (eds.), *Transitions and Transformations in the History of Religions* (Leiden, Netherlands: Brill): 56-94.

Robins, N., and S. Roberts (1998) 'Sense of Sustainable Consumption', *Development* (Rome: SID): 41.1.

Rothchild, K. (1992) *Ethics and Economic Theory* (London: Edward Elgar).

Roy, S. (1989) *Philosophy of Economics: On the Scope of Reason in Economic Enquiry* (London: Routledge, 1991 edn).

RSA (Royal Society for the Encouragement of Arts, Manufactures and Commerce) (1995) *RSA Inquiry. Tomorrow's Company: The Role of Business in a Changing World* (London: RSA).

Ruben, R., and N. Heerink (1996) 'Economic Approaches for the Evaluation of Low External Input Agriculture', draft paper for the Study Group, 'Mediating Sustainability', London; abridged version as 'Economic Evaluation of LEISA Farming', *ILEIA Newsletter* 11.2: 18-20.

Ruggie, J. (1983) 'International Regimes, Transactions and Change: Embedded Liberalism in the Postwar Economic Order', in S. Krasner (ed.), *International Regimes* (Ithaca, NY: Cornell University Press).

Sachs, J., G. Stone and A. Warner (1999) 'Year in Review', in *Global Competitiveness Report* (Geneva: World Economic Forum).

Sahlins, M. (1972) *Stone Age Economics* (London: Routledge, repr. 1988).

Said, E. (1994) *Representations of the Intellectual: The 1993 Reith Lectures* (London: Vintage).

SBN Bank (1993) *Ethical Accounting Statement 1993* (Denmark: SBN Bank).

Scholte, J.A. (2001) 'The IMF and Civil Society: An Interim Progress Report', in M. Edwards and J. Gaventa (eds.), *Global Citizen Action* (Boulder, CO: Lynne Rienner Publishers).

Schumacher, E.F. (1973) *Small is Beautiful: Economics as if People Mattered* (London: Blond & Briggs).

Scoones, I., and J. Thompson (1994) *Beyond Farmers First: Rural People's Knowledge* (Agricultural Research and Extension Practice; London: IT Books).

Scott, C. (1996) 'El Nuevo Modelo Económico en América Latina y la Pobreza Rural', in A.P. de Teresa and C. Cortés R. (eds.), *La Nueva Relación Campo–Ciudad y la Pobreza Rural* (Mexico: Plaza y Valdés): 83-121.

Scott, M. (2001) 'Danger—Landmines! NGO–Government Collaboration in the Ottawa Process', in M. Edwards and J. Gaventa (eds.), *Global Citizen Action* (Boulder, CO: Lynne Rienner Publishers).

Selden, T., and D. Song (1994) 'Environmental Quality and Development: Is there a Kuznets Curve for Air Pollution?', *Journal of Environmental Economics and Management* 27.

Sen, A. (1982) *Choice, Welfare and Measurement* (Oxford, UK: Blackwell).

—— (1987) *On Ethics and Economics* (Oxford, UK: Blackwell).

—— (1999) *Development as Freedom* (Oxford, UK: OUP).

Shared Earth (1994) *Shared Earth Social Audit 1993/94* (York, UK: Shared Earth).

Shell International (1999) *The Shell Report 1999. People, Planet and Profits: An Act of Commitment* (London: Shell International).

Shiva, V. (1993) *Monocultures of the Mind: Perspectives on Biodiversity and Biotechnology* (Penang: Zed Books and Third World Network).

Smillie, I., and L. Gberie (2001) 'Dirty Diamonds and Civil Society', CIVICUS World Assembly, Vancouver, Canada, 19–23 August 2001.

Sogge, D., with K. Biekart and J. Saxby (eds.) (1996) *Compassion and Calculation: The Business of Private Foreign Aid* (London: Pluto Press).

Spiegelmann, R. (1982) *Abundance and Scarcity: A Methodology of Reading Social Theory: Case Study of Marx* (unpublished PhD, City University of New York).

Stanley Foundation (2001) *Report of the Symposium on UN Civil Society Outreach* (New York: Stanley Foundation).

Stigler, G. (1981) 'Economics of Ethics?', in S. McMurris (ed.), *Tanner Lectures on Human Values: Volume II* (Cambridge, MA: Cambridge University Press).

Strannegård, L., and R. Wolff (1998) 'Discovering Sustainability: A Case Study of Learning through Environmental Scenarios', *Greener Management International* 23 (Autumn 1998): 53-67.

Suksamran, S. (1977) *Political Buddhism in Southeast Asia: The Role of the Sangha in the Modernisation of Thailand* (London: C. Hurst & Co.).

SustainAbility (2003) *The 21st Century NGO: In the Market for Change* (London: SustainAbility).

Tajfel, H. (1978) *Differentiation between Social Groups* (London: Academic Press).

Traidcraft (1993) *Traidcraft plc Social Audit 1992/93* (Gateshead, UK: Traidcraft).

—— (1994) *Traidcraft plc Social Audit 1993/94* (Gateshead, UK: Traidcraft).

TransOceanic Institute (1996) *The Private Agencies: Rulers or Ruled?* (Amsterdam: TransOceanic Institute).

Tussie, D., and M.F. Tuozzo (2001) 'Opportunities and Constraints for Civil Society Participation in Multilateral Lending Operations: Lessons from Latin America', in M. Edwards and J. Gaventa (eds.), *Global Citizen Action* (Boulder, CO: Lynne Rienner Publishers).

UNCTAD (United Nations Conference on Trade and Development) (1998) *World Investment Report 1998* (New York: UNCTAD).

UNDP (United Nations Development Programme) (1998) *Human Development Reports* (New York: UNDP).

—— (1999) *Human Development Reports* (New York: UNDP).

—— (2000) *Human Development Reports* (New York: UNDP).

UNEP (United Nations Environment Programme)/SustainAbility (2000) *Global Sustainability Reporters: A Benchmark Study* (London: SustainAbility).

United Nations (1999) *Views of Member States, Members of the Specialized Agencies, Observers, Intergovernmental and Non-governmental Organizations from all Regions on the Report of the Secretary-General on Arrangements and Practices for the Interaction of Non-governmental Organizations in All Activities of the United Nations System: Report of the Secretary-General* (Document A/54/329; New York: United Nations).

Utting, P. (2000) *Business Responsibility for Sustainable Development* (Occasional Paper, 2; Geneva: United Nations Research Institute for Social Development, January 2000).

Van der Does, M., and A. Arce (1995) 'The Use of Narrative in Project Evaluation: A Case from Ecuador', paper for the Study Group, 'Mediating Sustainability', Wageningen, Netherlands, November 1995.

Van Loon, L. (1990) ' "Why the Buddha did not Preach to the Hungry Man": Buddhist Reflections on Affluence and Poverty', *Bodhi Leaves* (Kandy, Sri Lanka: Buddhist Publication Society) 121.

Varela, F., E. Thompson and E. Rosch (1992) *The Embodied Mind: Cognitive Science and Human Experience* (Cambridge, MA: The MIT Press).

Von Weizsäcker, E.U., A. Lovins and L.H. Lovins (1997) *Factor Four: Doubling Wealth, Halving Resource Use* (London: Earthscan Publications).

Ward, H. (2001) *Governing Multinationals: The Role of Foreign Direct Liability* (Briefing Paper New Series, 18; London: RIIA, February 2001).

WBCSD (World Business Council for Social Development) (1999) *Corporate Social Responsibility* (Geneva: WBCSD).

—— (2000) *Framework for the New Economy* (Johannesburg: WBCSD)

WDM (World Development Movement) (1998) *Making Investment Work for People: An International Framework for Investment* (WDM Consultation Paper; London: WDM).

Weber, M. (1958) *Economy and Society: Volume II* (ed. G. Roth and C. Wittich; New York: Bedminster Press).

Weisbrot, M., D. Baker, E. Kraev and J. Chen (2001) *The Scorecard on Globalisation 1980–2000: Twenty Years of Diminished Progress* (Washington, DC: Center for Economic and Policy Research).

Weiser, J., and S. Zadek (2000) *Conversations with Disbelievers: Persuading Companies to Increase their Social Engagement* (Massachusetts: Brody & Weiser).

WFUNA (World Federation of United Nations Association) (2000) *Resolution on NGO Accreditation to the General Assembly* (New York: WFUNA).

Wheeler, D., and M. Sillanpää (1997) *The Stakeholder Corporation: A Blueprint for Maximising Stakeholder Value* (London: Pitman).

Winter, A. (1995) *Is Anyone Listening? Communicating Development in Donor Countries* (UN Non-Governmental Liaison Service Development Dossiers, UNCTAD/NGLS/57; Geneva: NGLS).

Wood, D., and R. Jones (1995) 'Stakeholder Mismatching: A Theoretical Problem in Empirical Research on Corporate Social Performance', *International Journal of Organisational Analysis* 3.3: 229-67.

World Bank (1990) *World Development Report 1990* (Washington, DC: International Bank for Reconstruction and Development).

—— (1997) *World Development Indicators 1997* (Washington, DC: World Bank).

World Economic Organisation/World Bank (1998) *Voluntary Action in the 21st Century: A Reassessment* (Tehran: World Economic Organisation).

World Wide Fund for Nature (1996) *Dangerous Curves: Does the Environment Improve with Economic Growth?* (Geneva: WWF).

WTO (World Trade Organisation) (2003) *Treatise Governing Self-Regulating Financial Systems* (Mexico City: World Trade Organisation).

Zadek, S. (1992) 'The Democratisation of Scarcity', unpublished paper presented at the Annual Conference of the European Association of Evolutionary Political Economy, Paris, 5 November 1992.

—— (1993a) *An Economics of Utopia: Democratising Scarcity* (Aldershot, UK: Avebury Press).

—— (1993b) *Bridging Spheres of Communication: Information Exchange for Sustainable Land-Use* (London: Overseas Development Institute, unpublished report).

—— (1994) 'Trading Ethics: Auditing the Market', *Journal of Economic Issues* 28.2 (June 1994): 631-45.

—— (1996) *Value-Based Organisation* (London: New Economics Foundation).

—— (1999) 'Reflections on a Factory Visit', in *Global Alliance for Workers and Communities: Progress Report*, Fall 1999: 3-4.

—— (2000a) *Doing Good and Doing Well: The Business Case for Corporate Citizenship* (New York: The Conference Board).

—— (2000b) *Ethical Trade Futures* (London: New Economics Foundation).

—— (2001a) *The Civil Corporation: The New Economy of Corporate Citizenship* (London: Earthscan Publications).

—— (2001b) *Third Generation Corporate Citizenship: Public Policy and Business in Society* (London: Foreign Policy Centre/AccountAbility).

—— (2001c) *Endearing Myths, Enduring Truths: Enabling Partnerships between Business, Civil Society and the Public Sector* (Washington, DC: Business Partners for Development).

—— (2002) *Working with Multilaterals* (San Francisco: Business for Social Responsibility).

—— and F. Amalric (1998) 'Consumer Works!', *Development* 41.1 (March 1998; Special Issue on Consumption, Civil Action, and Sustainable Development; Society for International Development): 7-15.

—— and J. Blauert (1998) *Mediating Sustainability: Growing Policy from the Grassroots* (West Hartford, CT: Kumarian Press, 1998): 1-18.

—— and J. Chapman (1998) *Revealing the Emperor's Clothes: How Does Social Responsibility Count?* (unpublished working paper; London: New Economics Foundation).

—— and R. Evans (1993) *Auditing the Market: A Practical Approach to Social Auditing* (Gateshead, UK: Traidcraft).

—— and M. Forstater (1999) 'Making Civil Regulation Work', in M. Addo (ed.), *Human Rights Standards and the Responsibility of Transnational Corporations* (The Hague: Kluwer): 69-75.

—— and A. MacGillivray (1994) *Accounting for Change: Indicators for Sustainable Development* (2 vols.; London: New Economics Foundation).

—— and M. Merme (2003–2004) *Mainstreaming Responsible Investment* (London: AccountAbility; Geneva: World Economic Forum).

—— and P. Raynard (2001) *The Digital Divide* (London: BT plc).

—— and S. Scott-Parker (2000) *Unlocking Potential: The New Disability Business Case* (London: Employers' Forum on Disability).

—— and S. Szabo (1993) *Buddhist Organisation: The Case of the Sarvodaya Shramadana Movement* (London: New Economics Foundation).

—— and P. Tiffen (1996) 'Fair Trade: Business or Campaign?', *Development* 3/1996: 48-53.

—— and C. Tuppen (2000) *Adding Values: The Economics of Sustainable Business* (British Telecommunications Occasional Paper, 4; London: BT).

——, P. Pruzan and R. Evans (eds.) (1997) *Building Corporate AccountAbility: Emerging Practices in Social and Ethical Accounting, Auditing, and Reporting* (London: Earthscan Publications).

——, S. Lingayah and S. Murphy (1998a) *Purchasing Power: Civil Action for Sustainable Consumption* (London: New Economics Foundation).

——, S. Lingayah and M. Forstater (1998b) *Social Labels: A Framework for Analysis* (Brussels: European Commission).

——, M. Forstater and P. Raynard (2002) *Social Development and the Private Sector: The Role of Corporate Social Responsibility* (unpublished paper prepared for the United Nations Department for Economics and Social Affairs: Division for Social Policy and Development, New York).

Zarsky, L. (1999) *Havens, Halos and Spaghetti: Untangling the Evidence about Foreign Direct Investment and the Environment* (Berkeley, CA: Nautilus Institute for Security and Sustainable Development).

index